Antitrust Law in the Online Economy: Selected Cases and Materials

Mark R. Patterson

Fordham University School of Law

Table of Contents

Preface

Most antitrust casebooks include the same traditional cases, and for good reason. Those cases, or many of them, set out the law as it currently stands. However, markets have changed dramatically since many of those cases were decided, and it is not always clear how the law will or should be applied in modern markets. It is important, therefore, that students consider the application of antitrust law to new markets, particularly in the information and high-technology industries.

This book seeks to provide a sampling of new cases and materials in each of the major areas of antitrust. In that respect, a course using this book could cover one of those areas in each week's class, but I have also sought to keep the materials independent of each other so that antitrust professors can supplement traditional casebooks with these materials as they choose. I have also aimed to connect these materials to the traditional cases so that students and practitioners can use this book on their own, again selecting the topics in which they are particularly interested.

Broadly speaking, the book contains cases addressing two types of issues: intellectual property (*Qualcomm*, *Huawei v. ZTE*, etc.) and the online economy (*Google*, *1-800 Contacts*, etc.). It also includes more secondary materials (on algorithmic collusion, personalized pricing, etc.) than is typical of a casebook, because some of these issues have not yet given rise to cases suitable for inclusion. In time, I expect to add problems for these issues to provide opportunities for factual analysis.

The book includes a greater portion of European materials than is usual for a U.S. antitrust book. The reason is obvious: the EU and its member states have been at the forefront of antitrust enforcement in these areas. For those readers who have studied primarily U.S. law, I have sought to provide enough context to appreciate the European materials. In today's world, and particularly given differences in enforcement priorities, even U.S. antitrust lawyers will benefit from attention to Europe and other jurisdictions.

My plan is to update this book frequently—more often than is practical for a standard casebook—to keep up with developments in these fast-moving areas. Self-publication allows me to do that without the delays that would accompany traditional casebook publication. To this end, I welcome suggestions for materials or citations to add (or delete), and of course I also welcome suggestions about how the material is presented.

I hope you find the book useful.

Teaching with this Book

This book is intended to be used either after a traditional antitrust course or as a supplement to one. I use it in a four-credit, two-day-a-week course with the first day covering the traditional material and the second day covering the related material in this book. Taking this approach requires cutting some material from the traditional three- or four-credit course, but it still allows adequate coverage, I believe. To facilitate using the book that way, it includes prior to some of the cases here short descriptions of cases that traditional books include but that might be omitted. That allows those cases to be presented briefly, followed by discussions of their application in the context of technology and information issues.

The book also seeks to indicate what traditional cases it assumes are covered prior to the cases here by making reference to those cases in short notes preceding the materials here. The notes after the materials then suggest some avenues for considering how those cases apply in the contexts on which this book focuses.

A side-effect of these efforts is a lessening of the more-or-less linear presentation of cases in a traditional antitrust casebook. Here there are more frequent references to cases and issues not yet addressed (*e.g.,* references to *Leegin* before coverage of vertical agreements) or not otherwise covered here (*e.g., Copperweld* and the intra-enterprise conspiracy doctrine, or *Brunswick* and antitrust injury). Some might object to this approach, but antitrust doctrine is sufficiently unitary and interrelated that presenting it in distinct categories is not always desirable. That is especially so for a supplement like this that is intended to follow or accompany presentation of traditional law.

In several instances, the materials provided for a particular area of law might not be sufficient for a typical two-hour class. In each such case, the notes before and after those provided point to related materials, and those materials can be used to supplement the materials here and set up the discussion of them.

A Note on Formatting

I have freely removed citations that are not of great value, even if the citation identifies the source of a quoted passage, on the view that the quotation marks themselves indicate that the passage does not come originally from the case or other source. I have also occasionally left short-form citations even after omitting the first, long-form citation. Again, I do not think this will be misleading.

I have generally left spelling, headings, and indentation internal to the materials as in the originals, which accounts for the inconsistencies in those formatting issues. Footnote numbers are also as in the original sources.

Acknowledgments

I acknowledge with gratitude the permissions granted by authors and publishers to reprint portions of the following works:

> Max Gulker, Hipster Antitrust Is Overdue for a Backlash, https://www.aier.org/article/hipster-antitrust-is-overdue-for-a-backlash/, Dec. 3, 2019.

> Geoffrey Manne & Ben Sperry, Debunking the Myth of a Data Barrier to Entry for Online Services, https://truthonthemarket.com/2015/03/26/debunking-the-myth-of-a-data-barrier-to-entry-for-online-services/, March 26, 2015.

> Mark R. Patterson, *Antitrust Law in the New Economy: Google, Yelp, LIBOR, and the Control of Information* (Harvard University Press 2017).

> Sanjukta M. Paul, Uber as For-Profit Hiring Hall: A Price-Fixing Paradox and its Implications, 38 *Berkeley Journal of Employment and Labor Law* 233 (2017), © 2017 by the Regents of the University of California, reprinted by permission.

> Daniel L. Rubinfeld & Michal S. Gal, Access Barriers to Big Data, 59 *Arizona Law Review* 339 (2017).

> Tim Wu, The Utah Statement: Reviving Antimonopoly Traditions for the Era of Big Tech, A new framework for holding private power to account, https://onezero.medium.com/the-utah-statement-reviving-antimonopoly-traditions-for-the-era-of-big-tech-e6be198012d7/, Nov. 18, 2019.

I also gratefully acknowledge helpful comments by John Newman and Geoff Manne, but of course any errors and all editorial bias are mine. I also thank my students for their engagement with these issues in class, and for their typo-hunting efforts outside class.

0. Introduction: "Big Tech" and Digital Markets

The first three readings below, in sections 0.1 and 0.2, introduce some problems of and perspectives regarding competition law in modern markets. Much of the first reading is a primer (or refresher) on U.S. antitrust law, so if that material is familiar one could skip to the section on "Antitrust and Big Tech: Possible Cases Against the Big Four."

The reading in section 0.3 is an excerpt from a careful and extensive effort to come to terms with the distinctive problems of digital and so-called platform markets, where many modern competition issues arise. It was produced by a committee appointed by a government agency in Germany, a jurisdiction that has approached these issues in an innovative way, particularly in a case against Facebook included below. (For some U.S. reactions to that Facebook decision, see Germany's Competition Agency Cracks Down On Facebook: But Is Antitrust The Right Tool For The Job?, March 18, 2018, https://www.forbes.com/sites/washingtonbytes/2019/03/18/germanys-competition-agency-cracks-down-on-facebook-but-is-antitrust-the-right-tool-for-the-job/#3a80708a260e.)

0.1. Introduction to the Issues

Congressional Research Service
Antitrust and "Big Tech"
Report R45910
September 11, 2019

Over the past decade, Google, Amazon, Facebook, and Apple—collectively known as the "Big Four" or "Big Tech"—have revolutionized the internet economy and affected the daily lives of billions of people worldwide. Google operates a search engine that processes over 3.5 billion searches a day (Google Search), runs the biggest online video platform (YouTube), licenses the world's most popular mobile operating system (Android), and is the largest seller of online advertising. Amazon is a major online marketplace, retailer, logistics network, cloud-storage host, and television and film producer. Facebook boasts 2.4 billion monthly active users worldwide, meaning more people use the social network than follow any single world religion. Apple popularized the smartphone, making the device so ubiquitous that consumers have grown accustomed to carrying a supercomputer in their pocket. Collectively, the Big Four generated over $690 billion in revenue in 2018—a sum larger than the annual GDPs of most national economies.

While these companies are responsible for momentous technological breakthroughs and massive wealth creation, they have also received scrutiny related to their privacy practices, dissemination of harmful content and misinformation, alleged political bias, and—as relevant here—potentially anticompetitive conduct. In June 2019, the Wall Street Journal reported that the Department of Justice (DOJ) and Federal Trade Commission (FTC)—the agencies responsible for enforcing the federal antitrust laws—agreed to divide responsibility over investigations of the Big Four's business practices. Under these agreements, the DOJ reportedly has authority over investigations of Google and Apple, while the FTC will look into Facebook and Amazon. The following month, the DOJ announced a potentially broader inquiry into Big Tech. Specifically, the Justice Department's Antitrust Division revealed that it intends to examine possible abuses of market power by unnamed "market-leading online platforms"—an announcement that has led some to speculate that a number of the Big Four may face investigations from both agencies despite the previously reported agreements.

Big Tech's business practices have also attracted congressional interest. In May 2019, the Senate Judiciary Committee held a hearing to investigate privacy and competition issues in the digital advertising industry. And in June and July, the House Judiciary Committee held two separate hearings examining the market power of online platforms.

This report provides an overview of antitrust issues involving the Big Four. The report begins with a general outline of the aspects of antitrust doctrine that are most likely to play a central role in the DOJ and FTC investigations—specifically, the case law surrounding monopolization and mergers. Next, the report discusses the application of this doctrine to each of the Big Four. Finally, the report concludes by examining policy options related to the promotion of digital competition.

Legal Background

General Principles

Contemporary antitrust doctrine reflects a commitment to the promotion of economic competition, which induces businesses to cut costs, improve their productivity, and innovate.

These virtues of competition are often illustrated with the stylized hypothetical of a "perfectly competitive" market with homogenous products, a large number of well-informed buyers and sellers, low entry barriers, and low transaction costs. In such a market, businesses must price their products at marginal cost to avoid losing their customers to competitors. However, real-world markets almost always deviate from this textbook model of perfect competition. When one or more of the structural conditions identified above is absent, individual firms may have *market power*—the ability to profitably raise their prices above competitive levels. At the extreme, a market can be *monopolized* when a single firm possesses significant and durable market power.

According to standard justifications for antitrust law, the exercise of significant market power harms consumers by requiring them to pay higher prices than they would pay in competitive markets, purchase less-desirable substitutes, or go without certain goods and services altogether. Moreover, significant market power harms society as a whole by reducing output and eliminating value that would have been enjoyed in a competitive market. Contemporary antitrust doctrine is focused on preventing these harms by prohibiting exclusionary conduct by dominant firms and anticompetitive mergers and acquisitions. The following subsections discuss these prohibitions in turn.

Section 2 of the Sherman Act: Monopolization

Section 2 of the Sherman Antitrust Act of 1890 makes it unlawful to monopolize, attempt to monopolize, or conspire to monopolize "any part of the trade or commerce among the several States, or with foreign nations." However, the statute itself does not define what it means to "monopolize" trade or commerce, leaving the courts to fill out the meaning of that concept through common law decisionmaking. Consistent with this approach, the Supreme Court's interpretation of Section 2 has evolved in response to changes in economic theory and business practice.

In its monopolization case law, the Court has made clear that the possession of monopoly power and charging of monopoly prices do not by themselves constitute Section 2 violations. Instead, the Court has held that a company engages in monopolization if and only if it (1) possesses monopoly power, and (2) engages in exclusionary conduct to achieve, maintain, or enhance that power.

Monopoly Power

To prevail in a Section 2 case, plaintiffs must show that a defendant possesses monopoly power. While the Supreme Court has explained that a firm has *market power* if it can profitably charge supra-competitive prices, the Court has described *monopoly power* as "the power to control prices or exclude competition," which requires "something greater" than market power. Lower federal courts have held that a firm possesses monopoly power if it possesses a *high degree* of market power.

A Section 2 plaintiff can establish that a defendant possesses monopoly power in two ways. First, plaintiffs can satisfy this requirement with *direct* evidence of monopoly power—that is, evidence that the defendant charges prices significantly exceeding competitive levels. However, such evidence is typically difficult to adduce because of complications in determining appropriate measures of a firm's costs, among other things. As a result, plaintiffs generally attempt to establish that a defendant has monopoly power with *indirect* evidence showing that the defendant (1) possesses a large share of a relevant market, and (2) is protected by entry barriers.

Market Share

To demonstrate that a defendant possesses a dominant market share, plaintiffs must define the scope of the market in which the defendant operates. Predictably, antitrust plaintiffs typically argue that a defendant operates in a narrow market with few competitors, while defendants ordinarily contend that they operate in a broad market with many rivals. Because the size of the market in which a defendant operates (the denominator in a market-share calculation) is generally harder to determine than its sales or revenue (the numerator in such a calculation), parties in antitrust litigation often vigorously contest the issue of market definition—so much, in fact, that more antitrust cases hinge on that question than on "any other substantive issue" in competition law.

Market Definition: Substitutability and the SSNIP Test. In analyzing market definition, the Supreme Court has explained that a relevant antitrust market consists of the product at issue in a given case and all other products that are "reasonably interchangeable" with it. According to the Court, whether one product is "reasonably interchangeable" with another product depends on demand substitution—that is, the extent to which an increase in one product's price would cause consumers to purchase the other product instead. The Court has further explained that a variety of "practical indicia" are relevant to an assessment of whether goods and services are reasonable substitutes, including

1. industry or public recognition of separate markets;

2. a product's peculiar characteristics and uses;

3. unique production facilities;

4. distinct customers;

5. distinct prices;

6. sensitivity to price changes; and

7. specialized vendors.

These criteria are sometimes called the *"Brown Shoe"* factors based on the name of the 1962 decision in which the Court identified them.

In addition to the *Brown Shoe* factors, the DOJ and FTC have provided specific market-definition guidance in their Horizontal Merger Guidelines. The 2010 version of the Guidelines endorses the "hypothetical monopolist" test for defining markets, which—like the Court's case law— principally focuses on demand substitution. Under this test, a group of products qualifies as a relevant antitrust market if a hypothetical monopolist selling those products would find it profitable to raise their price notwithstanding buyers' incentives to substitute other goods and services in response. Specifically, the test asks whether a hypothetical monopolist would be able to profitably impose a "small but significant and non-transitory increase in price" (SSNIP)— generally, a 5% increase. If buyer substitution to other products would make such a price increase unprofitable, then the candidate market must be expanded until a hypothetical monopolist would benefit from such a strategy.

One popular antitrust treatise illustrates the SSNIP test's application by comparing proposed markets consisting of *Ford passenger cars* and *all passenger cars.*

Because Ford—which has a "monopoly" over the sale of Ford passenger cars—would likely be unable to profitably raise its prices by 5% because of the business it would lose to other car companies, *Ford passenger cars* are unlikely to qualify as a properly defined antitrust market. However, because a hypothetical firm with a monopoly over *passenger cars* likely could profit from such a price increase, *passenger cars* likely qualify as a distinct antitrust market.

Market Definition and Big Tech: The Challenge of Zero-Price Markets. The SSNIP test's application to certain technology markets raises difficult issues. In a number of technology markets, firms do not charge customers for access to certain services like online search and social networking. The difficulty with applying the SSNIP test to such markets is clear: as one commentator notes, there is "no sound way" to analyze a 5% increase in a price of zero because such an increase would result in a price that *remains zero*. The SSNIP test as traditionally administered is accordingly "inoperable" in a number of zero-price technology markets.

. . .

. . . Some commentators have argued that regulators should modify the SSNIP test to account for *quality-adjusted* prices, creating a new methodology called the "small but significant and non-transitory decrease in quality" (SSNDQ) test. According to these academics, decreases in the quality of "free" services (e.g., a decline in the privacy protections offered by a social network) are tantamount to increases in the quality-adjusted prices of those services. Under the SSNDQ test, then, a firm offering "free" goods or services would possess monopoly power if it had the ability to profitably raise its quality-adjusted prices significantly above competitive levels.

In contrast, other analysts have proposed that courts and regulators evaluate the scope of zero-price markets by engaging in *qualitative* assessments of the degree to which various digital products and services are "reasonably interchangeable." For example, in a 2019 European Commission report on digital competition, a group of commentators proposed a "characteristics-based" approach to market definition for zero-price industries under which regulators would compare the functions of relevant digital services.

. . .

Finally, a number of courts employing the *Brown Shoe* criteria have emphasized "industry recognition" of the scope of certain markets. Specifically, these courts have relied on corporate conduct, internal strategy documents, and expert testimony to determine the types of companies that a defendant regards as competitors. Accordingly, courts and regulators may be able to rely on these types of qualitative evidence to determine the scope of certain zero-price digital markets.

Market Shares: How Much Is Enough? Once a Section 2 plaintiff has defined a relevant antitrust market, it must show that the defendant occupies a dominant share of that market. Courts have recognized that there is no fixed market-share figure that conclusively establishes that a defendant-company has monopoly power. However, the Supreme Court has never held that a party with *less* than 75% market share has monopoly power.

Lower court decisions provide a number of other useful data points. In the U.S. Court of Appeals for the Second Circuit's influential decision in *United States v. Aluminum Co. of America*, Judge Learned Hand reasoned that (1) a 90% market share can be sufficient to establish a prima facie case of monopoly power, (2) a 60% or 64% share is unlikely to be sufficient, and (3) a 33% share is "certainly" insufficient. Similarly, the Tenth Circuit has explained that courts generally require a market share between 70% and 80% to establish monopoly power. And the Third Circuit has reasoned that a defendant's market share must be "significantly larger" than 55%, while holding that a share between 75% and 80% is "more than adequate" to establish a prima facie case of monopoly power.

Entry Barriers

Several courts have held that proof that a defendant occupies a large market share is insufficient on its own to establish that the defendant has monopoly power. Instead, these courts have concluded that a defendant must also be insulated from potential competitors by significant entry barriers to possess the type of *durable* monopoly power necessary for a Section 2 case. Courts and commentators generally use the concept of entry barriers to refer to long-run costs facing new entrants but not incumbent firms, including (1) legal and regulatory requirements, (2) control of an "essential or superior resource," (3) "entrenched buyer preferences for established brands," (4) "capital market evaluations imposing higher capital costs on new entrants," and (5) in certain circumstances, economies of scale.

The significance of any entry barriers shielding Big Tech companies is a fact-intensive question that will depend on the specific evidence that the DOJ and FTC uncover. However, commentators have identified a number of plausible entry barriers in certain digital markets, including:

- *Network Effects.* A digital platform benefits from network effects when its value to customers increases as more people use it. A platform exhibits "direct" or "same-side" network effects when its value to users on one side of the market increases as the number of users on that side of the market increases. Social networks arguably exhibit this category of network effects because their value to users is dependent on the number of other users that they are able to attract. In contrast, a platform exhibits "indirect" or "cross-side" network effects when its value to users on one side of the market increases as the number of users on *the other side* of the market increases. Search engines arguably benefit from indirect network effects because they become more valuable to advertisers as they attract additional users who can be targeted with ads. Some courts and commentators have concluded that both categories of network effects represent entry barriers that make it difficult for small firms to meaningfully compete with larger incumbents in certain digital markets.

- ***The Advantages of Big Data.*** A number of commentators have argued that the significant volume of user data generated by certain digital platforms confers important advantages on established companies. According to this theory, large firms with access to significant amounts of data can use that data to improve the quality of their products and services (e.g., by increasing the accuracy of a search engine, improving targeted advertising, or offering targeted discounts)—a process that attracts additional customers, who in turn generate more data. Some commentators have accordingly argued that access to "big data" can result in a feedback loop that reinforces the dominance of large firms.

- ***Costs of Switching and Multi-Homing.*** Some commentators have argued that consumers in certain digital markets are unlikely to switch from one platform to another or use multiple platforms simultaneously—a phenomenon that advantages large established companies. These "lock-in" effects can have a variety of causes. A digital platform's customers may be dissuaded from switching to another platform by the prospect of losing their photos, contacts, search history, apps, or other personal data. To similar effect, technology companies may "tie" various products or services together through contractual requirements or technical impediments that prevent customers from simultaneously using competing products or services. Finally, some consumers may exhibit behavioral biases that render their initial choice of a platform "sticky," making them unlikely to switch platforms even when presented with superior alternatives. All of these factors can create a powerful "first-mover advantage" for incumbent firms that deters potential competitors.

In contrast, others have questioned whether digital markets exhibit significant entry barriers. For example, Google has repeatedly denied the claim that it is insulated from rivals, arguing that consumers incur low costs in switching to alternative search engines because competition is only "one click away." Similarly, other commentators have argued that the history of upstart rivals supplanting once-dominant technology companies suggests that any monopoly power in dynamic technology markets is unlikely to be durable.

Exclusionary Conduct

In addition to establishing that a defendant possesses monopoly power, Section 2 plaintiffs must demonstrate that the defendant engaged in exclusionary conduct to achieve, maintain, or enhance that power. While the Supreme Court has developed tests for evaluating whether specific categories of behavior qualify as prohibited exclusionary conduct, it has not endorsed a general standard for distinguishing such conduct from permissible commercial activities. However, courts have made clear that exclusionary conduct must involve harm to the *competitive process* and not simply harm to a defendant's *competitors*. . . .

. . .

Section 7 of the Clayton Act: Mergers and Acquisitions

While Section 2 of the Sherman Act is concerned with unilateral exclusionary conduct, Section 7 of the Clayton Antitrust Act of 1914 prohibits mergers and acquisitions that may "substantially lessen" competition. Section 7 applies to both "horizontal" mergers between competitors in the same market and "vertical" mergers between companies at different levels of a distribution chain. In evaluating horizontal mergers, the DOJ and FTC typically evaluate the merged firm's market share and the resulting level of concentration in the relevant market, in addition to any efficiencies that the combined company will likely realize as a result of the proposed merger.

In contrast, vertical mergers may raise competition concerns when they involve a firm with significant power in one market entering an adjacent market, which may foreclose potential sources of supply or distribution and raise entry barriers by requiring the firm's potential competitors to enter both markets to be competitive. For example, if a dominant widget manufacturer acquires a widget retailer, it may have incentives to discriminate against competing widget retailers by charging them higher prices or refusing to deal with them altogether. As a result of this vertical discrimination, such a merger may force prospective widget retailers to also enter widget manufacturing to be competitive, raising entry barriers in the retail market. Despite these potential concerns with certain vertical mergers, the DOJ and FTC police such mergers far less aggressively than horizontal mergers, largely on the basis of academic work suggesting that vertical integration can result in significant efficiencies and only rarely threatens competition. However, whether the antitrust agencies should scrutinize vertical mergers more closely remains a subject of ongoing debate.

The DOJ and FTC apply Section 7 by reviewing large proposed mergers before they are finalized, though the agencies also have the authority to unwind consummated mergers. Under the Hart-Scott-Rodino Antitrust Improvements Act of 1976 (the HSR Act), parties to certain large mergers and acquisitions must report their proposed transactions to the antitrust agencies and wait for approval before closing. If the agencies determine that a proposed merger threatens to "substantially lessen" competition, they can sue to block the merger or negotiate conditions with the companies to safeguard competition. Section 7 of the Clayton Act also gives the agencies the authority to challenge previously closed mergers that "substantially lessen" competition, though lawsuits to unwind consummated mergers have been "rare" since the enactment of the HSR Act.

. . .

Antitrust and Big Tech: Possible Cases Against the Big Four

Applying the general legal principles discussed above to specific technology companies is a highly fact-intensive enterprise that will depend on the specific evidence that the DOJ and FTC uncover during their investigations. Moreover, the agencies have yet to publicly release details on the categories of conduct that they are evaluating in the course of their Big Tech inquiries, making it difficult to confidently assess the strength of antitrust cases against the relevant companies. With these caveats in mind, the following subsections discuss certain categories of conduct that the antitrust agencies may be investigating at each of the Big Four.

Google

Google is no stranger to antitrust scrutiny. The technology giant—which runs Google Search, licenses the Android mobile operating system, and owns a major online ad-brokering platform (AdSense)—has found itself in the crosshairs of competition authorities several times over the past decade. In 2013, the FTC concluded a wide-ranging investigation into the company's business practices, including its alleged discrimination against vertical rivals, copying of content from other websites, restrictions on advertisers' ability to do business with competing search engines, and exclusivity agreements with websites that used AdSense. While agency staff had recommended that the FTC bring a lawsuit challenging some of these activities, the Commission unanimously declined to pursue such an action after Google committed to make certain changes to its business practices.

In contrast, European antitrust authorities have pursued three separate investigations of Google that have each resulted in large fines. In June 2017, the European Commission (EC) fined Google 2.4 billion euros for antitrust violations related to Google Search's preferential treatment of the company's comparison-shopping service, Google Shopping. The EC later levied an additional 4.3 billion-euro penalty in July 2018 for tying and exclusive-dealing arrangements related to Android. And in March 2019, the EC imposed a further 1.49 billion-euro penalty for exclusive- and restrictive-dealing agreements involving AdSense.

While the focus of the DOJ's inquiry into Google's conduct remains somewhat obscure, the investigation is likely to implicate some of the same practices that have occupied the attention of European antitrust authorities. . . .

. . .

Amazon

Commentators have identified a variety of competition-related issues surrounding Amazon. However, most of the antitrust discussion involving the e-commerce giant has concerned two general categories of conduct: discrimination against vertical rivals and predatory pricing. In addressing Amazon's alleged vertical discrimination, a number of analysts have focused on the company's dual role as both the operator of Amazon Marketplace—a platform on which merchants can sell their products directly to consumers—and as a merchant that sells its own private-label products on the Marketplace. Some commentators have alleged that Amazon exploits this dual role by implementing policies that privilege its own products over competing products offered by other sellers. According to a 2016 ProPublica investigation, for example, Amazon has designed its Marketplace ranking algorithm—which determines the order in which products appear to consumers—to favor its own products and products sold by companies that buy Amazon's fulfillment services. Similarly, certain merchants have complained that

Amazon has revoked their ability to use its Marketplace after deciding to move into the relevant markets with its own private-label products or products it distributes on behalf of other companies.

Some observers have also raised the possibility that Amazon may engage in predatory pricing by selling certain products at below-cost prices to eliminate rivals. A number of these allegations involve Amazon's 2010 acquisition of Quidsi—the parent company of the online baby-products retailer Diapers.com and several other online-retail subsidiaries. According to some commentators, Amazon aggressively cut its prices for baby products after Quidsi rebuffed its initial offer to purchase the company. When Amazon's below-cost prices began to impede Quidsi's growth, the company ultimately accepted Amazon's subsequent acquisition offer. And after the Quidsi acquisition, Amazon allegedly raised its prices for baby products. Other predatory-pricing allegations leveled against Amazon concern the company's sale of certain e-books. Specifically, some observers have argued that when it entered the e-book market in 2007, Amazon priced some categories of e-books below cost to eliminate potential competitors, ultimately securing 90% of the market by 2009.

. . .

Facebook

Most of the antitrust commentary directed toward Facebook has focused on its acquisitions of potential competitors—in particular, its 2012 acquisition of the photo-sharing service Instagram and its 2014 acquisition of the messaging service WhatsApp. In a March 2019 letter to the FTC, the Chairman of the House Antitrust Subcommittee urged the Commission to examine whether these acquisitions— which according to some estimates have resulted in Facebook owning three of the top four and four of the top eight social media applications—violated Section 7 of the Clayton Act. Other legislators and commentators have echoed calls for regulators to unwind these acquisitions.

The FTC appears to be taking these arguments seriously. In August 2019, the Wall Street Journal reported that Facebook's acquisition practices are a "central component" of the agency's investigation of the company. In addition to potentially focusing on the Instagram and WhatsApp deals, the Journal reported that the FTC could also be evaluating Facebook's 2013 acquisition of Onavo Mobile Ltd.—a mobile-analytics company that may have allowed Facebook to identify fast-growing social media companies and purchase them before they became competitive threats. Depending on the evidence that the FTC uncovers, Facebook's general acquisition strategy could plausibly serve as the basis for a Section 2 monopolization case to the extent that it suppressed competition.

. . .

Apple

Like Google, Apple has faced antitrust claims related to its mobile-device software. Specifically, the iPhone maker has faced separate class-action lawsuits related to its design of the device's operating system, iOS. In these lawsuits, classes of customers who purchased iPhone apps through the company's App Store and app developers claim that Apple has illegally monopolized the market for iPhone apps by designing iOS as a closed system and installing security measures to prevent customers from purchasing apps outside of the App Store. In May 2019, the Supreme Court rejected Apple's contention that App Store customers lacked standing to challenge this conduct, allowing their lawsuit to proceed. While these cases will accordingly continue to work their way through the courts, the DOJ may also be contemplating a similar action challenging Apple's design of iOS.

. . .

Options for Congress

While the antitrust action surrounding the Big Four is currently concentrated in the executive branch and the courts, digital competition issues have also attracted the interest of Congress, which may pursue legislation to address anticompetitive conduct by large technology companies. Such legislation could take two general forms. First, some commentators have proposed that Congress enact certain changes to existing antitrust doctrine to promote digital competition. Second, a number of lawmakers and academics have advocated legislation that would impose sector-specific competition regulation on large technology companies. The subsections below discuss each category of potential legislation in turn.

Changes to Antitrust Law

A number of commentators have proposed that Congress adopt certain changes to existing antitrust doctrine to promote competition in technology markets. These proposals include:

> • ***Changes to Predatory-Pricing Doctrine.*** Some observers have proposed changes to predatory-pricing doctrine with an eye toward addressing the pricing practices of dominant technology firms like Amazon. Specifically, one commentator has criticized *Brooke Group*'s "recoupment" requirement on the grounds that it does not adequately deter predatory pricing by dominant online platforms. According to this line of criticism, *Brooke Group*'s requirement that plaintiffs demonstrate a "dangerous probability" of recoupment fails to account for dominant platforms' unique ability to persist in charging below-cost prices for years and employ difficult-to-detect recoupment strategies like price discrimination among different categories of customers. As a result, this commentator has advocated a presumption that below-cost pricing by dominant platforms qualifies as prohibited exclusionary conduct.

Other academics have criticized the first *Brooke Group* requirement, which demands that predatory-pricing plaintiffs show that a monopolist charged below-cost prices. These commentators argue that pricing-cutting can be anticompetitive even when a firm prices its products above cost, especially in cases where a monopolist aggressively cuts prices in order to prevent a new rival from recovering its entry costs or realizing economies of scale. To address this concern, these observers contend that courts should evaluate whether challenged price-cutting strategies exclude potential entrants without screening predation claims with a price-cost test. Congress could accordingly remedy this alleged defect in current predatory-pricing doctrine with legislation eliminating the first *Brooke Group* requirement.

- ***Enhanced Merger Review for Dominant Technology Companies.*** Some commentators have advocated stricter scrutiny for mergers and acquisitions by dominant technology companies, including a rebuttable presumption that mergers and acquisitions between certain monopolist technology companies and their potential competitors are unlawful. A number of academics have also suggested that because promising technology startups often fall below the minimum-size thresholds that trigger DOJ and FTC review under the HSR Act, Congress should consider lowering or eliminating those thresholds for deals involving dominant technology companies.

- ***Enhanced Scrutiny of Product Design Decisions.*** Finally, some observers have argued that courts should be less deferential toward defendants' justifications of allegedly exclusionary product designs, arguing that product-design decisions are often "key elements" of large technology companies' business strategies. Congress could accordingly consider legislation to clarify the appropriate standards for evaluating exclusionary-design claims, perhaps by making clear that such claims are subject to full Rule-of-Reason scrutiny rather than the more permissive tests adopted by certain lower federal courts.

Sector-Specific Regulation

As discussed, academic commentators have argued that certain digital markets possess structural characteristics that advantage large incumbent firms. In some cases, dominant firms in these markets can enhance such entry barriers by making it difficult for consumers to "multi-home" or use complementary products offered by competitors, and courts evaluating challenges to these product-design choices hesitate to hold companies liable under existing antitrust doctrine. Moreover, vertically integrated technology monopolists do not face general nondiscrimination rules requiring them to deal evenhandedly with rivals in adjacent markets. Some analysts have accordingly argued that large technology platforms require sector-specific regulations to address these competition concerns. These proposed regulations include "data mobility" rules giving consumers greater ability to control their data and move it to competing platforms,

"interoperability" standards requiring companies to minimize technical impediments to the use of complementary products, and nondiscrimination requirements prohibiting vertically integrated technology monopolists from discriminating against rivals who use their platforms. Congress could legislate such requirements, direct an existing federal agency to develop them through rulemaking, or create a new agency tasked with regulating the technology industry.

A number of lawmakers and academics have also argued that the infrastructure-like features of certain digital services justify separation regimes prohibiting monopolists that provide those services from entering adjacent markets. Such separation regimes are not without precedent. Historically, Congress and federal regulators have imposed a variety of structural prohibitions limiting the lines of business in which certain categories of firms—including railroads, banks, television networks, and telecommunications companies—can engage. Commentators have justified these separation regimes on the grounds that they eliminate conflicts of interest that lead companies in key infrastructure-like sectors to discriminate against their vertical rivals. While the nondiscrimination requirements discussed above represent one means of addressing this concern, categorical separation rules are an alternative to such requirements that may prove easier to administer.

In March 2019, Senator Elizabeth Warren proposed one type of separation regime for dominant technology companies, arguing that large "platform utilities"—including "online marketplaces," "exchanges," and "platforms for connecting third parties"—should be prohibited from owing companies that participate on their platforms. The Chairman of the House Antitrust Subcommittee has also expressed support for similar separation requirements.

Congress may also be interested in broader separation regimes prohibiting dominant technology platforms from entering other types of markets. Specifically, many lawmakers have expressed concern about Facebook's announcement that it intends to develop a new cryptocurrency. These worries have generated a legislative proposal to prevent any large technology platform from entering the financial industry, with Members on the House Financial Services Committee circulating draft legislation titled the Keep Big Tech Out of Finance Act. This draft bill would prohibit "large platform utilities" from (1) affiliating with financial institutions, or (2) establishing, maintaining, or operating digital assets intended to be "widely used as a medium of exchange, store or value, or any other similar function.

0.2. Different Perspectives on "Big Tech"

Tim Wu
The Utah Statement: Reviving Antimonopoly Traditions for the Era of Big Tech
A new framework for holding private power to account
Nov. 18, 2019
https://onezero.medium.com/the-utah-statement-
reviving-antimonopoly-traditions-for-the-era-of-big-tech-e6be198012d7

Over the last several years, a movement to revive the anti-monopoly traditions of the United States has gained increasing momentum and even retaken its place in presidential political debate. While popularly known as a movement to "break up big tech," it is really a movement that reacts to the economic policies of the last 40 years. For we have, over that time, weakened and nearly abandoned the anti-monopoly tradition that, in various forms, has been part of the U.S. system since the Declaration of Independence and the original anti-monopoly tea-party protest. The result has been decades of economic consolidation across industries like agriculture, finance, pharmaceuticals, and telecommunications. It is a reaction also to the consolidation of tech into just a few platforms, like Google, Facebook, and Amazon.

We have been left with an economy dominated by well-protected oligopolies who maintain high profits, low levels of investment, and stagnant wages. Employers have gained disproportionate power over their workers, thanks to a weakening of labor law, declining unionization, and business models that coerce and restrict workers. The policies have also contributed to the widening gap between rich and poor, and the widespread economic dissatisfaction and anger that is a hallmark of our times.

The anti-monopoly movement is also a response to the undeniable sense that concentrated private interests have an unfairly disproportionate influence over government and Congress. The legislature regularly refuses to do what even supermajorities of citizens want, like control drug prices or provide paid maternity leave. Excessively concentrated industries, in other words, have become a threat to the basic idea of representative democracy.

The simple premise of anti-monopoly revival is that concentrated private power has become a menace, a barrier to widespread prosperity, and an indefensible division of the spoils of progress and economic security that yields human flourishing. It has sparked a wealth of new articles, books, studies and symposia. (A reading list can be found here.) And the revival movement has attracted important political adherents that cross ideological and party lines.

It is important to understand that the revival of an antimonopoly tradition is a broader project than revival of the antitrust law. While that project is a key front, a broad set of policy levers and legal interventions — including in labor law, intellectual property law, corporate law, banking law and financial regulation, and campaign finance law — can be used to structure markets and check private power in the service of anti-monopoly values.

Given the stakes, it may be no surprise to hear that the effort to revive the antimonopoly tradition has met resistance and sharp criticism — as such efforts always have. But in one area the critics have made an important point concerning antitrust revival. Those who believe in a strong revival of antitrust, and a return to its anti-monopoly roots, have a duty to specify what, exactly, they mean, in concrete, legal detail.

As a response to that criticism, the following statement was drafted over lunch by a group of participants at the "A New Future for Antitrust" conference at the University of Utah in the Fall of 2019. It followed a specific challenge from Professor Dan Crane, a prominent antitrust professor and treatise author from the University of Michigan, to declare what, exactly, were the positions taken by his co-panelists calling for antitrust revival.

In that spirit, a few of us at the conference put together an initial list of principles and proposed reforms. There are of course, healthy differences in approaches to reviving antitrust. We share this list in the spirit of promoting further conversation and view it as just one starting point in an ongoing discussion about how to reorient antitrust towards its antimonopoly roots.

The Utah Statement

(as authored by a group of participants at "A New Future for Antitrust," Oct 25, 2019, and edited thereafter)

We believe that:

(1) Subjecting concentrated private power to democratic checks is a matter of constitutional importance;

(2) The protection of fair competition is a means to a thriving and democratic society and an instrument for both the creation of opportunity and the distribution of wealth and power;

(3) Excessive concentration of private economic power breeds antidemocratic political pressures and undermines liberties; and

(4) While antitrust is not an answer to every economic distress, it is a democratically enacted and necessary element in achieving these aims.

In reflection of these principles, we therefore call for the following reforms to current antitrust doctrine and enforcement practice:

A. Doctrine

1. Vertical coercion, vertical restraints, and vertical mergers should enjoy no presumption of benefit to the public;

2. By rule or statute, non-compete agreements should be made presumptively unlawful;

3. The Trinko doctrine of implied regulatory preemption should be overruled;

4. The Brooke Group test for predatory pricing and Weyerhaeuser test for predatory bidding should be overruled;

5. The Berkley Photo standard for establishing monopoly leveraging should be restored;

6. The essential facilities doctrine should be reinvigorated for dominant firms that deny access to critical infrastructural services;

7. Structural presumptions in merger review should be restored;

8. The LinkLine doctrine holding that price squeeze allegations fail as standalone Section 2 claims should be overruled;

9. Noerr-Pennington should be overruled and replaced by a First Amendment defense and appropriate statutory protections for workers; and

10. The Clayton Act's worker exemption should be extended to all who labor for a living, regardless of statutory employment status, for horizontal coordination, collective bargaining, and collective action in service of either.

B. Method and Enforcement Practice

1. It is not true that "Congress designed the Sherman Act as a 'consumer welfare prescription'";

2. Antitrust rules should be created through case development, agency rule-making, and legislation;

3. The States, the laboratories of economic experimentation, are a critical vanguard of enforcement efforts;

4. Private enforcement is a critical complement to public enforcement;

5. The markets for labor — and in particular problems caused by labor market monopsony — should be subject to robust antitrust enforcement, and enforcers should treat business structures that restrict alternatives for or coerce working Americans as suspect;

6. The broad structural concerns expressed by Congress in its enactment of the 1950 Anti-Merger Act, including due concern for the economic and political dangers of excessive industrial concentration, should drive enforcement of Section 7 of the Clayton Act;

7. Anticompetitive conduct harming one party or class should never be justifiable by offsetting benefits to another party or class. Netting harms and benefits across markets, parties, or classes should not be a method for assessing anticompetitive effects;

8. False negatives should not be preferred over false positives, and the costs of erroneous lack of enforcement should not be discounted or assumed harmless, but given appropriate weight when making enforcement decisions;

9. Structural remedies are to be preferred;

10. Harms demonstrated by clear and convincing evidence or empirical study should never be ignored or discounted based on theories that might predict a lack of harm;

11. Clear and convincing evidence of anti-competitive intent should be taken as a presumptive evidence of harm;

12. Mergers should be subject to both prospective and retrospective analysis and enforcement practice; and

13. The determination by the antitrust agencies of relevant market definitions should receive judicial deference.

Max Gulker
Hipster Antitrust Is Overdue for a Backlash
https://www.aier.org/article/hipster-antitrust-is-overdue-for-a-backlash/
Dec. 3, 2019

The American Left has recently made an important shift. They've long justified redistributative policies by portraying wealthy individuals and big corporations as beneficiaries of an unfair system designed to reward greed and privilege. But as we stare down the barrel of a presidential election year, candidates like Senators Bernie Sanders and Elizabeth Warren now go at least one step further — billionaires and large corporations are not a symptom of an unfair system, but its cause.

The shift is important in that government policies aimed directly at weakening wealthy individuals and large corporations are an end unto themselves rather than a means to help those struggling. This approach was in full view during the recent controversy around Warren's proposed wealth tax, which seemed to focus more on reducing the political power of billionaires than on what the government might do with its extra cash.

Sanders, never one to gussie up his proclamations, tweeted that "Billionaires should not exist."

Less prominent in the recent debate, beyond its implications for big tech, is the parallel fight emerging with large corporations. Here, taxation takes a back seat to antitrust laws, where a new movement seeks nothing less than the full weaponization of antitrust law and enforcement to keep firms squarely in their lane.

The Utah Statement, a recent brief manifesto of the New Brandeisian or "hipster" antitrust movement, gets specific about what changes to antitrust law and enforcement the movement's leaders would like to see. Drafted by two of those leaders, Columbia Law Professor Timothy Wu and academic fellow Lina Khan, along with Marshall Steinbaum of the University of Utah, the document should galvanize those opposing the Left's return to the embrace of central planning.

Fighting Private Power

While not associated with any specific candidate, it's clear from the Utah Statement's introduction that the authors view the current U.S. commercial landscape through the same predatory lens as Sanders and Warren. They frequently change the term "antitrust" to "anti-monopoly," likely conjuring for many the robber barons of old:

The simple premise of anti-monopoly revival is that concentrated private power has become a menace, a barrier to widespread prosperity, and an indefensible division of the spoils of progress and economic security that yields human flourishing.

How do the authors wish to confront this menace? The 10 statements on legal doctrine and 13 statements on enforcement they put forward amount to a radical overhaul of American antitrust law and enforcement. They would shift from a system of rules spelled out by legal precedent that limit the hand of enforcers to one chiefly driven by what the executive branch would like to do.

The authors' desired changes to legal doctrine focus primarily on presumption — shifting the burden of proof from Justice Department enforcers to accused firms. Examples include:

- Vertical mergers should be presumed harmful to consumers rather than beneficial due to efficiency gains (#2)

- Courts could find incumbent firms guilty of predatory pricing without plaintiffs or prosecution demonstrating that the alleged scheme would have benefited its accused perpetrator (#4)

- Horizontal mergers in concentrated markets should be presumed anticompetitive (#7)

These desired changes in legal doctrine open the door to a far more aggressive approach to antitrust enforcement, detailed in its own 13-point plan:

- Explicitly scrapping the consumer welfare standard (#1)

- Making labor-market structure ("anti-monopsony") the explicit domain of antitrust enforcers (#5)

- Ordering regulators to not prefer "false negatives" over "false positives," in effect telling regulators not to worry about leveling false allegations if it means finding the bad guys (#8)

This laundry list of legal and regulatory changes makes antitrust enforcement discretionary rather than rules-based. Regulators can block mergers, break up firms, and police other market conduct in the way they and their elected bosses see fit, and defendants, due to the changes in legal doctrine, can't do much about it.

When faced with any such radical proposed expansion of executive power, we must ask two questions. First, what would those seeking to expand executive power do with it? Second, how else could future elected officials put such expended power to use?

The reasoning behind the New Brandeisians' antitrust approach seems to hinge on a cursory and selective reading of an Econ 101 textbook. The canonical "Chapter 1" model of "perfect competition" exists as a straw man throughout. Since every market departs from that model's assumptions of atomistic buyers and sellers, homogenous products, static rather than dynamic process, perfect information, and many others, there is always scope, even imperative, for the government to intervene.

According to the authors, much of the stagnation they observe in America's poor and middle class is traceable to big companies and their political allies who for decades eased off the antitrust gas pedal and laid out the red carpet for "concentrated private power":

We have been left with an economy dominated by well-protected oligopolies who maintain high profits, low levels of investment, and stagnant wages. Employers have gained disproportionate power over their workers, thanks to a weakening of labor law, declining unionization, and business models that coerce and restrict workers. The policies have also contributed to the widening gap between rich and poor, and the widespread economic dissatisfaction and anger that is a hallmark of our times.

Basic economic theory says that all else equal such market power would yield higher prices and lower wages. But nowhere in their analysis do the authors raise the possibility that some or many of their concerns are mitigated by new developments in technology, including the increased importance of network effects, or globalization that redefines markets and supply chains.

This is where the authors' Econ 101 myopia truly has teeth — it yields a vision of a static rather than dynamic economy. The best argument for giving firms more discretion over growing, shrinking, merging, and entering and exiting markets is that solutions to new and unforeseen facts on the ground emerge through evolution rather than being proclaimed by intelligent design.

Idealizing Public Power

The authors of the Utah Statement also offer a stark "good vs. evil" take on political economy. "Concentrated private power" is fundamentally extractive and exploitative, while concentrated public power is sanctified by democracy. Were the nature of power really so simple, the executive branch's discretion would obviously be the most direct means to achieve public well-being.

There's a certain hubris in touting democracy in order to expand government power in ways one wants while ignoring that like past elections, future ones will likely bring winners who will use that power in misguided or abusive ways. The Utah Statement's authors write as though they believe that their candidate of choice will win the 2020 election and usher in an era of such monumental progress for working families that the other party will become a permanent political minority. To expect or even entertain such an outcome neglects both logic and history.

Electoral politics in the 21st century has yielded unpredictable and diverse results. The kind of expansion of power proposed in the Utah Statement could be wielded in a variety of ways by future administrations. The proposed executive powers could be put to work just as easily in the service of protectionism or cronyism as they could to advance the authors' concept of consumer and worker rights.

In a 2018 paper, Elyse Dorsey of the FTC, Jan Rybnicek of Freshfields Bruckhaus Deringer LLP, and Joshua Wright of the George Mason University law school detail the many opportunities that expanded executive-branch power will afford incumbent firms to craft policy and enforcement in ways that confer a competitive advantage:

A primary theme of Hipster Antitrust is concern with regulatory capture and oversized corporate influence on regulation and market outcomes. We share those concerns. Yet, ironically, by expanding antitrust enforcers' discretion dramatically and removing institutional safeguards ensuring accountability, Hipster Antitrust would usher in a new era of rent-seeking by corporations hoping to misuse the antitrust laws to gain advantages over competitors.

The irony is even deeper when supporters of Sanders and Warren tout their policies as virtuous simply because they harm corporations and decrease their political power. Khan, Wu, and Steinbaum are clearly well aware of the potential for the rich and powerful to co-opt the tools of government. Their fatal flaw is to believe we can solve the problem by electing better people or making better rules.

Racing to the Bottom

The hipster antitrust movement may consider themselves intellectual heirs of Supreme Court Justice Louis Brandeis, but their marketing strategy takes inspiration from more recent, less lofty sources. Writing about Warren's tax plan, I said that "Our president has Mexican immigrants and Chinese trade officials. Warren and Sanders have billionaires." The neo-Brandeisians will ensure that the left scapegoats corporations the same as people.

The American left and right are becoming two sides of the same populist coin. Both peddle simplistic narratives that pin peoples' real struggles on some "other" group gaining in size, influence, or power. And both promise that new, executive-based government power will fix what's broken.

President Trump's brand of xenophobic right-populism has brought our politics to new lows and been terrible for the economy. When democrats mock "billionaire tears" they join the president in a populist race to the bottom. Persecution of CEOs is not high on my list of concerns, but we're all victims of this two-sided populism that seeks quick political victory by making one group of people hate another while solving nothing.

Democracy, upon which both sides somehow hang their hats, still has time to save the day. Every hipster trend worth remembering has an equally severe backlash. Democrats can reject neo-Brandeisian antitrust along with the other pillars of left-populism, or seek a victory that in many ways will prolong rather than end the Trump era.

Notes

1. An issue that is often raised in considering antitrust enforcement in the technology industries is the fast-moving nature of those industries. Some enforcers and commentators believe that the law is quite capable of dealing with dynamic industries, but others have more doubts. *Cf.* Fiona Scott-Morton, Deputy Assistant Attorney General, Antitrust Division, U.S. Department of Justice, "Antitrust Enforcement in High-Technology Industries: Protecting Innovation and Competition", Remarks prepared for the 2012 NYSBA Antitrust Forum: Antitrust in High-Tech Markets – Intervention or Restraint, 7 December 2012 *with* Douglas H. Ginsburg and Joshua D. Wright, "Dynamic Analysis and the Limits of Antitrust institutions", 78 Antitrust Law Journal 1 (2012).

2. To what extent do the proposals in the Utah Statement appear to respond to the problems identified in the first reading and in the next one? It is worth returning to the Utah Statement from time to time as you read the materials here to see whether it responds to the problems of the online economy.

3. Even if a wholesale revamping of competition law like that proposed by the Utah Statement is not necessary, it remains true that some conduct in technology industries does not fit neatly in the categorics of traditional competition law. *See* Nicolas Petit, "'Problem Practices" in EU Competition Law," https://antitrustlair.files.wordpress.com/2014/07/problem-practices-ccp-nicolas-petit.pdf. Many of these "problem practices" are presented in this book, and it is not always clear whether the "problems" are best solved by adaptation of current competition law, by replacing it with a different body or bodies of law, or by allowing the market's own methods of self-correction to work.

4. There is now a considerable quantity of scholarship addressing technology and information markets and the particular problems they raise. *See, e.g.,* NICOLAS PETIT, BIG TECH AND THE DIGITAL ECONOMY: THE MOLIGOPOLY SCENARIO (2020); TIM WU, THE ATTENTION MERCHANTS: THE EPIC SCRAMBLE TO GET INSIDE OUR HEADS (2016); MARK R. PATTERSON, ANTITRUST LAW IN THE NEW ECONOMY: GOOGLE, YELP, LIBOR, AND THE CONTROL OF INFORMATION (2017); ARIEL EZRACHI & MAURICE E. STUCKE, VIRTUAL COMPETITION: THE PROMISE AND PERILS OF THE ALGORITHM-DRIVEN ECONOMY (2016); John M. Newman, *Antitrust in Digital Markets*, 72 VAND. L. REV. 1497 (2019); John M. Newman, *Antitrust in Zero-Price Markets: Applications*, 94 WASH. U. L. REV. 49 (2016); John M. Newman, *Antitrust in Zero-Price Markets: Foundations*, 164 U. PA. L. REV. 149 (2015); Lina Khan, *Amazon's Antitrust Paradox*, 126 YALE L.J. 710 (2017).

0.3. Digital Markets

Germany, Federal Ministry for Economic Affairs and Energy
A new competition framework for the digital economy:
Report by the Commission 'Competition Law 4.0'
September 2019

I.   The mandate: Making EU competition law fit for the digital age

The Commission 'Competition Law 4.0' was set up by [German] Federal Minister for Economic Affairs and Energy Peter Altmaier in September 2018, and tasked with developing recommendations on how EU competition law could be amended to take account of new developments in the data economy, the increased relevance of platform-driven business models, and the emergence of 'Industry 4.0'.

In particular, the Commission 'Competition Law 4.0' was tasked to examine whether the overall framework of competition law needs to be revised in order to enable German and European digital companies to successfully compete internationally; what could be done to better respond to the needs of German and European digital companies to engage in cooperation and to scale up; whether there is a need to adapt the provisions governing access to data in a way that is compliant with the rules for data protection; how competition law can contribute to promoting innovation; how to update the competition rules as they apply to platform operators with a high level of market power; and whether procedural rules need to be adjusted to allow competition authorities to respond more swiftly to developments in highly dynamic markets. The Commission 'Competition Law 4.0' was asked to take into consideration the numerous intersections and overlaps between competition law, unfair commercial practices law, consumer protection law, data protection and liability law, and other fields of law that play a role in the digital economy. . . .

. . .

The report begins with an outline of the challenges associated with the digital economy and its effects on markets and economic structures. The new data economy, the rise of platform-based business models and the growing importance of digital ecosystems are the game changers leading us towards a digital economy (Chapter II). Following this outline, the report highlights the importance of effective competition for innovation as well as the value of innovation for competition and for consumers. Consumer choice is indispensable for undistorted competition. For this very reason, openness for innovation and the strengthening of consumer autonomy are leitmotifs of this report. Any substantive discussion on the various options for reforms requires an understanding of the trade-offs associated with the relevant regulatory regimes and law enforcement institutions in what is a highly dynamic area of regulation full of uncertainty. This is the basic understanding which underpins the discussion of the possible options for action (Chapter III). The digital economy is characterised by its ability to use digital technologies to supersede established business models, to create new markets, and to eliminate or fundamentally transform previously existing markets.   . . .

II. Structural challenges of the digital economy

The new data economy, the rise of platform-based business models and the growing importance of digital ecosystems spanning what had previously been several separate markets are the game changers in the digital economy. One of the characteristics of the digital economy is that it combines these different aspects into a single process which puts certain companies in new positions of great and ever increasing power, allowing them to extend their market power beyond the traditional market boundaries.

The role played by data as an input factor for numerous products, services, and processes along the value chain has considerably increased. The more that access to data translates into a competitive advantage, the greater the likelihood of the emergence of self-reinforcing 'feedback loops'. In other words, better access to data may result in competitive advantages, which may then give the company even more and better access to data. This type of mechanism is characteristic of platform-based business models which combine a trend towards greater concentration due to positive network effects with ever increasing access to data. The fact that the same set of data may translate into competitive advantages on several markets is in itself an expression of a new type of conglomerate effects which may contribute to the emergence of integrated digital ecosystems which have the ability to tear down and modify existing industry structures. All this presents new challenges to competition law and policy-makers. . . .

The following section is a summary of some of the most important features of the digital economy. . . .

1. Basic characteristics of the data economy: potential for innovation, asymmetrical information, and the danger of dominance

The new levels of data availability – personal and non personal user and usage data, location data, environmental data etc. – combined with lower data storage and processing costs are defining features of the digital economy. Much of today's digital innovation is linked to the storage, compilation and analysis of data – the stuff of which many business models of the digital age are made.

a. Data as an input for the creation of bespoke services and products and for efficiency gains in manufacturing

Systematic data mining makes it possible for customers to better recognise consumers' preferences and needs. User profiles first became important in marketing. They make it possible to increasingly target the products, services or information shown to consumers to fit their individual preferences. The same is true of adverts ('targeted advertising').

Furthermore, detailed insights into consumers' behaviour and profiles can also be used to individualise products and services, i.e. for innovation not only in sales, but also in the product portfolio. The continuous analysis of usage data can also be used to consistently improve and adjust products and services so that they meet users' needs. To the extent that this type of data analysis translates into innovative and better products, this can create positive feedback loops and also lock-in effects for the individual. Products and services that have been improved thanks to the use of collective user data are more attractive and will be more popular, resulting in a larger pool of data that can be used for further improvements and innovation. If it is precisely the individualised nature of a product or service that makes that product or service more useful to the consumer, this very same fact will also make it more costly for that consumer to switch suppliers – unless user profiles are portable. From the point of view of firms competing with the original supplier, these positive feedback loops and lock-in effects can be barriers to their entry into the market. Once a company is in a position of market power, these effects can perpetuate that power.

Besides individualised products and services, the data economy can also deliver other types of innovation, such as efficiency gains throughout the manufacturing and the sales processes. Usage data can be mined to help improve existing products. Classic examples of this are the error logs sent by software applications to their respective creators who use them to eliminate bugs.

b.   Versatile use across several markets: new economies of scope

One of the characteristics of user data, which provides insights into individual needs and preferences and makes it possible to predict consumers' behaviour in various different situations, is the ability of these data to be used in manifold ways and across several traditional markets. Data that was generated during the use of a particular service may decrease the marginal cost of innovation in other markets if they are used to spot gaps in the market, to enter new markets, or to develop new products that are exceptionally innovative. Economists refer to this as 'economies of scope' and, in this particular case, as 'data-driven indirect network effects'. Data generated in the course of developing or using one product may thus be used to improve a different, seemingly unrelated product. As soon as data of the type that can be used for other products has been collected, it will bring down the level of investment needed to enter a new market. This will make it cheaper to develop and create several different products or services within a single company rather than in separate companies. One example of this is Google, which uses data gathered for its search engine to better position Google Maps in the market for navigation systems.

One of the main reasons for the existence of these economies of scope is the fact that data can usually be used by several parties without rivalry. In other words, data will usually not vanish once it has been 'consumed' and can be used an infinite number of times for the purpose of developing or improving different products. At the same time, however, those holding the data may decide to use technical means to exclude other market participants from using the very same data. Whenever this happens, the benefits derived from access to these data will be limited to the "possessors" of the data – unless they decide to share them on a voluntary basis or as a result of a legal obligation under access rights.

c.   Marginal returns from data usage are increasing

It is argued by some that the marginal returns from the use of data are increasing, i.e. that the value of the data acquired by a company will be higher the more data the company already possesses. Where this is the case, it will be extremely difficult for companies with access to less data to compete with companies that are in control of large amounts of data. The answer to the question as to whether marginal returns are indeed increasing will differ between markets. Nevertheless, it is safe to assume that wherever data mining becomes a significant factor in the competition on a product or service market, those companies competing with 'data-rich' firms will be on the back foot. This is especially true wherever self-learning algorithms are used, the training and optimisation of which crucially depend on regular access to large amounts of data or at least access to highly diverse data. If algorithms are trained with too little data or with data that is too uniform, this will have a negative impact on the algorithms' abilities to deal with the problems they were supposed to solve.

At what point exactly the marginal returns of data can be expected to significantly fall will depend on the respective application of the data. Training a self-learning algorithm for diagnosing rare diseases, for instance, will require a very large and diverse pool of data, whereas smaller data volumes will suffice for establishing sufficiently reliable correlations between location data and visits to local coffee shops.

. . .

d.   The data economy as a new source of information asymmetries

Companies' access to user and consumer data is by no means an issue for competition law alone. It also establishes a new level of information asymmetry between companies and consumers. Detailed user profiles and the ability to predict consumers' behaviour in different situations can tempt companies to manipulate and exploit certain groups of consumers. If the interests of data-rich companies diverge from consumers' interests, the exploitation of information asymmetries may result – depending on the company's position on the market – in welfare losses and considerable distortions of competition.

All of this shows that the new data economy presents a challenge to the legislator – a challenge which goes beyond competition law in a narrow sense and which requires legislators to adjust the legal framework to ensure that competition remains a process of invention to the benefit of consumers.

2.   Concentration tendencies in platform markets

One of the key characteristics of the digital economy are platform-based business models which are increasingly integrated into the sales chain. The emergence of platform companies is resulting in changes to the structures of industries and value chains as well as to the global distribution of value creation. Thus, platform companies are causing structural changes in our economic system at large.

a.   Platforms come in various different forms

For analytical purposes, it makes sense to distinguish between advertising platforms and intermediation platforms. Advertising platforms are platforms that sell to one user group the attention of other user groups. Intermediation platforms, by contrast, are designed to bring together and connect members of different user groups according to their individual preferences and wishes.

Within this group of platforms one can further distinguish between transaction and non-transaction platforms. Transaction platforms are designed to facilitate economic transactions whereas non-transaction platforms mediate other types of interaction, such as 'matches' on dating websites. These latter interactions are often impossible for the platforms to observe. While this classification may be theoretically valid, it may be difficult to distinguish between these different types of platforms in practice. Search engines, for instance, often share characteristics of advertising and intermediation platforms.

Besides two-sided and multi-sided platforms that bring together two or more different groups of users, there are also one-sided networks which facilitate interaction within one single user group. This is typically the starting-point for pure social networks. However, since this type of service is often financed by advertisements, many of these networks do feature a second user group – the advertisers – which means that these networks are two-sided platforms after all. This report uses a broad definition of 'platform', which also includes networks that only cater to one group of users.

We can also differentiate between platforms that are aimed at consumers (B2C or business-to-consumer platforms) and platforms that are part of the value chain between businesses (B2B or business-to-business platforms). Retail platforms, hotel booking platforms, travel platforms, payment service providers, real estate, vehicle, and job-hunting portals as well as social networks are all examples of B2C platforms. Operating systems such as Android or iOS are also platforms, as they connect users with app providers. B2C platforms tend to strive for high user numbers.

B2B platforms, by contrast, act as intermediaries between companies. They come in the form of purchasing or sales platforms or service or software platforms. All of the users on both sides of the platform are companies, resulting in more individualised contracts between users and between users and the platform. The overall number of users of this type of platform also tends to be smaller than that of B2C platforms.

b.   Network effects as a key feature of the platform economy

The network effects manifested on platforms are a defining characteristic of the platform economy. It is important to distinguish between direct and indirect network effects. Positive direct network effects are present when the usefulness of a network increases with the number of participants or, in the case of a platform, with the size of a user group on one side. Positive indirect network effects occur when there is a growing number of users on one side of the platform that makes using that platform more interesting for those on the other side of the platform. Put more simply, this means that users will derive the greatest benefit from using the platform that has the most users already, either on the same side (positive direct network effects) or on the other side of the platform (positive indirect network effects). For example: Those seeking to sell goods or services will usually have a preference for an online market place that brings them into contact with the largest possible number of potential customers; conversely, customers will tend to visit online market places that offer the largest possible range of products or services that are relevant to them.

Negative (direct or indirect) network effects operate the opposite way around: if the number of users on one side of the platform is too big, the platform becomes less attractive for users on the same or opposite side of the platform. In the case of advertising-financed products or services, for instance, any network effects observed will often be asymmetrical, i.e. they will benefit those placing the advertisement whilst driving other users away.

c.   Specific features of platforms and platform-based markets

Platforms are a new element in the value chain and are transforming our economy. The following characteristics of platforms and platform-based markets are important for the purposes of this report:

In an economy that is based on the division of labour, platforms can generate value by bringing together upstream and downstream market participants. The platform can turn into a gatekeeper if it is able to control access to the other side of the market, for instance where customers tend to be active only on that one platform ('single homing').

The (direct and indirect) network effects that are characteristic of platforms enable companies to scale up their digital business models more easily and quickly. This also makes it easier to market innovative products and services. It is therefore common for newly founded platforms to focus on generating network effects by covering as much of the market as possible.

Platforms factor indirect network effects into their pricing, which often results in those on the consumer side paying less than the marginal cost, if anything at all, for a service.

Platforms creating market places or other spaces for online interaction set the rules governing the social interactions taking place in these virtual spaces. This can take the form of explicit rules (e.g. terms and conditions), implicit rules (e.g. those underpinning the ranking algorithms used by a platform) or the market or forum design including all of the institutions belonging to the platform (recommendation schemes, buy boxes etc.).

In the case of hybrid platforms (vertically integrated platforms) the operator itself also acts as a user of the platform—for instance by selling goods or services there. While this can lead to efficiency gains, e.g. by allowing the platform operator to respond more swiftly to changes on the market, it also creates room for distortion as platform operators may favour their own products and services.

3.   Digital ecosystems and conglomerate effects

Due to the rapid increase in the use of data and platforms for the creation and selling of products and services, value chains and economic structures are changing and new types of digital ecosystems emerge. While there is still plenty of uncertainty about the future development of this process in most industries, some patterns have already emerged.

One of these is referred to as 'Industrie 4.0' or the 'Industrial Internet'. In the industrial context, this is understood to mean an increased use of data that is available through the greater use of sensors as well as data processing with the help of software-based solutions, and the inter-connection of products with one another and with users and manufacturers (Internet of Things (IoT)). For instance, the wear and tear on a vehicle's brake pads is recorded by sensors and transmitted to the manufacturer who can use it to build a database that will allow him to optimise his brake pads; at the same time, the user of the car receives a message to have the defect fixed at a repair shop. This kind of technology can help create new value chains and modify existing ones, e.g. by modifying or replacing previous value creation stages. Companies seeking to create value in this environment may have to generate data themselves, so that it can be pooled with other data and used to build new platforms. This in turn may result in greater cooperation between different companies.

a.   Formation of new types of conglomerate structures

Another defining characteristic and pattern observed in digital ecosystems is the fact that data from several different markets are increasingly pooled by a single company. This allows new types of conglomerates to emerge.

Over the last few decades, conglomerates have become less prominent in traditional industries. In fact, many corporate groups that used to be active in different sectors have divested and focused on their core business. By contrast, conglomerate structures are experiencing a revival in the digital economy. Prominent examples of the growing importance of conglomerates have been leading US-based digital corporations including Facebook, Apple, Amazon, Netflix and Google. Large Chinese platform operators such as Tencent operate in a similar fashion. What all these companies have in common is that they are expanding into new markets which seem to have little to do with their core business. Amazon, for instance, is not only a retailer and market place provider, but also one of the world's largest providers of cloud-computing. Google is not only a search engine, but also active in online streaming, online advertising, smart phone operating systems, smart homes, self-driving cars etc. The increasingly conglomerate structures of many digital corporations is fed both by new companies established by these corporations as well as acquisitions of other companies, notably small and innovative start-ups.

The reasons why conglomerate structures are becoming more important in the digital world are manifold. There are supply-side and demand-side factors that sometimes reinforce each other (feedback loops), and which provide incentives for conglomerate activities.

On the supply side, this is particularly true of economies of scope in product development, as many different digital products or services are based on similar input factors. These include cloud services, identification and payment services, coding capacities and most importantly data.

These economies of scope provide an incentive to digital companies to widen their product range and branch out. The incentive for sharing such input factors only within the corporation is further increased by the absence of a market for unused resources such as personal data. Data, especially user data, is a key factor for economies of scope. Pooling user data is a way to create ever more detailed user profiles which can be used for continuous optimisation and personalisation of existing services and for identifying potential new products or services; in the best-case scenario, this will lead to a growing competitive advantage compared to other companies seeking to sell to the very same customers. In addition, access to large amounts of personal data also makes it possible to optimise personal advertising, which is the key source of financing for many digital products and services.

Those able to combine data from different sources are often able to achieve a significantly better position for their own services on the market. They are also better positioned to develop new products and to enter new markets. The use of user data across separate markets is a characteristic feature of the digital economy and can be regarded as a sub-type of economies of scope ('data-driven economies of scope'). Unlike in the case of traditional conglomerates, the various activities performed by digital conglomerates are closely linked by the user profiles being used. Against this background we need to interpret statements by digital companies saying that rather than competing on distinct product markets they compete for access to users.

Maximising access to data is also of crucial importance in the growing number of market segments in which the use of artificial intelligence, especially machine learning, is turning into a key enabling technology.

In addition to these supply-side factors, there can also be factors on the demand side that lead to conglomerate activities. Of special importance are consumption synergies. These exist where consumers derive a benefit from buying different products from the same supplier (e.g. through product bundling). Moreover, every additional digital service provided by a supplier also has the effect of strengthening the supplier's digital brand and builds consumer trust. There can also be incentives for companies to link up their various individual products and services to form their own ecosystem designed to inspire customer loyalty.

. . .

b.   Conglomerate structures may encourage anti-competitive conduct

Looking at conglomerate activities from a competition angle, it is important to assess whether a digital company is abusing its market power in a given market. For instance, it could leverage its power onto other markets rather than competing on the merits. Furthermore, there are circumstances where conglomerate mergers may result in significant impediments to effective competition.

In general terms – irrespective of the latest developments in the digital economy – the potential for restrictions to competition caused by conglomerates is often seen as a result of their 'deep pockets'. Financial strength may allow conglomerates to sell their products or services at a loss for a longer period, thus forcing their competitors out of the market or stopping them from entering it in the first place. Restraints of competition may also be caused by tying or bundling different products or by portfolio effects. At the same time, the resulting economies of scope may also lead to efficiency gains. From an economic point of view this means that any review of conglomerate corporate strategies or of conglomerate mergers must weigh up the potential harm to effective competition against the potential for efficiency gains. Legally, the competition rules do allow for considering efficiency gains, but set out strict criteria for this.

. . .

Problems under competition law may also arise if individual companies have exclusive access to certain resources or technologies that give them a competitive edge on other product markets. Exclusive access to data can be of key importance here. As has been explained above, the ability to collect and pool data from different sources can generate information that is important not only for the improvement of existing products and services, but also for the development of new ones. Access to data from one market and the ability to combine it with data from other markets could be a way of expanding into promising markets or strengthening one's position on these markets in ways that are similar to the 'classical' financial strength.

We would also like to point out that there is a danger that individual digital corporations that are widening their product and service ranges to create ecosystems of their own may become gatekeepers that control access to their users, where these are reluctant to leave the ecosystem (e.g. because of convenient product bundling). Examples of companies that are acting as gatekeepers are AppStores vis-à-vis web developers and operating systems vis-à-vis complementary service providers. Where third-party suppliers seeking to market their products are dependent on access to these users, the digital corporations controlling these ecosystems may be able to dictate the terms on which they are willing to grant access to these users.

III. Strengthening innovation and consumer autonomy in a dynamic economy

German and European legislators are currently faced with the task of adapting the existing legal framework to take account of the many changes taking place in the digital economy. The task of the Commission 'Competition Law 4.0' was to identify options for action that could help protect competition and the capacity for innovation and competitiveness of German and European companies under the new conditions created by the digital economy. The Commission 'Competition Law 4.0' was led in its considerations and the development of its recommendations by three guiding principles: the importance of innovation for competition and competition law (I.); the importance of informed and autonomous demand-side decisions for undistorted competition (II.); and the need for rules and institutions that can respond to the speed of change that is characteristic of the digital economy in a way that is flexible and is based on sufficient information (III.). These guiding principles are outlined below.

1. Objective: protecting competition as a driver of innovation

Innovation is a key driver of competition and economic development. The ability of companies to thrive in the race for innovation is key for their international competitiveness. This is particularly true in the current state of the digital economy: platform-driven business models have proven to be a disruptive innovation in many markets and are challenging the market positions of established companies. Efforts to identify new fields of application for platforms that link up businesses with consumers (B2C) and businesses with businesses (B2B) are continuing. The Internet of Things (IoT) is, in many different ways, designed to enable new types of networking. Using data to make production and sales processes more efficient and to design new products and services carries enormous potential for innovation for the foreseeable future.

The digital economy is, however, characterised by trends towards greater concentration. These tendencies are driven by large economies of scale and vast network and connectivity effects, and can create significant advantages for first movers. At a theoretical level, the way that innovation and competition affect one another remains a contentious issue. The permanent contest between businesses for positions of power on the market is, however, widely recognised to create important incentives for innovation. Companies that make risky investments must – once they manage to develop a successful innovation – be able to make a profit which, multiplied by the probability of success, exceeds the cost of the investment. For companies that are shielded from competition or that are able to shield themselves from competition, the incentive to develop innovations becomes weaker as they do not need to innovate in order to make high profits. If radical innovations emerge on the market, they can therefore expect their own returns to be cannibalised (replacement effect). Dominant companies that are not subject to the pressure of competition therefore have considerable incentives to focus on developing innovations which do not jeopardise their own business model. It is therefore crucial to maintain opportunities for companies to pursue decentralised innovations. Maintaining the contest between businesses to attain a position of power on the market also serves to protect innovation.

. . .

Dominant companies have a special responsibility to maintain the competition that still exists: they must not be allowed to take any action that hinders this competition or the development of this competition by acting in a way that is not compatible with the basic principles of competition. The stronger the position of dominance, the greater the probability that actions meant to secure this position will result in anti-competitive foreclosure. In an environment that is characterised by highly concentrated, strongly entrenched market power, the risk of permanent damage to competition and innovation is particularly high. The non-intervention of competition authorities against action that could potentially weaken contestability can therefore lead to high-level welfare losses.

The general thrust of innovation policy thus reinforces competition law in its goal to ensure contestability. The rising significance of innovation-based theories of harm in competition law reflects the role of innovation in competition. Recent decisions of the European Commission stress the importance of protecting both competition to innovate and consumers' freedom of choice.

Developing innovations can require cooperation – a fact that is broadly recognised in EU competition law. However, there is currently a high level of uncertainty regarding the (il)legality of new forms of cooperation – such as the exchange and sharing of data. A competition law that seeks to promote innovation needs to be designed in a way that allows companies to gain legal certainty on the lawfulness of new types of innovation projects with high investment potential.

2.   Objective: ensuring freedom of choice for consumers

In open markets with undistorted competition, the allocation of resources is driven by the choices made on the demand side. Competition as a discovery process draws an important part of its societal legitimacy from the fact that innovations and efficiency gains generated by competition ultimately benefit the consumer.

The digital economy has led to a massive increase in consumer options and has made it much easier to exercise choice. At the same time, it changes the conditions under which consumers decide. In particular, consumers are increasingly relying on the services provided by intermediaries. The availability of user data and user profiles allows for the personalisation of products and services, frequently to the benefit of consumers.

Under certain conditions, however, data-driven competition in products and sales can jeopardise the ability of consumers to steer competition in their interest. A growing literature points to the fact that digital intermediaries with access to detailed consumer user profiles may have the ability, and the incentive, to systematically exploit information asymmetries and/or bounded rationality. Furthermore, where certain product and service providers have exclusive access to individual user data, 'lock-in' effects may result and increase switching costs for consumers. This effect may be reinforced where a digital platform bundles a variety of interlocking services, including services that enable consumers to participate in the digital market in the first place, like communication services, digital identities, payment methods, cloud data storage and digital content management.

A legal framework that strives to protect open markets and undistorted competition, it is vital to give special consideration to these new conditions created by the digital economy. Such a legal framework must protect the ability of consumers to make meaningful choices and to determine how "their" data are processed and used. In this report, particular emphasis is therefore placed on strengthening the position of consumers in a variety of contexts.

One measure that can serve this objective is the creation of "data intermediaries" which are committed to upholding the interests of the data subjects whose data are processed. This objective can also justify legislation that strengthens the right to data portability vis-à-vis dominant companies and facilitates switching in typical lock-in situations. Reinforcing the position of consumers vis-à-vis dominant companies also increases contestability and contributes to an environment in which decentralised innovation can thrive. Consumer empowerment thus contributes to the objectives of competition policy.

3.   Objective: adapting regulatory structures to the conditions created by the digital transformation

European competition law is characterised by its broadly formulated general clauses. They have allowed competition authorities to analyse the new market conditions created by the digital economy case-by-case and to respond flexibly to the changes in market structures that it has brought about. However, applying competition rules often involves a great deal of time and resources. Based on experience and widely accepted economic insights, certain types of behaviour have been identified which, by their very nature, are considered harmful to the proper functioning of competition and are therefore generally prohibited (subject to an objective justification in an individual case) with no extensive effects analysis being required. This is so in the context of both the ban on cartels and the ban on the abuse of dominant positions.

However, in most cases the likely effects of a given conduct will need to be analysed with a view to the actual economic and legal context. The demands on this effects analysis have increased as the "more economic approach" has gained acceptance over the past 20 years. On the positive side, this leads to a considerable amount of knowledge about the changing market conditions being generated case by case and, ideally, to a high degree of fairness in each individual case. However, the number of cases that the competition authorities are able to process based on such a resource-intensive approach are limited.

. . .

The Commission 'Competition Law 4.0' works from the assumption that the following basic principles can be helpful in identifying an optimum structure of rules that foster competition and innovation in the digital economy:

Ideally, rules should be structured such that they minimise the overall costs for society resulting from welfare losses caused by wrong decisions (false positives and false negatives) and of the costs of enforcing the law.

If rules of conduct are simplistically divided into two groups – clear, simple and unambiguous rules of conduct which leave little room for interpretation (rules), and broad general clauses formulated to allow for interpretation (standards), the advantages and disadvantages of each type carry different weight in different contexts. If the factual information relevant to deciding a case is readily available, clear, simple and unambiguous rules of conduct can be implemented comparatively quickly and at low cost. Such rules send out clear signals to all concerned and facilitate planning. The rigidity and "formalism" of such rules can, however, have negative effects: if the particular circumstances of a given case are not taken into account, the number of decisions that are economically wrong may increase. In addition, such rules often leave less room for a rule evolution in reaction to new developments. Consequently, the legislator may be required to intervene more frequently. Developing the right rules at legislative level can be time-consuming and difficult given the variety and complexity of the economic issues involved, and in the face of a quickly changing environment.

The use of standards [as opposed to rules] is therefore particularly suitable if the legislator does not (yet) have sufficient knowledge about the breadth of the issues that are relevant to individual cases and the effects that certain behaviours will have. The relevant information can then be generated case by case. The decisions made can take account of actual differences in a flexible manner. Hence, standards lend themselves more towards an evolutionary development of law. The addressees of standards can feed relevant information into the decision-making process and thus contribute to the development of legal stipulations. However, the use of standards is associated with greater legal uncertainty, and application of the law requires a great deal of time and resources.

In very basic terms, rules and standards represent two opposite styles of legal stipulations. In practice, there is a variety of intermediate stipulations which seek to combine the advantages of both rules and standards depending on the specific contexts in which such stipulations are used. For example, where rules have been designed based on the presumption that a particular behaviour will have undesirable effects, a list of clearly defined exceptions can be issued. These then take account of a defined set of exceptional circumstances that can occur in individual cases. Similarly, rebuttable presumptions are frequently used. These, too, are based on the presumption that a particular behaviour will have undesirable effects, but enable the rule addressees to rebut this presumption by drawing upon information that is primarily available to them.

The Commission 'Competition Law 4.0' proposes that in markets that tend towards fast concentrations of power and therefore call for a particularly speedy intervention against anti-competitive practices by dominant companies, the best approach is for relatively simple rules of conduct to be applied. These send clear signals to the market as to what the "rules of the game" are and are easier and quicker to apply. Granting companies the opportunity to justify their conduct ensures that, with each application of the law, important information about new economic interrelationships is generated, which can then feed into the future development of rules of conduct. In the view of the Commission 'Competition Law 4.0', simple, generalised rules of conduct are not currently a suitable approach for other problem areas, such as obligating dominant companies to provide access to data. This is because the circumstances involved are too varied and the effects on competition too complex. The cost of making bad decisions when imposing simple, clear bans and obligations would be too high. Instead, the recommendation is to develop sector-specific rules on access to data, which would enable experience to be gathered and solutions to be tested in more narrow settings.

Reflections on the optimal structure of rules are closely linked to law enforcement structures. The changes in the digital economy raise the question of whether competition authorities alone are capable of providing sufficient protection for the competitive process, or whether new institutions need to be established. Furthermore, questions as to the relationship between the enforcement of competition law by competition authorities and the enforcement of other areas of digital law, particularly data protection law arise – areas of law which can also impact competition. . . .

In the past, the discussion about the advantages and disadvantages of having additional regulation that applies and is enforced alongside general competition rules has focused on the network industries in their transformation from a monopolistic regime to a competitive situation. Far-reaching interventions into the economic freedoms of the addressees of regulation (i.e. permanent supervision and monitoring, special obligations to provide information, codes of conduct and possibly licensing requirements) are justified here partly as transformational regimes and partly due to the economic characteristics of network infrastructures. The question as to which markets should be subject to regulation is examined according to three criteria: Markets should be regulated only if   i)   there   are significant and permanent barriers to entry, whether structural or legal, and ii) if no trend towards competition can be identified. The third precondition for regulation is that iii) general competition law alone is not enough to counter market failure.

Despite certain parallels to the conventional network industries, the digital economy is different. Among other things, the positions of power have emerged on the basis of competition. In addition to ensuring contestability, a key challenge is to deal with the conglomerate effects outlined above which can facilitate the leveraging of market power to new markets. As a result of the process of digitalisation, nearly all sectors are subject to rapid and complex changes that are often difficult to predict. In an environment in which there is a considerable degree of market dynamism and a high level of innovative potential, a regulatory regime characterised by heavy-handed intervention can entail high costs. At the same time, it is precisely these disruptive processes of change – compared to a relatively stable market environment characterised by more incremental innovation – which call for a continuous generation of not only case-specific, but cross-sectoral information, and for a close dialogue between competition authorities and other authorities (e.g. consumer protection and data protection authorities) so that a coherent legal framework for the digital economy can be developed that adequately considers the special features of the digital economy and the interaction between different areas of law. Moreover, an evolutionary approach towards rule development may be too slow, such that a more rapid rule-setting is needed.

All of these aspects argue against the idea of establishing a public utilities-style regulation for the digital economy; at the same time, they also indicate that the conventional mechanisms of implementing competition rules are not always sufficient in order to respond to emerging trends towards a concentration of power. This may make it necessary to develop other instruments for systematically generating information, developing rules and implementing the law. Whilst the Commission 'Competition Law 4.0' does not arrive at unanimous recommendations on how such a regime should be designed, it does agree on this initial finding. There is also agreement that it can be helpful to develop sectoral rules that can be used to target the particular problems found on specific markets. Sector-specific rules – for example on data access, data portability, or interoperability – can also serve as a regulatory sandbox for rules that could subsequently be generalised.

. . .

Notes

1.   This report is only one of a number of reports focusing on competition in the digital economy. These reports include the following (by date of publication): Heike Schweitzer et al., Modernisierung der Missbrauchsaufsicht für marktmächtige Unternehmen (2018), available at https://www.bmwi.de/Redaktion/ DE/Publikationen/Wirtschaft/modernisierung-der-missbrauchsaufsicht-fuer-marktmaechtige-unternehmen.pdf, with Modernising the law on abuse of market power: Summary of the report's recommendations in English at https://www.bmwi.de/Redaktion/DE/Downloads/Studien/modernisierung-der-missbrauchsaufsicht-fuer-marktmaechtige-unternehmen-zusammenfassung-englisch.pdf; Unlocking Competition: Report of the Digital Competition Expert Panel (2019) (the "Furman Report"), https://assets.publishing.service. gov.uk/government/uploads/system/uploads/attachment_data/file/785547/ unlocking_digital_competition_furman_review_web.pdf; European Commission, Competition policy for the digital era: Final report (2019), http://ec.europa.eu/ competition/publications/reports/kd0419345enn.pdf; Australian Competition & Consumer Commission, Digital Platforms Inquiry: Final Report (2019), https://www.accc.gov.au/system/files/. A very useful review of most of these reports is Wolfgang Kerber, "Updating Competition Policy for the Digital Economy? An Analysis of Recent Reports in Germany, UK, EU, and Australia," https://papers.ssrn.com/sol3/papers.cfm?abstract_id=3469624, September 14, 2019.

2.   What are economies of scope? Increasing marginal returns? Network externalities? Are these phenomena unique to the digital environment? See section 2.1 below.

3.   To what extent does this report support or undermine the arguments made in the preceding readings? Are you convinced that the digital economy is different? In what way?

4.   Is it a valid goal for competition law "to enable German and European digital companies to successfully compete internationally"? As you go through this book, consider whether the European cases would have produced a different result in the U.S.

Some of the Utah Statement's proposals are arguably designed to enable smaller digital companies to successfully compete with larger ones. Is that a valid goal for competition law?

5.   Should a dominant firm have a special responsibility to maintain any competition that remains despite its dominance? What might that mean? Should a dominant firm have to operate according to different, more restrictive

rules (or standards) than a non-dominant firm? Is the answer to that question different in the digital economy? See section 2.2 below.

6.   Is individualized pricing a good or a bad thing? Does it depend on which buyers get high prices and which get low prices? See section 2.2.3 below.

1. Horizontal Restraints of Trade

1.1 Price-Fixing Agreements

Despite the analytical problems many traditional price-fixing cases pose, many such cases are conceptually straightforward compared to some recent cases. For example, *Broadcast Music* and *Maricopa* both involve alleged price-fixing of final products offered for sale by the agreeing sellers. In contrast, the article excerpt and case below address conceptual problems regarding the nature of competition that the law should regulate. These problems are created in part because there is some distinction between (for Uber) the parties providing the services at issue or (for LIBOR) the product at issue and the final product offered for sale. That leads to questions about where the analysis should be applied.

1.1.1 The "Gig Economy"

The reading immediately below considers Uber and by extension other providers in the "gig economy." Should the setting of prices by Uber, Airbnb, and other such providers be viewed as an agreement to which Sherman Action section 1 should apply? If so, who are the parties to the agreement? From one perspective, Uber serves as a vehicle for coordinating price among its drivers. In this respect, it is important to note that an early U.S. Supreme Court case, *United States v. Socony-Vacuum Oil Co., Inc.*, 310 U.S. 150 (1940), held that agreements "with the effect of raising, depressing, fixing, pegging, or stabilizing" prices are illegal *per se*. From another perspective, though, Uber is an independent, risk-bearing entity that differs from the medical societies at issue in *Maricopa* in a way that the Supreme Court in that case appeared to conclude was important.

Another Supreme Court case, *Copperweld Corp. v. Independence Tube Corp.*, 467 U.S. 752 (1984), is useful for considering the Uber situation. *Copperweld* involved an alleged price-fixing agreement between a corporation and its wholly-owned subsidiary. The Supreme Court held that such entities are part of a single enterprise and thus cannot conspire for the purposes of Sherman Act section 1, establishing the "intra-enterprise conspiracy" doctrine. This doctrine also applies to exclude "conspiracies" between a firm and its employees from Sherman Act section 1. The "intra-enterprise conspiracy doctrine" is thus at least similar to what the author calls the "firm exception" to antitrust law.

The author also discusses two cases that are often part of a traditional antitrust course, *National Society of Professional Engineers v. United States*, 435 U.S. 679 (1978), and *FTC v. Superior Court Trial Lawyers Association*, 493 U.S. 411 (1990). *Professional Engineers* involved an agreement among engineers to refuse to disclose price to their customers until those customers had chosen an engineer. The Supreme Court condemned the agreement without considering the engineers' quality justifications for it, though without using the *"per se"* label. In *Trial Lawyers*, the agreement was one among lawyers to refuse to represent indigent defendants in the District of Columbia unless the rates for doing so were raised. Again the Court condemned the agreement without regard to the defendants' justification, in this case explicitly applying a *per se* rule.

The article briefly mentions the state-action exemption to U.S. antitrust law. That doctrine, stemming from *Parker v. Brown*, 317 U.S. 341 (1943), exempts from antitrust scrutiny acts of the states as well as acts of private parties that are "clearly articulated and affirmatively expressed as state policy" and "actively supervised" by a state. *See* California Retail Liquor Dealers Assn. v. Midcal Aluminum, Inc., 445 U.S. 97 (1980).

Sanjukta M. Paul
Uber as For-Profit Hiring Hall: A Price-Fixing Paradox and its Implications
38 Berkeley Journal of Employment and Labor Law 233 (2017)

INTRODUCTION

. . . In two recent high-profile cases, *Meyer v. Kalanick*[1] and *Chamber of Commerce v. City of Seattle*,[2] Uber has pressed against drivers' coordination on antitrust grounds, while seeking to protect its own price-coordination activity from antitrust scrutiny. These litigation positions serve to dramatize a tension that inheres in status quo regulation of Uber and of independent contractor service providers more generally.

Antitrust law generally forbids sellers of a commodity from coordinating among each other regarding the price of that commodity. That prohibition on price-fixing extends to express agreements to set a price, to joint bargaining with buyers, and to lesser coordination that would affect price, such as an agreement to restrict supply. Sellers of labor are exempted from this prohibition, and may coordinate the price of their labor. This exemption— the labor exemption—creates the space for affirmative protections of collective bargaining by workers with their employers over wages and working conditions. Historically, the rationale for the labor exemption was that there are many reasons to treat labor differently from other commodities – or that perhaps it is not a commodity at all. The debate about those reasons and what they require of regulation is ongoing today, particularly as questions of labor law failure and potential reform increasingly predominate. This paper sets aside these important questions, and focuses on a slightly different

---

[1] Complaint, Meyer v. Kalanick, 174 F. Supp. 3d 817 (S.D.N.Y. 2016) (No. 1:15-CV-9796), 2015 WL 9166194.

[2] Complaint, Chamber of Commerce of the U.S. v. City of Seattle, 2016 WL 836320 (W.D. Wash. Mar. 3, 2016) (No. 2:16-CV-00322).

matter, that nevertheless has implications for a broad swath of contemporary workers and perhaps ultimately also for labor law reform. To wit, while it is near-axiomatic that firms have the right to set prices, Uber tests the limits of intra-firm immunity from price-fixing liability, and it does so by reorganizing its relationship to those who perform work. It turns out that the "firm exemption" from antitrust, as I will call it, has significant implications for workers and work regulation.

. . . The key statutory sources of the labor exemption are the Norris-La Guardia Act and the Clayton Act . . . . The labor exemption has been understood to be delineated by the boundaries of the employment relationship, a coextension that resulted from foundational case-law rather than express statutory language (in contrast to other key statutes that regulate work relationships, such as the Fair Labor Standards Act, etc.). In fact, the distinction between employees and non-employees was simply not a very legally salient one prior to the New Deal, partly because of the relative paucity of legislative work regulation. Although there are limited exceptions to that coextension, those recognized exceptions are nevertheless still derivative of the employment relationship in concept and purpose, and their applicability to the growing number of workers who labor outside the bounds of employment is very limited. . . .

. . .

I.

A PUZZLE ABOUT PRICE-FIXING

The regulatory structure in which Uber and other similar ride-services firms currently operate enacts an inconsistency: it permits Uber to engage in price coordination of ride services and bars Uber drivers from engaging in price coordination of the very same commodity. This regulatory structure, however, is somewhat unstable and dynamic, as the litigation discussed here shows. Seattle's ordinance would effectively undo the inconsistency by extending the right to engage in price coordination to Uber drivers, and the antitrust lawsuit against Uber would undo the inconsistency in the opposite direction—by eliminating Uber's ability to engage in price coordination. Meanwhile, the Chamber of Commerce's challenge to the Seattle ordinance on antitrust grounds, together with Uber's defense of its own price coordination in the lawsuit against it, together give voice to the *status quo* and its contradictions.

Uber wants to deny its drivers the right to collectively bargain over their payment, while also setting prices that raise costs for riders and enhance profits for Uber. Taking Uber's position in *Kalanick* together with the U.S. Chamber of Commerce's position in *City of Seattle*, we derive the following proposition: price-fixing norms ought to regulate the market in which Uber and Uber drivers bargain with each other, and price-fixing norms ought *not* regulate the bargain between Uber and Uber riders. This is paradoxical, for it implies that Uber is entitled to derive an economic benefit from a premium from coordination in the price of ride services, at the expense of Uber riders, while Uber drivers are not entitled to benefit

from the premium, for precisely the antitrust reasons that—if one accepts them—
ought to prevent Uber for doing so.

A. *Price-Fixing in City of Seattle*

In the final month of 2015, the City of Seattle passed an ordinance that
grants collective bargaining rights to drivers for taxicab, limo, and "transportation
network companies" (encompassing Uber, Lyft and other companies in the ride
services sector) who are classified as independent contractors rather than
employees (hereinafter "the Seattle ordinance"). The ordinance creates a process
for the certification of an exclusive worker representative, which will negotiate on
behalf of drivers who contract with a particular "driver coordinator" or
transportation network company as to "terms and conditions of work," including
entering into a contract on behalf of those drivers that sets out such terms and
conditions. In this the ordinance parallels the basic function and structure of the
National Labor Relations Act: it provides a mechanism for workers to collectively,
rather than individually, bargain for the terms and conditions of their work, on the
premise that they are not able to do so effectively on an individual basis. Yet the
ordinance is novel in that it guarantees collective bargaining rights to workers
without requiring the threshold showing of employee status, as the NLRA and its
state analogues generally do. Seattle subsequently released some of the key
regulations implementing the ordinance.

The Chamber of Commerce sued the City of Seattle, challenging the
ordinance as preempted by federal antitrust law. The lawsuit characterized the
purpose of the Sherman Act as protecting and promoting "market freedom," and
described the "on-demand economy" typified by Uber and similar firms as the
natural consequence of this market freedom and of the "exceptional" American
"entrepreneurial tradition." The lawsuit challenged the Seattle ordinance on the
ground that the regulation threatens the operation of market freedom and the
entrepreneurial model of the on-demand economy. Suggesting that they are the
same thing, it alleged that the Seattle ordinance constitutes an illegal restraint of
trade under the Sherman Act, because the collective bargaining contemplated by
the ordinance constitutes illegal price-fixing in ride services.

Although the actual contest in *City of Seattle* is likely to take place to a
large extent upon the terrain of the state action exception to antitrust, lurking
beneath that issue is the deeper question of the proper interpretation of price-fixing
law itself. The dominant interpretation of price-fixing law, which is enthusiastically
adopted by the Chamber's lawsuit, punishes all cooperation between sellers without
regard to their material circumstances and without regard to the existing
concentrations of power in the market at issue. The linchpin of the Chamber's
complaint aggressively extends this interpretation to the rapidly growing sector of
gig economy workers, to whom it has never before been applied. While that
interpretation is partially the result of the limits of the labor exemption, it is also
the result of developments that are entirely internal to the law of price-fixing, rather
than about fixing its borders. Over much of the last century, the law of price-fixing
grew away from considering market power and related considerations, and toward

an intensification of the per se rule about price coordination (and economically equivalent coordination by sellers, such as coordination of supply). The apotheosis of this tendency is well-represented by *Trial Lawyers* and *Professional Engineers*. Both cases involved groups of individual or microenterprise service-providers whose coordination or collective action the Court deemed to be price-fixing while refusing to consider whether the coordination or resultant prices were reasonable. In *Professional Engineers*, even coordination over non-price elements of consumer bargains (safety and quality standards) within a professional trade group was deemed anticompetitive. *Trial Lawyers* censured collective action by a group of panel attorneys who represented indigent defendants and were paid low hourly rates, rates that essentially all the relevant agreed did not serve public policy. These are precisely the cases cited in the *City of Seattle* complaint for its core theory:

> Under § 1 of the Sherman Antitrust Act, a "contract, combination in the form of trust or otherwise, or conspiracy, in restraint of trade or commerce among the several States" is illegal. 15 U.S.C. § 1. As the Supreme Court has repeatedly held, this provision forbids independent economic actors— such as independent contractors—from colluding on the prices they would accept for their services or otherwise engaging in concerted anticompetitive action in the marketplace. [citing *Trial Lawyers* and *Professional Engineers*] Specifically, collective bargaining by independent contractors over the price and terms of a service is per se illegal under § 1 of the Sherman Act. [citing *Professional Engineers*].

This tendency is mostly *latent* in the sense that the labor exemption has protected most individual workers from this aspect of price-fixing law for most of the twentieth century and has blunted or obscured some of its more extreme implications. Of course, the reach of the labor exemption is waning precisely to the extent that the performance of services in the contemporary economy shifts from firms operating on an employment model to (various) organizational forms that do not involve the employment relationship. This receding of the labor exemption thus exposes the starker implications of the law of price-fixing for sellers who lack wealth and market power.

The theory of the complaint, and the rule of price-fixing law upon which it relies, implies that any price premium realized by coordination in the price of services, such as ride services, is a violation of the Sherman Act. The Chamber of Commerce in *City of Seattle* seeks to maintain the regulatory space that Uber has relied upon thus far, to wit, one in which Uber drivers do not have the right to engage in collective action or collective bargaining regarding the terms and conditions of their work. In its attack on the ordinance, the Chamber's litigation position draws out commitments embedded in that status quo: that price-fixing should prohibit price coordination among sellers of a service (regardless of their size, wealth or market power).

B. *Price-Fixing in Kalanick*

In *Kalanick*, as in *City of Seattle*, Uber is also defending an aspect of the *status quo*, but here that entails shielding rather than prohibiting coordination in the price of ride services. The *status quo* regulatory structure in which Uber operates currently permits Uber's price coordination activity.

Kalanick is a putative class action lawsuit brought on behalf of Uber riders, alleging an illegal price-fixing conspiracy in violation of Section of 1 of the Sherman Act. In this, its basic legal theory is identical to that of *City of Seattle*. The core issue it presents is this: "plaintiff alleges that Uber drivers agree to participate in a conspiracy among themselves when they assent to the terms of Uber's written agreement . . . and accept riders using the Uber app." The plaintiff thus posits Uber itself, in place of *City of Seattle*'s "exclusive worker representative," as the mechanism of the illegal price coordination. At its essence, *Kalanick* surfaces a long-buried issue that parallels the more visible matter of the labor exemption: the limits of the firm exemption from price-fixing law, whereby intra-firm price coordination is immunized. Ironically, it is Uber's innovative self-conception—which has lent legal traction to its bypassing of traditional *labor* regulation—that is ultimately responsible for this resurfacing.

Kalanick's basic theory of liability also implies that collective action by Uber drivers ought not to be permitted. Thus, on its own it should be seen as cold comfort by critics of Uber who are also worker advocates. Some such advocates have criticized the Uber "disruption" for wreaking havoc on existing workers', mainly taxi drivers', livelihoods as well as being bad for Uber drivers. A loss for Uber in *Kalanick* would only worsen both of these effects by driving down rates of pay even further.

The Uber app matches riders with drivers based on location, uses a pricing algorithm to set the fare for a ride, and provides a mechanism for riders to pay drivers. It collects a percentage of the fare, characterizing that portion as a "software licensing fee." The price set by Uber is mandatory: drivers do not have the ability to set their own price or to depart from the price set by the app.

The lawsuit is motivated in large part by Uber's "surge pricing" practice, wherein fares may rise up to tenfold the standard in times of high demand, and much of the attention on the case (as well as a good portion of the complaint and motion practice) has been focused on this. In its ruling on Kalanick's motion to dismiss, the court analyzed the plaintiff's allegations in terms of two possible species of price-fixing liability: a horizontal or a vertical price-fixing agreement or conspiracy. A horizontal conspiracy is an agreement between direct competitors on price; it is the paradigm case of price-fixing. As such, it is subject to the *per se* rule, which means that the agreement is prohibited on its face, regardless of its consequences or context. Not even the reasonableness of the resultant prices, nor other procompetitive effects of the agreements, are a defense. Generally speaking, vertical restraints involve agreements or conditions, regarding or affecting price, imposed by an actor upon downstream sellers. The regulation of vertical restraints affecting price is more complex and subject to more exceptions than that of horizontal restraints; courts consider such restraints' overall effects under the *rule of reason*. Unlike the *per se* rule, the rule of reason allows a decision-maker to consider the effects of an agreement or arrangement to decide whether it ought to be permitted under antitrust. A court's analysis of vertical restraints under the rule of reason may include consideration of the primary actor's market power (whereas market power is not considered in the evaluation of horizontal restraints or agreements). Thus, for example, Uber's surge pricing practice may be relevant to liability under the vertical restraint theory, because it may tend to show that Uber has the market power to unilaterally set prices. However, the surge pricing issue is secondary under the core, horizontal restraint analysis. While it would certainly affect the extent of damages, liability ought to either attach or not attach on the basis of the app's mandatory pricing mechanism. This follows from the general rule that it is the fact of coordination in prices that is the issue, not whether the resultant price is reasonable or exorbitant, nor even whether the resultant price ultimately benefits the seller.

Thus, the core issue in the case, and the one with which this paper is primarily concerned, is this: "As to the horizontal conspiracy, plaintiff alleges that Uber drivers agree to participate in a conspiracy among themselves when they assent to the terms of Uber's written agreement . . . and accept riders using the Uber app." This framing of the contest puts Uber in the position of arguing that the agreements and relationships to be assessed are vertical, not horizontal. It argues that the fact that "a condition of [the agreement between drivers and Uber] was that the driver-partner agree to use Uber's pricing algorithm" is not sufficient to establish a single multilateral horizontal agreement, rather than many vertical bilateral agreements. Uber then cites a body of cases involving resale price maintenance agreements, in which manufacturers' agreements with retailers or other downstream sellers to charge minimum prices are subject to rule of reason rather than per se treatment, and are sometimes permitted under that analysis.

Apart from the merits of the analogy to resale price maintenance agreements, it is interesting that Uber, which presses the strong version of the *per se* rule against coordination by Uber drivers in *City of Seattle* and in its articulations of its business model elsewhere, invokes resale price maintenance in its own defense. Resale price maintenance as a practice –and as a practice tolerated or sanctioned by antitrust and related regulation– has its roots in the "fair trade" movement spearheaded by small business-people, notably a group of California pharmacists in the 1920's and 1930's, to influence industry practice as well as to influence antitrust regulators and lawmakers. Resale price maintenance is an aspect of a minor strain in antitrust law that sometimes permits arrangements that may not maximize short-term competition between existing sellers in a given market, but which are justified on other grounds. But not only in litigation positions espoused by its representatives and principals, but also in its general self-proclaimed ethos, Uber usually purports to embody the pure competition-maximizing strain.

The court rejected the resale price maintenance argument, correctly noting that the analogy to resale price maintenance is incoherent because on Uber's own account of its business model, Uber is not selling a commodity to drivers that drivers are then reselling to riders—which is the core structure of resale price maintenance. The court holds that the plaintiff's horizontal conspiracy claim is legally cognizable, under a "hub and spoke" theory of conspiracy whereby multiple express vertical agreements effect a single instance of horizontal coordination. Uber is the hub in this picture: both the architect and, via the app and the pricing algorithm, the mechanism of the price coordination. Like the "exclusive worker representative" at issue in City of Seattle, it effects horizontal coordination in the price of ride services.

I note now, and will further discuss below, that this theory of liability would be unintelligible if Uber *did* hold itself out as a transportation company and engaged Uber drivers on an employment model, for a very simple reason: Uber drivers' coordination, around which the alleged conspiracy is expressly built, would be immunized by the labor exemption to antitrust. It is Uber's skirting of the employment model that raises the specter of price-fixing in the first place. Conversely, the *Kalanick* lawsuit also relies upon the same contention that drives the antitrust challenge to the Seattle ordinance: that coordination by individuals selling their services—perhaps nothing more than their labor—ought to be prosecuted as a price-fixing conspiracy, regardless of reasonableness of price and regardless of market power, so long as those individuals are not employees.

Critics and boosters of Uber often tend to either undervalue or overvalue the role of the app. A skeptic may cast the app as little more than a diversionary tactic for regulatory avoidance by Uber. Meanwhile, Uber and many of its defenders seem to characterize the app as so powerful that it may dispense a wisdom that is independent of the humans who control it. In fact, Uber's model, which matches drivers to riders by use of a smartphone app, dispensing with a dispatcher or with the need to physically sight and hail a cab, seems to be a genuine operational innovation. This technology affects the speed of the transaction, the cost, and the wait-time. As a result of all these—and probably *also* as a result of regulatory avoidance that gives Uber and similar firms an obvious competitive advantage over taxi services that are compelled to follow existing regulations— many more riders and drivers are brought into the market for exchanging rides for money. But there is no need to suppose that the changes that Uber has wrought in this market must all be due either to operational innovation on one hand, or to regulatory arbitrage on the other.

A specific peril of overvaluing the app is the conflation of a new *means* of accomplishing an old purpose with the undertaking of an entirely new purpose, particularly where the applicability of a set of regulations turns on that distinction. This sometimes leads, in the context of Uber and other gig economy firms, to the attempted erasure of human agency. This point has been made generally about the gig economy and Uber, for example in the context of racial and other illegal discrimination. The point applies just as forcefully to any price coordination performed by Uber and executed by means of the app. The *Kalanick* court seems to share this view, namely that the app may be the *means* of the price coordination:

> . . .[T]he capacity to orchestrate such an agreement is the 'genius' of Mr. Kalanick and his company, which, through the magic of smartphone technology, can invite hundreds of thousands of drivers in far-flung locations to agree to Uber's terms. The advancement of technological

means for the orchestration of large-scale price-fixing conspiracies need not leave antitrust law behind.

The court thus rejects the conflation of the economic function of the pricing algorithm and the technological functioning of the software.

The regulatory status quo with respect to Uber seems to permit a "supracompetitive price premium" in such services, but to allocate that premium entirely to Uber. Absent a loss in *Kalanick*, Uber continues to derive such a premium from its price coordination; absent enforcement of a regulation like Seattle's, drivers cannot coordinate in bargaining a share of that premium. To put it another way, the regulatory *status quo* permits Uber to evade price-fixing norms in its bargaining with consumers, but does not allow drivers to evade them in its bargaining with Uber. If we agree that price-fixing norms either ought to govern the price of a given service, in this case ride services, or not, then status quo regulation contains a tension.

. . .

Notes

1.   Is it true, given any traditional antitrust cases you have read, that "[t]he dominant interpretation of price-fixing law . . . punishes all cooperation between sellers without regard to their material circumstances and without regard to the existing concentrations of power in the market at issue"?

2.   We will take up the distinction between horizontal and vertical agreements in more detail later, but given the descriptions in the article, could the agreements in *Broadcast Music* and/or *Maricopa* be seen as vertical agreements?

3.   Should the application of antitrust law differ depending on whether workers are employees or independent contractors? Should the answer to that question depend on the nature or degree of "independence" of the independent contractors? Is it desirable for firms like Uber to decide between using employees and using independent contracts in part based on antitrust? Would it be desirable for antitrust rules to be based on labor or employment policy? Is that what the author is proposing?

4.   Does the digital economy facilitate the switch by an employer/coordinator from employees to independent contractors. In this respect, one might consider Ronald H. Coase, "The Nature of the Firm," 4 *Economica* 386 (1937), where Coase argued that firms arise (or, presumably, persist) when it is easier or less costly to coordinate through the employer-employee relationship than through the market.

1.1.2 Information-Fixing in LIBOR

The case below considers the distinction between cooperation and competition in a recent high-profile case. It refers to a Supreme Court case from 1988, *Allied Tube & Conduit Corp. v. Indian Head, Inc.*, 486 U.S. 492 (1988). In *Allied Tube*, one of several Supreme Court cases in this area, the Court addresses joint standard-setting activities. Many standard-setting organizations adopt standards for a variety of products, and the members of such organizations are often the sellers of the products at issue. In *Allied Tube* the defendant arranged with others to vote against a proposal that would have permitted market entry by a competitor.

The Court in *Allied Tube* said that "[w]hen . . . private associations promulgate safety standards based on the merits of objective expert judgments and through procedures that prevent the standard-setting process from being biased by members with economic interests in stifling product competition, those private standards can have significant procompetitive advantages." It also said, though, that "the hope of procompetitive benefits depends upon the existence of safeguards sufficient to prevent the standard-setting process from being biased by members with economic interests in restraining competition."

Gelboim v. Bank of America Corp.
823 F.3d 759 (2d Cir. 2016)

JACOBS, Circuit Judge:

Appellants purchased financial instruments, mainly issued by the defendant banks, that carried a rate of return indexed to the London Interbank Offered Rate ("LIBOR"), which approximates the average rate at which a group of designated banks can borrow money. Appellees, 16 of the world's largest banks ("the Banks"), were on the panel of banks that determined LIBOR each business day based, in part, on the Banks' individual submissions. It is alleged that the Banks colluded to depress LIBOR by violating the rate-setting rules, and that the payout associated with the various financial instruments was thus below what it would have been if the rate had been unmolested. Numerous antitrust lawsuits against the Banks were consolidated into a multi-district litigation ("MDL").

The United States District Court for the Southern District of New York (Buchwald, J.) dismissed the litigation in its entirety on the ground that the complaints failed to plead antitrust injury, which is one component of antitrust standing. The district court reasoned that the LIBOR-setting process was collaborative rather than competitive, that any manipulation to depress LIBOR therefore did not cause appellants to suffer anticompetitive harm, and that they have at most a fraud claim based on misrepresentation. The complaints were thus dismissed on the ground that they failed to allege harm to competition.

. . .

BACKGROUND

"Despite the legal complexity of this case, the factual allegations are rather straightforward." *In re: LIBOR-Based Fin. Instruments Antitrust Litig.*, 935 F.Supp.2d 666, 677 (S.D.N.Y. 2013) ("LIBOR I"). Appellants entered into a variety of financial transactions at interest rates that reference LIBOR. Because LIBOR is a component or benchmark used in countless business dealings, it has been called "the world's most important number." Issuers of financial instruments typically set interest rates at a spread above LIBOR, and the interest rate is frequently expressed in terms of the spread. LIBOR rates are reported for various intervals, such as one month, three months, six months, and twelve months.

The LIBOR-based financial instruments held by the appellants included: (1) asset swaps, in which the owner of a bond pegged to a fixed rate pays that fixed rate to a bank or investor while receiving in return a floating rate based on LIBOR; (2) collateralized debt obligations, which are structured asset-backed securities with multiple tranches, the most senior of which pay out at a spread above LIBOR; and (3) forward rate agreements, in which one party receives a fixed interest rate on a principal amount while the counterparty receives interest at the fluctuating LIBOR on the same principal amount at a designated endpoint. These examples are by no means exhaustive.

The Banks belong to the British Bankers' Association ("BBA"), the leading trade association for the financial-services sector in the United Kingdom. During the relevant period, the BBA was a private association that was operated without regulatory or government oversight and was governed by senior executives from twelve banks. The BBA began setting LIBOR on January 1, 1986, using separate panels for different currencies. Relevant to this appeal, the U.S. Dollar ("USD") LIBOR panel was composed of 16 member banks of the BBA.

The daily USD LIBOR was set as follows. All 16 banks were initially asked: "At what rate could you borrow funds, were you to do so by asking for and then accepting inter-bank offers in a reasonable market size just prior to 11 a.m.?" Each bank was to respond on the basis of (in part) its own research, and its own credit and liquidity risk profile. Thomson Reuters later compiled each bank's submission and published the submissions on behalf of the BBA. The final LIBOR was the mean of the eight submissions left after excluding the four highest submissions and the four lowest. Among the many uses and advantages of the LIBOR-setting process is the ability of parties to enter into floating-rate transactions without extensive negotiation of terms.

Three key rules governed the LIBOR-setting process: each panel bank was to independently exercise good faith judgment and submit an interest rate based upon its own expert knowledge of market conditions; the daily submission of each bank was to remain confidential until after LIBOR was finally computed and published; and all 16 individual submissions were to be published along with the final daily rate and would thus be "transparent on an ex post basis." Thus any single bank would be deterred from submitting an out-lying LIBOR bid that would risk negative media attention and potential regulatory or government scrutiny.

Collectively, these three rules were intended as "safeguards ensuring that LIBOR would reflect the forces of competition in the London interbank loan market."

Although LIBOR was set jointly, the Banks remained horizontal competitors in the sale of financial instruments, many of which were premised to some degree on LIBOR. With commercial paper, for example, the Banks received cash from purchasers in exchange for a promissory obligation to pay an amount based, in part, on LIBOR at a specified maturity date (usually nine months); in such transactions, the Banks were borrowers and the purchasers were lenders. Similarly, with swap transactions, the Banks received fixed income streams from purchasers in exchange for variable streams that incorporated LIBOR as the reference point.

A LIBOR increase of one percent would have allegedly cost the Banks hundreds of millions of dollars. Moreover, since during the relevant period the Banks were still reeling from the 2007 financial crisis, a high LIBOR submission could signal deteriorating finances to the public and the regulators.

Appellants allege that the Banks corrupted the LIBOR-setting process and exerted downward pressure on LIBOR to increase profits in individual financial transactions and to project financial health. In a nutshell, appellants contend that, beginning in 2007, the Banks engaged in a horizontal price-fixing conspiracy, with each submission reporting an artificially low cost of borrowing in order to drive LIBOR down. The complaints rely on two sources.

The vast majority of allegations follow directly from evidence collected in governmental investigations.[5] The United States Department of Justice ("DOJ") unearthed numerous potentially relevant emails, communications, and documents, some of which are referenced in the complaints and only a few of which are referenced for illustrative purposes. Prompted by the DOJ investigations, three banks — Barclays, UBS, and RBS — have reached settlements over criminal allegations that they manipulated and fixed LIBOR.

In addition, the complaints rely on statistics. The DOJ compiled evidence that from June 18, 2008 until April 14, 2009, UBS's individual three-month LIBOR submissions were identical to the later-published LIBOR benchmark that was based

---

[5] *See, e.g.,* "Second Amended Complaint," The City of Philadelphia & The Pennsylvania Intergovernmental Cooperation Authority v. Bank of America Corporation et al., *In re: LIBOR–Based Fin. Instruments Litig.*, No. 1:11–md–2262 (S.D.N.Y. Oct. 6, 2014) at 33 ¶ 104 (Doc. 667) ("[A] Barclays manager conceded in a recently-disclosed liquidity call to the FSA **to the extent that, um, the LIBORs have been understated, are we guilty of being part of the pack? You could say we are.**" (bolding and emphasis in original) (internal quotation marks omitted)); id. at 41 ¶ 122 ("UBS managers directed that the bank's USD Libor submissions be artificially suppressed so as to **place UBS in the middle of the pack of panel bank submissions** ." (bolding and emphasis in original) (internal quotation marks omitted)); id. at 47 ¶ 140 ("One RBS trader gloated, [i]t's just amazing how Libor fixing can make you that much money. **It's a cartel now in London.**" (bolding and emphasis in original) (internal quotation marks omitted)).

on all 16 submissions; the statistical probability that UBS independently predicted LIBOR exactly over approximately ten consecutive months is minuscule. Furthermore, prior to 2007, the value of LIBOR had moved in tandem with the Federal Reserve Eurodollar Deposit Rate ("FRED"), with LIBOR tracking slightly above FRED. Beginning in 2007, however, the two rates switched positions, and LIBOR did not consistently again rise above FRED until around October 2011, when the European Commission began an inquiry into allegations of LIBOR-fixing. The complaints adduce other analyses and phenomena to support the hypothesis that the Banks conspired to depress LIBOR.

Procedural History

. . .

The motions to dismiss were granted based on the finding that none of the appellants "plausibly alleged that they suffered antitrust injury, thus, on that basis alone, they lack standing." *LIBOR I*, 935 F. Supp. 2d at 686. This ruling rested on three premises:

[1] "Plaintiffs' injury would have resulted from [d]efendants' misrepresentation, not from harm to competition," because the LIBOR-setting process was cooperative, not competitive. *Id.* at 688.

[2] Although the complaints "might support an allegation of price fixing," antitrust injury is lacking because the complaints did not allege restraints on competition in pertinent markets and therefore failed to "indicate that plaintiffs' injury resulted from an anticompetitive aspect of defendants' conduct." *Id.*

[3] Supreme Court precedent forecloses a finding of antitrust injury if "the harm alleged . . . could have resulted from normal competitive conduct" as here, because LIBOR could have been depressed if "each defendant decided independently to misrepresent its borrowing costs to the BBA." *Id.* at 690.

The district court rejected the notion that LIBOR operated as a proxy for competition and distinguished cases cited by appellants on the ground that they involved "harm to competition which is not present here." *Id.* at 693.

. . .

DISCUSSION

. . .

I. ANTITRUST VIOLATION

To avoid dismissal, appellants had to allege an antitrust violation stemming from the Banks' transgression of Section One of the Sherman Act: "Every contract, combination in the form of trust or otherwise, or conspiracy, in restraint of trade or commerce among the several States, or with foreign nations, is declared to be illegal." 15 U.S.C. § 1. Schematically, appellants' claims are uncomplicated. They allege that the Banks, as sellers, colluded to depress LIBOR, and thereby increased the cost to appellants, as buyers, of various LIBOR-based financial instruments, a cost increase reflected in reduced rates of return. In short, appellants allege a horizontal price-fixing conspiracy, "perhaps the paradigm of an unreasonable restraint of trade."

Since appellants allege that the LIBOR "must be characterized as an inseparable part of the price," and since we must accept that allegation as true for present purposes, the claim is one of price-fixing. *Catalano, Inc. v. Target Sales, Inc.*, 446 U.S. 643, 648 (1980). In urging otherwise, the Banks argue that LIBOR is not itself a price, as it is not itself bought or sold by anyone. The point is immaterial. LIBOR forms a component of the return from various LIBOR-denominated financial instruments, and the fixing of a component of price violates the antitrust laws. *See id.; see also United States v. Socony-Vacuum Oil Co.*, 310 U.S. 150, 222 (1940) ("[P]rices are fixed . . . if the range within which purchases or sales will be made is agreed upon, if the prices paid or charged are to be at a certain level or on ascending or descending scales, if they are to be uniform, or if by various formulae they are related to the market prices. They are fixed because they are agreed upon." (emphasis added)); *Plymouth Dealers' Ass'n of No. Cal. v. United States*, 279 F.2d 128, 132 (9th Cir.1960) (holding that use of a common fixed list price constituted price-fixing despite independently negotiated departures from said list price).

Horizontal price-fixing conspiracies among competitors are unlawful *per se*, that is, without further inquiry. The unfamiliar context of appellants' horizontal price-fixing claims provides no basis to disturb application of the *per se* rule. *See Arizona v. Maricopa Cty. Med. Soc'y*, 457 U.S. 332, 349 (1982) ("We are equally unpersuaded by the argument that we should not apply the per se rule in this case because the judiciary has little antitrust experience in the health care industry. The argument quite obviously is inconsistent with *Socony-Vacuum*. In unequivocal terms, we stated that, '[w]hatever may be its peculiar problems and characteristics, the Sherman Act, so far as price-fixing agreements are concerned, establishes one uniform rule applicable to all industries alike.'" (alteration in original) (quoting *Socony-Vacuum*, 310 U.S. at 222)).

Appellants have therefore plausibly alleged an antitrust violation attributable to the Banks, for which appellants seek damages.

Who should be suing here?   ## II. ANTITRUST STANDING

Although appellants charge the Banks with hatching and executing a horizontal price-fixing conspiracy, a practice that is per se unlawful, they are not "absolve[d]. . . of the obligation to demonstrate [antitrust] standing." Two issues bear on antitrust standing:

[1] have appellants suffered antitrust injury?

[2] are appellants efficient enforcers of the antitrust laws?

The second raises a closer question in this case.

The efficient enforcer inquiry turns on: (1) whether the violation was a direct or remote cause of the injury; (2) whether there is an identifiable class of other persons whose self-interest would normally lead them to sue for the violation; (3) whether the injury was speculative; and (4) whether there is a risk that other plaintiffs would be entitled to recover duplicative damages or that damages would be difficult to apportion among possible victims of the antitrust injury. Built into the analysis is an assessment of the "chain of causation" between the violation and the injury.

The district court, having found that appellants failed to plausibly allege antitrust injury, had no occasion to consider the efficient enforcer factors. We conclude that, although the district court erred in finding that appellants suffered no antitrust injury, remand is necessary for proper consideration of the efficient enforcer factors.

A. ANTITRUST INJURY

. . .

Appellants have pled antitrust injury. Generally, when consumers, because of a conspiracy, must pay prices that no longer reflect ordinary market conditions, they suffer "injury of the type the antitrust laws were intended to prevent and that flows from that which makes defendants' acts unlawful." *Brunswick Corp. v. Pueblo Bowl-O-Mat, Inc.*, 429 U.S. 477, 489 (1977).

True, appellants remained free to negotiate the interest rates attached to particular financial instruments; however, antitrust law is concerned with influences that corrupt market conditions, not bargaining power. "Any combination which tampers with price structures is engaged in an unlawful activity. Even though the members of the price-fixing group were in no position to control the market, to the extent that they raised, lowered, or stabilized prices they would be directly interfering with the free play of market forces." *Socony-Vacuum*, 310 U.S. at 221; *see also Plymouth Dealers' Ass'n*, 279 F.2d at 132 ("[T]he fact that the dealers used the fixed uniform list price in most instances only as a starting point, is of no consequence. It was an agreed starting point; it had been agreed upon between competitors; it was in some instances in the record respected and followed; it had to do with, and had its effect upon, price." (footnote omitted)). This consideration may well bear upon contested issues of causation, but it does not foreclose antitrust injury.

This conclusion is settled by Supreme Court precedents beginning with Socony-Vacuum, the "seminal case" holding that horizontal "price fixing remains per se unlawful." *Todd v. Exxon Corp.*, 275 F.3d 191, 198 (2d Cir. 2001). The defendant oil companies in *Socony-Vacuum* collusively raised the spot market prices for oil, which (like LIBOR) were determined by averaging submitted price quotes; this conduct violated Section One because "[p]rices rose and jobbers and consumers in the Mid-Western area paid more for their gasoline than they would have paid but for the conspiracy. Competition was not eliminated from the markets; but it was clearly curtailed, since restriction of the supply of gasoline . . . reduced the play of the forces of supply and demand." *Socony-Vacuum*, 310 U.S. at 220. Although the price-fixing conspiracy was not solely responsible for the increased prices, "[t]here was ample evidence that the buying programs at least contributed to the price rise and the stability of the spot markets, and to increases in the price of gasoline sold in the Mid-Western area. . . . That other factors also may have contributed to that rise and stability of the markets is immaterial." *Id.* at 219 (emphasis added). Similarly, "the fact that sales on the spot markets were still governed by some competition [wa]s of no consequence." *Id.* at 220.

Socony-Vacuum deemed horizontal price-fixing illegal without further inquiry because horizontal price-fixing is anathema to an economy predicated on the undisturbed interaction between supply and demand. *See id.* at 221 ("If the so-called competitive abuses were to be appraised here, the reasonableness of prices would necessarily become an issue in every price-fixing case. In that event the Sherman Act would soon be emasculated; its philosophy would be supplanted by one which is wholly alien to a system of free competition; it would not be the charter of freedom which its framers intended."); *id.* at 224 n. 59 ("The effectiveness of price-fixing agreements is dependent upon many factors, such as competitive tactics, position in the industry, [and] the formula underlying price policies. Whatever economic justification particular price-fixing agreements may be thought to have, the law does not permit an inquiry into their reasonableness. They are . . . banned because of their actual or potential threat to the central nervous system of the economy." (emphasis added)).

. . .

Appellants have plausibly alleged antitrust injury. They have identified an "illegal anticompetitive practice" (horizontal price-fixing), have claimed an actual injury placing appellants in a "'worse position' as a consequence" of the Banks' conduct, and have demonstrated that their injury is one the antitrust laws were designed to prevent.

* * *

The district court's contrary conclusion rested in part on the syllogism that since the LIBOR-setting process was a "cooperative endeavor," there could be no anticompetitive harm. *LIBOR I*, 935 F.Supp.2d at 688. But appellants claim violation (and injury in the form of higher prices) flowing from the corruption of the rate-setting process, which (allegedly) turned a process in which the Banks jointly participated into conspiracy. "[T]he machinery employed by a combination for price-fixing is immaterial." *Socony-Vacuum*, 310 U.S. at 223.[12] The district

---

[12] A leading antitrust treatise has similarly seized on this defect. See IIA Areeda & Hovenkamp, Antitrust Law ¶ 337 p. 100 n. 3 (4th ed.2014) (labeling LIBOR I a "troublesome holding that purchasers of instruments subject to LIBOR rate manipulation

court drew a parallel between the LIBOR-setting process and the collaborative venture in *Allied Tube* (though the standard-setting in *Allied Tube* likewise posed antitrust concerns): "Like the LIBOR-setting process, the process of forming the safety standard [in *Allied Tube*] was a cooperative endeavor by otherwise-competing companies under the auspices of a trade association." *LIBOR I*, 935 F.Supp.2d at 693. The Banks were indeed engaged in a joint process, and that endeavor was governed by rules put in place to prevent collusion. But the crucial allegation is that the Banks circumvented the LIBOR-setting rules, and that joint process thus turned into collusion. *See, e.g., Allied Tube*, 486 U.S. at 506-07 ("[P]rivate standard-setting by associations comprising firms with horizontal and vertical business relations is permitted at all under the antitrust laws only on the understanding that it will be conducted in a nonpartisan manner offering procompetitive benefits . . . .").

. . .

Appellants have alleged an anticompetitive tendency: the warping of market factors affecting the prices for LIBOR-based financial instruments. No further showing of actual adverse effect in the marketplace is necessary. This attribute separates evaluation of per se violations — which are presumed illegal — from rule of reason violations, which demand appraisal of the marketplace consequences that flow from a particular violation.

The district court observed that LIBOR did not "necessarily correspond to the interest rate charged for any actual interbank loan." *LIBOR I*, 935 F.Supp.2d at 689. This is a disputed factual issue that must be reserved for the proof stage. But even if none of the appellants' financial instruments paid interest at LIBOR, *Socony-Vacuum* allows an antitrust claim based on the influence that a conspiracy exerts on the starting point for prices. See *In re High Fructose Corn Syrup Antitrust Litig.*, 295 F.3d 651, 656 (7th Cir. 2002) ("The third trap is failing to distinguish between the existence of a conspiracy and its efficacy. The defendants point out that many of the actual sales . . . were made at prices below the defendants' list prices, and they intimate . . . that therefore even a bald-faced agreement to fix list prices would not be illegal in this industry. . . . That is wrong. An agreement to fix list prices is . . . a per se violation of the Sherman Act even if most or for that matter all transactions occur at lower prices.").

The district court deemed it significant that appellants could have "suffered the same harm under normal circumstances of free competition." *LIBOR I*, 935 F.Supp.2d at 689. True; but antitrust law relies on the probability of harm when evaluating per se violations. See *Catalano*, 446 U.S. at 649 ("[T]he fact that a practice may turn out to be harmless in a particular set of circumstances will not prevent its being declared unlawful per se.").

---

did not suffer antitrust injury because LIBOR agreements were never intended to be anticompetitive but rather the product of joint production").

The test fashioned by the district court was based on an over-reading of *Brunswick* and of *Atlantic Richfield Co. v. USA Petroleum Co.*, 495 U.S. 328 (1990) ("*ARCO*"). At most, these cases stand for the proposition that competitors who complain of low fixed prices do not suffer antitrust injury. See *ARCO*, 495 U.S. at 345-46 ("We decline to dilute the antitrust injury requirement here because we find that there is no need to encourage private enforcement by competitors of the rule against vertical, maximum price fixing . . . . [P]roviding the competitor a cause of action would not protect the rights of dealers and consumers under the antitrust laws."). Neither *ARCO* nor *Brunswick* treated antitrust injury as one that could not have been suffered under normal competitive conditions.[15] As *ARCO* explains: "[t]he antitrust injury requirement ensures that a plaintiff can recover only if the loss stems from a competition-reducing aspect or effect of the defendant's behavior"; rigging a price component to thwart ordinary market conditions is one such "aspect or effect." 495 U.S. at 344. The district court opinion emphasizes that appellants "have not alleged any structural effect wherein defendants improved their position relative to their competitors." *LIBOR I*, 935 F.Supp.2d at 692. However, appellants sustained their burden of showing injury by alleging that they paid artificially fixed higher prices. Whether the Banks' competitors were also injured is not decisive, and possibly not germane.

* * *

"Congress did not intend to allow every person tangentially affected by an antitrust violation to maintain an action . . . . [T]he potency of the [§ 4] remedy implies the need for some care in its application." *McCready*, 457 U.S. at 477. At the same time, the "unrestrictive language of the section, and the avowed breadth of the congressional purpose" in enacting this remedial provision "cautions [courts] not to cabin § 4 in ways that will defeat its broad remedial objective." *Id.* Accommodation of both aims requires courts to consider "the relationship of the injury alleged with those forms of injury about which Congress was likely to have been concerned, in making . . . conduct unlawful and in providing a private remedy under § 4." *Id.* at 478. The Sherman Act safeguards consumers from marketplace abuses; appellants are consumers claiming injury from a horizontal price-fixing conspiracy. They have accordingly plausibly alleged antitrust injury.

B. THE EFFICIENT ENFORCER FACTORS

The second question that bears on antitrust standing is whether appellants satisfy the efficient enforcer factors. The district court did not reach this issue because it dismissed for lack of antitrust injury. We are not in a position to resolve

---

[15] The district court's musing that the same harm could have occurred if the defendants each "independently" submitted a "LIBOR quote that was artificially low" is similarly inapt and amounts to forcing antitrust plaintiffs to rule out the possibility of unilateral action causing their asserted injury; this notion is unsupported by precedent. *LIBOR I*, 935 F.Supp.2d at 691.

these issues, which may entail further inquiry, nor are we inclined to answer the several relevant questions without prior consideration of them by the district court.

. . .

IV.

This decision is of narrow scope. It may be that the influence of the corrupted LIBOR figure on competition was weak and potentially insignificant, given that the financial transactions at issue are complex, LIBOR was not binding, and the worldwide market for financial instruments — nothing less than the market for money — is vast, and influenced by multiple benchmarks. The net impact of a tainted LIBOR in the credit market is an issue of causation reserved for the proof stage; at this stage, it is plausibly alleged on the face of the complaints that a manipulation of LIBOR exerted some influence on price. The extent of that influence and the identity of persons who can sue, among other things, are matters reserved for later.

Moreover, common sense dictates that the Banks operated not just as borrowers but also as lenders in transactions that referenced LIBOR. Banks do not stockpile money, any more than bakers stockpile yeast. It seems strange that this or that bank (or any bank) would conspire to gain, as a borrower, profits that would be offset by a parity of losses it would suffer as a lender. On the other hand, the record is undeveloped and it is not even established that the Banks used LIBOR in setting rates for lending transactions. Nevertheless, the potential of a wash requires further development and can only be properly analyzed at later stages of the litigation.

Although novel features of this case raise a number of fact issues, we think it is clear that, once appellants' allegations are taken as true (as must be done at this stage), they have plausibly alleged both antitrust violation and antitrust injury and thus, have cleared the motion-to-dismiss bar. It is accordingly unnecessary for us to reach or decide whether the district court erred by denying appellants leave to amend their complaints.

pay attention to standard to determine scope of holding

CONCLUSION

For the foregoing reasons, we vacate the judgment of the district court and remand for further proceedings consistent with this opinion.

Notes

1.   Were the relationships among the composers in *Broadcast Music* and among the doctors in *Maricopa* cooperative or competitive?

2.   Is cooperation the same as collusion or conspiracy?

3.   Generally speaking, antitrust treats an agreement on the nature of a product in much the same way as it treats an agreement on price. *See, e.g.,*

National Macaroni Manufacturers Association v. Federal Trade Commission, 345 F.2d 421 (7th Cir. 1965) (agreement on the composition of pasta *per se* illegal). Why, then, is standard-setting ever permissible? Is an agreement on the composition of pasta relevantly different from an agreement on LIBOR or on the composition of electrical conduit (as in *Allied Tube*)?

4.   Which is preferable, viewing the LIBOR conspiracy as price-fixing or viewing it as fixing the nature of an information product, the LIBOR rate? Does it matter?

5.   If *Allied Tube* is a good analogy to the facts of the LIBOR conspiracy, should liability rest on the banks or on the BBA or on both? See Mark R. Patterson, "Who Is Responsible for Libor Rate-Fixing?," Harvard Law School Forum on Corporate Governance and Financial Regulation, https://blogs.law.harvard.edu/ corpgov/2013/12/26/who-is-responsible-for-libor-rate-fixing/ (Dec. 26, 2013). Is your answer consistent with cases such as *Broadcast Music* and *Maricopa*?

6.   The *LIBOR* case is not the only one involving the setting of an index that affects or controls the price of other products. *See, e.g., Knevelbaard Dairies v. Kraft Foods, Inc.*, 232 F.3d 979 (9th Cir. 2000).

1.2 Horizontal Market Allocation

There are a variety of ways in which firms can allocate markets: by geography, as in *Palmer v. BRG of Georgia, Inc.*, 498 U.S. 46 (1990); by customers; by time, as in *F.T.C. v. Actavis, Inc.*, 570 U.S. 136 (2013); by the manner in which potential customers seek information, as in the case below; etc. Although market allocation is generally said to be *per se* illegal, the case below does not apply that rule, presumably because of the novel aspects of the case.

As you read the case, consider whether it involves a straightforward restriction on information. That is also a way to think about *Actavis* and similar cases, in which brand-name drug manufacturers and generic manufacturers agree to settlements that eliminate challenges to the validity of the brand-name manufacturers' patents. The grant of a patent does not make the patent immune from challenge. To be entitled to a patent, an invention must be new, useful, and nonobvious, and an alleged infringer may argue that an invention does not have those characteristics; if the challenge prevails, the patent will be invalidated. The implication is that an issued patent might or might not prove to be valid, and thus might or might not entitle the patentee to exclude others from the invention. *See* Mark A. Lemley & Carl Shapiro, *Probabilistic Patents,* 19 J. OF ECON. PERSP. 75 (2005).

It is possible, then, to view *Actavis* and like cases either as involving restrictions on competition in drug markets or as agreements to suppress the information that would be produced by patent validity challenges. As the case below illustrates, parties can use agreement to try to avoid competition in court regarding patent validity just as they can use agreement to try to avoid competition in the market. In fact, in a case cited by *Actavis* that involved a somewhat similar settlement, *United States v. Singer Mfg. Co.*, 374 U.S. 174 (1963), Justice White's concurring opinion arguably took this approach:

> [C]ollusion among applicants to prevent prior art [*i.e.*, information about previously-available products that might invalidate a patent] from coming to or being drawn to the Office's attention is an inequitable imposition on the Office and on the public. In my view, such collusion to secure a monopoly grant runs afoul of the Sherman Act's prohibition against conspiracies in restraint of trade—if not bad per se, then such agreements are at least presumptively bad.

See also Mark R. Patterson, *Confidentiality in Patent Dispute Resolution: Antitrust Implications*, 93 WASH. L. REV. 827 (2018). The following case presents the information-suppression issue more directly.

Opinion of the Commission (Public Record Version)
In re 1-800 Contacts, Inc.
Docket No. 9372
November 7, 2018

*[handwritten: * INFORMATION SUPPRESSION SEARCH ENGINE]*

By Chairman Joseph J. Simons, for the Commission:

This proceeding considers Complaint Counsel's challenge to a number of agreements among horizontal competitors—in most instances, trademark litigation settlements—that, allegedly, anticompetitively limit internet search advertising and restrict bidding in internet search auctions to the detriment of consumers. Respondent 1-800 Contacts sued rival contact-lens sellers for trademark infringement when sellers' online advertising appeared in response to consumers' internet searches for "1-800 Contacts." In nearly all cases, the litigation settled before trial. The resulting settlement agreements require the parties, when bidding at search engine advertising auctions, to take steps to ensure their ads do not appear in response to searches for the other party's trademark terms.

At first glance, this proceeding may appear to contemplate little more than a few terms embedded in a document that purports to resolve a trademark dispute among internet sellers of contact lenses. But, in reality, this case grapples with issues of enormous import. We consider here consumer marketplaces that embody the very basic institutions of 21st century commerce. Increasingly, consumers no longer shop for goods by walking down Main Street and looking at the price tags on window displays or by wandering through the aisles of retail establishments comparing prices on shelves and product characteristics written on packages. Rather, consumers now frequently—and with increasing frequency—open their web browsers, enter desired product names or qualities into a search engine, and wait for Main Street or supermarket aisles to be digitally transported to them. This phenomenon is comparatively recent, but e-commerce already comprises a significant and growing share of our economy's retail sales. Indeed, the Census Bureau estimated that e-commerce retail sales in the United States totaled $127.3 billion in the second quarter of 2018, which comprised approximately 9.6 percent of total retail sales.

. . .

I. BACKGROUND

A. Respondent, 1-800 Contacts

1-800 Contacts sells contact lenses to consumers throughout the United States. It started as a mail-order contact lens business in a college dorm in 1992. The business changed its name in 1995 when it obtained the 1-800 Contacts telephone number. The company launched its website in 1996, and beginning in 2004, its internet sales exceeded its telephone sales. In 2015, 1-800 Contacts' revenues were approximately $460 million. Its annual volume of contact lenses sold via the Internet to U.S. consumers currently exceeds the online sales of contact lenses to U.S. consumers by any other company.

B. The Contact Lens Industry

Contact lenses are a billion dollar industry in the United States. Contact lenses are medical devices that can be sold only pursuant to a prescription written by an optometrist or ophthalmologist, also called eye care practitioners ("ECPs"). A consumer interested in wearing contact lenses must first visit an ECP for a lens fitting and prescription. A consumer's prescription specifies the brand as well as the power and other characteristics of the contact lenses. A consumer's prescription expires in one year in most states, and two years in others; consequently, the consumer must regularly return to an ECP.

In 2003, Congress enacted the Fairness to Contact Lens Consumers Act, which, along with the FTC's implementing regulations, gives patients an automatic right to their contact lens prescriptions upon completion of a fitting. 15 U.S.C. § 7601 (2003). This facilitates their ability to fill contact lens prescriptions through any retail channel they choose. Because prescriptions identify the power, base curve, and specific lens brand, the lenses a consumer receives are identical in every way, irrespective of the choice of retailer. Consumers often buy contact lenses from ECPs when they return every 1-2 years for a new prescription. Other contact lens retailers compete mostly for consumers' "refill" sales.

There are four types of retailers in the industry. First, many ECPs operate independent practices ("independent ECPs") and sell both their services (eye exams) and the products they prescribe (contact lenses). Independent ECPs sell contact lenses directly to consumers and, in 2015, accounted for 40 percent of all contact lens sales in the United States. Second, national and regional optical retail chains, such as LensCrafters and Visionworks, accounted for 20 percent of contact lens sales in 2015. Third, mass merchants, such as Walmart and Target, and club stores, such as BJ's and Sam's Club, sell contact lenses and accounted for 23 percent of contact lens sales in 2015. Fourth, so-called "pure-play" online retailers, such as 1-800 Contacts, sell only online and do not have brick-and-mortar locations; pure-play online sellers accounted for 17 percent of contact lens sales in 2015. In 2015, 1-800 Contacts accounted for approximately ███████ percent of online sales, which is more than four times the sales of the second-largest online retailer.

The price for contact lenses varies significantly based on the retail channel. Among brick-and-mortar retailers, independent ECPs typically have the highest prices for contact lenses, followed by optical retail chains, which, on average, sell contact lenses priced just below those sold by ECPs. Mass merchants offer lower contact lens prices than independent ECPs and optical retail chains. Membership club stores have the lowest contact lens prices.

Online contact-lens retailers—other than 1-800 Contacts—generally offer prices well below those of independent ECPs, optical retail chains, and mass merchants.

But 1-800 Contacts' prices are higher than those of other online retailers. It sets its prices below ECPs' and optical retail chains' prices, but above prices offered by mass merchants and club stores. Importantly, 1-800 Contacts' prices are approximately ██████ percent higher than other online retailer prices.

C. Paid Search Advertising

Online retailers use online advertising to attract new customers. Internet search engines, such as Google, Bing, and Yahoo!, allow internet users to search and retrieve content on the World Wide Web. In response to a user's search query, the search engine employs algorithms to match the text of the query with portions of the Web that may contain relevant content. Links to webpages deemed potentially responsive to the user's search are ranked and presented to the user on a search engine results page ("SERP").

A typical SERP displays two sorts of search results: "organic" links and "sponsored" links, which are advertisements. Organic search results are links to websites that the search engine has identified as relevant to the user's query. No one can pay the search engine to have an organic result appear or to change a result's rank on the SERP. Rather, the appearance and rank of organic links are based on relevance to the user's search, with the most relevant results at the top of the SERP.

Sponsored links typically are displayed above, below, or to the side of the organic results, and often appear in a different colored box labeled with the word "Ad." Google and Bing display up to four search advertisements at the top of the page, above the organic search results. As the name suggests, advertisers pay to have sponsored links appear on a SERP. To determine which ads appear, and in what order, search engines use an auction to sell advertising positions. Advertisers bid on "keywords," which are words or phrases that trigger the display of ads when they are determined to "match" a user's search. But the auction bids alone do not determine whether a particular ad appears. Search engines evaluate other factors, such as an ad's quality and its relevance to a user's search query, in determining the ad's location on a SERP and whether it displays at all. Thus, even a high auction bid will not result in an ad appearing if the search engine does not find the ad relevant to the user's search. Search engines have an incentive to show relevant ads because search engines are paid for displaying an ad only if the user clicks on the ad.[3]

Google, the leading search engine in the United States, receives more than eight out of every ten dollars spent on paid search advertising. Google's paid search platform is called "AdWords." When bidding on keywords in AdWords, advertisers may designate a keyword as "broad match," "phrase match," "exact match," or "negative match." When an advertiser designates a keyword as "broad match," its ad may appear when a Google search contains the specific keyword, any of its plural forms, synonyms, or phrases similar to the word.[4] When designated as "phrase match," the ad may appear when a search contains the keyword with additional words before or after. And when designated as "exact match," the ad may appear when a search contains the exact keyword and nothing more. In contrast, an advertiser may use "negative keywords" to ensure its ad does not appear when a user performs a search for a selected word or phrase. Similar to other keywords, negative keywords can be designated as broad match, phrase match, or exact match.

Generally, search engines do not currently restrict keywords available for bidding in advertising auctions. In fact, it is common for companies to pay search engines to present their ads in response to a user's search query of another company's brand name. Before the agreements at issue in this case were in place, Google displayed ads for many of 1-800 Contacts' retail competitors when those retailers bid on, and Google determined the ads were relevant to searches for 1-800 Contacts' trademarks.

Paid search advertising is an important method for marketing contact lenses online to obtain new customers and increase brand awareness. The paid search ad is presented to the consumer at a time when the consumer is more likely looking to buy. In fact, many online retailers devote most of their advertising expenditures to search advertising.

---

[3] The price that an advertiser pays to the search engine each time its advertisement is clicked is the cost-per-click ("CPC"). The CPC for each advertiser is based on the outcome of a generalized second-price auction. Advertisers are not charged the amount they bid. Instead, the CPC is the bid amount needed to beat the rank of the advertiser in the next lower position.

[4] Broad match seeks to match within the meaning of the user's search, rather than focusing on the text of any particular keyword. For example, if an advertiser purchases the keyword "low-carb diet plan" and selects broad match, Google may select that advertiser's ad in response to searches for "carb-free foods" or "Mediterranean diets" even though the advertiser did not bid on those particular keywords.

In contrast to other online contact lens retailers, 1-800 Contacts also advertises heavily offline, including printed matter, radio, television, and other means. According to Respondent, the company has "made enormous investments" in building its brand and convincing consumers to buy contact lenses online rather than from brick-and-mortar retailers. Between 2002 and 2014, 1-800 Contacts spent a total of ████████ on television advertising. Yet online advertising is still important to 1-800 Contacts. Between 2002 and 2014, it spent a total of ████████ on online advertising. In 2014, ██████ percent of 1-800 Contacts' advertising budget was spent on internet advertising, and between ████████ percent of 1-800 Contacts' internet advertising budget was spent on paid search advertising each year from 2004 through 2014. When 1-800 Contacts bids on its trademark keywords, it bids high enough to ensure that 1-800 Contacts' sponsored ad is the first advertisement displayed in response to searches for its own trademark.

D. 1-800 Contacts' Conduct, Litigation, and the Settlement Agreements

In 2002, 1-800 Contacts filed a complaint against Vision Direct alleging, inter alia, trademark infringement, claiming Vision Direct caused pop-up ads to appear when internet users visited the 1-800 Contacts website. The complaint did not include allegations regarding the use of 1-800 Contacts' trademarks as keywords to trigger search engine advertisements. 1-800 Contacts filed a similar action challenging pop-up ads against Coastal Contacts in March 2004. 1-800 Contacts resolved its disputes with Vision Direct and Coastal Contacts by executing settlement agreements that included terms related to pop-up advertising and the use of trademark keywords.

In addition to addressing pop-up ads, 1-800 Contacts monitored whether sponsored ads of its online competitors appeared on SERPs for queries involving the 1-800 Contacts trademarks. Between 2005 and 2010, the company sent cease-and-desist letters to many of the online contact lens retailers whose ads appeared in the monitoring. The company later filed suit against several of these online retailers alleging federal trademark infringement and unfair competition under the Lanham Act §§ 32 and 43(a),[10] trademark dilution, state and common law unfair competition, and unjust enrichment based on the retailers' ads appearing on SERPs in response to searches for 1-800 Contacts' trademark terms. . . .

---

[10] Under federal trademark law, to succeed on a trademark infringement claim, a plaintiff must prove (1) that it has a protectable mark, and (2) that the defendant used the mark without the plaintiff's consent in a manner that is likely to cause consumer confusion. "The most traditional form of trademark confusion is generally known as 'source confusion,' which is confusion as to the source of a good or service. . . . [C]ourts also recognize confusion as to affiliation, connection, or sponsorship. . . . because the Lanham Act . . . prohibits activity likely to cause '[t]he public's belief that the mark's owner sponsored or otherwise approved the use of the trademark[.]'" Courts have recognized that confusion is possible even if it does not occur at the point of sale. "Initial interest confusion . . . refers to the use of another's trademark in a manner calculated to capture initial consumer attention."

1-800 Contacts settled most of the cases. In the suit against Lens.com, however, the case went to a judge. In December 2010, the U.S. District Court for the District of Utah issued an opinion granting summary judgment in favor of Lens.com on 1-800 Contacts' trademark litigation claims. See 1-800 Contacts, Inc. v. Lens.com, Inc., 755 F. Supp. 2d 1151 (D. Utah 2010). The court found "insufficient evidence for a jury to conclude that Defendant infringed on Plaintiff's mark for all advertisements that did not use Plaintiff's mark in them." Id. at 1181. In July 2013, the Tenth Circuit upheld this portion of the district court judgment. See 1-800 Contacts, Inc. v. Lens.com, Inc., 722 F.3d 1229 (10th Cir. 2013). The appellate court, however, did not resolve the question of whether use of challenged trademark keywords, divorced from the text of the resulting ads, could result in a likelihood of confusion, because it found that 1-800 Contacts' infringement claim "fail[ed] for lack of adequate evidence" of confusion. Id. at 1242- 43.

Between 2004 and 2013, 1-800 Contacts entered into thirteen settlement agreements (including the agreements with Vision Direct and Coastal Contacts) to resolve its trademark disputes. The settlement agreements include recitals that describe the litigation between the parties and state "the Parties have determined that, in order to avoid the expense, inconvenience, and disruption" of litigation, "it is desirable and in their respective best interests to terminate" the litigation and "settle any claims related thereto." The settlement agreements release the parties of "any and all liability" arising from the claims and require dismissal of the litigation.

Although the language of the agreements varies, each includes provisions that prohibit the parties from using the other party's trademarks, URLs, and variations of marks as search advertising keywords. The settlement agreements also require the parties to employ "negative" keywords to prevent their ads from displaying whenever a search includes (or, as stated in some of the agreements, "contains") the other party's trademarks---even in situations when the advertiser did not bid on the other party's actual trademark and the ad appears due to the search engine's determination that the ad is relevant and useful to the consumer. The agreements, however, do not specify whether negative keywords must be implemented under broad-match, phrase-match, or exact-match protocols. The settlement agreements do not prohibit parties from bidding on generic keywords such as "contacts" or "contacts lens," so long as they employ negative keywords as required.

. . .

E. Procedural History

1.   The FTC's Complaint

In August 2016, the FTC issued an administrative Complaint against 1-800 Contacts, alleging that the thirteen settlement agreements and the sourcing agreement (collectively, the "Challenged Agreements") and subsequent policing of the agreements unreasonably restrain both price competition in search advertising auctions and the availability of truthful, non-misleading advertising in violation of Section 5 of the FTC Act. The Complaint alleges that the Challenged Agreements prevented the parties from disseminating ads that would have informed consumers that identical products were available at different prices, which reduced price competition among online contact lens retailers and made it costlier for consumers to search prices offered by the retailers. As a result, the Complaint alleges, at least some consumers paid higher prices for contact lenses.

The Complaint also alleges that Respondent's conduct undermined the efficiency of search advertising auctions, distorted the prices in those auctions by eliminating bidders, and degraded the quality of service offered by search engines, including the quality of the SERP displayed to users.

. . .

IV. 1-800 CONTACTS' SETTLEMENTS ARE NOT IMMUNE FROM ANTITRUST SCRUTINY

A. *Actavis* Does Not Immunize Commonplace Settlement Agreements or Settlements within the Scope of Potential Judicial Relief

Respondent contends the settlement agreements between 1-800 Contacts and thirteen rival online sellers of contact lenses are not subject to antitrust scrutiny. Respondent asserts that *Actavis* stands for the proposition that there can be no antitrust challenge to a settlement agreement that is commonplace in form. Here, Respondent claims its settlements of trademark litigation took the form of common, non-use agreements. According to Respondent, *Actavis* exempted commonplace forms of settlement from antitrust scrutiny and held that "a party challenging a settlement must show that the settlement's form is unusual." Respondent, however, reads *Actavis* much too broadly; the Court created no such shield from antitrust review.

As support for its argument, Respondent quotes the following sentence fragment in *Actavis*: "commonplace forms have not been thought for that reason alone subject to antitrust liability." The Court's wording is much more limited than Respondent suggests. The Supreme Court presented two examples of settlements: (1) where "Company A sues Company B for patent infringement and demands, say $100 million in damages" and receives "some amount less than the full demand as part of the settlement – $40 million, for example"; and (2) where "B has a counterclaim for damages against A" and "the original infringement plaintiff, A ... end[s] up paying B to settle B's counterclaim." The Court then explained: "Insofar as the dissent urges that settlements taking these commonplace forms have not been thought for that reason alone subject to antitrust liability, we agree, and do not intend to alter that understanding." The Court did not state a general rule that removes settlement agreements from antitrust scrutiny, but rather characterized two specific types of settlements as commonplace, and made it clear that the form of the settlement alone is not what subjects an agreement to antitrust scrutiny.

. . .

In any case, the challenged settlements are in fact unusual. Respondent directs us to consider the "form" of the settlements, not their substance. Thus, Respondent describes each settlement as "a standard, non-use agreement whereby a party agreed not to use another's trademark," a form that practicing lawyers allegedly recognize as regularly used to settle trademark litigation. Antitrust law, however, "has consistently prioritized substance over form."

When we consider the substance of these settlement agreements, we find they are unusual. Trademark litigation typically seeks to bar the use on the infringer's labels, ads, or other promotional materials of the plaintiff's trademark or a similar mark in a way likely to confuse consumers. *Clorox Co. v. Sterling Winthrop, Inc.*, 117 F.3d 50 (2d Cir. 1997), cited repeatedly by Respondent, provides a classic example where Clorox's PINE-SOL products allegedly confused consumers of Sterling Winthrop's LYSOL products. The settlement agreement upheld by the court restricted Clorox's ability to market products as disinfectants or as special purpose cleansers under the PINE-SOL mark. There the agreement did "no more than regulate how the name PINE-SOL may be used" in direct competition with LYSOL and did not restrict Clorox or other firms from selling products that compete with LYSOL under a brand name other than PINE-SOL. It therefore raised none of the competition concerns attached to agreements that divide markets. Given this limited restraint upon one competitor among many, the court concluded that Clorox had not shown that the agreement significantly restricted Clorox, or restricted at all any of the other large potential entrants, from competing.

Here, as discussed below, the settlement agreements effectively shut off an entire—and very important—channel of advertising triggered by an alleged use of the trademark in the generation of search advertising. Stated differently, each settlement reaches farther than a cure based on rewording a label or an ad—effectively eliminating an entire channel of competitive advertising at the key moment when the consumer is considering a purchase. Furthermore, 1- 800 Contacts systematically applied similar restrictions to rival after rival that sought to challenge its position. And, contrary to Clorox's premise, the agreements did achieve a market division through their reciprocal prohibitions on bidding in specific search auctions. Thus, from the perspective of substance, the settlement agreements between 1-800 Contacts and its thirteen rivals were indeed unusual.

. . .

B. The "*Actavis* Considerations"

Respondent argues that even if the Commission finds the challenged settlements were unusual, dismissal still would be appropriate because Complaint Counsel did not prove any of the five "*Actavis* considerations" that, taken together, could outweigh the desirability of settlements, to favor antitrust scrutiny. The *Actavis* Court identified five factors that convinced it to give the FTC an opportunity to prove its antitrust claim: (1) the specific restraint's potential for genuine adverse effects on competition; (2) the potential that the anticompetitive consequences will sometimes prove unjustified; (3) the likelihood that the patentee possesses the power to bring about unjustified competitive harm in practice; (4) the administrative feasibility of an antitrust action; and (5) the risk that finding antitrust liability for a particular form of settlement would prevent litigants from settling (i.e., the litigants' ability to settle in other ways that do not harm competition). Respondent treats these factors as threshold requirements for conducting antitrust review and argues that the ALJ erred by ignoring these considerations. We disagree that *Actavis* requires this five-factor test to be applied to antitrust review of all settlements of intellectual property litigation. Moreover, even if the Court had created such a requirement, the litigation in this case would pass.

. . .

V. ANTITRUST ANALYSIS OF THE CHALLENGED AGREEMENTS

The Complaint alleges that the series of agreements between 1-800 Contacts and numerous online sellers of contact lenses are agreements to restrain competition in violation of Section 5 of the FTC Act and constitute unfair methods of competition in or affecting commerce in violation of Section 5 of the FTC Act. To assess whether the Challenged Agreements violate Section 5 of the FTC Act, we are guided by case law concerning Section 1 of the Sherman Act.

. . .

In [*Polygram Holding, Inc.*, 136 F.T.C. 310 (2003), aff'd, 416 F.3d 29 (D.C. Cir. 2005)], the Commission traced the Supreme Court's development of the rule of reason. 136 F.T.C. at 325-44 [!]. One feature of the Court's jurisprudence is that the rule of reason calls for "an enquiry meet for the case, looking to the circumstances, details, and logic of a restraint," with a goal to reach "a confident conclusion about the principal tendency of a restriction." Cases such as "*BMI, NCAA,* and *IFD* indicate[] that the evaluation of horizontal restraints takes place along an analytical continuum in which a challenged practice is examined in the detail necessary to understand its competitive effect." *Polygram*, 136 F.T.C. at 336 (citing Broadcast Music, Inc. v. Columbia Broadcasting Sys., Inc., 441 U.S. 1 (1979); *Nat'l Collegiate Athletic Ass'n v. Bd. of Regents of the Univ. of Oklahoma*, 468 U.S. 85 (1984); *FTC v. Indiana Fed'n of Dentists*, 476 U.S. 447 (1986) ("*IFD*")).

The Court has defined three separate but not entirely distinct ways for a plaintiff to show that a challenged restraint resulted in anticompetitive effects under a rule of reason analysis. First, the *IFD* Court observed that the particular horizontal restraint at issue, by its very nature established that anticompetitive effects were likely; it did not require "elaborate industry analysis. . . to demonstrate the anticompetitive character of such an agreement." In *Massachusetts Board of Registration in Optometry*, 110 F.T.C. 549 (1988), and *Polygram*, we labeled such restraints "inherently suspect." Second, the Court in *IFD* held that, even if the restriction in question was "not sufficiently naked" to be considered inherently suspect based on the nature of the restraint, the plaintiff's prima facie case was established, even without a detailed market analysis, because the record contained direct evidence of anticompetitive effects. Third, the Court's discussion made clear that the traditional mode of analysis—inquiring into market definition and market power to determine whether an arrangement has the potential for genuine adverse effects on competition—was also available. Any one of these modes of analysis is sufficient to establish a prima facie case.

In this case, we use two of these modes of analysis to assess whether 1-800 Contacts' agreements resulted in anticompetitive effects: (1) we consider whether the Challenged Agreements are inherently suspect; and (2) we examine whether there is direct evidence of anticompetitive effects. Each mode of analysis provides an independent basis for finding that the Challenged Agreements have substantial anticompetitive effects and leads us to find liability.

We explain the structure of the analysis based on the case law for these modes in the sections devoted to each. We also examine Complaint Counsel's allegation that the Challenged Agreements have substantial anticompetitive effects on competition with respect to bidding on search terms, which again leads us to find a violation of Section 5 of the FTC Act.

. . .

Qnick
Look

A. Analysis of the Challenged Agreements for Effects on Consumers Under *Polygram*'s Inherently Suspect Framework

In *Polygram*, we held that in a limited but significant category of cases, "the conduct at issue is inherently suspect owing to its likely tendency to suppress competition." In these cases, "scrutiny of the restraint itself . . . without consideration of market power" is sufficient to condemn the restraint, unless the defendant can "articulate a legitimate justification" for that restraint. *See also California Dental Ass'n v. FTC*, 526 U.S. 756, 770 (1999) (describing a "quick-look analysis" applicable when "an observer with even a rudimentary understanding of economics could conclude that the arrangements in question would have an anticompetitive effect on customers and markets"); *IFD*, 476 U.S. at 459 (finding "no elaborate industry analysis" was required to demonstrate the anticompetitive character of a "horizontal agreement among participating dentists to withhold from their customers a particular service that they desire").

Drawing from the Supreme Court's analysis in *California Dental*, 526 U.S. at 779, *Polygram* spelled out the structure of the "inherently suspect" analysis for the plaintiff's demonstration that a restraint has anticompetitive effects. A plaintiff must

> demonstrate[] that the conduct at issue is inherently suspect owing to its likely tendency to suppress competition. . . . [T]he defendant can avoid summary condemnation only by advancing a legitimate justification for those practices. . . . When the defendant advances such cognizable and plausible justifications, the plaintiff must make a more detailed showing that the restraints at issue are indeed likely, in the particular context, to harm competition. Such a showing still need not prove actual anticompetitive effects or entail "the fullest market analysis." Depending upon the circumstances of the cases and the degree to which antitrust tribunals have experience with restraints in particular markets, such a showing may or may not require evidence about the particular market at issue, but at a minimum must entail the identification of the theoretical basis for the alleged anticompetitive effects and a showing that the effects are indeed likely to be anticompetitive. Such a showing may, for example, be based on a more detailed analysis of economic learning about the likely competitive effects of a particular restraint, in markets with characteristics

comparable to the one at issue. The plaintiff may also show that the proffered procompetitive effects could be achieved through means less restrictive of competition.

On review, then Chief Judge Douglas Ginsburg, writing for the D.C. Circuit, "accept[ed] the Commission's analytical framework."

1.   The Anticompetitive Nature of the Restraints

Inherently suspect conduct "ordinarily encompasses behavior that past judicial experience and current economic learning have shown to warrant summary condemnation." Consequently, our analysis considers whether there is a "close family resemblance between the suspect practice and another practice that already stands convicted in the court of consumer welfare." determination is based on the conduct's "likely tendency to suppress competition." "At this stage, the focus of the inquiry is on the nature of the restraint rather than on the market effects in a particular case." *North Texas Specialty Physicians*, 140 F.T.C. 715, 733 (2005) ("*NTSP*").

We previously recognized that an inherently suspect analysis and a per se analysis are "close neighbors." *NTSP*, 140 F.T.C. at 719. Consequently, the Commission previously condemned conduct as inherently suspect that approximates conduct that had otherwise been characterized as per se violations of the antitrust laws. For instance, in *Polygram*, we condemned as inherently suspect an agreement between record album distributors to suspend temporarily advertising and discounting of particular performers' earlier concert albums. The D.C. Circuit agreed, explaining that "[a]n agreement between joint venturers to restrain price cutting and advertising with respect to products not part of the joint venture looks suspiciously like a naked price fixing agreement between competitors, which would ordinarily be condemned as per se unlawful. The Supreme Court has recognized time and again that agreements restraining autonomy in pricing and advertising impede the 'ordinary give and take of the market place.'" Similarly, in *NTSP*, we condemned as inherently suspect certain contracting practices of a physician trade association, while also recognizing that "NTSP's activities could be characterized as per se illegal because they are closely analogous to conduct condemned per se in this and other industries . . . ."

In the present case, the agreements between 1-800 Contacts and its rivals prohibit each party from causing or allowing advertisements to appear in response to an internet search for the other party's trademarks or URLs, or variations of the trademarks or URLs. Those agreement terms and 1-800 Contacts' subsequent enforcement of them prevent the agreeing parties from offering advertising in response to an internet search for "1-800 Contacts" or similar queries. Thus, the Challenged Agreements are, in essence, agreements between horizontal competitors to restrict the information provided by advertising to consumers when they search for 1-800 Contacts' trademark terms and URLs; consumers could have used that withheld information to compare and evaluate the prices and other features of competing online sellers. Ultimately, the effect of the advertising restrictions is to make information enabling consumer comparisons more difficult and costly to obtain.

. . .

Economic theory indicates that restrictions on this type of advertising are likely to harm competition. A flow of information between buyers and sellers is an essential part of the market system. Buyers have to find out who they can buy from and on what terms, and sellers must let consumers know how to find them, what they have to offer, and on what terms. Restrictions on advertising interfere with that flow of information and raise the cost to consumers of finding the most suitable offering of a product or service. Faced with these higher search costs, consumers must either spend more time and money looking for a lower- priced supplier or end their search because the cost of continued search exceeds the likelihood of finding a lower price. Ultimately, as a result of the reduced information flow, some consumers will pay higher prices for the particular good or service while others stop their search before they find a price that induces them to buy, which reduces the quantity sold. In addition, advertising restrictions "reduce[] sellers' incentives to lower prices. One reason a restriction on advertising may reduce a seller's incentives to lower prices is that, absent an ability to advertise, lower per-unit prices may not be sufficiently offset by higher volume."

. . .

Consistent with the economic literature, over the past 40 years, the Commission has repeatedly found that advertising restrictions harm competition and consumers. See *Am. Med. Ass'n*, 94 F.T.C. 701, 1010 (1979) (condemning an agreement among physicians not to advertise), *aff'd*, 638 F.2d 443 (2d Cir. 1980), *aff'd by an equally divided Court*, 455 U.S. 676 (1982) (per curiam); *Mass. Board*, 110 F.T.C. at 598 (condemning a licensing board's ban on advertising). Among the more recent cases, in *Polygram*, we concluded that an agreement between music companies not to advertise two recordings for a short time period was inherently suspect. Courts have similarly recognized the role of advertising in fostering competition and have condemned advertising restrictions. The Supreme Court explained that advertising "serves to inform the public of the availability, nature, and prices of products and services, and thus performs an indispensable role in the allocation of resources in a free enterprise system." *Bates v. State Bar of Ariz.*, 433 U.S. 350, 364 (1977). The Supreme Court further explained, "[I]t is clear as an economic matter that . . . restrictions on fare advertising have the forbidden significant effect upon fares. . . . Restrictions on advertising 'serve to increase the difficulty of discovering the lowest cost seller . . . and [reduce] the incentive to price competitively.'" *Morales v. Trans World Airlines, Inc.*, 504 U.S. 374, 388 (1992) (quoting *Bates*, 433 U.S. at 377).

More recently, in *California Dental*, the Court found "unexceptionable" the Ninth Circuit's "statements that 'price advertising is fundamental to price competition' and that 'restrictions on the ability to advertise prices normally make it more difficult for consumers to find a lower price and for [sellers] to compete on the basis of price.'" The Court, however, found that the professional services market at issue permitted "the possibility that the particular restrictions on professional advertising could have different effects from those 'normally' found in the commercial world." Thus, even when the Court did not affirm liability in *California Dental*, it recognized that in ordinary commercial markets, bans on truthful advertising normally are likely to cause competitive harm.

. . .

Our conclusion that the particular advertising restrictions imposed by the Challenged Agreements are inherently suspect is a limited finding. We do not contend that all advertising restrictions are necessarily inherently suspect. The restrictions in this particular case prohibit the display of ads that would enable consumers to learn about alternative sellers of contact lenses and give them the opportunity to make price comparisons at the time they are likely to make a purchase. Importantly, the restrictions at issue here are not limitations on the content of an advertisement a consumer would otherwise see; they are restrictions on a consumer's opportunity to see a competitor's ad in the first place. Moreover, the record shows that the suppressed ads often emphasize lower prices. In this context, we find the advertising restrictions are inherently suspect. Because the Challenged Agreements restrict the ability of lower cost online sellers to show their ads to consumers, it is easy to see how "an observer with even a rudimentary understanding of economics could conclude that the arrangements in question would have an anticompetitive effect on customers and markets." *California Dental*, 526 U.S. at 770.

2.   Preliminary Analysis of Respondent's Justifications

Burden shifted to defendant

That conclusion is not the end of the analysis. As we explained in *Polygram*,

> If the challenged restrictions are . . . inherently suspect, then the defendant can . . . advanc[e] a legitimate justification for those practices. . . . At this early stage of the analysis, the defendant need only articulate a legitimate justification. . . . [T]he proffered justifications must be both cognizable under the antitrust laws and at least facially plausible. . . . When the defendant advances such cognizable and plausible justifications, the plaintiff must make a more detailed showing that the restraints at issue are indeed likely, in the particular context, to harm competition.

Moreover, Respondent bears the burden of "articulat[ing] the specific link between the challenged restraint and the purported justification." this case, Respondent must articulate the specific link between restraints on its competitors' use of search advertising and the protection of its own trademark rights.

"[C]ognizability allows the deciding tribunal to reject proffered justifications that, as a matter of law, are incompatible with the goal of antitrust law to further competition. Cognizable justifications ordinarily explain how specific restrictions enable the defendants to increase output or improve product quality, service, or innovation." "A justification is plausible if it cannot be rejected without extensive factual inquiry. The defendant . . . must articulate the specific link between the challenged restraint and the purported justification to merit a more searching inquiry into whether the restraint may advance procompetitive goals . . . ."

Here, Respondent has articulated two legitimate justifications that are cognizable and, at least, facially plausible: avoidance of litigation costs through settlement and trademark protection. Settling costly litigation is a cognizable and facially plausible justification for the settlement agreements. As the Supreme Court explained in *Actavis* and we recognized in *Schering-Plough*, 136 F.T.C. 956, 1003 (2003), there is a "general legal policy favoring settlement of disputes." *Actavis*, 570 U.S. at 153; see also *In re Tamoxifen Citrate Antitrust Litig.*, 466 F.3d 187, 202 (2d Cir. 2006) (noting public's "strong interest in settlement" of complex and expensive cases). While this public policy favoring settlements does not create antitrust immunity, see *supra* Section IV, it is, nonetheless, a legitimate justification that we do not ignore.

. . .

Similarly, at this stage of the analysis, we consider protecting trademark rights to be a legitimate procompetitive justification. As Respondent's experts, Drs. Landes and Murphy, explained, trademarks provide informational benefits to consumers about product and quality attributes that reduce consumers' search costs. Trademark protection preserves those quality signals for consumers and encourages firms to invest in both product quality and the trademark. Also, at least facially, Respondent's contention that the settlement agreements advance this procompetitive goal is plausible; "it cannot be rejected without extensive factual inquiry." . . . Also, the record shows that 1-800 Contacts had a brand identity that it wished to preserve. It had a marketing strategy to create brand awareness and during the period 2002 through 2014 had spent ███████ on television advertising and ███████ on internet advertising to build that brand.

It is important to note that our determination that two of 1-800 Contacts' procompetitive justifications are legitimate at this stage of the analysis is not the end of our evaluation. We return to Respondent's procompetitive justifications with an "extensive factual [and legal] inquiry" when we move farther into the rule of reason analysis. In Sections V.A.3.a and V.A.5, we consider Complaint Counsel's contention that the procompetitive benefits could be reasonably achieved through less anticompetitive means and examine whether Respondent's procompetitive rationales are supported by the facts.[22]

3.   Complaint Counsel's More Detailed Showing

Because Respondents have advanced legitimate procompetitive justifications, we do not summarily condemn the Challenged Agreements based only on an initial

---

[22] We recognize the current limited inquiry regarding 1-800 Contacts' procompetitive justifications and the later steps in the rule of reason burden-shifting analysis "could be combined, [but] we think it analytically superior and consistent with the relevant case law to first screen the purported justification for legitimacy before engaging in a more extensive, and therefore longer and more resource-intensive, inquiry whether detailed analysis supports or refutes the justification. Antitrust courts have long held that preliminary analysis of purported justifications is appropriate." *Polygram*, 136 F.T.C. at 348 n.43.

review of the nature of the restraints. Instead, to satisfy their burden under the rule of reason, Complaint Counsel must make a further showing. As we explained in *Polygram*,

> When the defendant advances such cognizable and plausible justifications, the plaintiff must make a more detailed showing that the restraints at issue are indeed likely, in the particular context, to harm competition. Such a showing still need not prove actual anticompetitive effects or entail "the fullest market analysis." Depending upon the circumstances of the cases and the degree to which antitrust tribunals have experience with restraints in particular markets, such a showing may or may not require evidence about the particular market at issue, but at a minimum must entail the identification of the theoretical basis for the alleged anticompetitive effects and a showing that the effects are indeed likely to be anticompetitive. . . . The plaintiff may also show that the proffered procompetitive effects could be achieved through means less restrictive of competition.

In short, Complaint Counsel may meet their burden to show that the restraints at issue are likely to harm competition by either (i) identifying the theoretical basis for the alleged anticompetitive effects and showing that these effects are likely in this particular setting or (ii) explaining how Respondent could have minimized the anticompetitive effects of its conduct or accomplished its procompetitive justifications through less restrictive alternatives. Here, Complaint Counsel show both that, in the context of online sales of contact lenses, the proffered procompetitive effects of the advertising restraints in the Challenged Agreements could be achieved through means less restrictive of competition, and that restraints "are indeed likely . . . to harm competition." We address each of these approaches separately.

a. Respondent's Proffered Procompetitive Justifications Could Be Achieved Through Less Anticompetitive Means

. . .

i.   Overbreadth

When an agreement limits truthful price advertising on the basis of trademark protection, it must be narrowly tailored to protecting the asserted trademark right. The agreements here are not—they restrict advertising regardless of whether the ads are likely to be confusing and, apparently, regardless of whether competitors actually use the trademark term (requiring negative keywords).

. . .

Here, no company names are alleged to be the cause of any confusion, and as noted above, non-use restrictions cut off an important channel of truthful price advertising. Whereas a typical trademark non-use remedy affects how a product may be labeled or what language may be used in the text of an ad, the non-use restriction here limits the number of times competitor ads are shown and insulates some 1-800 Contacts' consumers from becoming aware of its rivals.

Respondent also points to cases in which courts have issued orders that would prohibit use of trademarks in internet advertising, but most of those cases are either consent judgments or default judgments and involve infringing conduct beyond mere keyword bidding. In any event, decisions about the appropriate remedy are inherently case-specific, and the fact that a court in some other context, with no or little consideration of the effects on competition, granted a broad injunction does not constitute an endorsement of the private agreements here or render them procompetitive.

ii.   Less Anticompetitive Alternatives

Complaint Counsel identify three alternatives to the restrictions in the Challenged Agreements. They suggest that Respondent could (1) bar the rival from using specific text alleged by 1-800 Contacts to cause confusion, including prohibiting the rival from using a name confusingly similar to its own; (2) require clear disclosure in each search advertisement of the identity of the rival seller; or (3) require the rival to refrain from using confusing or deceptive language in its search ads.

These options present alternative ways for avoiding litigation costs and achieving the procompetitive benefits that flow from trademark protection. The first and third proposed alternatives would adequately address consumer confusion stemming from the content of the ad. Respondent, however, claims that its trademark was infringed by the mere appearance of competitor ads in response to a trademark search, not from any confusing ad content. Assuming, arguendo, and contrary to our findings below, that protection against such infringement has been established as a valid procompetitive benefit here, alternatives one and three would not adequately address it. But the second proposed alternative—requiring clear disclosure of the identity of the rival seller—is a workable option that would achieve both litigation cost savings and protection of trademark rights, including prevention of the consumer confusion associated with infringement, in a significantly less anticompetitive manner. Respondent's arguments to the contrary are unpersuasive.

Respondent contends that a disclosure requirement would be unworkable because "clear and conspicuous disclosure" is an amorphous standard that would likely generate future litigation. [25] We, however, do not find a requirement to clearly disclose the seller's identity to be "amorphous." The Commission has

---

[25] Courts have been inconsistent in their burden allocation in assessing less restrictive alternatives, "[b]ut the difference in assignment of this proof burden is more apparent than real." 11 Herbert Hovenkamp, Antitrust Law ¶ 1914c (3rd ed. 2011). As a leading antitrust treatise explains:

> The most workable allocation gives the plaintiff the burden of suggesting, or proffering, a particular alternative claimed to achieve the same benefits but less restrictive of competition. The defendant then has the burden of showing that the proffered alternative is either unworkable or not less restrictive.

Id.

ordered parties to implement clear and conspicuous disclosures in numerous cases involving misleading advertising and did not find the requirements too amorphous or otherwise problematic to serve its remedial goals. Moreover, nothing prevents the parties, as part of their settlement, from agreeing on the specific language of the disclosure that would need to be included in the ads to dispel any purported consumer confusion.

. . .

Respondent additionally argues that this proposed alternative is "merely theoretical" because the record does not contain any real-world trademark settlements embodying such terms. But insistence on identifying examples of other settlements that incorporate Complaint Counsel's specific proposal is unrealistic given the relatively new context of search- based keyword advertising, particularly in light of the large number of cases dismissing claims based on keyword bidding altogether. Moreover, settlement agreements are often subject to confidentiality provisions and consequently unavailable. In any event, an absence of such settlement examples in the record does not determine whether the proposed alternative is workable. The idea that disclaimers can be used to eliminate consumer confusion is not new, and courts have ordered disclaimers as a remedy in internet-based trademark infringement cases. *See, e.g., Nissan Motor Co., Ltd. v. Nissan Computer Corp.*, 89 F. Supp. 2d 1154 (C.D. Cal. 2000), *aff'd*, 246 F.3d 675 (9th Cir. 2000) (preliminary injunction requiring defendant Nissan Computer Corporation, owner of the websites nissan.com and nissan.net, to clearly identify itself on the website, disclaim affiliation with, and identify the correct website for, Nissan Motor Co., and not to display any automobile-related information or web links.); *Tempur-Pedic N. Am., LLC v. Mattress Firm, Inc.*, 2017 WL 2957912, at *11 (S.D. Tex. July 11, 2017) (permitting defendant to continue to use plaintiff's trademark in Google AdWords, but limiting number of times defendant could use the mark on its webpage and requiring disclaimer of affiliation); *Simone v. VSL Pharm., Inc.*, 2016 WL 3466033, at *27 (D. Md. June 20, 2016) (allowing competitor to post AdWords ads containing trademark term if such ads also include adequate disclaimer of affiliation, to be pre-approved by the court).

The FTC, too, in its decades of experience preventing and remedying false advertising claims and consumer deception, has ordered respondents to provide disclosures to avoid consumer confusion. In fact, in 2013, the Commission published guidelines to assist businesses in providing clear, effective disclosures in space-constrained internet ads. We thus have successfully employed remedial mechanisms similar to those urged by Complaint Counsel. We see no reason why a brief statement identifying the ad sponsor and/or disclaiming affiliation with 1-800 Contacts would be ineffective or unworkable.

Given the inherently suspect nature of Respondent's advertising restraints and our finding that the procompetitive benefits asserted to justify those restraints could be achieved by significantly less anticompetitive means, we can conclude that Respondent has engaged in unfair methods of competition in violation of Section 5 of the FTC Act. Although Complaint Counsel have met their burden by demonstrating that Respondent could have chosen a less restrictive alternative to achieve the same procompetitive benefit, we also consider whether Complaint Counsel has satisfied its further showing by focusing alternatively on the particular restraints and context presented here.

b. Complaint Counsel's Showing that the Restraints Are Likely, in the Particular Context, to Harm Competition

Our review of the record shows that the restraints "are indeed likely, in the particular context, to harm competition." Online search advertising is a key method for consumers to discover, compare, and reach online contact lens vendors and for lower-priced retailers to compete. It enables online sellers to increase brand awareness and to obtain new customers. It is displayed at the key moment when the consumer is more likely to be looking to buy.

For 1-800 Contacts, search advertising is important. From 2004 to 2014, between ▉▉▉▉▉▉ percent of 1-800 Contacts' internet advertising budget was spent on paid search

advertising each year. 1-800 Contacts earns approximately ▉▉▉▉▉▉ of its sales from paid search advertising.

Search advertising is similarly important for 1-800 Contacts' online competitors. The record shows that online retailers have found search advertising much more effective in reaching potential buyers than other types of advertising. For example, AC Lens has found that, compared to other marketing channels, search advertising generates the most new customer orders and the most revenue, at a cost consistent with AC Lens' financial goals. Thus, for AC Lens, search advertising is the most effective and important marketing channel to grow its business. Other online competitors reported similar reliance on search advertising. Vision Direct advertised almost exclusively online. Search advertising "was a major driver" in building its business, including driving traffic to Vision Direct's website and generating new and repeat sales. Web Eye Care predominantly relies on paid search advertising, because it has determined that search advertising "drives the most traffic" and orders at an acceptable cost. For LensDirect, paid search advertising constitutes its most important marketing channel and has been effective in generating growth. Lens Discounters found that paid search advertising is "essential" to its ability to attract new customers because it reaches customers who are seeking to purchase contact lenses online. For Memorial Eye, search advertising was the "most efficient," form of advertising, which was "critical" to the company's growth. Similarly, search advertising was "[e]specially important" for Walgreens when it began selling contact lenses online because it helped let people know that Walgreens sold contact lenses; it was "an essential form" of advertising for Walgreens to remain competitive with other online retailers of contact lenses.

Not only is search advertising in general important, the record shows that search advertising generated by searches for 1-800 Contacts' trademark terms is important. Trademark search is a significant source of 1-800 Contacts' business. It accounts for the substantial majority of 1-800 Contacts' new customer orders attributable to paid search advertising. In 2006, 2007, and 2008, trademark search generated far more orders than non-trademark searches. In 2015, between 20 and

31 percent of 1-800 Contacts' initial web orders came from users searching for 1-800 Contacts' trademark terms. 1-800 Contacts' trademark terms have higher conversion rates[34] than non-branded search terms.

Similarly, for 1-800 Contacts' online rivals, advertising displayed for searches on 1-800 Contacts' trademark terms is important. During the period from 2002 through 2016, Google displayed advertisements for nine of the 14 contact lens retailers that are parties to the Challenged Agreements, as a result of their direct bidding on 1-800 Contacts' trademark terms prior to entering into the agreements. These nine firms found such keyword bidding to be worth the cost, and Google determined their advertisements were sufficiently relevant to warrant display. Id. In addition, parties to the Challenged Agreements consistently testified that, absent the agreements, they would bid, or test bidding, on 1-800 Contacts' trademark terms and/or remove negative keywords from their advertising accounts.

. . .

The reason that 1-800 Contacts' rivals' ads are so important at this key moment is that the rival online sellers offer lower prices, and advertising for those retailers often emphasizes those lower prices. That information is valuable: online shoppers for contact lenses are primarily concerned with low prices. Yet, in a 2012 consumer survey of 1-800 Contacts' customers, more than one-third of respondents explained that they initially purchased from 1-800 Contacts because "It Was the Only Online Contacts Site of Which I Was Aware," and a 2015 AEA Investors Fund analysis based on another survey found that actual price variances were "much more" than consumers thought them to be.

. . .

This examination of the context of the particular advertising restraints in the Challenged Agreements demonstrates that anticompetitive effects are likely. Economics and prior cases counsel that the challenged advertising restrictions prevent consumers from obtaining information that would permit price and service comparisons. The record evidence showing the significance of search advertising and searches for 1-800 Contacts trademark terms in particular; the price competition offered by 1-800 Contacts' rivals; and the consumer responses to online competitors' ads generated by searches for 1-800 Contacts trademarks confirm that the Challenged Agreements are "indeed likely, in [this] particular context, to harm competition."

4.   1-800 Contacts' Response to Complaint Counsel's Showing of Anticompetitive Effects

1-800 Contacts responds to Complaint Counsel's showing that the restraints are inherently suspect and likely to have substantial anticompetitive effects by

---

[34] A "conversion" refers to a sale made over the internet. The conversion rate is the number of times a conversion occurs divided by the total number of ad clicks.

challenging the factual, economic, and legal support for the demonstration of those anticompetitive effects. These challenges are <u>not persuasive.</u>

Respondent and the Dissent argue that the Challenged Agreements affected advertising by only some companies, in only one medium, in response to only a portion of internet searches related to contact lenses. Of course, the fact that some advertising remained unrestrained does not excuse a restraint affecting a competitively significant subset of ads. While the Challenged Agreements do not prevent all advertising for the online sale of contact lenses, they affect a particularly significant type of advertising for online sales at the crucial moment when sales are about to be made. The suppressed ads would have enabled consumers to learn about alternative, lower-priced sellers of contact lenses and to make price comparisons. Prohibiting this particular type of advertising is likely to have substantial anticompetitive effects.

Respondent argues that the ads banned by the settlements could have different effects from advertising in other markets. Although Respondent points to some attributes of search advertising—some consumers may be conducting navigational searches and expect to see the most relevant results appearing first, [36] and some consumers may be unable to distinguish between paid search ads and organic results—Respondent does not identify any record evidence demonstrating that consumers' purchasing behavior in response to search ads generated by 1-800 Contacts' trademark terms differs from their response to other advertising. . . .

5.   Validity of the Asserted Procompetitive Justifications

As discussed in Section V.A.2, the avoidance of litigation costs through settlement and the protection of trademark rights are cognizable and facially plausible procompetitive justifications because, under the right circumstances, both cost savings and trademark protection can result in enhanced competition and innovation. But Complaint Counsel have shown that the purported procompetitive benefits could have been accomplished through means less restrictive of competition. See supra Section V.A.3.a. Even if no less restrictive alternative were available, however, Respondent's case would falter because it has not shown that its purported justifications have a basis in fact, i.e., that they are valid as well as plausible and cognizable. As we noted in *Polygram*, the respondent "has the burden of producing factual evidence in support of its contentions."

---

[36] Respondent suggests that absent the advertising restrictions rivals' ads would appear first. Yet "1-800 Contacts' strategy to search advertising was to spend as much as necessary when bidding on its trademark keywords to meet its goal of ensuring that 1-800 Contacts' advertisement was the first advertisement displayed in response to searches for its trademark." Viewed in light of this strategy, the advertising restrictions may enable 1-800 Contacts to reduce its bids and pay lower prices, but they do not better satisfy consumer expectations.

At this point, then, we look closer at Respondent's asserted justifications and require sufficiently detailed evidence to establish that the justifications are not merely plausible, but actually valid. We find that Respondent has not met this burden.

a.   Avoidance of Litigation Costs through Settlement

Although Respondent has identified litigation cost savings, it has not demonstrated that these cost savings would have procompetitive effects. Respondent must provide "some explanation connecting [its] practice[s] to consumers' benefits." Chicago Prof'l Sports, L.P. v. Nat'l Basketball Ass'n, 961 F.2d 667, 674 (7th Cir. 1992); see also *Polygram*, 136 F.T.C. at 345 (describing legitimate justifications as "reasons why the practices are likely to have beneficial effects for consumers"). But Respondent provides no basis for finding that the litigation cost savings would be passed through to consumers or would otherwise benefit competition in a way that could offset the anticompetitive effects. Capital savings are not cognizable efficiencies in and of themselves, though they may be cognizable if defendant demonstrates that avoidance of capital expenditures provides a tangible, verifiable benefit to consumers by lowering prices or improving service quality. "While increasing output, creating operating efficiencies, making a new product available, enhancing product or service quality, and widening consumer choice have been accepted by courts as justifications for otherwise anticompetitive agreements, mere profitability or cost savings have not qualified as a defense under the antitrust laws." Respondent has not demonstrated that the litigation cost savings provide benefits to consumers that could or would offset the competitive harms attributable to its conduct.

b.   Trademark Protections

Respondent and the Dissent argue that 1-800 Contacts' agreements facilitate trademark protection, which allows retailers to market products in a way that reduces the likelihood of consumer confusion and incentivizes brand-building. Both maintain that brand-building, in turn, assures consumers of consistent quality and reduces consumer costs of making purchasing decisions. Although trademark protection can be a legitimate justification, it does not justify the restraints challenged in this case.

. . .

Although claims based on keyword bidding have sometimes withstood dispositive motions, apart from a single district court summary judgment decision from over ten years ago, no court has found bidding on trademark keywords to constitute trademark infringement, absent some additional factor, such as a misleading use of the trademark in the ad text that confuses consumers as to the advertisement's source, sponsorship, or affiliation. Rather, "[c]ourts have consistently rejected the notion that buying or creating internet search terms, alone, is enough to raise a claim of trademark infringement." *Tempur-Pedic N. Am.*, 2017 WL 2957912, at *7 (holding, on motion for preliminary injunction, that "[b]ecause the court has concluded that the purchase of AdWords alone, without directing consumers to a potentially confusing website, is unlikely to cause customer confusion, the AdWords will not be included in the injunction"); *see Acad. of Motion Picture Arts & Sciences v. GoDaddy.com, Inc.*, 2015 WL 5311085, *50 (C.D. Cal. Sept. 10, 2015) ("There is a growing consensus in the case authorities that keyword advertising does not violate the Lanham Act.").43 Indeed, Respondent lost the one infringement case that it pursued to judgment. *See 1-800 Contacts, Inc. v. Lens.com, Inc.*, 722 F.3d 1229 (10th Cir. 2013) (affirming, in relevant part, summary judgment in favor of defendant). As the appellate court explained:

> Perhaps in the abstract, one who searches for a particular business with a strong mark and sees an entry on the results page will naturally infer that the entry is for that business. But that inference is an unnatural one when the entry is clearly labeled as an advertisement and clearly identifies the source, which has a name quite different from the business being searched for.

Despite the accumulating evidence regarding the weakness of trademark infringement claims, 1-800 Contacts continued to police and enforce the Challenged Agreements and, consequently, continued to extend their anticompetitive effects.

. . .

We are neither deciding matters of trademark law nor suggesting that to determine whether the Challenged Agreements unreasonably restrain competition, we need to conduct a mini-trial on the merits of the underlying trademark litigations. Respondent's justifications, however, must meet at least a minimum threshold of validity—more than merely surviving challenges as shams. In this case, the agreements restrict a type of competitive advertising that has never been found to violate the trademark laws, and the weight of authority overwhelmingly points to non-infringement. We are not convinced that trademark protection in this case is a valid procompetitive benefit that merits suppressing truthful advertising.

. . .

Rule of Reason

B. Analysis of the Challenged Agreements for Effects on Consumers Using Direct Evidence of Anticompetitive Effects

Even if we did not rely on the inherently suspect nature of the restraints in the Challenged Agreements to conclude that there is liability, a second way independently to establish plaintiff's initial burden to show that a particular horizontal restraint has anticompetitive effects is to consider direct evidence of those effects. When there is direct evidence of anticompetitive effects, detailed market analysis and proof of market power is unnecessary. "[S]ince the purpose of the inquiries into market definition and market power is to determine whether an arrangement has the potential for genuine adverse effects on competition, proof of actual detrimental effects, such as a reduction of output can obviate the need for an inquiry into market power, which is but a surrogate for detrimental effects." *IFD*, 476 U.S. at 460-61 (internal quotation marks omitted); see also *Ohio v. American Express Co.*, 138 S. Ct. at 2285 n.7 (explaining that market definition is unnecessary for the analysis of horizontal restraints when actual anticompetitive effects have been demonstrated).

When plaintiff satisfies the initial burden to show anticompetitive effects using direct evidence, the burden then shifts to the defendant. The defendant can challenge plaintiff's support underlying the initial showing. In addition, defendant can seek to establish procompetitive justifications for its conduct. Ultimately, the fact-finder must consider whether the anticompetitive harms outweigh any procompetitive benefits.

1.   Direct Evidence of Anticompetitive Effects for Consumers

Like Judge Chappell, who considered the evidence only under this mode of analysis, we conclude that Complaint Counsel successfully established their prima facie case through direct evidence of two anticompetitive effects: the restriction of truthful advertising and an increase in contact lens prices sold online.

a.   Restriction of Truthful Advertising

Respondent and the Dissent argue that a restriction on truthful advertising does not qualify as an anticompetitive effect; according to Respondent, only reduced output or higher prices for the underlying product is sufficient. Respondent and the Dissent rely on California Dental's statement that "the relevant output for antitrust purposes here is presumably not information or advertising, but dental services themselves" so that "the question is not whether the universe of possible advertisements has been limited (as assuredly it has), but whether the limitation on advertisements obviously tends to limit the total delivery of [the product being advertised]."

But the Court's concern in *California Dental* was that the normal linkage between advertising restrictions and price/output effects in the underlying product market was attenuated in the context of professional services because consumers may not be able to make valid assessments regarding advertising claims about the quality, comfort, or other non-price aspects of dentists' services. *See, e.g.,* 526 U.S. at 778 (citing the "plausibility of competing claims about the effects of the professional advertising restrictions" as the basis for concluding that "[t]he obvious anticompetitive effect that triggers abbreviated analysis has not been shown").

We find Respondent's and the Dissent's reliance on *California Dental* misplaced because there is no similar concern that consumers may be unable to assess the information contained in advertising for the sale of contact lenses. The record shows a focus on price advertising by many of 1-800 Contacts' online rivals. When consumers have a prescription and are shopping for contact lenses, the lenses they purchase are identical—by prescription, brand name, and even type (e.g., daily or biweekly)—regardless of the retailer. For such commodity products, consumers can comparison shop. In fact, the Fairness to Contact Lens Consumers Act, which requires prescribers to provide a patient with a portable copy of his or her prescription, "promotes competition in retail sales of contact lenses by facilitating consumers' ability to comparison shop for contact lenses." FTC Contact Lens Rule, 81 Fed. Reg. 88526 (Dec. 7, 2016) (review of Rule). Congress apparently had no concern that consumers would be unable to assess competing offers and prices for contact lenses.

Restricting the availability of truthful information that guides consumer decisions in the marketplace is a competitive harm. As the Supreme Court explained in *IFD*, "a concerted and effective effort to withhold (or make more costly) information desired by consumers for the purpose of determining whether a particular purchase is cost justified is likely enough to disrupt the proper functioning of the price setting mechanism of the market that it may be condemned even absent proof that it resulted in higher prices or . . . the purchase of higher priced services than would occur in its absence." *IFD*, 476 U.S. at 461-62. We similarly found direct evidence of competitive harm from a showing that there were "significantly fewer discount [residential real estate] listings" available to consumers after an association of real estate brokers adopted rules that limited consumers' access to information about the availability of lower-priced real estate services.

. . .

Respondent and the Dissent also dispute that *IFD* finds that a restriction on truthful advertising is sufficient as evidence of actual anticompetitive effects. According to Respondent, in that case, the withholding of x-rays from insurance companies was an express restriction on output because x-rays were a service customers wanted. We disagree. X-rays were taken to assess the need for, and to guide the provision of dental treatment. X-rays were not offered as a separate product independent of dental treatment. Moreover, the Supreme Court's analysis focused on the informational role of x-rays and the harm to market mechanisms that would flow from withholding that information. See *IFD*, 476 U.S. at 461-62 ("A concerted and effective effort to withhold (or make more costly) information desired by consumers for the purpose of determining whether a particular purchase is cost justified is likely enough to disrupt the proper functioning of the price-setting mechanism of the market that it may be condemned even absent proof that it resulted in higher prices or, as here, the purchase of higher priced services, than would occur in its absence.").

b.   Increased Online Contact Lens Prices

In addition to evidence of reduced advertising, Complaint Counsel presented direct evidence of a price effect, which provides a persuasive, independent basis for Complaint Counsel's prima facie case. As the ALJ found, "the evidence in this case proves . . . that at least some consumers have paid, or will pay, prices that are higher than they would otherwise be, absent the Challenged Agreements." As we previously discussed, the record contains evidence that the Challenged Agreements reduced the number of competitor ads, and increased sales for 1-800 Contacts while reducing the sales for its rivals.

At the same time, prices charged by 1-800 Contacts were on average ███████ higher than those of its online competitors. . . .

. . .

2. 1-800 Contacts' Response to the Direct Evidence of Anticompetitive Effects

Because Complaint Counsel have demonstrated anticompetitive effects, the burden now shifts to Respondent. 1-800 Contacts challenges the factual support for the direct evidence of anticompetitive effects and proffers procompetitive justifications for the restraints.

a. Respondent's Challenges to the Direct Evidence

Respondent and the Dissent challenge the direct evidence of anticompetitive effects on several grounds. First, Respondent argues that Complaint Counsel have presented only the theories of experts, not direct evidence of price effects. We reject this characterization. The opinions of Complaint Counsel's experts derive from the facts in the record and econometric analysis of those facts. The experts use known facts to quantify the impact of the advertising restrictions on the ads that would otherwise appear and on the consumer responses—including clicks and purchases—thereto. They provide empirical evidence, not economic theory isolated from facts, and the underlying facts are in the record.

Respondent and the Dissent next challenge the premise of higher prices, arguing that 1- 800 Contacts offers a higher quality of service, so there is no reason to conclude that its prices are higher on a quality-adjusted basis. Certainly, customer service can be a differentiating factor when a firm sells a commoditized product. But the record shows that without the Challenged Agreements, consumers would have shifted purchases from 1-800 Contacts to its rivals, which reveals customer preferences for the price/quality combination offered by rivals. At least for these customers, 1-800 Contacts was offering a higher price, even after adjusting for quality.

Other aspects of the record show that 1-800 Contacts' service levels do not fully explain its higher prices. Professor Athey testified that "[D]irect facts and market data support that there is a price premium [for 1-800 Contacts] and that that price premium is not fully accounted for by service differentials." This testimony reflects numerous market facts.

Other online sellers judge that they offer comparable service to 1-800 Contacts. See, e.g.,

██████████████████████████

. The competitors' view of service levels was shared by independent evaluators. The investment memorandum prepared by Berkshire Partners as part of the consideration of 1-800 Contacts stated, "[W]e are concerned that 1-800's premium pricing positioning versus its competitors is unsustainable in the medium- to long-term given the commodity-like nature of contact lenses and 1-800's insufficiently distinguishable service."

Other evidence supports the conclusion that 1-800 Contacts' higher prices are not fully explained by the firm's service level. Some statements by 1-800 Contacts' employees express doubt that its service level is sufficient to justify the price premium. See, e.g., CX1086 (email expressing concern that ads by lower priced competitors would lead to reduced 1-800 Contacts sales; comment in the email chain states, "The only other option I see is trying to convince customers that our existing prices are better than they really are or worth the cost. Tough challenge considering that we sell the exact same thing as everyone else."). Similarly, some of 1-800 Contacts' documents question the firm's supposed quality advantage. See CX1117-022 ("Other online suppliers achieve satisfaction scores as high as us"). Finally, the need for 1-800 Contacts to offer a price-match policy suggests that the service differential is insufficient to offset the price premium.

. . .

Consequently, we find that Complaint Counsel have established a prima facie case of anticompetitive harm through direct evidence of the restriction of truthful advertising and through direct evidence of price increases.

b. Respondent's Procompetitive Rationales for the Advertising Restraints

Respondent may rebut Complaint Counsel's prima facie case by establishing procompetitive justifications that outweigh the anticompetitive harms. Respondent has identified two justifications—the settlement of costly litigation and trademark protection—that we have found cognizable and facially plausible. See supra Section V.A.2. But, as discussed above in our analysis of the challenged restraints as inherently suspect, Respondent fails to sufficiently support its asserted justifications, and Complaint Counsel have demonstrated that the challenged advertising restraints are not reasonably necessary to achieve the asserted benefits. See supra Sections V.A.5 and V.A.3.a. In these circumstances, direct evidence of anticompetitive harm provides a second, independent basis for concluding that Respondent has engaged in unfair methods of competition in violation of Section 5 of the FTC Act.

C. Analysis of the Challenged Agreements for Effects on Search Engines

In addition to harm to consumers, the Complaint alleges that the Challenged Agreements harm search engines by, inter alia, unreasonably restraining price competition in certain search advertising auctions, preventing search engine companies from displaying to users the array of advertisements that are most responsive to a user's search, and impairing the quality of service provided to consumers by search engine companies. Despite the allegations in the Complaint and the presentation of evidence on the issue, and contrary to Commission rules, Judge Chappell determined that the "Initial Decision need not, and does not, . . . determine whether or not the Challenged Agreements have anticompetitive effects in the form of harm to search engines."

[The Commission found that a prima facie case of such harm was established and that although the Respondent offered legitimate procompetitive justifications, the Respondent did not counter the likelihood of anticompetitive effects, that there were less restrictive ways to achieve the Respondent's procompetitive justifications, and that the Respondent did not show that those justifications were valid.]

****

In this opinion, we have evaluated traditional concerns of antitrust law—the anticompetitive harms that flow when rivals agree to restrict truthful advertising and to limit their participation in auctions—in a contemporary context involving online shopping and advertising via internet search engines. Our analysis has accounted for and given weight to justifications based on trademark protection as well as the benefits of settling costly litigation. We hold that Complaint Counsel have shown competitive harm by demonstrating the inherently suspect nature of the restraints at issue. We have determined that Respondent has asserted cognizable and plausible procompetitive justifications, requiring Complaint Counsel to make a further showing. Complaint Counsel have made that showing, both by demonstrating the availability of less anticompetitive alternatives to the challenged restraints and by showing in greater detail that those restraints are indeed likely in the particular context to harm competition. In contrast, Respondent has failed to establish that its justifications are not merely plausible, but in fact valid. We also hold that Complaint Counsel have shown competitive harm by providing direct evidence that the challenged agreements resulted in actual anticompetitive effects. Respondent, however, failed to rebut Complaint Counsel's direct evidence and could not provide sufficient efficiency justifications that would outweigh the evidence of anticompetitive effects.

Consequently, we conclude that the advertising restrictions in the Challenged Agreements between Respondent and 14 of its rival online sellers of contact lenses constitute unfair methods of competition, in violation of Section 5 of the FTC Act, and we require Respondent to cease and desist from enforcing the unlawful provisions in its existing agreements and from entering into similar agreements in the future.

Issued: November 7, 2018

Commissioner Rebecca Kelly Slaughter submitted a concurring opinion.

Commissioner Noah Joshua Phillips submitted a dissenting statement.

Notes

1.   How does the F.T.C.'s "inherently suspect" approach differ from and resemble the *per se* rule? The "quick look" approach? The rule of reason?

2.   How does the Commission's analysis in part V.A.1 differ from that in part V.B.1? How does V.A.1 differ from V.A.3? V.A.2 from V.A.5? Can you place all of these sections in the context of *Broadcast Music*, *Maricopa*, and *NCAA*?

3.   Does the "inherently suspect" approach rely on market characteristics? Actual market effects?

4.   Do you agree with the opinion's statement that "[w]e are neither deciding matters of trademark law nor suggesting that to determine whether the Challenged Agreements unreasonably restrain competition, we need to conduct a mini-trial on the merits of the underlying trademark litigations"?

5.   In recent years the Department of Justice has pursued a number of cases in which employers agreed not to "poach" employees from competitors. One of the first no-poach arrangements that the Department of Justice pursued was among high-tech companies. *See* Press Release, Department of Justice, "Justice Department Requires Six High Tech Companies to Stop Entering into Anticompetitive Employee Solicitation Agreements: Settlement Preserves Competition for High Tech Employees," https://www.justice.gov/opa/pr/justice-department-requires-six-high-tech-companies-stop-entering-anticompetitive-employee, September 24, 2010. More recently it has also challenged an agreement not to poach college students. *See* Press Release, Department of Justice, "Justice Department Files Antitrust Case and Simultaneous Settlement Requiring Elimination of Anticompetitive College Recruiting Restraints," December 12, 2019, https://www.justice.gov/opa/pr/justice-department-files-antitrust-case-and-simultaneous-settlement-requiring-elimination.

Should no-poach agreements be characterized as market allocations or as group boycotts (see next section), or are they better characterized as practices that facilitate price-fixing? Or do they not fit neatly into any of these categories? Sherman Act § 1 refers only to agreements "in restraint of trade," so a restraint need not fit into one of the *per se* categories to be condemned. Presumably the use of long-term contracts, rather than at-will employment, would have effects similar to those of no-poach agreements. Should long-term contracts be illegal also? What if a trade association agreed on a standard stating that job security and long-term contracts were the ethical obligation of employers?

1.3. Group Boycotts/Concerted Refusals to Deal

As discussed above, standards are sometimes used by sellers to coordinate on aspects of the products they provide. Some such standards are primarily informational, as with the "voluntary" movie ratings of the Motion Picture Association of America (MPAA) and the similar video-game ratings of the Entertainment Software Ratings Board, though they could still have coercive effects. Other standards, however, seem more to resemble legal enforcement mechanisms, as in the reading below, a joint product of the MPAA, The Recording Industry Association of America, and large internet service providers. In reading this document, you might want to consider the *per se* treatment of the boycott in Fashion Originators' Guild of America v. FTC, 312 U.S. 457 (1941).

Center for Copyright Information
Memorandum of Understanding
July 6, 2011

MEMORANDUM OF UNDERSTANDING

Whereas:

- Copyright infringement (under Title 17 of the United States Code) on the Internet ("Online Infringement") – including the illegal distribution of copyrighted works such as music, movies, computer software, gaming software, e-books and the like via Peer-to-Peer ("P2P") file exchanges and other illegal distribution via Internet file hosting, streaming or other technologies – imposes substantial costs on copyright holders and the economy each year. Online Infringement also may contribute to network congestion, negatively affecting users' Internet experiences. . . .

- While the government maintains a critical role in enforcing copyright law, it should be readily apparent that, in an age of viral, digital online distribution, prosecution of individual acts of infringement may serve a purpose, but standing alone this may not be the only or best solution to addressing Online Infringement. If Online Infringement is to be effectively combated, law enforcement must work with all interested parties, including copyright holders, their licensees, artists (and the guilds, unions and other organizations that represent them), recording companies, movie studios, software developers, electronic publishers, Internet Service Providers ("ISPs"), public interest groups, other intermediaries and consumers on reasonable methods to prevent, detect and deter Online Infringement. Such efforts must respect the legitimate interests of Internet users and subscribers in protecting their privacy and freedom of speech, in accessing legitimate content, and in being able to challenge the accuracy of allegations of Online Infringement. . . . This work also should include the development of solutions that are reasonably necessary to effectuate the rights that are granted by copyright without unduly hampering the legitimate distribution of copyrighted works online or impairing the legitimate rights and interests of consumers and ISPs. Such efforts serve not only the shared interests of creators and distributors of creative works, but also the interests of Internet users who benefit from constructive measures aimed at education and deterrence in lieu of litigation with its attendant costs and legal risk.

. . .

- whereas, the Content Owner Representatives, the Participating ISPs, and the members of the Participating Content Owners Group (all, as defined in Section 1 below) and independent record labels and film production companies (Independent Content Owners , as defined in Section 5C below) represented by the American Association of Independent Music ("A2IM") and the Independent Film and Television Alliance ("IFTA"), respectively, seek to establish a consumer-focused process for identifying and notifying residential wired Internet access service customers of the Participating ISPs ("Subscribers") (other than dial-up Subscribers) who receive multiple notifications of allegations of Online Infringement made via P2P networks and applications ("P2P Online Infringement"), in an effort to educate consumers, deter Online Infringement, and direct consumers to lawful online legitimate sources of content.

- Whereas, having considered the desirability of implementing such a process as a means to encourage lawful and legitimate use of copyrighted content, the Parties (as defined in Section 1 below) hereby voluntarily enter into this Memorandum of Understanding (the "Agreement").

IT IS HEREBY UNDERSTOOD AND AGREED AMONG THE PARTIES THAT:

1. Parties to the Agreement

The parties to this Agreement (the "Parties") are The Recording Industry Association of America, Inc. ("RIAA"), The Motion Picture Association of America, Inc. ("MPAA" and together with RIAA, the "Content Owner Representatives"); the entities set forth in Attachment A (as may be amended from time to time) (collectively, the "Participating ISPs"); and solely for the purposes of Sections 2(E), 4(C), 4(D), 4(H), 4(I), 5(A), 5(C), 6, 7, 8, 9(E), 9(F), and 10 of this Agreement, MPAA members Walt Disney Studios Motion Pictures, Paramount Pictures Corporation, Sony Pictures Entertainment Inc., Twentieth Century Fox Film Corporation, Universal City Studios LLC, and Warner Bros. Entertainment Inc. (such MPAA members, together with MPAA, the "MPAA Group"), RIAA members UMG Recordings, Inc., Warner Music Group, Sony Music Entertainment, and EMI Music North America (such RIAA members, together with RIAA, the "RIAA Group" and together with the MPAA Group, and any other entities set forth in Attachment B (as may be amended from time to time), the "Participating Content Owners Group").

2. Establishment of CCI

A.   Not later than sixty (60) days after the Effective Date (as defined in Section 8(A) below), the Content Owner Representatives and the Participating ISPs will establish the Center for Copyright Information ("CCI") to assist in the effort to combat Online Infringement by, among other things, . .

. (iii) assisting in the design and implementation of a process that provides for consumer and Subscriber education through the forwarding of Copyright Alerts to, and application of Mitigation Measures (as defined in Section 4(G)(iii) below) on, Subscribers engaged in persistent P2P Online Infringement, including reviewing the accuracy and efficacy of Content Owner Representative processes for identifying instances of P2P Online Infringement and ISP processes for identifying the Subscriber accounts associated with such P2P Online Infringement; . . . .

B.   CCI will be governed by a six (6) member executive committee (the "Executive Committee") that will be selected as follows: three (3) members to be designated collectively by the Content Owner Representatives, and three (3) members to be designated collectively by the Participating ISPs. Each member shall serve without compensation for a term of two (2) years, which may be renewed.

. . .

3. System for Reducing Instances of P2P Online Infringement

A.   The Content Owner Representatives will develop and maintain written methodologies, which shall be adopted by the applicable Content Owner Representative, for identifying instances of P2P Online Infringement that are designed to detect and provide evidence that the identified content was uploaded or downloaded or copied and offered on a P2P network to be downloaded through a bit torrent or other P2P technology. Each Participating ISP will develop and maintain methodologies, which shall be adopted by the applicable Participating ISP, to match Internet Protocol ("IP") addresses identified by the Content Owner Representatives to the Participating ISP Subscribers' accounts, to keep a record of repeat alleged infringers, and to apply Mitigation Measures (as defined in Section 4(G)(iii) below). Such Content Owner Representative and Participating ISP methodologies are collectively referred to herein as the "Methodologies". . . .

B.   In conformance with its budget, CCI shall retain an independent and impartial technical expert or experts (the "Independent Expert") to review on a periodic and ongoing basis the Methodologies and any modifications thereto, and recommend enhancements as appropriate, with the goal of ensuring and maintaining confidence on the part of the Content Owner Representatives, the Participating ISPs, and the public in the accuracy and security of the Methodologies. If a Content Owner Representative Methodology is found by the Independent Expert to be fundamentally unreliable, the Independent Expert shall issue a confidential finding of inadequacy ("Finding of Inadequacy") to the affected Content Owner Representative to permit the affected Content Owner Representative to modify or change the Methodology for review. The selection of the Independent Expert shall require approval by a majority of the members of the Executive Committee. . . . .

C.   Each Participating ISP agrees to communicate the following principles in its Acceptable Use Policies ("AUP") or Terms of Service ("TOS"): (i) copyright infringement is conduct that violates the Participating ISP's AUP or TOS and for which a Subscriber may be legally liable; (ii) continuing and subsequent receipt of Copyright Alerts (as defined in Section 4(G) below) may result in the Participating ISP taking action by the application of Mitigation Measures (as defined in Section 4(G)(iii) below); and (iii) in addition to these Mitigation Measures, the Participating ISP may also adopt, in appropriate circumstances, those measures specifically authorized by section 512 of the Digital Millennium Copyright Act ("DMCA") and/or actions specifically provided for in the Participating ISP's AUP and/or TOS including temporary suspension or termination, except that nothing in this Agreement alters, expands, or otherwise affects any Participating ISP's rights or obligations under the DMCA.

D.   Each Participating ISP will develop, implement and independently enforce a Copyright Alert program as described in this Section 4(G) (each such program a "Copyright Alert Program"), provided that each Participating ISP shall not be required to exceed the notice volumes pertaining to its Copyright Alert Program as established in Section 5 of this Agreement. Each Participating ISP's Copyright Alert Program will be triggered by the Participating ISP's receipt of an ISP Notice that can be associated with a Subscriber's account and will result in the Participating ISP sending one (1) or more alert notices to the applicable Subscriber concerning the ISP Notice, as further described below (each such alert notice a "Copyright Alert").

G.   . . .

Each Participating ISP's Copyright Alert Program shall be comprised of [sic] six (6) Copyright Alerts, except that a Participating ISP may elect to send a single Educational Step Copyright Alert (as defined in Section 4(G)(i) below). However, to give an affected Subscriber time to review each Copyright Alert pertaining to such Subscriber's account and to take appropriate steps to avoid receipt of further Copyright Alerts, a Participating ISP and its Subscriber will be afforded a grace period of seven (7) calendar days after the transmission of any Copyright Alert before any additional Copyright Alerts will be directed to the account holder (the "Grace Period"). The same Grace Period shall apply following the sending of a Mitigation Measure Copyright Alert (as described in Section 4(G)(iii) and (iv) below) and during the pendency of any review requested by a Subscriber following the receipt of either such Copyright Alert. During such Grace Period, any further ISP Notices received by the Participating ISP that the Participating ISP determines to be associated with the applicable Subscriber's account will be handled as described in sub-paragraphs (i), (ii), (iii), and (iv) below.

Each Participating ISP shall use commercially reasonable efforts to develop a Copyright Alert Program in accordance with this Section 4(G), and shall work in good faith to complete all technical development work necessary for implementation of its Copyright Alert Program by a target launch date set forth in the applicable Implementation Agreement (each Participating ISP's target launch date referred to herein as its "Copyright Alert Program Launch Date").

Each Participating ISP's Copyright Alert Program shall be substantially similar to the following four (4) step sequential framework, which shall include an educational step (the "Initial Educational Step"), an acknowledgement step (the "Acknowledgement Step"), a mitigation measures step (the "Mitigation Measures Step"), and a post mitigation measures step (the "Post Mitigation Measures Step") as further described below. Under this framework, each Participating ISP will send Copyright Alerts with escalating warning language to Subscribers who are the subject of continuing ISP Notices. Specifically, each Participating ISP (1) shall send the Subscriber up to two (2) Copyright Alerts during the Initial Educational Step; (2) shall send two (2) more Copyright Alerts during the Acknowledgement Step; (3) shall send one (1) Mitigation Measure Copyright Alert (as defined in Section 4(G)(iii) below) during the Mitigation Measures Step and shall apply the specified Mitigation Measure (as defined in Section 4(G)(iii) below), subject to the Subscriber's right to challenge (or the Participating ISP's discretion to waive) the Copyright Alert(s) at this step; and (4) during the Post Mitigation Measures Step, shall send one (1) Mitigation Measure Copyright Alert and shall apply the specified Mitigation Measure, and may, at the Participating ISP's sole discretion, send additional Mitigation Measure Copyright Alerts and apply additional Mitigation Measures, subject to the Subscriber's right to challenge Copyright Alerts at this step.

Each Participating ISP's Copyright Alert Program shall follow the following format:

(i) Initial Educational Step: Upon receipt of an ISP Notice associated with a Subscriber's account and taking into account the parameters of the Grace Period (if applicable), the Participating ISP shall direct a Copyright Alert to the account holder (an "Educational Step Copyright Alert"). The Educational Step Copyright Alert shall notify the Subscriber of receipt of an ISP Notice alleging P2P Online Infringement and shall include, at a minimum, the information contained in the ISP Notice regarding the alleged infringement and shall inform the Subscriber that: (a) copyright infringement is illegal as well as a violation of the Participating ISP's AUP or TOS, (b) users of the Subscriber's account must not infringe copyrighted works, (c) there are lawful methods of obtaining copyrighted works, (d) continuing and subsequent receipt of Copyright Alerts may result in the Participating ISP taking action by the application of Mitigation Measures, (e) in addition to these Mitigation Measures, the Participating ISP may also adopt, in appropriate circumstances, those measures specifically authorized by section 512 of the DMCA and/or actions specifically provided for in the Participating ISP's AUP and/or TOS including temporary suspension or termination, (f) the Subscriber will have an opportunity to challenge any Copyright Alerts associated with the Subscriber's account before a Mitigation Measure is applied and may therefore wish to preserve records or information that could be used to show that the Subscriber's conduct was non-infringing, and (g) additional information regarding the Copyright Alert program may be found at CCI's web site. The number of Educational Step Copyright Alerts shall be at the discretion of the Participating ISP, not to exceed two (2) Copyright Alerts per Subscriber account, taking into account the parameters of the Grace Period. The second Educational Step Copyright Alert shall note specifically that it is in fact the Subscriber's second Educational Step Copyright Alert.

If the Participating ISP receives one (1) or more additional ISP Notices attributable to such Subscriber's account during the Grace Period associated with one of the Educational Step Copyright Alerts, the Participating ISP may at its discretion emphasize the educational and warning nature of its Copyright Alert Program by directing to the account holder additional Copyright Alerts that are similar in style to the Educational Step Copyright Alert. Such supplemental Copyright Alerts sent during the Grace Period shall not count toward the limit of two (2) Educational Step Copyright Alerts.

(ii) Acknowledgement Step. At the Acknowledgement Step, upon receipt of further ISP Notices determined to be associated with a Subscriber's account and taking into account the parameters of the Grace Period, the Participating ISP shall direct two (2) Copyright Alerts to the account holder that, as further described below, will require acknowledgement of receipt (but not require the user to acknowledge participation in any allegedly infringing activity) (each such Copyright Alert an "Acknowledgement Step Copyright Alert"). Each such Acknowledgement Step Copyright Alert shall state that the Subscriber, by acknowledging the notice, agrees immediately to cease, and/or agrees to instruct other users of the Subscriber's account to cease infringing conduct, if any exists. Each such Copyright Alert shall also state that, upon receipt of lawful process requiring production of records or pursuant to a qualifying claim that the Subscriber has made via the Independent Review Program (as defined in Section 4(H) below and Attachment C hereto), the Participating ISP may provide relevant identifying information about the Subscriber and the Subscriber's infringing conduct to third parties, including Content Owner Representatives or their agents and law enforcement agencies.

The mechanism provided for the Subscriber to acknowledge an Acknowledgement Step Copyright Alert may be in the form of (a) a temporary landing page to which the Subscriber's browser is directed prior to permitting general access to the Internet ("Landing Page") that shall state that the Subscriber has received prior warnings regarding P2P Online Infringement, and shall require the user of the

Subscriber's account to acknowledge receipt by clicking through the page prior to accessing additional web pages, (b) a "pop-up" notice which shall be designed to persist until the user of the Subscriber's account acknowledges receipt by clicking through the pop-up notice, or (c) such other format as determined in the Participating ISP's reasonable judgment which shall require acknowledgement of receipt of the Acknowledgement Step Copyright Alert.

If the Participating ISP receives one (1) or more additional ISP Notices attributable to such Subscriber's account during the Grace Period associated with one of the Acknowledgement Step Copyright Alerts, the Participating ISP may at its discretion emphasize the educational and warning nature of its Copyright Alert Program by directing to the account holder additional Copyright Alerts that are similar in style to the Educational Step Copyright Alert or the Acknowledgement Step Copyright Alert.

Such supplemental Copyright Alerts sent during the Grace Period shall not count toward the limit of two (2) Acknowledgement Step Copyright Alerts.

(iii) Mitigation Measures Step: At the Mitigation Measures Step, upon receipt of further ISP Notices determined to be associated with a Subscriber's account and taking into account the parameters of the Grace Period, the Participating ISP shall direct a Copyright Alert (a "Mitigation Measure Copyright Alert") to the account holder that (a) requires acknowledgement of receipt of the Copyright Alert as described in the Acknowledgement Step, (b) shall state that the Subscriber has received prior warnings regarding alleged P2P Online Infringement, and (c) informs the Subscriber that, per the Participating ISP's AUP and/or TOS and as set forth in prior Copyright Alerts, additional consequences shall be applied upon the Subscriber's account as described more fully in this subparagraph (iii) (each such measure a "Mitigation Measure").

The Mitigation Measure Copyright Alert shall set forth the specific Mitigation Measure to be applied and shall inform the Subscriber that, unless the Subscriber has requested review under one of the dispute resolution mechanisms specified in Section 4(H) below, the Participating ISP shall apply the selected Mitigation Measure after the expiration of a notice period of ten (10) business days or fourteen (14) calendar days from the time the Mitigation Measure Copyright Alert is delivered. The term of the notice period (i.e., ten (10) business days or fourteen (14) calendar days) shall be at the Participating ISP's discretion. If no review is requested by the Subscriber, the Participating ISP shall apply the specified Mitigation Measure on the applicable Subscriber's Internet access service account after such ten (10) business day or fourteen (14) calendar day period has expired.

The Mitigation Measure applied at the Mitigation Measures Step shall be one of the following, determined by the Participating ISP and applied in a manner reasonably calculated, in the Participating ISP's reasonable discretion, to help deter P2P Online Infringement: (a) temporary reduction in uploading and/or downloading transmission speeds; (b) temporary step-down in the Subscriber's service tier to (1) the lowest tier of Internet access service above dial-up service that the Participating ISP makes widely available to residential customers in the Subscriber's community, or (2) an alternative bandwidth throughput rate low enough to significantly impact a Subscriber's broadband Internet access service (*e.g.*, 256 - 640 kbps); (c) temporary redirection to a Landing Page until the Subscriber contacts the Participating ISP to discuss with it the Copyright Alerts; (d) temporary restriction of the Subscriber's Internet access for some reasonable period of time as determined in the Participating ISP's discretion; (e) temporary redirection to a Landing Page for completion of a meaningful educational instruction on copyright; or (f) such other temporary Mitigation Measure as may be applied by the Participating ISP in its discretion that is designed to be comparable to those Mitigation Measures described above. Participating ISPs shall not be obligated to apply a Mitigation Measure that knowingly disables or is reasonably likely to disable a Subscriber's access to any IP voice service (including over-the-top IP voice service), e-mail account, or any security service, multichannel video programming distribution service or guide, or health service (such as home security or medical monitoring) while a Mitigation Measure is in effect.

The foregoing provisions notwithstanding, the Participating ISP will retain the discretion, on a per Subscriber account basis, (a) to decide whether appropriate circumstances exist to waive such Mitigation Measure (a "Waiver"), provided that the Participating ISP will only issue one (1) such Waiver per Subscriber account, or instead of applying the Mitigation Measure specified in the Mitigation Measure Copyright Alert, to apply an alternate Mitigation Measure on the Subscriber's Internet access service account and to so inform the Subscriber.

If the Participating ISP elects to use a Waiver, the Participating ISP will direct to the account holder a final warning (a "Fifth Warning Copyright Alert") that will contain each of the elements contained in the Mitigation Measure Copyright Alert as described in this Section 4(G)(iii) and will inform the Subscriber that, in the event that the Participating ISP receives one (1) or more further ISP Notices from a Content Owner Representative, the Subscriber's Internet access service account will be subject to a Mitigation Measure per the Participating ISP's AUP and/or TOS and as set forth in prior Copyright Alerts, unless the Subscriber requests review under one of the dispute resolution mechanisms specified in <u>Section 4(H)</u>. If, after the expiration of the Grace Period following issuance of a Fifth Warning Copyright Alert, a Participating ISP receives one (1) or more further ISP Notices determined to be related to a Subscriber's account for which a Waiver has been granted, the Participating ISP will proceed with the transmission of a Mitigation Measure Copyright Alert and the associated activities described above.

(iv) <u>Post Mitigation Measures Step</u>: In the event that a Participating ISP receives a further ISP Notice determined to be associated with a Subscriber's account after a Mitigation Measure has been applied on that Subscriber's account, the Participating ISP shall direct a further Mitigation Measure Copyright Alert to the account holder and after ten (10) business days or fourteen (14) calendar days, as applicable, either re-apply the previous Mitigation Measure or apply a different Mitigation Measure, unless the Subscriber requests review under one of the dispute resolution mechanisms specified in <u>Section 4(H)</u>. The Mitigation Measure Copyright Alert at this step shall also inform the Subscriber that the Subscriber may be subject to a lawsuit for copyright infringement by the Copyright Owners and that continued infringement may, in appropriate circumstances, result in the imposition of action consistent with section 512 of the DMCA and/or actions specifically provided for in the Participating ISP's AUP and/or TOS including temporary suspension or termination. Upon completion of the Post Mitigation Measures Step, a Participating ISP may elect voluntarily to continue forwarding ISP Notices received for that Subscriber account, but is not obligated to do so. The Participating ISP will, however, continue to track and report the number of ISP Notices the Participating ISP receives for that Subscriber's account, so that information is available to a Content Owner Representative if it elects to initiate a copyright infringement action against that Subscriber.

(v) <u>Reset</u>: If a Participating ISP does not receive an ISP Notice relating to a Subscriber's account within twelve (12) months from the date the Participating ISP last received an ISP Notice relating to that same Subscriber's account, (a) the next ISP Notice associated with that Subscriber's account shall be treated as the first such ISP Notice under the provisions of this Copyright Alert Program and the Subscriber may be afforded an additional Waiver as set forth in <u>Section 4(G)(iii)</u> above; and (b) the Participating ISP may expunge all prior ISP Notices and Copyright Alerts from the Subscriber's account.

(vi) <u>Transmission of Copyright Alerts to Subscribers</u>: Copyright Alerts should be directed by the Participating ISP to the account holder by means that are designed to ensure prompt receipt (*e.g.*, via email, physical mail, auto-dialer notification, ISP account management tool pop-ups requiring user click through, electronic or voice communications with Subscribers or such other means of delivery as the Participating ISP deems commercially practicable), and the Participating ISP shall design such Copyright Alerts in a manner reasonably calculated, in the Participating ISP's discretion, to be received by the Subscriber. Each Copyright Alert after the initial Educational Step Copyright Alert will include the educational and general information required in the Educational Step Copyright Alert and in any other Copyright Alerts that were forwarded to the Subscriber after the Educational Step, together with a summary of the pertinent information regarding the alleged P2P Online Infringement related to prior ISP Notices or a link or other mechanism by which the Subscriber can access or obtain such information. Each Participating ISP will provide the form of its Copyright Alerts to the Independent Expert as part of the Independent Expert's review of each Participating ISP's Methodology, and will in good faith consider any suggestions from the Independent Expert.

(vii)   Notification of Ability to Request Review: Copyright Alerts directed to account holders at the Mitigation Measures Step and the Post Mitigation Measures Step shall inform the Subscriber of the Subscriber's ability to request review within ten (10) business days or fourteen (14) calendar days, as applicable, under one of the dispute resolution mechanisms described in Section 4(H). If the Subscriber requests such review, the Participating ISP shall, upon receiving notice of the request for such review and pending a final decision via the chosen dispute resolution mechanism, defer taking any further action under its Copyright Alert Program.

E.   Independent Review Program

(i)   A Subscriber may seek review of a Mitigation Measure Copyright Alert via the dispute resolution program set forth in Attachment C (the "Independent Review Program") or as otherwise permitted in the Participating ISP's AUP or TOS or as permitted by law, at the election of the Subscriber. The Independent Review Program shall allow for the Subscriber to remain anonymous to the Content Owner Representatives and the members of the Participating Content Owners Group, except in cases where the Subscriber elects a defense in which the Subscriber's identity will be disclosed. The decision from the Independent Review Program shall be binding on the Parties solely for purposes of the Notice Process and the affected Copyright Alert Program but shall have no force or effect beyond the Notice Process and the affected Copyright Alert Program, and shall not be deemed to adjudicate any rights outside of this limited context. In any judicial proceeding between a Subscriber and a Copyright Owner concerning subject matter that is or has been the subject of the Independent Review Program, as provided in the procedures governing the Independent Review Program, neither the Subscriber nor the Copyright

Owner shall seek to enter into evidence, or otherwise refer to or cite, either the fact of the Independent Review or any outcome of the Independent Review.

(ii)   The costs of establishing and administering the Independent Review Program shall be borne fifty percent (50%) by the Participating Content Owners Group and fifty percent (50%) by the Participating ISPs.

. . .

Notes

1.   More on the Copyright Alert system can be found at THE ROLE OF VOLUNTARY AGREEMENTS IN THE U.S. INTELLECTUAL PROPERTY SYSTEM, U.S. HOUSE OF REPRESENTATIVES, COMMITTEE ON THE JUDICIARY, SUBCOMMITTEE ON COURTS, INTELLECTUAL PROPERTY, AND THE INTERNET, ONE HUNDRED THIRTEENTH CONGRESS, FIRST SESSION, September 18, 2013, https://www.hsdl.org/?view&did=745185.

2.   The system was discontinued in 2017, apparently because it was not effective.

3.   The Copyright Alert system relied on Thomson Reuters-owned firm MarkMonitor to detect infringement, though that was apparently not specified in the Memorandum of Understanding or in its subsequent amendments. The report by the Independent Expert required in the MoU (Stroz Freidberg) was confidential. Was Copyright Alert a boycott of MarkMonitor's competitors? Were there any efficiencies from having all the ISPs use the same monitor? Were there any efficiencies from having all the ISPs use the same "six strikes" formula? What did they gain (or avoid losing) by all using the same approach?

4.   A law-student note analyzing the antitrust implications of the system is Sean M. Flaim, *Copyright Conspiracy: How the New Copyright Alert System May Violate the Sherman Act*, 2 N.Y.U. J. OF INTELL. PROP. & ENT. L. 142 (2012).

5.   Is the Copyright Alert system like the blanket licenses in *Broadcast Music*, like the boycott in *Fashion Originators' Guild*, like the reverse-payment agreement in *Actavis*, or like the trademark litigation settlements in *1-800 Contacts*?

The following letter responds to what has become a common context in modern electronics markets: the development of product standards that may incorporate patented inventions. Standard-setting organizations (SSOs) often develop and promulgate technical standards for products like cellphones that must use a common system in order to interact successfully with each other. If, however, a patented invention is part of a technical standard, the patentee could demand very high royalties in exchange for the ability to produce products that conform to the standard. As a result, SSOs have generally required firms participating in the standard-setting process to agree to license their patents on "reasonable and non-discriminatory" (RAND) terms (or, more commonly today, "fair, reasonable, and non-discriminatory, or FRAND, terms). The SSOs often fail to define RAND further, and we will discuss later the implications of the resulting uncertainty. Here, though, the IEEE sought to provide a more specific definition.

As you will see, the composition of an SSO is very important. Although most SSOs include both technology developers, which will be patent licensors, and technology implementers, which will be licensees, the decision-making balance of power becomes critical. *Cf.* NCAA v. Board of Regents of the University of Oklahoma, 468 U.S. 85 (1984). The predominant view has been that the activities of SSOs are on balance procompetitive, as reflected in the letter below, but the ascendancy of Makan Delrahim to the leadership of the Department of Justice's Antitrust Division has brought about a more complicated picture. In private practice, Assistant Attorney General Delrahim represented Qualcomm, a company that is both a patentee and an implementer, and under him the Department of Justice has become more hostile to the activities of SSOs, as is apparent in his speech include here after the letter and in connection with the *Qualcomm* case below.

Renata B Hesse, Acting Assistant Attorney General, U.S. Department of Justice
Response To Institute Of Electrical And Electronics Engineers, Incorporated
February 2, 2015

U.S.   DEPARTMENT   OF
JUSTICE
Antitrust Division

RENATA B. HESSE
Acting Assistant Attorney General

Main Justice Building
950 Pennsylvania Avenue, N.W.
Washington, D.C. 20530-0001
(202) 514-2401 / (202) 616-2645
(Fax)

February 2, 2015

Michael A. Lindsay, Esq.
Dorsey & Whitney LLP
50 South Sixth Street
Suite 1500
Minneapolis, MN 55402-1498

Dear Mr. Lindsay:

This letter responds to your request on behalf of the Institute of Electrical and
Electronics Engineers, Incorporated ("IEEE") for a business review letter from the
Department of Justice pursuant to the Department's Business Review Procedure,
28 C.F.R. § 50.6. You have asked for a statement of the Department's antitrust
enforcement intentions with respect to a proposed update (the "Update") to the
IEEE Standards Association's ("IEEE-SA's") Patent Policy (the "Policy"). . . .

The Department's task in the business review process is to advise the requesting
party of the Department's present antitrust enforcement intentions regarding the
proposed conduct. It is not the Department's role to assess whether IEEE's policy
choices are right for IEEE as a standards-setting organization ("SSO"). . . .

I.   IEEE and IEEE-SA

IEEE, a non-profit professional association with over 400,000 members, is
engaged in the advancement of technology. It is governed by a Board of Directors,
which includes the current and immediately former IEEE presidents, the president-
elect, the president of IEEE-SA, and a number of other organizational leaders.

The IEEE-SA, an operating unit of IEEE, is a leading developer of international
standards. It is governed by a Board of Governors, whose members either are

elected by IEEE-SA members or appointed by existing members of that Board. The IEEE-SA president serves as the chair of the Board of Governors. The IEEE-SA Standards Board (the "Standards Board") oversees the IEEE standards-development process, and its members are appointed by the Board of Governors.

The Standards Board relies on various committees to study issues and make recommendations for Standards Board actions. Among those committees is the Patent Committee (the "PatCom"), which is responsible for overseeing the use of patents in the development of IEEE standards. The Standards Board chair appoints the PatCom chair and members for one-year terms. The PatCom must have no fewer than four and no more than six members, including the chair, all of whom must be voting members of the Standards Board or the Board of Governors. All those serving in a governance role at IEEE have a fiduciary duty to act in the best interests of IEEE when exercising their governance responsibilities.

II. Development of the Proposed Policy Update

The Policy governs the incorporation of patented technology in IEEE standards. Participants in IEEE-SA working groups are invited to disclose patent claims that may be essential to a standard under development. Any holder of potentially essential patent claims is asked to submit a Letter of Assurance (an "LOA"), in which the holder chooses one of four options for licensing those claims:

> (1) It will make a license available, without compensation, for its essential patent claims, to an unrestricted number of applicants for uses implementing the standard;

> (2) It will make a license available for its essential patent claims "under reasonable rates, with reasonable terms and conditions that are demonstrably free of any unfair discrimination," to an unrestricted number of applicants for uses implementing the standard (the "IEEE RAND Commitment");

> (3) It will not enforce its essential patent claims against any person (or entity) complying with the standard; or

> (4) It is unwilling or unable to license its essential patent claims without compensation or under reasonable rates, or to agree that it will not enforce those patent claims.

IEEE-SA does not require that a patent holder provide an LOA. However, it considers the absence of an LOA when deciding whether to approve a draft standard that includes patented technology.

III. Overview of Analysis

Standards offer significant procompetitive benefits. For example, standards can facilitate product interoperability, ensuring that products from a variety of suppliers will work together efficiently, thereby reducing costs for consumers and producers, making products more valuable, and promoting innovation both in and around the standard. In addition, the standards-setting process can increase competition among technologies for inclusion in standards, benefiting consumers through increased functionality or lower prices (and sometimes both).

Transactional and market efficiencies are achieved when market participants are well-informed and can engage in negotiations in the absence of significant informational asymmetries. Clear patent policies at SSOs promote these goals by allowing for informed participation in standards-setting activities and more knowledgeable decision making when considering whether to adopt or implement a standard. SSOs use licensing commitments–such as commitments to license on RAND terms–to promote inclusion of the best technologies in standards and to ensure access to those technologies. The inherent ambiguity in the meaning of the terms "reasonable" and "nondiscriminatory," however, can limit the benefits of RAND licensing commitments. Greater clarity and transparency may facilitate further the adoption and implementation of standards, thereby increasing the benefits that consumers derive from standards that include patented technologies.

By bringing greater clarity to the IEEE RAND Commitment, the Update has the potential to facilitate and improve the IEEE-SA standards-setting process. First, the Update may provide participants in IEEE-SA standards-setting processes with better ex ante knowledge about licensing terms, potentially broadening ex ante competition among technologies for inclusion in a standard. Second, this information could facilitate both ex ante and ex post licensing negotiations, and reduce patent infringement litigation. A patent holder seeking compensation for patented technology it contributed to a standard should be compensated for its invention in a way that reflects the value of that technology; otherwise patent holders may become reluctant to contribute technology to standards or to invest in future research and development that leads to innovation. In the standards-setting context, voluntarily negotiated licensing agreements between a licensee and licensor that give each the benefit of the bargain they seek–implementers of the standard receive access to the technology they need to manufacture, market, and sell their products, while patent holders receive compensation that reflects the value of their technology–is the optimal result. Clarification of the IEEE RAND Commitment may help parties reach such outcomes. Finally, the Update's provisions also may further help to mitigate hold up,[28] ensure access to technology

---

[28] A patent holder can engage in hold up "after its technology has been chosen by the SSO and others have incurred sunk costs which effectively increase the relative cost of switching to an alternative standard. Before, or ex ante, multiple technologies may compete to be incorporated into the standard under consideration. Afterwards, or ex post, the chosen technology may lack effective substitutes precisely because the SSO chose it as the standard. Thus, ex post, the owner of a patented technology necessary to implement the standard may have the power to extract higher royalties or other licensing terms that reflect the absence of competitive alternatives." IP2 Report, supra note 24, at 36-37 (internal citations omitted). The economic bargaining model underlying claims of hold up has been studied extensively and applied to the standards-setting context. See, e.g., Mark Lemley & Carl Shapiro, Patent Holdup and Royalty Stacking, 85 Texas L. Rev. 1991 (2007); Joseph Kattan & Chris Wood, Standard-Essential Patents and the Problem of Hold-Up, in William E. Kovacic, An Antitrust Tribute – Liber Amicorum 409 (Nicolas Charbit & Elisa Ramundo

necessary to implement IEEE–SA standards, and eliminate certain potentially anticompetitive practices.

IV. Process Concerns

Some critics of the Update contend that parties desiring lower royalty rates commandeered IEEE-SA and that the Update was the product of a closed and biased process antithetical to the consensus-based goals of open SSOs. Many of these concerns centered on the composition, formation, and conduct of the Ad Hoc, which was responsible for generating the Update. The Department takes seriously these concerns. If a standards-setting process is biased in favor of one set of interests, there is a danger of anticompetitive effects and antitrust liability. As the Supreme Court has observed, SSOs "may not . . . (without exposing [themselves] to possible antitrust liability for direct injuries) . . . bias the process by . . . stacking the private standard-setting body with decision makers sharing their economic interest in restraining competition."

Despite these concerns, it appears that the overall process afforded considerable opportunity for comment on and discussion of the Update, and the duly constituted governing bodies of IEEE-SA and IEEE will have approved the Update before it takes effect. There were numerous opportunities for presenting divergent views as part of the multiple-level review process. The PatCom issued four public drafts of

---

eds., 2014); see also Benjamin Klein et al., Vertical Integration, Appropriable Rents, and the Competitive Contracting Process, 21 J.L. & Econ. 297 (1978); Oliver E. Williamson, The Economic Institutions of Capitalism: Firms, Markets, Relational Contracting 52-56 (1985) (discussing the economics of hold up generally). Competition authorities in the United States and Europe have taken enforcement actions against owners of RAND-encumbered standards-essential patents engaging in hold up by using the threat of injunctive relief to exploit the market power that they acquired through the standards-setting process. See, e.g., Complaint, In the Matter of Motorola Mobility LLC and Google, Inc., File No. 121-0120 (F.T.C. July 24, 2013), available at http://www.ftc.gov/sites/default/files/documents/cases/2013/07/130724googlemotorolacm pt.pdf; Complaint, In the Matter of Robert Bosch GmbH, File No. 121-0081 (F.T.C. Nov. 21, 2012), available at http://www.ftc.gov/sites/default/files/documents/cases/2012/11/121126boschcmpt.pdf; European Commission, Commission finds that Motorola Mobility infringed EU competition rules by misusing standard essential patents (Apr. 29, 2014), available at http://europa.eu/rapid/press-release_IP-14-489_en.htm; European Commission, Commission accepts legally binding commitments by Samsung Electronics on standard essential patent injunctions (Apr. 29, 2014), available at http://europa.eu/rapid/press-release_IP-14-490_en.pdf. In addition, litigated cases demonstrate the potential for hold up when owners of RAND-encumbered standards-essential patents make royalty demands significantly above the adjudicated RAND rate. See, e.g., In re Innovatio IP Ventures, LLC Patent Litig., No. 11 C 9308, 2013 WL 5593609, at *43 (N.D. Ill. Oct. 3, 2013) (for 19 asserted patents, assessing damages of $0.0956 per unit as compared to the proposed royalty of $16.17 per unit for tablet computers); Microsoft Corp. v. Motorola, Inc., No. C10-1823, 2013 WL 2111217, at *100 (W.D. Wash. Apr. 25, 2013) (determining, inter alia, a RAND rate of $0.03471 per Microsoft's xBox unit, as compared to Motorola's initial demand of $6-$8 per xBox unit).

the Update for comment and received 680 comments on those drafts. It voted 3-2 to approve the Update. The Standards Board received submissions regarding the Update and allowed both supporters and opponents to provide their views orally. It then voted by a super-majority of 14-5 to approve the Update. The Board of Governors similarly heard from supporters and opponents of the Update before it approved the Update by a super-majority vote of 9-3. Finally, there will be an additional level of review as the IEEE Board of Directors must approve the Update by majority vote for it to go into effect. It is clear that the Board is aware of the wide range of views regarding the Update. Its members have a fiduciary duty to IEEE and can be expected to vote in the best interests of IEEE (the same is true for all those IEEE-SA members who voted on the Update). Given the numerous opportunities for comment, discussion, and voting at different levels within IEEE, the Department cannot conclude that the process raises antitrust concerns.

V. Analysis of the Update's Provisions

The Department has analyzed whether the Update's provisions on (1) the availability of prohibitive orders; (2) the meaning of "Reasonable Rate"; (3) permissible demands for reciprocal licensing; and (4) the production levels to which IEEE licensing commitments apply will harm competition by anticompetitively reducing royalties and thereby diminishing incentives to innovate. The Department has concluded that such harm is unlikely to occur as a result of the Update given that, inter alia, licensing rates ultimately are determined through bilateral negotiations, the Update's specific provisions are not out of step with the direction of current U.S. law interpreting RAND commitments (or the evolution of U.S. patent damages law for complex products that incorporate many patented technologies, whether or not these patents are RAND-encumbered), and patent holders can avoid the updated IEEE RAND Commitment and still participate in standards-setting activities at IEEE-SA (or can depart to other SSOs). The balance of this letter describes the Department's analysis of these issues.

  A. Prohibitive Orders

The Update recognizes that a voluntarily negotiated licensing agreement between a licensor and licensee is a preferred outcome. When parties cannot agree on licensing terms and need to resort to neutral third parties to resolve their licensing dispute–a dispute likely relating to differences over the value, validity, or enforceability of the patented technology or its infringement–the Update gives specific guidance on the availability of a prohibitive order under the IEEE RAND Commitment. It states that companies agreeing to the IEEE RAND Commitment "shall neither seek nor seek to enforce a Prohibitive Order . . . unless the implementer fails to participate in, or to comply with the outcome of, an adjudication, including an affirming first-level appellate review . . . by one or more courts that have the authority to determine Reasonable Rates and other reasonable terms and conditions; adjudicate patent validity, enforceability, essentiality, and infringement; award monetary damages; and resolve any defenses and counterclaims."

The threat of exclusion from a market is a powerful weapon that can enable a patent owner to hold up implementers of a standard. Limiting this threat reduces the possibility that a patent holder will take advantage of the inclusion of its patent in a standard to engage in patent hold up, and provides comfort to implementers in developing their products.

Under the current Policy, and in SSOs generally, a patent holder that makes a RAND commitment agrees that licensing its essential patent claims on reasonable rates and other reasonable terms and conditions is appropriate compensation for their use in implementing the standard. Inherent in such a RAND commitment is a pledge to make licenses available to those who practice such essential patent claims as a result of implementing the standard–in other words, not to exclude these implementers from using the standard unless they refuse to take a RAND license. Over the past several years, U.S. patent courts have recognized this principle, making it unlikely that a patent holder bound by a RAND commitment, even one that does not address explicitly the availability of injunctive relief, can secure an injunction (in addition to monetary damages) in an infringement action.

The Update's express limitation on the availability of exclusionary relief may reduce any remaining uncertainty among implementers of IEEE-SA standards by limiting the ability of patent holders who have made an IEEE RAND Commitment to seek prohibitive orders that would prevent those willing to license from making, using, or selling products that comply with the standard. This provision may place additional limits on patent holders' ability to obtain injunctive relief in a U.S. court, but it appears that, in practice, it will not be significantly more restrictive than current U.S. case law, and the added clarity may help parties reach agreement more quickly. Although this provision is more restrictive than recent guidance on this issue from the U.S. government, the U.S. government does not dictate patent policy choices to private SSOs. If IEEE determines that these limitations on exclusionary relief will benefit its standards-setting activities, it may decide to implement a policy that includes them, as long as such limitations do not violate the antitrust laws and are otherwise lawful.

Importantly, this provision does not affect the rights of patent holders (who have made an IEEE RAND Commitment) to seek patent damages, in the form of RAND compensation, for infringement of their patents when the parties cannot agree to a negotiated license. Nor does it purport to alter U.S. law regarding whether companies resolve patent infringement disputes on a claim-by-claim basis for individual patents or on the basis of a licensor's entire portfolio of patents relevant to a standard. Nevertheless, patent holders have expressed concern that this damages remedy is insufficient because it permits potential licensees to benefit by delaying paying reasonable compensation for a portfolio of patents until a patent holder has litigated each patent in its portfolio individually. The Department encourages patent holders and implementers to negotiate licensing agreements that are mutually acceptable, and there are incentives favoring a negotiated outcome. For example, implementers have incentives to reach agreement on licensing terms to reduce cost uncertainty as they bring products to market. In addition, litigation is expensive for both parties and licensees risk that a court will award a higher royalty for a patent that is found to be valid and infringed than a discounted pre-litigation rate offered by a licensor.

. . .

In sum, this provision furthers the procompetitive goal of providing greater clarity regarding the IEEE RAND Commitment concerning the availability of prohibitive orders, which could facilitate licensing negotiations, limit patent infringement litigation, and enable parties to reach mutually beneficial bargains that appropriately value patented technology. Moreover, because the provision is consistent with the direction of U.S. case law and patent holders can avoid its requirements by declining to submit an LOA, the Department concludes that it is unlikely to result in competitive harm.

B. Definition of Reasonable Rate

The Update adds a definition of "Reasonable Rate" as used in the Policy and the LOA. Your request states that this revision is aimed at improving licensing negotiations by adding clarity to this key term. The Update mandates consideration of one factor in determining a Reasonable Rate and recommends consideration of three other factors.

The mandatory factor states that a Reasonable Rate "shall mean appropriate compensation . . . excluding the value, if any, resulting from the inclusion of [the patent claim's] technology in the IEEE standard." IEEE explains in its frequently asked questions that this requirement is meant to exclude from the rate the value arising from the cost or inability of implementers to switch from technologies included in a standard.

This provision aligns with generally accepted goals of RAND commitments, namely, providing the patent owner with appropriate compensation, while assuring implementers that they will not have to pay any hold-up value connected with the standardization process. U.S. courts addressing patent damages for RAND-encumbered patents have recognized these goals; for example, the U.S. Court of Appeals for the Federal Circuit recently stated that "the patentee's royalty must be premised on the value of the patented feature, not any value added by the standard's adoption of the patented technology." This provision reduces the possibility that a patent holder that has made an IEEE RAND Commitment could hold up implementers of a standard and obtain higher prices (or more favorable terms) for its invention than would have been possible before the standard was set.

The Update also includes three recommended factors, stating that the determination of Reasonable Rates "should" include consideration of (1) "[t]he value that the functionality of the claimed invention or inventive feature within the Essential Patent Claim contributes to the value of . . . the smallest saleable Compliant Implementation that practices the Essential Patent Claim"; (2) "[t]he value that the Essential Patent Claim contributes to the smallest saleable Compliant Implementation that practices that claim, in light of the value contributed by all Essential Patent Claims for the same IEEE Standard practiced in that Compliant Implementation"; and (3) "[e]xisting licenses covering use of the Essential Patent Claim, where such licenses were not obtained under the explicit or implicit threat of a Prohibitive Order, and where the circumstances and resulting licenses are otherwise sufficiently comparable to the circumstances of the contemplated license." Significantly, the Update makes clear that the determination of Reasonable Rates "need not be limited to" these factors. The Update, then, does not mandate any specific royalty calculation methodology or specific royalty rates.

These factors focus attention on considerations that may be likely to lead to the appropriate valuation of technologies subject to the IEEE RAND Commitment. Regarding the first factor, the IEEE's focus on the smallest saleable Compliant Implementation may be appropriate in calculating a royalty that is correctly tied to the patented invention, particularly when the product is complex and incorporates many patented technologies. This factor does not mandate the use of the smallest saleable Compliant Implementation as the correct base. For example, the provision does not exclude evidence of the role of the relevant patented functionality in driving demand for the end product, or bar using end-product licenses to help determine the appropriate value to attribute to the technology. Regarding the second recommended factor, appropriately apportioning the value of all essential patent claims in an IEEE standard addresses royalty stacking, which may hamper implementation of a standard. Finally, regarding the third recommended factor, courts consider whether licenses offered as evidence are comparable and hence relevant to calculating a reasonable royalty. The Update does not prevent consideration of licensing agreements other than those specifically identified therein.

The Update's Reasonable Rate definition provides additional clarity regarding the IEEE RAND Commitment, which could help speed licensing negotiations, limit patent infringement litigation, enable parties to reach mutually beneficial bargains that appropriately value the patented technology, and lead to increased competition among technologies for inclusion in IEEE standards. Consistent with U.S. case law, the definition appears designed to help ensure that reasonable royalties for patents that are essential to an IEEE standard, like royalties for other patents, compensate the patent holder for the value attributable to the essential patent or patents. For these reasons, it does not appear likely that the Update's definition of Reasonable Rate will result in competitive harm.

. . .

VI. Conclusion

The Department concludes that the Update has the potential to benefit competition and consumers by facilitating licensing negotiations, mitigating hold up and royalty stacking, and promoting competition among technologies for inclusion in standards. The Department cannot conclude that the Update is likely to harm competition. Further, to the extent that there are any potential competitive harms, the Department concludes that the Update's potential procompetitive benefits likely outweigh those harms. Accordingly, the Department has no present intention to take antitrust enforcement action against the conduct you have described. The Department's analysis in this letter applies only to the Update's impact on future LOAs; the Department offers no statement regarding its intentions concerning the application of the Update retroactively to previously submitted LOAs.

This letter expresses the Department's current enforcement intention and is predicated on the accuracy of the information you have provided. In accordance with our normal practices, the Department reserves the right to bring an enforcement action in the future if the actual operation of the proposed conduct proves to be anticompetitive.

This statement is made in accordance with the Department's Business Review Procedure, 28 U.S.C. § 50.6. Pursuant to its terms, your business review request and this letter will be made publicly available immediately, and any supporting data you have submitted will be made publicly available within thirty days of the date of this letter, unless you request that part of the material be withheld in accordance with paragraph 10(c) of the Business Review Procedure.

Sincerely,

/s/

Renata B. Hesse

Notes

1.   Which is preferable, to require a "reasonable" rate while leaving the terms undefined, or to require a particular understanding of the term? Does "preferable" mean procompetitive?

2.   The Office of Management and Budget has issued OMB Circular No. A-119, which defines "voluntary consensus standards." Does the IEEE Policy satisfy this criterion from that definition: "Consensus, which is defined as general agreement, but not necessarily unanimity, and includes a process for attempting to resolve objections by interested parties, as long as all comments have been fairly considered, each objector is advised of the disposition of his or her objection(s) and the reasons why, and the consensus body members are given an opportunity to change their votes after reviewing the comments." If you cannot answer that question on the information provided, what further information would you need?

As noted above, the appointment of Assistant Attorney General Makan Delrahim has resulted in significant changes in Department of Justice (DoJ) policy regarding standard-setting. See Mark R. Patterson, The Patent-Antitrust Debate Annotated, Patently-O, July 23, 2018, https:// papers.ssrn.com/sol3/papers.cfm?abstract_id=3400228. It has also resulted in significant conflict between the DoJ and the F.T.C., as evidenced by the DoJ's recent request to argue for Qualcomm in the F.T.C.'s case against Qualcomm, below.

Speech, Assistant Attorney General Makan Delrahim, U.S. Department of Justice
The Long Run: Maximizing Innovation Incentives Through Advocacy and Enforcement
LeadershIP Conference on IP, Antitrust, and Innovation Policy, Washington, DC
April 10, 2018

Good afternoon. It is great to be here at the Leadership IP conference. This conference for many years now has brought together a broad network of experts and policymakers with diverse viewpoints to discuss what I view as some of the most important issues of our day. Thanks to the organizers, and especially to my friend, the Honorable Jim Rill, for inviting me to speak.

. . .

As I see it, the Division wears two hats in this space. One is the hat of the competition advocate; the other is the hat of the competition enforcer. Both important, but distinct, roles.

. . .

Both of these roles are important to the Division's core mission of protecting and promoting competition, but they are distinct, to be sure. So in the interest of transparency, let me elaborate on how we carry out our dual roles in the area of antitrust and IP; and then I will highlight a few risks associated with conflating the Division's advocacy and enforcement work in this area, with the goal of avoiding such risks.

Competition Advocacy

There is a great deal of work that we do in our role as an advocate for competition. A primary method of advocacy is giving speeches. Conferences like today's allow us to share with the public—in person and on our website, where many of the Division leadership's speeches are published—the Division's views about what conditions will make the market most dynamic, innovative and competitive. Although we speak often about the application of the antitrust laws, our advocacy extends more broadly. For example, when I spoke at USC, I addressed remedies in patent infringement litigation, and described my concern that by denying injunctive relief to standard essential patent holders except in the rarest circumstances, courts in the U.S. run the risk of turning a FRAND commitment into a compulsory license. As a defender of competitive markets, I am concerned that these patent law developments could have an unintended and harmful effect on dynamic competition by undermining important incentives to innovate, and ultimately, have a detrimental effect on U.S. consumers.

Another advocacy position we have taken relates to how patent holders are held to their commitments to license on FRAND terms. At Penn last month, I noted that so-called unilateral patent hold-up is not an antitrust problem. Where a patent holder has made commitments to license on particular terms, a contract theory is adequate and more appropriate to address disputes that may arise regarding whether the patent holder has honored those commitments. The Division will not hesitate to bring a sound antitrust case, but as competition advocates, we must strive to ensure that we use the antitrust laws for their intended purpose, which is to address practices that harm competition. Using the antitrust laws to impugn a patent holder's efforts to enforce valid IP rights risks undermining the dynamic competition we are charged with fostering. So when it comes to disputes that arise between intellectual property holders and implementers regarding the scope of FRAND commitments, we advocate for the application of more appropriate theories, other than the blunt instrument of antitrust.

. . .

While I have focused so far today on speech-related advocacy work, the Division has many other mechanisms for promoting the discussion of pro-competitive policies.

Our business review letter process might, in one sense, be viewed as a mechanism to share our policies on competition. While a business review letter is, of course, a statement of our enforcement intentions with respect to the particular arrangement described in the request, others in the antitrust community look to these letters for insight about our prospective enforcement views. It is in that context that I include our business review letters as a facet of our advocacy function. And as many of you know, the Antitrust Division has had a number of occasions to opine on issues of antitrust and IP through the business review process over the years.

. . .

Having described in more detail our competition advocacy role, let me turn to the Division's role as an **enforcer.** As I have said previously, in the context of antitrust and IP, we will be inclined to investigate and enforce when we see evidence of collusive conduct undertaken for the purpose of fixing prices, or excluding particular competitors or products. So what type of conduct in particular might attract enforcement scrutiny?

In the context of standard setting, cases like *Radiant Burners*, *Hydrolevel*, and *Allied Tube* provide helpful guidance regarding the kinds of collusive conduct that, naturally, would garner our attention. They are particularly helpful in illuminating our concern about situations in which competitors either corrupt the standard setting process so that decisions are not made by a balanced group of IP holders and implementers, or where competitors reach anticompetitive agreements outside of the scope of a legitimate standard setting exercise, with a detrimental effect on competition.

Let me describe two related situations that would raise concerns in the context of voluntary consensus standards development. First, if a group of patent implementers were to engage in concerted efforts to exclude a patent holder from meaningful participation in standard setting unless the patent holder agreed to offer particular licensing terms dictated by the group of implementers, those facts would raise red flags. Similarly, if patent holders A, B and C were to agree to exclude from consideration for inclusion substitute technology owned by their competitor patent holder D—for the purpose of harming patent holder D, rather than as a result of good-faith efforts to incorporate the most effective technology—that would also raise concerns.

While I believe in a very restrained approach to antitrust enforcement when it comes to the legitimate exploitation of valid IP rights, the Division will not hesitate to enforce against anticompetitive collusive conduct, particularly in an area as high-stakes for the American consumer as this one.

. . .

I point out the distinction between advocacy and enforcement, and the Division's efforts to highlight it, because I believe there are some risks associated with conflating the two. First, it can be the case that advocacy positions lead to unsupportable or even detrimental legal theories when taken out of context. As I explained at Penn, as a result of past speeches and position statements about hold-up that may have been intended to be limited to the context of competition advocacy, I worry that putative licensees have been emboldened to stretch antitrust theories beyond their rightful application, and that courts have indulged these theories at the risk of undermining patent holders' incentives to participate in standard setting at all.

Another risk of conflating advocacy positions with enforcement intentions is that industry leadership in standard setting could be stifled or undermined if business leaders are concerned that each decision they make will be called into question by antitrust enforcers in the context of an investigation. That is why our statements regarding antitrust and IP aim to clarify what conditions are ideal, and at the opposite end of the spectrum, what conduct might attract enforcement scrutiny. As a prior Division official said,

> "The great strength of the competitive marketplace is its ability to experiment, recover from false starts, and seek an efficient equilibrium through an organic development process. We should not expect to be able to predict where the best ideas will come from, but with all respect to my colleagues in the enforcement community, I doubt they will be developed entirely from the top down by antitrust enforcers in the U.S. or elsewhere."

While the Division will not hesitate to advocate for the conditions that are most likely to attract robust participation in standard setting, we want standard setting bodies to be industry-led, and we encourage them to experiment, to compete with one another, and to be creative. This is a point we have supported making to foreign governments in the trade context—something I will be talking more about in the coming months.

With respect to the difference between advocacy and enforcement, a final point I want to make is how important it is that foreign enforcers are aware of our two distinct roles. Recently, I have noticed that some of the Division's work, including business review letters, has been cited to support foreign enforcement actions that we would not bring under U.S. antitrust law. For example, while the Division decided that it would not challenge as unlawful the IEEE's patent policy update in 2015—including the portion of the policy that limits the availability of injunctions to holders of FRAND-encumbered patents—for the reasons I have just explained, this letter should never be cited for the proposition that what IEEE did is required, or that a patent holder who seeks an injunction is somehow in violation of the antitrust laws.

. . .

Finally, we adhere to sound and transparent enforcement procedures, because doing so is a fundamental part of operating according to the rule of law, and also because providing parties with opportunities to test our evidence and to push back on our legal theories helps us refine our thinking. This ultimately allows us to reach the right substantive conclusions. As we engage with our foreign counterparts on this topic, we are considering some innovations of our own regarding how we and other jurisdictions might increase our mutual commitments to these principles.

Ultimately, it is the people in this room—who work for some of the most innovative companies in our country and the world—who will enable the next great technological leap. My responsibility is first, to ensure we don't implement policies that unduly limit your incentives; and second, to leverage actively all of the tools at the Division's disposal to ensure that you are motivated and able to thrive in a market-based system. As part of that responsibility, I want to ensure that our policies and enforcement intentions are clear and well-understood, so that you can proceed with the business of developing the next generation of technology for the benefit of all of us. I also want to ensure that our enforcement intentions are clear to our enforcer colleagues outside the U.S., given the interconnectedness of the world when it comes to high technology.

Thank you very much for inviting me to speak today.

Notes

1.   To what extent do you think it is safe to rely on the IEEE business review letter after this speech? To what extent do you think it is safe to rely on *any* business review letter after this speech?

2.   What is "the scope of a legitimate standard setting exercise"? Is that a substantive or procedural criterion?

2. Unilateral Conduct

2.1. Market Power

2.1.1. Market Share

Market share is usually thought to be a good proxy for market power because a it is likely that a firm or firms with a large market share will be capable of reducing output, thus creating an increase in price. This strategy is likely to be successful because if other firms in the market have small shares, they will probably be incapable of increasing their output sufficiently to meet the unmet consumer demand.

The material below argues that in markets for information, another mechanism is at work. When a firm or firm provides information that is not entirely accurate, it could be viewed as reducing the supply of accurate information, but one could also view the problem not as one with supply, but with demand. That is, the obstacle to competing firms meeting unmet demand may not be limitations on capacity—which are not likely be significant in information markets in any event—but the ability to demonstrate to consumers that they should switch to the competing firms.

In some respect, the approach this material suggests has similarities with the information-cost discussion in *Eastman Kodak Co. v. Image Technical Servs., Inc.*, 504 U.S. 451 (1992). The explanation in *Kodak* was that the costs of acquiring information can prevent a small market share from constraining market injury. The material below suggests a broader applicability for this approach, one that is consistent with recent arguments that the focus on market definition and market share is misguided. *See* Louis Kaplow, *Why (Ever) Define Markets?*, 124 HARV. L. REV. 437 (2010).

Mark R. Patterson
Information and Market Power
from Antitrust Law in the New Economy:
Google, Yelp, LIBOR, and the Control of Information
(Harvard University Press 2017)

Market power—the power of a seller to act unconstrained by competitors—is a central element in antitrust law, both conceptually and doctrinally. Antitrust law is not concerned with minor or short-lived deviations from effective competition, because many such deviations are self-correcting through the competitive process. By focusing on market power, antitrust law is in part identifying those cases in which such self-correction is unlikely. It is in those circumstances in which consumers can be subject to significant injury. Conversely, firms that lack significant power, which even large firms sometimes do when they operate in markets in which entry by competitors is easy, are constrained by competition to serve consumers well. Until recent years, providers of information seldom had power, because information did not yet occupy the structural role that it has now acquired in the market. In the current economy, though, informational market power is common.

Market power is therefore an important part of antitrust doctrine. Although some obviously anticompetitive conduct—like price-fixing—can be condemned without a showing of market power (or monopoly power, which is a large amount of market power), proof of power is a requirement for most violations. The proof of single-firm antitrust violations requires, in the United States, proof of either monopoly power or a dangerous threat of acquiring it and, in Europe, proof of a dominant position in the market. Establishing a violation as the result of an anticompetitive agreement is said by many courts also to require proof of market power, though the U.S. Supreme Court has said that a showing of actual anticompetitive effects can obviate the need for an independent showing of power. Generally speaking, though, where there is ambiguity regarding the effects of challenged conduct, the role of market power in an important one.

Unfortunately, the usual definition of market power is not particularly useful for information. Market power is typically defined as the ability to profit from raising the price of a good or service above marginal cost (understood to include a reasonable profit). As described in the previous chapter, however, the marginal cost of information is often near zero. Although one could still apply a marginal cost-based definition of power, almost all information providers would be found to have power, so the result would not be meaningful as a means of identifying providers that can significantly harm competition. Market share, which is often used as a proxy for market power, as will be discussed below, is also problematic as a measure in the informational context, for related reasons.

There is a problem, then. Information has acquired a greater significance and independence in the economy, resulting in the creation of what are quite clearly markets for information. And the control of injurious effects on markets is a task allocated to antitrust law. But antitrust's rules have evolved in the context of tangible goods and services, and those rules, particularly the ones that apply to the assessment of market power, do not apply in a straightforward way to information products. Nevertheless, market-power measures adapted to the information context can be developed. As described below, there is an increasing emphasis in antitrust on determining power by specific reference to the nature of the anticompetitive conduct alleged, and this approach is well suited to informational issues.

Market Power, Market Share, and Information

As noted above, market power is typically defined as the ability to profit from raising the price of a good or service above marginal cost. In fact, though, the usual method of assessing market power is to rely on market share. Antitrust law rarely uses actual price-cost comparisons because the necessary data are rarely available and because market share often accurately reflects the ability of a firm to act without regard to competition. Generally speaking, if a firm with a large market share seeks to act anticompetitively—by raising price, for example—smaller competitors will be unable to compensate for the anticompetitive acts by selling at a lower price themselves because they will be too small to produce the unmet demand. So market share usually serves as an accurate proxy for market power.

Although antitrust law typically uses sales to measure market share, capacity is actually the relevant measure. Unused capacity, not current sales, allows competitors to meet the needs of consumers who are priced out of the market by the high prices of a dominant firm. For example, suppose that a firm with only a small amount of sales in a particular market has the capacity to easily, and at low cost, switch some of its large production facilities into that market. In such circumstances, if prices increased in the market, the firm would likely make that switch, and if it could bring significant production to bear, it could prevent the price increase. In that case, its initial small sales would not have been a good indicator of its market significance because its capacity was much larger.

In traditional product markets, capacity and size are usually closely related, so the distinction between sales and capacity is unimportant. For most products and services, the expansion of capacity requires an increase in plant size or the number of employees. Therefore, additional capacity can be expensive, and producers of tangible products and services typically have capacities that are not significantly greater than their sales. As described above, in some cases, capacity may be larger than current sales, perhaps because the extra capacity is not unused but is being used in another market. In such cases, it may be possible for firms to make capacity changes at relatively low cost when a market becomes newly profitable. However, it will often be expensive for firms producing tangible goods or services to expand capacity significantly without considerable expense.

For information, that may not be true, at least if, as is often the case, an expansion of capacity would involve only the delivery of more "copies" of information that has already been produced. In that case, it may be necessary only, say, to purchase more advertising time or to expand Internet server capacity, neither of which is likely to require expenditures or time on a scale comparable to that required for tangible goods or services. Consider a search engine that competes with Google, for example. If Google were to act anticompetitively, its competitor would easily be able to "produce" products to meet the demand of those consumers who sought search results elsewhere. After all, the products at issue are search results, and the algorithm for producing them is already available to a competing search engine, so the only obstacle to producing more of them would be the installation of more server capacity to deliver the results to customers. Although expanding server capacity imposes some costs and takes some time, those limitations are small compared with, say, expansion of capacity in the production of the archetypal widget.

Hence, market share of current sales will at least sometimes be a relatively poor proxy for power when the product at issue is information. But neither doctrine nor theory requires that market power be measured through market share. The U.S. Supreme Court has said that where there is a showing of actual anticompetitive effects, there is no need to make an independent showing of market power, let alone the definition of market boundaries that is needed to calculate market share:

Since the purpose of the inquiries into market definition and market power is to determine whether an arrangement has the potential for genuine adverse effects on competition, "proof of actual detrimental effect, such as a reduction of output," can obviate the need for an inquiry into market power, which is but a "surrogate for detrimental effect."

In theory, too, there has been a move away from market definition and market share to what are sometimes called "first principles." The "first principles" approach advocates, as the Supreme Court described in the quotation above, a focus on the anticompetitive effects of the conduct at issue. This approach, as advocated by Steven Salop and Louis Kaplow and discussed further below, contends that by focusing on those competitive effects and assessing market power by considering the defendant's ability to cause competitive harm, antitrust can avoid being misled by the flaws and gaps in the evaluation of market share. Moreover, a careful focus on competitive harm is especially important in novel contexts, such as that of information.

That does not mean, however, that market definition, as opposed to market share, has no role to play. Indeed, Gregory Werden, a vigorous advocate of market definition, describes its value, at least in part, in a way that can be seen as echoing the "first principles" approach: "Delineating the relevant market specifies the product and geographic scope of the particular competitive process allegedly harmed and thereby clarifies the claim and facilitates its assessment." Again, that is particularly true for information, where markets often have distinctive characteristics. Hence, before examining the "first principles" of power in information markets, the following paragraphs discuss the problems of defining those markets.

Defining Markets for Information

Information is available from a wide variety of sources. That is true not only of information in general, but also for many of the particular items of information that are important for competition. Product prices, for example, can be obtained from Google, from other search engines and websites like NexTag, from the stores that carry the products, and often from the product manufacturers themselves. A particular piece of information may be available not only from different sources but also in different forms. For example, the price of product X from manufacturer A may be available from the manufacturer, in which case it would presumably come alone, but the same information obtained from Google might come with the prices of other, competing products from other manufacturers.

In other instances, it may not be clear whether one is receiving comparable information. For example, as discussed in the previous chapter, the requirements for posting reviews are different on Expedia and TripAdvisor. That makes it difficult to know whether the reviews the two sites deliver are comparable, or "reasonably interchangeable," the test for determining whether two products are in the same market for antitrust purposes. Other forms of product information, like product certifications, are also often available from multiple sources. On the other hand, certifications and other types of information may also be protected by intellectual-property laws or by contract. The new provider of LIBOR, for example, purports to limit its availability to those who directly or indirectly obtain a license for its use (though the legal basis for this requirement is somewhat mysterious). And some providers of financial information have sought to deny use of the identifiers of their information to competitors, making it harder for competition to arise, though providers in two European Commission (EC) commitment decisions agreed to provide greater access.

The disparate ways in which information is provided make market definition a valuable exercise. Market definition seeks to identify which products compete with each other. So, for example, if the problem at issue is the provision of deceptive information, then an important question would be whether the recipients of that information also had available to them more accurate information, i.e., whether there was accurate information in the same market. If so, the competition from that accurate information could make a provider's efforts at deception less successful. But that constraint would only be present to the extent that consumers, or at least some consumers, were provided with multiple competing sources of information. If, instead, a significant number of consumers could obtain information from only one or a few sources, then deception from those sources could cause competitive harm even if accurate information were available somewhere else. That makes identifying the sources of competing information—defining the market—an important task in the informational context.

Research has shown that the simple availability of information somewhere is not always sufficient, practically speaking, to inform consumers in a way that allows competition to work effectively. The most accessible of this research focuses on advertising and its effect on prices. Generally speaking, advertising does not affect the ultimate availability of information on prices because the information is typically available directly from—e.g., though a telephone call to—the providers of the goods at issue. The role, or one role, of advertising is to make the information more easily available to consumers. Although there is some controversy regarding the effect of advertising on prices, and some inconsistency in the evidence, the weight of the evidence appears to show that the availability of advertising lowers consumer prices. The implication, then, is that information obtained directly from providers of goods is not an effective substitute for advertising and, more generally, that there may not be effective competition between information provided through different means.

Thus, the definition of information markets, like the definition of many other markets in recent years, can turn largely on the viability of different distribution channels. Does price information online compete with price information obtained at brick-and-mortar stores? Does price information from a price-comparison site compete with information from individual sellers? As the advertising example suggests, this is partly an issue of the cost of obtaining information. To what extent are consumers willing to seek out multiple sources of, say, price information, or will they simply rely on Google, or Expedia, or whatever is their favorite source of price information? As discussed below, the answer will depend not only on the cost of seeking out information from additional sources, but on whether consumers have any knowledge of inaccuracies in the sources they use.

Markets for Individuals?

Attention to distribution channels is particular [*sic*] important because information channels can be very narrow. Providers are not only delivering information *to* consumers but also know a great deal *about* consumers. Some have argued that this will allow sellers to better serve the needs of buyers, and of course it could do so. But others have offered a different perspective, responding to what they call the "myth" that better information about consumers will allow customization of products in a way that consumers will find valuable:

> However, we propose there is an alternative perspective (counter-myth). Suppliers using powerful computers and comprehensive databases could exploit smaller and smaller market niches, by making inferences about an individual buyer's flexibility on product and price, propensity to shop around, etc. In doing so, they could inhibit competition and charge higher prices in these market niches.

The authors here refer to price discrimination, which was discussed in the previous chapter and will be discussed further in Chapter 7, but also to product discrimination, or tailoring the product provided to individual consumers. This tailoring may be difficult to do for tangible products without the cooperation of consumers, but it can be much easier for information products. For example, if an online price-comparison site knows that a user came to its site from another, similar site, it is likely to deliver good prices to that user. If, on the other hand, the user is a frequent visitor to the site, and the site has no reason to think that the user has visited competing sites, it might deliver higher prices. This approach would make sense, of course, only if the site received some form of compensation, presumably from sellers whose products are shown on the site, for delivering higher prices. That could happen, though, if sellers were able to charge higher prices to users who clicked on links with those prices. In this way, an information provider could use information about its users to discriminate in the quality of information it provides them, just as other sellers use price discrimination.

What would be the implications of such practices for market definition, though? If users could easily switch to another information provider, perhaps none. But a problem arises when a firm has both information it can use to provide low-quality information to its users and information that makes its competitors less useful for consumers. For example, suppose an information provider knew that one of its users was planning a trip to Italy and also knew the user's preferences in hotels. If the user did a search for, say, "hotels Florence," the provider might deliver information that reflected the user's hotel preferences, but that showed higher prices than were actually available. If the user were to go to another provider, she might receive better prices, but would likely receive less relevant results. The user might prefer to see lower prices than the most relevant results, if she knew that she were receiving high prices at her usual site. But it would take some effort to determine that fact, and the user might not make the effort absent a reason to expect the delivery of low-quality information.

The gathering of user information that makes the information a site delivers particularly valuable to users is a big part of what many online sites do. Amazon has its users' purchasing history, Google has their search history and information from their e-mail accounts, and Facebook has the information the users post. All of this information gives those sites an advantage over their competitors and potentially allows them to tailor the information they provide to their users with relatively little threat of the users leaving for other information providers. As a result, the site-user relationship devolves from a market in which a user can seek information from multiple providers to a situation in which one site is uniquely valuable to the user—in a market by itself—and the user, for that reason and because of the information the site possesses, is highly exploitable.

This is only one example of the way in which information providers can seek to make the information their competitors provide less useful. The concept of "confusopoly," where sellers design complicated pricing plans that make it difficult for their customers to compare prices, is one example. Another example is the case brought in 1998 by the Federal Trade Commission (FTC) against Toys "R" Us in 1998 for various practices that Toys "R" Us had used to try to reduce competition between it and warehouse clubs. One of these practices was to insist in agreements with toy manufacturers that they would not package products sold by the clubs and by Toys "R" Us in the same way. The goal, the FTC said, was to try to make it difficult for consumers to compare prices. The online approaches discussed above accomplish similar goals, but in a much more sophisticated and individually tailored way.

The "First Principles" of Informational Power

What constrains competitors' ability to respond to anticompetitive information practices by a competing firm or firms? Sometimes, particularly where misleading or incomplete information is at issue, consumers may not be able to determine what would be the benefits of switching to another provider. That is so because consumers may not know whether they are receiving high-quality or low-quality information. As a result, it may not be the unavailability of information, or the cost of obtaining it, that is the problem. Instead, it may be the cost of determining whether the information that one already possesses or has been offered is sufficient or accurate.

Indeed, it is almost necessary that this is so. As Kenneth Arrow said of information, "its value for the purchaser is not known until he has the information." Therefore, "the potential buyer will base his decision to purchase information on less than optimal criteria." It is not far wrong to say that whenever a consumer is seeking information, she will be unable to evaluate the quality of the information she receives. (Recall the discussion of credence goods above.) That makes information very different from other products, where comparisons are usually much more straightforward. Consumers have no trouble comparing prices of traditional goods, of course—lower prices are better, all other things being equal.

Evaluation can also be easy for many aspects of product quality, at least for traditional goods. But when consumers are seeking information, they often lack the ability to evaluate it.

As a result, the constraint on competition may not be the inability of competitors to respond, but the inability of consumers to determine whether a competitor is offering a better product. It may be more productive, therefore, when assessing the power of information providers, to focus on competitors' means of responding, in a manner akin to the way that the market-share measure captures competitors' ability to respond to an increase in price. If consumers do not know that they are receiving inaccurate or otherwise low-quality information, competitors will have to incur not just the cost of providing accurate information, but also the cost of pointing out the shortcomings of other information. Again, this is not a problem for price; consumers do not generally have to be persuaded that lower prices are better than higher ones. But for other types of information it may not be enough to provide better information; it may also be necessary to *prove* that the information is better. And there may be behavioral factors that come into play here, in that consumers may be more inclined to accept the first information received than to have their opinions changed.

The problem may be compounded by a tendency of consumers to be overly optimistic about missing information. That tendency is especially important in light of the "layers" of information that are relevant in some instances. For example, where information is provided by an entity like Yelp or TripAdvisor, at least three independent types of information are important. First, there are the individual reviews themselves, which generally are not provided by the platform itself. Second, there is the Yelp or TripAdvisor collection of reviews, perhaps with star ratings, which *is* provided by the platform. Third, there is information *about* the reviews, which often is also provided by the platform. The enforcement actions against TripAdvisor focused on this last type of information, taking the view that the platform had been misleading in its representations of the objectivity of the reviews it provided.

In many instances, platforms may simply provide the underlying information without stating all they know about the quality of that underlying information. A recent experimental study suggests that consumers faced with a lack of information may systematically overestimate the quality of the underlying good. The study is far from conclusive, of course, but as the authors say, it calls into question previous work that suggested that markets force firms to disclose quality information because consumers, in the absence of disclosure, will draw adverse inferences about the quality of the goods provided.

The focus, then, should be on market characteristics that would prevent correction of inadequate or misleading information. Those characteristics could be of at least four kinds. First, competitors of the information provider might not themselves have access to accurate information that would allow them to correct any information deficiencies. As will be seen below, one reason for this is that correction may require information about how the information was produced, and the information might be the product of a competitor's "black box." Second, competitors must be able to provide corrective information when it is useful to consumers. Third, although the competitors might have access to information that would allow them to correct information problems, they might lack the incentive to correct those problems. Fourth, even with access to correct information and the incentive to provide it, consumers might not readily accept the correct information as a substitute for the information deficiencies.

Can Competitors Identify Low-Quality Information?

As described above, consumers will often lack the ability to identify false or misleading information because they do not have access to correct information with which to compare it. One might expect competitors to fill the void, but competitors might not be able to provide the comparison, either. The U.S. Supreme Court made this point in a well-known case, *Eastman Kodak Co. v. Image Technical Services, Inc.* At issue was information regarding the repair costs of Kodak copiers and similar products. Consumers' lack of access to that information could be, the Court said, a source of market power for Kodak. The Court pointed out the difficulty and expense for consumers of obtaining such information, and it rejected Kodak's argument that the gap would necessarily be filled by competitors:

> Kodak acknowledges the cost of information, but suggests, again without evidentiary support, that customer information needs will be satisfied by competitors in the equipment markets. It is a question of fact, however, whether competitors would provide the necessary information. A competitor in the equipment market may not have reliable information about the lifecycle costs of complex equipment it does not service or the needs of customers it does not serve.

The point is a general one, in that firms often will not have good information about their competitors' products. Sometimes that will not be the case, of course. In a market for price information, for example, competitors presumably would easily be able to tell whether other firms were providing good information (though, as noted below, an information provider might deliver good information to its competitors but lower-quality information to consumers). For prices, there exists an external reference point, the actual price, assuming there is a single actual price, and a firm that is in the business of providing that price would normally know that actual price. It could therefore judge whether its competitors are delivering the information accurately.

For other information, however, there may be no objective reference point, or, even if such a reference exists, it may not be public. The LIBOR case is an example of the latter possibility. The LIBOR rate was designed to be a benchmark interest rate, primarily for use in variable-rate loans, and it was to be calculated by averaging the interest rates that leading banks would have had to pay to borrow for their own accounts. As will be discussed in more detail in the next chapter, though, the banks provided false estimates of their borrowing costs, sometimes to make their financial status look better than it was and sometimes at the behest of other, conspiring banks that stood to benefit from a distorted LIBOR rate. The estimates were "false" in the sense that the banks deliberately reported (mostly) lower rates than what they knew their borrowing costs to be. The banks' actual borrowing costs were thus an objective reference point, but those actual costs would not have been known by competitors. (When the false rates were requested by another bank, then the co-conspirator would also presumably have known that the reported rate was incorrect, but it would not necessarily have known what the correct rate was.) The banks were thus relatively free to provide (slightly) inaccurate information without fear of detection.

To be sure, individual rates of the banks submitting estimates were also published, so they could have been scrutinized. And they were. The *Wall Street Journal* raised concerns about LIBOR in 2008. Why were those concerns—warnings—not heeded? The problem might have been that it was just too difficult to tell if any misreporting was really misreporting and, if so, whether it was due simply to mistakes or to deliberate acts. Some support for this view is provided in a 2008 memo from Timothy Geithner, then at the U.S. Federal Reserve, to Sir Mervyn King at the Bank of England:

> To improve the integrity and transparency of the rate-setting process, we recommend the BBA work with LIBOR panel banks to establish and publish best practices for calculating and reporting rates, including procedures designed to prevent accidental or deliberate misreporting. The BBA could require that a reporting bank's internal and external auditors confirm adherence to these best practices and attest to the accuracy of banks' LIBOR rates.

The sort of auditing that Geithner recommended requires access to the banks' internal information, of course, so although it might be a viable approach for a government mandate or for internal compliance procedures, it would not enable competitors to detect the misreporting to which Geithner refers.

Somewhat similar procedural protections were suggested in *Allied Tube & Conduit Corp. v. Indian Head, Inc.,* a U.S. Supreme Court decision on standard-setting. That case involved a trade organization's promulgation of a safety standard that was alleged to have been improperly influenced by a member of the organization. The possibility of exploitation of standard-setting processes raises antitrust concerns, the Court said, but such concerns can be lessened when "private associations promulgate safety standards based on the merits of objective expert judgments and through procedures that prevent the standard-setting process from being biased by members with economic interests in stifling product competition. As will be discussed in the next chapter, one way—perhaps the only way—in which these protections can be implemented is to have a decision-making body that is composed of a variety of perspectives, including those of both competitors and consumers. In that way, the decision that is reached will ideally be a "correct" one, and, even if it is not, competitors and consumers who are disadvantaged by the decision will at least have access to any problems in the process.

This sort of access to an information provider's decision-making process is especially important when the information at issue has an element of subjectivity, i.e., when there is no objective benchmark against which the information can be measured. In that case, it may not even be clear what "accurate" information would be. With knowledge of the provider's decision-making process, however, it can be clear that the information provided was less accurate—of lower quality—than it could have been. It was that sort of access that allowed the Department of Justice to determine that Standard & Poor's had avoided issuing lower credit ratings because it was concerned about losing business if it did so. Thus, the Justice Department's complaint alleged that "S&P's desire for increased revenue and market share in the [residential mortgage-backed security (RMBS)] and [collateralized debt obligation (CDO)] ratings markets led S&P to downplay and disregard the true extent of the credit risks posed by RMBS and CDO tranches in order to favor the interests of large investment banks and others involved in the issuance of RMBS and CDOs who selected S&P to provide credit ratings for those tranches."

As noted above, though, often only the government will have access to the internal processes that reveal this sort of information distortion. That means that when firms are providing information that has this sort of subjectivity, competitors may be unable to determine whether the information that is being provided is as accurate as it could be, or is at least what it purports to be. And much competitively significant information is of this subjective kind. Not only credit ratings, but search results, product reviews, and many product standards lack objective benchmarks against which they can be compared. As described above, consumers will also often lack the ability to determine whether they receive high-quality information. In these circumstances, the competitive information-quality constraints on information providers are likely to be quite limited.

Black Boxes

The difficulty described here is insightfully analyzed from a broader perspective by Frank Pasquale in his recent book *The Black Box Society*. Pasquale addresses the problem of opacity more generally, focusing on three important areas: production of reputation information such as credit scores, search, and evaluation of financial innovation. He compellingly describes the extent to which we are dependent on firms' internal algorithmic results and decisions whose correctness we cannot review because the algorithms are proprietary. As a result, we are unable to assess the fairness and accuracy of broad swaths of the economy. Moreover, he suggests that this "knowledge problem" is not an accident but is the intended result of the business strategies of the firms in these markets.

As Pasquale describes, "[b]lack boxes embody a paradox of the information age: Data is becoming staggering in its breadth and depth, yet often the information most important to us is out of our reach, available only to insiders." Pasquale's concerns are broader than competition, extending to accountability more generally, and he suggests public alternatives to private credit reporting companies and Internet firms. That suggestion echoes the point above that often only the government will have access to the algorithms that produce these sorts of information. If we do not want to make the provision of information a public function but leave it in the market, we must, as Pasquale emphasizes, solve the problems that hidden information poses "to assure the competitive process is itself fair." He states that "[a]ntitrust law flirts with irrelevance if it disdains the technical tools necessary to understand a modern information economy." His point is that it is important to look into the algorithms that firms, particularly Internet firms, use, because only in that way can we determine if the firms are operating in an evenhanded manner:

> We should expect any company aspiring to order vast amounts of information to try to keep its methods secret, if only to reduce controversy and foil copycat competitors. However wise this secrecy may be as a business strategy, it devastates our ability to truly understand the social world Silicon Valley is creating. Opacity creates ample opportunity to hide anticompetitive, discriminatory, or simply careless conduct behind a veil of technical inscrutability.

Furthermore, each firm can act not just as a single black box, but potentially as a different black box to different users, which presents its own competition problems. Pasquale suggests a variation on the "markets for individuals" issue described above, noting that a site demoted in Google's search results might not know it was demoted, because "[i]f it looked for itself from its own IP address it might well appear near the top of the results, its own personalized signals for salience having locally overwhelmed the signals for demotion." The ultimate implication here, then, is that not only consumers, but also competitors and antitrust enforcement agencies, may have difficulty obtaining information about the accuracy of and alternatives to information they receive.

When a firm operates as a "black box" in this way, delivering information that is to some extent subjective in a way that both competitors and consumers will find it difficult to evaluate, the firm will have some degree of market power. Power alone does not constitute an antitrust violation, of course, but in these circumstances, the law should move to the next step of evaluating conduct. The result has been exactly the opposite, though. In fact, the courts have dismissed cases challenging credit ratings and search results specifically on the ground that such ratings and results are subjective "opinions" protected by the First Amendment. As will be discussed in Chapter 9, these dismissals are incorrect as a matter of First Amendment law, but more importantly, they dispose of these cases before there is any opportunity to assess the information providers' conduct. The effect of the dismissals is that firms that provide the *least* easily evaluated (though still competitively important) information get the *most* freedom from scrutiny regarding how that information is produced. That is bad law, and it is bad policy.

Can Competitors Provide Better Information When It Matters?

Another problem, one related to the question of individual markets above, is that of access to consumers when it matters. If a consumer is using, for example, Bing, and the consumer is delivered a search result that is problematic, how is Google to obtain access to the consumer to show it an alternative result? One might ask how this is different from the brick-and-mortar world, in which a consumer at one store will not be easily accessible to other stores. There are two important differences, however. First, a consumer at a store knows that he or she is seeing only that store's offerings. The consumer is therefore on notice that he or she has incomplete information, in a way that a user of a search engine or price-comparison site that purports to display the best options may not be. Second, a consumer in a store will generally be presented with the same products, at the same prices, as are presented to other consumers. That is, there will generally be no customization of the kind that is possible online.

To some extent, this situation echoes those cases in which one information provider, like a newspaper or magazine, has refused to allow competitors to advertise in its pages. Several antitrust cases have presented these facts. In *Home Placement Service, Inc. v. Providence Journal Co.*, for example, the defendant *Providence Journal* refused to allow plaintiff, a competing provider of apartment rental advertising, to advertise in the *Journal*'s classified pages. In defining the relevant market, the court focused on the importance of advertising in the newspaper:

> Thus, the relevant product is not all advertising, or even all classified advertising, but merely daily newspaper rental advertising. Defendant offered no rebuttal of plaintiff's substantial evidence, through numerous witnesses, that there was no effective substitute therefor. The court's reference to the alternatives of "radio, television, (and) billboard," overlooked the uncontradicted testimony of experts, and those in the business, that these are effective only for institutional advertising, in conjunction with, but not in substitution for, more specific daily newspaper ads. Nor are weekly newspapers an adequate substitute, precisely because they offer competition only once a week. In short, on the evidence, none of the alternative media identified by the court could be said to be "reasonably interchangeable" with, or competing "on substantial parity" with, the rental columns of daily newspapers.

In contrast, a similar claim in *Twin Laboratories, Inc. v. Weider Health & Fitness* was decided in favor of the defendant. The plaintiff and defendant were competing providers of nutritional supplements for bodybuilders, and Weider refused to allow Twin Labs to advertise in Weider's magazines, which were the two leading ones in the field. Despite the Weider magazines' 66 percent share, though, the court rejected the view that advertising in them was essential. Twin Labs's supplements continued to be successful after the advertising ban, and, presumably more importantly, the court noted that only five of the top ten supplement sellers advertised in the magazines.

One interpretation of these cases is that it is critical to provide information when consumers are seeking it. In *Home Placement,* potential renters seeking rental information would turn, the court said, to the *Journal*'s classified pages, so that is where Home Placement needed to provide its information, even though those pages were controlled by its competitor. But bodybuilders apparently did not get all their information about supplements from advertising in the Weider magazines. They could get such information from friends, stores, and other magazines. As the court said, even Weider itself did only 50 percent of its advertising in its own magazines, so there was information available more broadly, and consumers could, and apparently did, turn to multiple sources. This issue, then, is simply a variation on that of distribution channels noted above: it is important in defining markets not just to include only distribution channels that actually compete, but also to include such channels only if they actually compete at the time of purchase.

The difference can be illustrated by considering search engines. In the Bing-Google context suggested above, the analogous issue would be whether Google would have means of gaining access to Bing users to correct any misinformation that Bing was providing at the time it mattered. Google and Bing are obviously competitors, and Google could even run independent advertising to consumers in general, seeking to inform them of any misinformation Bing provided. Perhaps that could be effective, but the key question is whether access to consumers is valuable only at the time they are doing the searching and thus presumably ready to make a purchase. A consumer who expects that he is receiving accurate information—a complete list of sellers, or the sellers with the best prices—may have no reason to look further. That is, he may conduct his search on one site without going anywhere else. This is why vertical search engines argue so vigorously that placement on Google's pages is critical to their success. Being pushed down, either in Google's "organic" search results or in its paid ads, can eliminate them from competition at the time that competition actually occurs.

This is exactly the theory of the European Commission's case against Google. The EC's statement of objections "alleges that Google treats and has treated more favourably, in its general search results pages, Google's own comparison shopping service 'Google Shopping' and its predecessor service 'Google Product Search' compared to rival comparison shopping services." Competitors of Google's shopping services of course have other ways of reaching consumers, as by advertising, and consumers can go directly to those competing services. But that is not enough, because being excluded from Google's results, the EC says, "hinder[s] their ability to compete." In other words, it is being there, in those results when the consumers seeks information, that is necessary for competition; in effect, Google has created a distinctive forum for competition, and the Commission argues that in that forum, it must treat competitors fairly.

Do Competitors Have Incentives to Provide Better Information?

In the U.S. Supreme Court's *Kodak* case, cited above, the Court noted that "[e]ven if competitors had the relevant information, it is not clear that their interests would be advanced by providing such information to consumers." The Court explained that it might in fact be more profitable to adopt the same practices themselves:

> To inform consumers about Kodak, the competitor must be willing to forgo the opportunity to reap supracompetitive prices in its own service and parts markets. The competitor may anticipate that charging lower service and parts prices and informing consumers about Kodak in the hopes of gaining future equipment sales will cause Kodak to lower the price on its service and parts, cancelling any gains in equipment sales to the competitor and leaving both worse off. Thus, in an equipment market with relatively few

sellers, competitors may find it more profitable to adopt Kodak's service and parts policy than to inform the consumers.

Even in a market with many sellers, any one competitor may not have sufficient incentive to inform consumers because the increased patronage attributable to the corrected consumer beliefs will be shared among other competitors.

This passage illustrates what antitrust refers to as the tacit collusion problem. Firms in many industries, such as the airline industry, are able to observe their competitors' prices. If firms can guess their competitors' cost structures, and they can often assume that their competitors' costs are similar to their own, they will then be able to know whether their competitors are pricing above cost. If there is, in fact, above-cost pricing, a firm could decide either to compete by undercutting that pricing or to go along by charging a comparable supracompetitive price. Undercutting might, of course, lead to a price war that would cut the profits of both firms, while going along with the higher prices could, if maintained, lead to higher profits for both.

Tacit collusion is not an antitrust violation in the United States because it involves neither an agreement among competitors nor a single dominant firm. It therefore falls in a "gap" between Sherman Act section 1, which condemns agreements in restraint of trade, and Sherman Act section 2, which condemns anticompetitive conduct by single powerful firms. That is not to say, though, that tacit collusion is not a competitive problem. The harm it causes is the same as the harm caused by price-fixing agreements, and some have argued that it should be illegal. If the concept of an "agreement" were construed expansively, for example, perhaps tacit collusion could be pursued under section 1. Or if the parallel conduct were viewed as creating a shared monopoly, the conduct could be pursued under section 2, in a way analogous to the European application of collective-dominance theory under Article 102 TFEU, discussed below.

In any event, the information analogy would be that of a firm that knew or suspected that its competitor was providing low-quality information. The firm would have the choice of doing the same or of competing with higher-quality information, perhaps with the addition of marketing to point out the low quality of its competitor's product. The incentive for providing the low-quality information might be simply the lower cost of creating it, or it might be, as with the allegations against Google, that it benefits the firm in some other way. In Google's case, the benefits are alleged to come from pushing competitors' websites down in its search results, thus benefiting Google's own, lower-quality sites. Bing then might have the incentive to engage in similar conduct, though it does not have quite the same constellation of related sites that Google does. Alternatively, as discussed above, Google might benefit by making it more difficult for sellers to reach consumers through Google's organic search results, thus making those sellers more likely to buy more advertising. Because Bing's business model also relies on advertising, Bing might find it desirable to support rather than challenge that approach.

Information providers also have less incentive to point out and challenge their competitors' self-interest rather than adopt it themselves because of the difficulties of establishing that competitors are providing low-quality information, as discussed above. Despite the basic conceptual similarity between parallel supracompetitive pricing and parallel low-quality information delivery, in practice the competitive contexts seem quite different. For example, it is generally easy for a firm—consider again an airline—to attract customers by lowering prices, but it is not obviously so easy for a firm to attract customers by providing, say, better search results. As is discussed below, the quality of search results may be difficult to evaluate and may only be appreciated by consumers over the long run. In that respect, it is interesting that there in fact is little information available about informational competition. To what extent do consumers compare Google and Bing? Yelp and TripAdvisor? There are some web postings that compare competing sites, but the services provided by the various sites are so varied and extensive that it would be difficult to provide useful comparisons.

Will Consumers Respond to Better Information?

Suppose that all of the conditions above are met. That is, suppose that competitors are able to obtain accurate information to correct misinformation or the absence of information provided by other firms, that the competitors have access to consumers at the time that providing accurate information could be useful, and that the competitors have the incentive to distribute the accurate information. Will consumers be persuaded by it? When will they be? As described above, consumers often will not be able to assess the correctness of the information that they are provided, so it is not clear that in the presence of both correct and incorrect information consumers will choose the correct information. Whether consumers will be persuaded depends on the kind of information at issue, of course. If it were price information that were at issue, and competitors had access to lower prices than a site was showing, the competitors could presumably provide that information to consumers in a way that would be effective.

But if there is an element of subjectivity, as, for example, if a restaurant received four stars on TripAdvisor and three on Yelp, would a consumer be able to determine which site to believe? It seems likely that without an opinion about which site is more reliable, the consumer would not. That is, the consumer would have to turn to some *other* sort of information to help assess which version of the information it seeks is correct. This is an implication of the fact that much information is an experience good, as described in the previous chapter; consumers will not know the value of the information they receive until they have used it, which in this case they would do by relying on it to go to the restaurant. This is also, of course, why Yelp and TripAdvisor market the reliability of their information, and why government enforcement agencies have challenged these sorts of marketing statements when companies do little to ensure that they are correct.

The issue is even more complicated if a competing website seeks to correct misinformation on another site. Suppose that Bing contended that Google has ranked certain sites too high or too low in its search results. Aside from the difficulty of assessing the contentions as a factual matter, a consumer would have to consider what weight to place on the different context in which Bing provided the information. Specifically, it would be clear that Bing was providing the information for competitive purposes, to seek an advantage over Google. But the Google search results likely would not be seen so clearly, if at all, as an effort to gain a competitive advantage. Consumers to some extent discount self-interested information, so that this sort of information might be much more valuable if provided by disinterested third parties. But such evaluators—information provider raters—have not developed, at least in most of the contexts at issue here, so consumers are left to rely to some extent on reputational information.

Reputation is particularly problematic for search engines. Many searches that a consumer performs on a search engine are for information that a search engine would have no incentive to distort. For example, if one performed a search for "national parks New England," there would presumably be no reason for Google or another search engine to deliver information on parks in, say, the upper Midwest. In contrast, a search for "Bosch refrigerators" might, if other refrigerator manufacturers were willing to pay to have their sites provided for that search, be more problematic. The point is that most, and maybe a great majority of, searches are of the former kind. Therefore, the experience of consumers is that Google and other search engines deliver exactly the information they want the great majority of the time. Even if the information received is not exactly what consumers want when they search for commercial information that it might be profitable to distort, consumers may not separate the two sorts of searches in their evaluations.

In that respect, a search engine—unlike, presumably, a review site like Yelp, for which a greater number of searches are related to purchases—could establish a reputation based on non-commercial searches and exploit that reputation in commercial ones. This would be similar to, but probably even more effective than, the "reputation mining" that is discussed by George Akerlof and Robert Shiller in their book *Phishing for Phools*. Their discussion is of credit-rating agencies mining their previously established reputations for trustworthiness to successfully market low-quality information in the form of inaccurate credit ratings. In the search engine example, the idea would be one of mining a reputation for trustworthiness established in non-commercial searches to market low-quality information in commercial searches. The reason this might be an even more effective strategy is that the search engines would continue, even while producing low-quality commercial search results, to produce high-quality noncommercial results. To detect the difference in quality, consumers would have to be quite sophisticated in how they evaluated the different search results they received.

All of this suggests that it would be desirable to have more information on how reputation works in these contexts. Authority and reputation are characteristics that allow firms to persuade, and thus, in some sense, they provide firms with informational power. In fact, we hear frequent references to "mindshare," which reflects consumer awareness and perhaps reputation as well. Although a direct analogy between "mindshare" and market share is not likely to be fruitful, some factors may be useful in assessing the power of an information provider. The frequency with which the statements of a particular provider are cited is an example; that is a factor often used in academic contexts to measure "impact."

Perhaps one could even find proxies for mindshare. If Google charges twice as much for comparable advertising as does Bing, would that show that Google has twice the mindshare? Or would it show power even more directly, in that Google's costs are presumably similar to Bing's, so that a higher price could be direct evidence of power? How, in general, could informational power be proved?

Proving Informational Power

These proof issues will be taken up further in the chapters below, in the context of particular types of potentially anticompetitive informational conduct. As suggested above, the "first principles" focus is on the form of power relevant to the particular informational conduct at issue. That is, it is on the ability of competitors to respond to the conduct. As the Supreme Court has said, the power of concern in antitrust is "the power to control prices or exclude competition." In the context of horizontal agreements, that power typically comes from the collective nature of the joint venture, and often from the fact that if many firms are part of the venture, there are not sufficient other firms available to form a competing one. This source of power will be of particular concern in Chapter 4. In the single-firm context addressed in Chapter 5, the focus will generally be on the latter part of the Court's definition, the power to exclude competition.

Admittedly, looking to conduct for evidence of power is problematic, particularly in the single-firm context, in that part of the value of the power inquiry is that of providing an independent check on evaluations of conduct. As the Supreme Court has said, an independent power inquiry "reduces the risk that the antitrust laws will dampen the competitive zeal of a single aggressive entrepreneur." But an inquiry into market power can be independent of conduct without being based traditionally on market share, as outlined above. Although the Supreme Court has insisted on definition of the market where single-firm conduct is being challenged, it has not required an inquiry into market share. Instead, it has appeared to allow a more open inquiry into power: "In order to determine whether there is a dangerous probability of monopolization, courts have found it necessary to consider the relevant market and the defendant's ability to lessen or destroy competition in that market."

Thus, the important point is to find independent evidence that a firm has the power to injure competition and that it has engaged in conduct that could cause that injury. Or, to reverse the order of these requirements and restate them, it is important to find evidence that the firm has sought to injure competition and that some obstacle prevents competitors from responding to those efforts. In many antitrust contexts, the relevant obstacle is an insufficient market share. In the informational context, it will instead be the inability to counter effectively the information provided by the defendant.

Notes

1.   Are informational issues better addressed by consumer protection law than antitrust? Another chapter in the book from which this chapter comes addresses that question.

2.   Is proof of informational power likely to be more or less satisfactory than proof of market share? Is market share's real advantage that it provides the (spurious) precision of a number?

3.   The book from which this chapter comes devotes more attention to assessing conduct than to devising remedies for anticompetitive conduct. In the exclusion section below, consider whether remedying anticompetitive effects from informational conduct is more challenging than remedying other anticompetitive effects. A significant problem in remedying anticompetitive refusals to deal is the determination of the price at which dealing should be required. Is that problem more difficult for information? Is information difficult to value?

2.1.2.   Barriers to Entry

algorithms look like IP

Daniel L. Rubinfeld & Michal S. Gal
Access Barriers to Big Data
59 Ariz. L. Rev. 339 (2017)

INTRODUCTION

"Big data" were recently declared to represent a new and significant class of economic assets that fuel the information economy. While data were always valuable in a range of economic activities, the advent of new and improved technologies for the collection, storage, mining, synthesizing, and analysis of data has led to the ability to utilize vast volumes of data in real-time in order to learn new information. Big data is a game changer because it allows for regularized customization of decision-making, thereby reducing risk and improving performance. It also changes corporate ecosystems by moving data analytics into core operational and production functions, and it enables the introduction of new products—for example, self-driving cars and digital personal assistants such as Siri.

. . .

I. CHARACTERISTICS OF BIG DATA

Big data is a generic name for data that share several characteristics with regard to their aggregation, rather than content. Big data's main characteristic, as the name signifies, is volume. A simple definition relates to amounts of data that cannot be analyzed by traditional methods. Rather, the data can only be analyzed through the establishment of a unique platform that can manage substantial volumes of information in a reasonable timeframe. The concept of big data is thus a moving target, given that the volume of data captured under the definition today may change over time as storage and analysis capabilities grow. What is possible today with terabytes was not possible with gigabytes only a few years ago.

The fact that the term *big data* relates to volume rather than content leads to several observations. First, big data can relate to a wide range of content—for example, earthquakes, calories, consumer preferences—and consequently may be used as inputs in a variety of markets. Second, there is no market that requires generic big data, as such. Rather, different markets often need different types of big data as inputs. For example, both a book publisher and a sports-car manufacturer would find information on the preferences of potential buyers, such as income and spending habits, to be valuable. Yet while the book publisher is less interested in income, given the relatively low prices of books, a sports-car manufacturer has a greater interest in it. Therefore, the users of big data often do not compete with each other, depending on the product and geographic market in which they operate. This also implies that simply because vast amounts of data are collected, one cannot conclude that data are fungible.

This leads to a third observation: due to its nonrivalrous nature, the same data set can be useful to a variety of users and consequently is likely to have different values for different users. Fourth, the collectors, aggregators, and analyzers of big data do not necessarily compete if they adopt or analyze different types of data—for example, one collects data on geological phenomena and another on drug use. Fifth, the data need not be collected from the same sources or in the same way in order to be competitive—for example, collection from the Internet, from wearables, from smart appliances, or from personal interviews. Finally, at least some of the data collected are a byproduct of other productive activities, a fact which does not affect the importance of the data but which could affect the ability of multiple firms to collect it. Taken together, these facts imply that determining whether a big-data collector possesses market power mandates that one define the market in which the data collector operates, as well as the use(s) of such data, much like any other market analysis.

While big-data markets may differ substantially from one another, most big data sets share four main characteristics which contribute to their value: volume, velocity, variety, and veracity. *Volume* is arguably the most important characteristic. Developments in collection, storage, and analytical capabilities have exponentially increased the volume of data that can be collected and analyzed. *Velocity*—sometimes referred to as the "freshness" of the data—relates to the speed of change. Especially in dynamic markets, new data might render some old data obsolete.

Variety is characterized by the number of different sources from which the data are gathered. Indeed, the vast amount of data often implies that several types of data are gathered together. Alternatively, data sources can be multivaried. Such sources can be human actions, such as a user of Facebook or WhatsApp, or maybe machines— Internet of things and wearables. Sources can also be primary—a post on a blog—or secondary—data already gathered by someone else. The integration of data from different sources may significantly increase the value of the data set. Variety can also relate to the time period covered by the data.

Finally, *veracity* relates to the truthfulness of the data—in essence, its accuracy. This characteristic can relate to the accuracy of the building blocks of the database (implying that not all data are equal), or to the database as a whole, because what we lose in accuracy at the micro level might be gained in insights at the macro level.

The importance of each of these characteristics might differ among the myriad of markets in which big data serves as an input. For example, where velocity is of small importance relative to the other three parameters, the data might not have to be constantly updated. Rather, old data can serve as a sufficiently effective input for firms competing in the market.

These four characteristics relate to the collection of big data and serve as the basis for its value. Yet what often gives big data its real advantage is not these characteristics alone, but rather the ability to synthesize and analyze the big data, characterized by the "four Vs," in ways not previously available, thereby creating metadata. Advancements in data science have contributed to the ability to learn fast and deep from big data by analyzing correlations among variables. Such advancements include data-mining techniques, such as association analysis, data segmentation and clustering, classification and regression analysis, anomaly detection, and predictive modeling. They also include Business Performance Management ("BPM"), which helps one "analyze and visualize a variety of performance metrics" based on the data. These technological advancements allow algorithms to find patterns and make predictions extremely quickly and efficiently in ways that no human analyst could—without getting sick, tired, or bored. Furthermore, the change in quantity has led to a change in quality: due to its size, big data provide insights that are not possible to glean from traditional data. Finally, new analytical tools enable algorithms to automatically "learn" from past actions, creating a positive feedback loop, to become more efficient in mining the data.

. . .

III. Some Economic Implications

The above findings have implications for the analysis of competitive conditions in big-data markets which, in turn, affect social welfare as well as optimal regulatory policy. Accordingly, this Part attempts to tie together the findings discussed above, to indicate how the characteristics of big data and the entry barriers at each level of the data-value chain affect the competitive analysis.

A. Entry Barriers

We begin with seven observations regarding entry barriers. A first and basic observation is that barriers can arise in all parts of the data-value chain. Such barriers may be technological, legal, or behavioral. Often there exists a combination of barriers in each part of the value chain, as well as across parts, which has the potential to create a cumulative negative effect on competition. At the same time, high entry barriers in one part of the chain might at least be partly overcome by another part of the chain. For example, better algorithms can allow a firm to learn more from less data.

Second, while some barriers are unique to big data, others such as barriers arising from two-sided markets or network economies apply more broadly.

Third, the existence and strength of such barriers may differ among markets for big data, depending on their specific characteristics. Therefore, in order to evaluate the importance of such barriers, one needs to understand the unique characteristics of the data that serve as an input for each specific market, as well as the ways in which the data-based information reaches the consumer. To give an example, the velocity of data necessary in order to determine optimal traffic routes at any given time is significantly different from the velocity of data required to determine past trends in the purchase of toys. Where economies of scope are significant, firms may benefit from a network of data sources, thereby possibly increasing entry barriers for those outside the network. Any analysis of big-data markets without such groundwork—what Balto and Lane call "lazy talk"—is therefore problematic.

Fourth, and relatedly, big data is nonrivalrous, and collecting it does not prevent others from collecting identical data by comparable or different means. This has led some to claim that low entry barriers exist in big-data markets. Our analysis of entry barriers challenges this assumption, at least in some big-data markets. This is because data gathering is only part of the data-value chain, because there may still exist high entry barriers in the collection of some types of data, and because of the cumulative effect of entry barriers in several parts of the data-value chain, each of which, on its own, might not seem to create a high entry barrier. The focus of analysis should therefore not be limited to the data-collection stage, unless it is the only relevant activity.

Fifth, in some markets, relevant data-based information can be based on substitutable sources of data, thereby increasing the ability to compete in its collection. The example of data on the average speed of drivers on dark streets exemplifies this point. The same is true with regard to storage, synthesis, and analysis tools.

Sixth, the strength of entry barriers at any part of the data-value chain *6* might affect the strength of related barriers. For example, the lowering of one barrier might affect the incentives of firms to erect higher barriers in another part of the data-value chain, in order to protect their data-based advantages. Alternatively, if high and durable technological entry barriers exist in one part of the chain, we might more easily justify imposing legal barriers of lower or similar height on the same part of the chain that would protect privacy or other social goals.

Seventh, firms may use a variety of strategies in order to erect entry *7* barriers, some observable and some less observable, some objectionable and some less objectionable.

B. Effects on Competition and Welfare

The above observations, combined with the unique characteristics of big data, allow us to reach some conclusions with regard to the competitive conditions in big-data markets. Entry barriers in such markets may create competitive effects similar to those created by traditional goods—for example, foreclosure, market power—and firms enjoying data-based advantages will be motivated to engage in exclusionary conduct and erect artificial barriers to entry in order to maintain or strengthen their advantage, just as in any other market. Yet, as we show below, the unique characteristics of big-data markets, which create interesting twists on the regular analysis, affect the nature, scale, and scope of such competitive effects. We also show that due to the unique characteristics of at least some big-data markets, the mere existence of high entry barriers into these markets, by itself, does not automatically lead to the conclusion that social welfare will be harmed.

barriers ≠ ↓ social welfare

1. Data Are Multidimensional

As observed above, the quality and value of data are affected not only by their volume, but also by their velocity, variety, and veracity. As a result, once one characteristic of big data exhibits high entry barriers, another characteristic might grow in importance in order to overcome the competitive advantages created by the first. For example, where past data are not easily available (therefore reducing the volume or temporal variety of data available), veracity or variety might gain importance in order to create a higher level of predictive certainty based on a smaller data panel. Firms might also invest more resources in creating better analytical tools rather than in gathering more data. Therefore, in analyzing the competitive effects of entry barriers in big-data markets, it is essential that one explore alternative routes of reaching data-informed conclusions based on the data's various characteristics. Failure to account for this fact may imply that potential implications for innovation—i.e., dynamic efficiency—will be disregarded.

The issue can be illustrated with respect to the U.S. DOJ/FTC 2010 Horizontal Merger Guidelines. The Guidelines make clear that U.S. agencies are concerned with mergers and acquisitions that are likely to increase barriers to entry created by the presence of scale economies, but there is no mention of similar barriers that could be created if there are substantial economies of scope or speed.

Another implication of the multidimensional characteristic of big data, which may have opposite competitive effects than the previous one, is that data from different sources can create important synergies. While entry barriers generally do not prevent own-use synergies, they might prevent synergies between different data owners, for example, by limiting data portability. This, in turn, may affect welfare, depending on the importance of the synergies to the quality of the data-based decisions. To illustrate, consider the analysis of the reactions of patients to a certain medical treatment, which, only if gathered across a very large panel of data gathered from many doctors, can generate essential insights for better care. In such situations, the ability to share data within and possibly across health maintenance organizations can substantially increase welfare.

Synergies are often, technologically, relatively easy to create among data sets, given that data are nonrivalrous and can often be easily replicated at low costs. Yet for synergies to take place, two conditions must be met: the relevant parties must be aware of possible synergies ("the informational obstacle"); and all relevant parties must find it worthwhile to invest in the realization of potential synergies ("the motivation obstacle").

Big data may involve both types of obstacles. In particular, the fact that each data owner organizes its data in accordance with its own preferences might create obstacles even if access to the data is allowed. But more importantly, the motivational problem might be affected by the technological, legal, or behavioral barriers observed above. This creates an important policy concern—how can we design regulatory rules and institutions and evaluate mergers and acquisitions so that socially desirable synergies will be created?

In fact, obstacles to achieving these synergies produce an anti-commons problem, in which goods controlled by more than one right holder are underutilized. With respect to big data, the problem arises because even if the data owner can give access to its database and will have an incentive to do so if such conduct benefits him economically, barriers to achieving potential synergies might remain.

Any synergies that can be created through the existence of big data must be balanced against market-power concerns. Such considerations were taken into account, for example, in the FTC's evaluation of the proposed merger of Nielsen and Arbitron. Nielsen has long been active in the provision of various television audience measurement services to content providers and advertisers. Arbitron had been the leading provider of radio measurement services. Each had separately expended substantial resources to develop a panel of individuals that served as the source of TV and radio ratings, respectively. As a result of their investments, each had "the most accurate and preferred sources of individual-level demographic data for [TV and radio] audience measurement purposes." In recent years, both Nielsen and Arbitron had made efforts to expand their services in the "cross-platform" arena. Cross-platform audience measurement services report the overall unduplicated audience size—i.e., reach—and frequency of exposure for programming content and advertisements across multiple media platforms, with corresponding individual audience demographic data. The FTC had concerns about competition within the market for cross-platform ratings. The FTC claimed that Nielsen and Arbitron were the best-positioned firms to develop cross-platform services in the future, because of their large, representative data panels, which created synergies (data economies of scale and scope). In settling the case, Nielsen agreed to divest and license assets and intellectual property needed to develop national syndicated cross-platform audience measurement services. Nielsen also agreed that ownership of all the data generated by the Arbitron Calibration Panel would belong to another rating firm, while Nielsen would retain ownership of the data from the Arbitron general panel.

A third and final implication of the fact that the data are vast and multidimensional is that it strengthens the possibility that the data set could be valuable to many different users, operating in unrelated and distinct markets. This is further strengthened by the fact that recent advancements in data science have led to the development of algorithms that can engage in deep learning, whereby the algorithm seeks correlations in the data set without specific directions. This, in turn, enables the data analyzer to find correlations that otherwise would not be explored. To give but one example, deep learning with respect to online transactions found a correlation between people who engage in online fraud and use of capital letters in writing online messages. Such information is relevant to both enforcement agencies as well as to private companies operating in a wide range of online markets. This characteristic of the data affects their value, which in turn affects incentives to collect and analyze data.

2. The Nonrivalrous Nature of Data

We now move to an exploration of the competitive effects of big data being nonrivalrous, because it can easily and cheaply be copied and shared, at least technologically. In this case, data collectors and analyzers have the potential to sell or license their data sets to multiple users. Yet legal and technological barriers in all parts of the data-value chain may limit data portability. For example, legal limitations on data portability based on privacy concerns, or technological data compatibility limitations, might reduce the potential benefits that are available due to the nonrivalrous characteristic of the data. With or without these potential barriers, there are likely to be strong economic incentives to maintain control over large data sets and to create structural barriers, potentially rendering at least parts of the chain noncompetitive.

If the source of the barriers is inherently structural, and sharing the data is socially beneficial, a regulatory solution may be appropriate, perhaps by requirements that the data be made widely available at a reasonable and nondiscriminatory cost. A potentially instructive model might be FRAND (fair, reasonable, and nondiscriminatory) licensing-rate requirements that are central to the operation of standard-setting organizations. Of course, any regulation should be sensitive to the fact that relative advantages of big data are often nuanced and complex. It is also important to stress that the data being nonrivalrous does not alter the fact that their collection, organization, storage, or analysis generally transforms data into a private good.

Another notable implication of the nonrivalrous characteristic of big data is that the comparative advantages resulting from a unique data set might be shortlived. Assume, for example, that an insurance company used a unique panel of data regarding the geological conditions in deep drillings to more accurately calculate the risks associated with insuring drilling operations. This, in turn, might lead the data-holder to set lower insurance prices that reflect reduced risk. Other insurers, acknowledging the fact that the price reducer has access to the relevant data, might follow suit and reduce their prices, without ever observing the data set themselves. The increased use of algorithms to track price changes of competitors may further limit the life of a data-based comparative advantage. This reduces the market value of the data, as well as the incentive to collect and analyze it in the first place. Note that no intellectual property rights are infringed because the copying relates to the results of the analysis on actions, rather than to the copying of the database itself. Another example involves content scraping: practices that make use of data collected by competing firms, such as scraping journalistic information or consumer reviews by adding them to one's webpage. Here, however, intellectual-property protection might kick in.

Indeed, due to the nonrivalrous aspects of the dataset, free riding is likely to be an issue. Free riding can broaden the benefits flowing from big data, but it can also reduce reward, and therefore, the incentive to invest in creating the database in the first place. Assume, for example, that a firm enjoys monopoly power over the collection and analysis of a certain kind of big data, and that the data enable the firm to create better-targeted offers to consumers. If these consumers seek better offers, they may share the information regarding the first firm's offer with the firm's rivals, thus enabling the latter through free riding to base their offers on second-hand information. Alternatively, if the first offer is made online and is widely observable, successive suppliers can rely on the publicly available information to create a better one of their own. In today's world, where the calculation of most online offers is made by algorithms that can observe and analyze information regarding competitors' offers in split seconds, the comparative advantage of the first data-based offer might be reduced.

Free riding thus creates mixed effects on social welfare. The tension between the advantages of free riding (greater competition, synergies) and the disadvantages (reduced incentive to innovate, market power) is inherent. This raises both regulatory and competition enforcement issues. Below we suggest some additional factors that affect welfare.

One factor involves the degree of harm to data collection and analysis. If, for example, an initial internet offer stands only for a very limited time and may change based on new data arriving or on the consumer seeking offers elsewhere, then it will be difficult for competitors to match offers. Alternatively, if the unique data set which affects the conditions of the offer is one-dimensional, such as price, whereas the offer is based on a multidimensional calculation, the data-based offer might not enable others to indirectly observe the data.

Another factor involves the externalities and internalities created by the erection of entry barriers in markets that use big data. To illustrate, suppose that there is vertical integration with respect to data collectors and data analysts. On the one hand, such integration might create high (two-level) entry barriers into data markets which, in turn, might create market power and could lead to foreclosing behavior. On the other hand, the vertical integration might overcome free riding and could increase synergies in the collection and use of data. For example, once the actions of a user indicate his potential interest in a certain product, it may be efficient to immediately provide him with offers about that product on the platform that he is currently using. Yet, the nonrivalrous characteristic of data, combined with the increased use of algorithms to determine trade conditions and the speed of internet connection, might reduce the comparative advantage of vertical integration if competitors can speedily copy the online offers made by their rivals.

This, in turn, might lead to the erection of barriers to reach the information regarding the first offer by the vertically integrated firm, so that its first offer could not be easily integrated into its rivals' price algorithms. Alternatively, if the integrated firm also operates an online platform or a search engine, it might erect barriers for users to reach the trade offers of low-cost suppliers, for example, by placing their results lower in the search algorithm's results. These considerations should be taken into account when evaluating the welfare effects of vertical integration.

Finally, it is important to emphasize that, as our analysis shows, the nonrivalrous nature of big data does not mean that its collection does not exhibit entry barriers. Rather, it is these very barriers which create an incentive for firms to compete over the provision of products or services from which they can get access to such information, sometimes even providing them free of charge. These products or services then may increase social welfare if the added value of the widgets to consumers (in lower prices or higher quality) plus the positive externalities big data creates—for example, learning to cure diseases faster—exceeds the value of the data to the consumer, plus the potential harm that the gathering of big data might create—for example, discrimination against certain social groups which results from correlations in the data set.

3. Data as an Input

The fact that big data usually serves as an input into other product or service markets, rather than a product of its own, leads to four observations that have broad relevance. First, the analysis of entry barriers should often extend beyond the specific market under scrutiny to related parts of the data-value chain. To illustrate, consider the use of free goods and services in online markets. The availability of free goods creates a two-level barrier to entry into data collection. Suppose that Firm A has a comparative advantage in market A which provides data-access points. It then uses the data in order to compete more effectively in market B. Firm B wishes to compete in market B. Firm B faces two entry options: contract with firm A for access to its data; or incur the high costs of entering not only market B but also market A. This implies that some firms will not enter market B, even if they can supply a more efficient product than is currently supplied. This entry obstacle might also lead to a situation in which market B will be monopolized. At the same time, consumers may enjoy lower-priced and higher-quality products that are intended to "lure them" to use particular online services. An analysis that is based on the realization of barriers in related vertical markets is essential if an analysis of competition and welfare is to be accurate and effective. It is also relevant to market definition.

This observation has not, as of yet, been recognized in all relevant regulatory decisions. For example, in analyzing the advertising-based media, both the FTC and the European Union focused on advertising markets and disregarded the dynamics of the markets in which these advertisements were placed, on the grounds that there is no trade relationship between the online user and the content provider. Such an analysis is, in our view, flawed because it disregards the competitive effects of the free online-services market, which affect the market for the collection of consumer data, and which in turn affect the dynamics in the advertising market.

2.   The second observation is that a comparative advantage unrelated to data might help overcome entry barriers in big-data markets. Tinder serves as a case in point. Its innovation among the online-dating sites was based on a simple change in how to use the site (left swipe versus right swipe) which catered to consumer needs, rather than on a comparative advantage based on big data. Other examples abound, including the recent entry of Qwant into the search market, which gains its comparative advantage from offering a less data-voracious search service. Indeed, because big data almost never serve as the final product (exceptions might occur where information, by itself, is sought), their effect on competition for the final product must always be determined by a holistic analysis focused on the relative weight of different factors that affect consumer choice. As noted above, this fact can explain competition and innovation in many markets that use big data as an input, including Facebook's replacement of MySpace and Google's successful entry into the search market. At the same time, where big data serve as a product of their own (mostly as an input into other markets), this has only indirect effects on the analysis of entry barriers and market power.

Furthermore, the fact that entry occurs into markets in which big data serve as an input or as an output does not necessarily lead to the conclusion that low entry barriers also exist in the relevant big-data markets. This seemingly simple differentiation appears to be disregarded by some scholars. At the same time, however, it may signal that even if high barriers exist, their welfare effects on the final consumer might not be high.

Finally, any analysis of the role of big data must also relate to new 3. technological developments—most importantly, the move from traditional vertically structured industries to networks. In the latter, big data, which are collected from multiple sources, including the Internet of things, serve as an input into automated machines, which are digitally connected, to automatically produce or supply the consumer. An automated car serves as an example: information about weather, traffic, low-cost gas stations, road difficulties, and the routes requested by other potential users who might wish to share the car, may all automatically affect the route of the car, without requiring any decision by the user. As a result, firms that control all or large parts of these networks might enjoy significant comparative advantages in smart products or smart supply chains. This, in turn, might change the industrial landscape as we know it. Where big data serve as an essential input into such networks, the analysis of the effect of entry barriers into their collection, storage, analysis, and usage must also relate to their effects on the larger picture.

4. Collection as a Byproduct

As elaborated above, another characteristic of many types of data is that their collection may be a byproduct of other activities. This, in turn, might create a two-level entry problem that may erect high entry barriers in the data-collection market.

Moreover, the fact that each level of the data-value chain is potentially characterized by an additional set of entry barriers may affect incentives to share such data. For example, if entry barriers in data storage and analysis are high, firms whose business model is not necessarily based on big data might have stronger incentives to sell the raw data they collect, thereby limiting the two-level entry barrier. Yet it is important to emphasize that the fact that the data would have been harvested in any case, or that the data's collector has no other use for the data, does not necessarily affect the data's market value or price.

5. Big Data May Exhibit Strong Network Effects

As noted previously, some types of big data may exhibit strong network effects. These include network effects arising from the fact that the scale, scope, or speed of data collection may positively affect the accuracy of information that can be discerned from the data. Multi-sidedness of a market strengthens such network effects.

These entry barriers have led the OECD to observe that big data favor market concentration and dominance, and that "data-driven markets can lead to a 'winner takes all' result where concentration is a likely outcome of market success." As our research has shown, this is not true of all data-driven markets. Much depends on the height of entry barriers that characterize the specific market. It also depends on market structure: whether several services are provided together through an intermediary, or whether each service is provided by a stand-alone provider. Yet, when network effects are substantial, and especially when they are coupled with other entry barriers, they can generate significant competitive effects. This is especially so when first-mover data-based comparative advantages are high or when some firms are poised to become "super platforms" of data and services.

6. Data Might Strengthen Discrimination

A final characteristic of some types of big data that may affect the competitive analysis centers on the ability to price discriminate more easily among downstream consumers, should the big data provide information regarding consumer preferences. Usually, price discrimination affects only immediate consumers. With big data, this implies that the data collector or analyzer often has the ability to demand different prices from those buying the data, depending on the buyers' elasticities of demand. Yet the more important price discrimination effects are often created at a lower level of the supply chain. In big-data driven markets, in which the data reveal consumer preferences, the ability to price discriminate may be substantial. The question then becomes whether such price discrimination increases overall welfare, or simply (or mostly) benefits the user of the data.

A related question is how, if at all, the competitive conditions in big-data markets affect price discrimination in the consumer-goods market? Much depends on the structure of the market exploiting such data. A monopolistic user of data may engage in first-degree price discrimination. Should such discrimination be based on the data regarding consumers' preferences rather than on the relative quality of the product purchased, this could reduce consumer welfare substantially given the ability of the monopolist controlling the data to effectively extract consumer surplus.

Introducing competition among the users of such data might not, however, necessarily increase welfare. Much depends on consumer conduct and the ultimate competitive equilibrium. Assume, for example, that consumers do not have much knowledge about other suppliers, or that they exhibit behavioral traits and biases, such as accepting the first offer they receive while not spending time comparing it with other offers, or exploring only the first links in their search query for comparable products. Such conduct might be rational, especially with regard to low-priced products. Under scenarios such as this, the fact that multiple data users have access to similar data would not necessarily reduce the price discrimination problem. Rather, it would allow all owners of data sets to engage in discrimination. If, however, consumers engage in substantial (albeit costly) searches, some suppliers might respond by offering better trade conditions, which would reduce the use and effects of price discrimination. Algorithms that search for better offers for consumers might serve to reduce this problem. The welfare effects of the erection of barriers for such searches should be analyzed.

Observe further that entry barriers into big-data markets do not necessarily affect consumer welfare. This is because such welfare effects depend, other things equal, on the effect of the data-based information on the price and quality of the final product or service. Assume, for example, that information on consumer preferences significantly increases the ability of one competitor to market his products effectively by targeting potentially interested consumers.

Other suppliers of competing goods, which lack such targeted marketing information, may nonetheless enjoy other comparative advantages, such as patents, location, unique human and physical resources, and reputation. In other situations, big-data advantages may increase the incentives for firms to compete not only on the big-data-based information, but also on other dimensions of the product, including quality and price. The higher the market reward for informational accuracy, the larger the advantage of big data that must be overcome by other advantages. Where this is true, big data should be treated no differently than other inputs that create comparative advantages. Further observe that, as noted above, big data might affect wider aspects of social welfare, such as equal opportunity.

7. Additional Observations

Due to its above features, often a multi-faceted balance needs to be struck between anticompetitive effects and pro-competitive and public-good justifications—for example, synergies, motivations for innovation, privacy concerns—with regard to the erection or lowering of entry barriers. An important part of the welfare analysis focuses on the uses of the data and how such uses affect welfare. Big data used by doctors on how best to treat an illness is not the same as big data used by firms on betting habits that offer gaming opportunities.

It is also noteworthy that big data might change the competitive dynamics across many markets. One example involves the market for advertising. Traditional ways to reach potential consumers include banners and newspaper advertising. More accurate information on consumers' characteristics, arising from big data that either relate to the specific consumer or to groups the consumer belongs to, allow for more targeted advertising, often through internet sites that reach each consumer specifically. This, in turn, also affects the delineation of relevant markets.

8.Adding an International Dimension

To this point, we have largely disregarded the international dimension: how the data's characteristics affect the conduct of, and competition between, international firms. While this is a subject that justifies a paper of its own, several observations are in order. Entry barriers into big-data markets may differ from one jurisdiction to another, thereby creating higher obstacles to the collection, storage, analysis, or usage of big data in certain jurisdictions. However, the characteristics of the data may allow for cross-border spillovers in data analysis. For example, where consumers across certain jurisdictions are likely to be relatively similar, data collected with regard to consumers in one jurisdiction can be used in other jurisdictions, thereby overcoming barriers to the collection and analysis of such data in the latter. A large international scale might also make it easier for firms to enjoy scale and scope economies in data collection and analysis, and for consumers to enjoy stronger network effects. This, in turn, creates a comparative advantage to firms operating in multiple jurisdictions. It might also make it more difficult for national firms to compete in their own jurisdictions. Yet firms do not necessarily need to operate in other jurisdictions in order to use some of their advantages to overcome entry barriers. Storage provides a good example. Due to the data's transferability, storage can be performed in jurisdictions with better storage capabilities while data is used in others. Such cross-border effects must be taken into account when analyzing the height of entry barriers.

Another issue arising from the internationalization of big data involves regulation. In today's world, regulation is mainly based on local welfare considerations (mostly country-specific and in some instances region-specific). Moreover, such regulation might not necessarily be based on competition considerations, but rather on wider ones, including industrial policy and human rights. An interesting set of questions arises regarding whether differences in legal barriers may lead to a race to the bottom, whether limitations in certain jurisdictions might create significant externalities that would affect welfare elsewhere, and whether some type of harmonized global regulation might be more efficient.

To sum up, big data creates new and sometimes complex issues regarding competition and social welfare. The implications are widespread, ranging from data-motivated acquisitions to the erection of artificial barriers to markets in the data-value chain. The challenge is to find the optimal balance between the clashing effects on social welfare analyzed above.

While beyond the scope of this paper, we have on occasion noted implications for regulatory and competition policy. Any analysis which groups together all big-data markets in a broad-brush analysis, or assumes that all big-data markets are open to competition because of the nonrivalrous nature of data, is likely to be problematic. To exemplify, a recent OECD report suggested that the economics of big data "[favors] market concentration and dominance." Yet, unless one recognizes the entry barriers into each relevant market under scrutiny, such suggestions are not helpful. To take another example, in *Big Mistakes Regarding Big Data*, Tucker and Wellford claim that, "[r]elevant data are widely available and often free," and therefore antitrust has a limited role to play. To the contrary, we have shown that this assumption is not necessarily true, once one recognizes entry barriers down the data-value chain.

Finally, this Article has shown that antitrust may well be relevant with respect to some aspects of big-data markets. While much depends on case-specific facts, some features of big-data markets create a solid basis for theories of harm to competition and welfare that should not be ignored. The U.S. merger of Baazarvoice/Power-Reviews serves as such an example: there, the DOJ found that the data created an entry barrier into the market for rating and review platform. Other cases may well follow, especially where the antitrust authorities exhibit the necessary flexibility to incorporate the unique features of big-data markets into their analysis.

. . .

Notes

1.   Rubinfeld and Gal state that "[a]ny synergies that can be created through the existence of big data must be balanced against market-power concerns," suggesting that synergies, in contrast to market power, are procompetitive. Is that true? Are synergies the same as economies of scope? If so, are they procompetitive?

2.   What is the significance of the fact that data are nonrivalrous? Does that mean that gathering the data is not costly? Isn't the problem with requiring sharing of any input that a price must be determined, at least if the incentive to produce the input is to be maintained? What effect should nonrivalrousness have on price?

Geoffrey Manne & Ben Sperry
Debunking the Myth of a Data Barrier to Entry for Online Services
March 26, 2015
https://truthonthemarket.com/2015/03/26/
debunking-the-myth-of-a-data-barrier-to-entry-for-online-services/

Recent years have seen an increasing interest in incorporating privacy into antitrust analysis. The FTC and regulators in Europe have rejected these calls so far, but certain scholars and activists continue their attempts to breathe life into this novel concept. Elsewhere we have written at length on the scholarship addressing the issue and found the case for incorporation wanting. Among the errors proponents make is a persistent (and woefully unsubstantiated) assertion that online data can amount to a barrier to entry, insulating incumbent services from competition and ensuring that only the largest providers thrive. This data barrier to entry, it is alleged, can then allow firms with monopoly power to harm consumers, either directly through "bad acts" like price discrimination, or indirectly by raising the costs of advertising, which then get passed on to consumers.

A case in point was on display at last week's George Mason Law & Economics Center Briefing on Big Data, Privacy, and Antitrust. Building on their growing body of advocacy work, Nathan Newman and Allen Grunes argued that this hypothesized data barrier to entry actually exists, and that it prevents effective competition from search engines and social networks that are interested in offering services with heightened privacy protections.

According to Newman and Grunes, network effects and economies of scale ensure that dominant companies in search and social networking (they specifically named Google and Facebook — implying that they are in separate markets) operate without effective competition. This results in antitrust harm, they assert, because it precludes competition on the non-price factor of privacy protection.

In other words, according to Newman and Grunes, even though Google and Facebook offer their services for a price of $0 and constantly innovate and upgrade their products, consumers are nevertheless harmed because the business models of less-privacy-invasive alternatives are foreclosed by insufficient access to data (an almost self-contradicting and silly narrative for many reasons, including the big question of whether consumers prefer greater privacy protection to free stuff). Without access to, and use of, copious amounts of data, Newman and Grunes argue, the algorithms underlying search and targeted advertising are necessarily less effective and thus the search product without such access is less useful to consumers. And even more importantly to Newman, the value to advertisers of the resulting consumer profiles is diminished.

Newman has put forth a number of other possible antitrust harms that purportedly result from this alleged data barrier to entry, as well. Among these is the increased cost of advertising to those who wish to reach consumers. Presumably this would harm end users who have to pay more for goods and services because the costs of advertising are passed on to them. On top of that, Newman argues that ad networks inherently facilitate price discrimination, an outcome that he asserts amounts to antitrust harm.

FTC Commissioner Maureen Ohlhausen (who also spoke at the George Mason event) recently made the case that antitrust law is not well-suited to handling privacy problems. She argues — convincingly — that competition policy and consumer protection should be kept separate to preserve doctrinal stability. Antitrust law deals with harms to competition through the lens of economic analysis. Consumer protection law is tailored to deal with broader societal harms and aims at protecting the "sanctity" of consumer transactions. Antitrust law can, in theory, deal with privacy as a non-price factor of competition, but this is an uneasy fit because of the difficulties of balancing quality over two dimensions: Privacy may be something some consumers want, but others would prefer a better algorithm for search and social networks, and targeted ads with free content, for instance.

In fact, there is general agreement with Commissioner Ohlhausen on her basic points, even among critics like Newman and Grunes. But, as mentioned above, views diverge over whether there are some privacy harms that should nevertheless factor into competition analysis, and on whether there is in fact a data barrier to entry that makes these harms possible.

As we explain below, however, the notion of data as an antitrust-relevant barrier to entry is simply a myth. And, because all of the theories of "privacy as an antitrust harm" are essentially predicated on this, they are meritless.

First, data is useful to all industries — this is not some new phenomenon particular to online companies

It bears repeating (because critics seem to forget it in their rush to embrace "online exceptionalism") that offline retailers also receive substantial benefit from, and greatly benefit consumers by, knowing more about what consumers want and when they want it. Through devices like coupons and loyalty cards (to say nothing of targeted mailing lists and the age-old practice of data mining check-out receipts), brick-and-mortar retailers can track purchase data and better serve consumers. Not only do consumers receive better deals for using them, but retailers know what products to stock and advertise and when and on what products to run sales. For instance:

- Macy's analyzes tens of millions of terabytes of data every day to gain insights from social media and store transactions. Over the past three years, the use of big data analytics alone has helped Macy's boost its revenue growth by 4 percent annually.

- Following its acquisition of Kosmix in 2011, Walmart established @WalmartLabs, which created its own product search engine for online shoppers. In the first year of its use alone, the number of customers buying a product on Walmart.com after researching a purchase increased by 20 percent. According to Ron Bensen, the vice president of engineering at @WalmartLabs, the combination of in-store and online data could give brick-and-mortar retailers like Walmart an advantage over strictly online stores.

- Panera and a whole host of restaurants, grocery stores, drug stores and retailers use loyalty cards to advertise and learn about consumer preferences.

And of course there is a host of others uses for data, as well, including security, fraud prevention, product optimization, risk reduction to the insured, knowing what content is most interesting to readers, etc. The importance of data stretches far beyond the online world, and far beyond mere retail uses more generally. To describe even online giants like Amazon, Apple, Microsoft, Facebook and Google as having a monopoly on data is silly.

Second, it's not the amount of data that leads to success but building a better ~~mousetrap~~ — INNOVATION

The value of knowing someone's birthday, for example, is not in that tidbit itself, but in the fact that you know this is a good day to give that person a present. Most of the data that supports the advertising networks underlying the Internet ecosphere is of this sort: Information is important to companies because of the value that can be drawn from it, not for the inherent value of the data itself. Companies don't collect information about you to stalk you, but to better provide goods and services to you.

Moreover, data itself is not only less important than what can be drawn from it, but data is also less important than the underlying product it informs. For instance, Snapchat created a challenger to Facebook so successfully (and in such short time) that Facebook attempted to buy it for $3 billion (Google offered $4 billion). But Facebook's interest in Snapchat wasn't about its data. Instead, Snapchat was valuable — and a competitive challenge to Facebook — because it cleverly incorporated the (apparently novel) insight that many people wanted to share information in a more private way.

Relatedly, Twitter, Instagram, LinkedIn, Yelp, Pinterest (and Facebook itself) all started with little (or no) data and they have had a lot of success. Meanwhile, despite its supposed data advantages, Google's attempts at social networking — Google+ — have never caught up to Facebook in terms of popularity to users (and thus not to advertisers either). And scrappy social network Ello is starting to build a significant base without data collection for advertising at all.

At the same time it's simply not the case that the alleged data giants — the ones supposedly insulating themselves behind data barriers to entry — actually have the type of data most relevant to startups anyway. As Andres Lerner has argued, if you wanted to start a travel business, the data from Kayak or Priceline would be far more relevant. Or if you wanted to start a ride-sharing business, data from cab companies would be more useful than the broad, market-cross-cutting profiles Google and Facebook have. Consider companies like Uber, Lyft and Sidecar that had no customer data when they began to challenge established cab companies that did possess such data. If data were really so significant, they could never have competed successfully. But Uber, Lyft and Sidecar have been able to effectively compete because they built products that users wanted to use — they came up with an idea for a better mousetrap. The data they have accrued came after they innovated, entered the market and mounted their successful challenges — not before.

In reality, those who complain about data facilitating unassailable competitive advantages have it exactly backwards. Companies need to innovate to attract consumer data, otherwise consumers will switch to competitors (including both new entrants and established incumbents). As a result, the desire to make use of more and better data drives competitive innovation, with manifestly impressive results: The continued explosion of new products, services and other apps is evidence that data is not a bottleneck to competition but a spur to drive it.

Third, competition online is one click or thumb swipe away; that is, barriers to entry and switching costs are low

Somehow, in the face of alleged data barriers to entry, competition online continues to soar, with newcomers constantly emerging and triumphing. This suggests that the barriers to entry are not so high as to prevent robust competition.

- Again, despite the supposed data-based monopolies of Facebook, Google, Amazon, Apple and others, there exist powerful competitors in the marketplaces they compete in:

- If consumers want to make a purchase, they are more likely to do their research on Amazon than Google.

- Google flight search has failed to seriously challenge — let alone displace — its competitors, as critics feared. Kayak, Expedia and the like remain the most prominent travel search sites — despite Google having literally purchased ITA's trove of flight data and data-processing acumen.

- People looking for local reviews go to Yelp and TripAdvisor (and, increasingly, Facebook) as often as Google.

- Pinterest, one of the most highly valued startups today, is now a serious challenger to traditional search engines when people want to discover new products.

- With its recent acquisition of the shopping search engine, TheFind, and test-run of a "buy" button, Facebook is also gearing up to become a major competitor in the realm of e-commerce, challenging Amazon.

- Likewise, Amazon recently launched its own ad network, "Amazon Sponsored Links," to challenge other advertising players.

Even assuming for the sake of argument that data creates a barrier to entry, there is little evidence that consumers cannot easily switch to a competitor. While there are sometimes network effects online, like with social networking, history still shows that people will switch. MySpace was considered a dominant network until it made a series of bad business decisions and everyone ended up on Facebook instead. Similarly, Internet users can and do use Bing, DuckDuckGo, Yahoo, and a plethora of more specialized search engines on top of and instead of Google. And don't forget that Google itself was once an upstart new entrant that replaced once-household names like Yahoo and AltaVista.

Fourth, access to data is not exclusive

Critics like Newman have compared Google to Standard Oil and argued that government authorities need to step in to limit Google's control over data. But to say data is like oil is a complete misnomer. If Exxon drills and extracts oil from the ground, that oil is no longer available to BP. Data is not finite in the same way. To use an earlier example, Google knowing my birthday doesn't limit the ability of Facebook to know my birthday, as well. While databases may be proprietary, the underlying data is not. And what matters more than the data itself is how well it is analyzed.

This is especially important when discussing data online, where multi-homing is ubiquitous, meaning many competitors end up voluntarily sharing access to data. For instance, I can use the friend-finder feature on WordPress to find Facebook friends, Google connections, and people I'm following on Twitter who also use the site for blogging. Using this feature allows WordPress to access your contact list on these major online players.

Further, it is not apparent that Google's competitors have less data available to them. Microsoft, for instance, has admitted that it may actually have more data.

And, importantly for this discussion, Microsoft may have actually garnered some of its data for Bing from Google.

If Google has a high cost per click, then perhaps it's because it is worth it to advertisers: There are more eyes on Google because of its superior search product. Contra Newman and Grunes, Google may just be more popular for consumers and advertisers alike because the algorithm makes it more useful, not because it has more data than everyone else.

Fifth, the data barrier to entry argument does not have workable antitrust remedies

The misguided logic of data barrier to entry arguments leaves a lot of questions unanswered. Perhaps most important among these is the question of remedies. What remedy would apply to a company found guilty of leveraging its market power with data?

It's actually quite difficult to conceive of a practical means for a competition authority to craft remedies that would address the stated concerns without imposing enormous social costs. In the unilateral conduct context, the most obvious remedy would involve the forced sharing of data.

On the one hand, as we've noted, it's not clear this would actually accomplish much. If competitors can't actually make good use of data, simply having more of it isn't going to change things. At the same time, such a result would reduce the incentive to build data networks to begin with. In their startup stage, companies like Uber and Facebook required several months and hundreds of thousands, if not millions, of dollars to design and develop just the first iteration of the products consumers love. Would any of them have done it if they had to share their insights? In fact, it may well be that access to these free insights is what competitors actually want; it's not the data they're lacking, but the vision or engineering acumen to use it.

Other remedies limiting collection and use of data are not only outside of the normal scope of antitrust remedies, they would also involve extremely costly court supervision and may entail problematic "collisions between new technologies and privacy rights," as the last year's White House Report on Big Data and Privacy put it.

It is equally unclear what an antitrust enforcer could do in the merger context. As Commissioner Ohlhausen has argued, blocking specific transactions does not necessarily stop data transfer or promote privacy interests. Parties could simply house data in a standalone entity and enter into licensing arrangements. And conditioning transactions with forced data sharing requirements would lead to the same problems described above.

If antitrust doesn't provide a remedy, then it is not clear why it should apply at all. The absence of workable remedies is in fact a strong indication that data and privacy issues are not suitable for antitrust. Instead, such concerns would be better dealt with under consumer protection law or by targeted legislation.

Notes

1.   The authors state that because data is useful in many markets, online and in the brick-and-mortar world, "[t]o describe even online giants like Amazon, Apple, Microsoft, Facebook and Google as having a monopoly on data is silly." Is "having a monopoly in data" the relevant issue? Is all data in the same relevant antitrust market, *i.e.*, is all data reasonably interchangeable? Might one or more of those firms have power over data that would be relevant for antitrust purposes?

2.   Is it true that if data were really important, Uber and Lyft would not exist?

3.   If it were indeed true that Facebook acquired Snapchat because of Snapchat's insight that people wanted to share information privately, would that show that the acquisition was not data-driven?

4.   Manne and Sperry, like Rubinfeld and Gal, focus on the nonrivalrous nature of data. In the view of Manne and Sperry, what are the implications of nonrivalrousness?

5.   Manne and Sperry argue if a merger were blocked, "[p]arties could simply house data in a standalone entity and enter into licensing arrangements." Does that show that there are no adequate antitrust remedies, or is that in fact a remedy?

The following decision focuses more on abuse of dominance than on dominance. It is useful to consider here in the context of data issues, though, also because it concerns an exploitation abuse, which it describes as a "manifestation of market power." That is, it concerns the use of power to exploit consumers, rather than an abusive exclusion of competitors. In Europe, article 102 (and its German equivalent in section 19(1)) covers not only "exclusionary" abuses of dominance that exclude competitors but also "exploitative" abuses that harm consumers; in the U.S., only the former are covered.

The decision refers to two relatively new subsections, (2a) and (3a), of section 18 of the German competition law:

§ 18
Market Dominance

(1) An undertaking is dominant where, as a supplier or purchaser of a certain type of goods or commercial services on the relevant product and geographic market, it

      1. has no competitors,

      2. is not exposed to any substantial competition, or

      3. has a paramount market position in relation to its competitors.

. . .

(2a) The assumption of a market shall not be invalidated by the fact that a good or service is provided free of charge.

. . .

(3a) In particular in the case of multi-sided markets and networks, in assessing the market position of an undertaking account shall also be taken of:

1. direct and indirect network effects,

2. the parallel use of services from different providers and the switching costs for users,

3. the undertaking's economies of scale arising in connection with network effects,

4. the undertaking's access to data relevant for competition,

5. innovation-driven competitive pressure.

. . .

Bundeskartellamt
Facebook
Exploitative business terms pursuant to Section 19(1) GWB
for inadequate data processing
(English Case Summary)
B6-22/16
February 6, 2019

In its decision of 6 February 2019 the Bundeskartellamt prohibited Facebook Inc., Menlo Park, USA, Facebook Ireland Ltd., Dublin, Ireland, and Facebook Germany GmbH, Hamburg, Germany (hereinafter: "Facebook") from making the use of the Facebook social network (hereinafter: "Facebook.com") by private users residing in Germany, who also use its corporate services *WhatsApp*, *Oculus*, *Masquerade* and *Instagram*, conditional on the collection of user and device-related data by Facebook and combining that information with the Facebook.com user accounts without the users' consent. The prohibition is based on Section 19(1) of the German Competition Act (GWB). The same applies to terms making the private use of Facebook.com conditional on Facebook being able to combine information saved on the "Facebook account" without the users' consent with information collected on websites visited or third-party mobile apps used via programming interfaces ("Facebook Business Tools") and use this data. There is no effective consent to the users' information being collected if their consent is a prerequisite for using the Facebook.com service in the first place.

The proceeding was initiated in March 2016 and aimed at user and device-related data which Facebook collects when other corporate services or third-party websites and apps are used and which it then combined with user data from the social network. The proceeding did not deal with the issue of information processed on the use of the social network that is generated after users have registered. The Bundeskartellamt saw no reason to intervene on the grounds of the prohibition of abusive practices under competition law. It is taken into account that an advertising-funded social network generally needs to process a large amount of personal data. However, the Bundeskartellamt holds that the efficiencies in a business model based on personalised advertising do not outweigh the interests of the users when it comes to processing data from sources outside of the social network. This applies in particular where users have insufficient control over the processing of their data and its allocation to their Facebook accounts. As far as this part of data processing is concerned, it was necessary to intervene from a competition law perspective because the data protection boundaries set forth in the GDPR were clearly overstepped, also in view of Facebook's dominant position.

1. Statement of facts

Facebook develops and operates various digital products, online services and applications for smartphones (apps). Facebook's core product is the social network Facebook.com, which has been offered in Germany since 2008. Its user base has been increasing continuously worldwide. In 2018 the number of daily active users in Germany was 23 million, while 32 million users were classified as monthly active users.

Private users can access Facebook.com via the websites www.facebook.com, www.facebook.de or via a mobile app. Facebook offers private users a range of functions to connect with their friends and acquaintances and share contents with them. Private Facebook.com use is conditional upon registration by creating a user profile. Using their real names, users can enter information on themselves and their personal situation and set a profile picture. Based on this information, a personalised site is created for each user, which is subdivided into three subsites: the "profile", "home" and the "find friends" pages. Users can see the latest news ("posts") of other private and commercial users in the "Newsfeed" on their start pages. The order of appearance is based on an algorithm to match the user's interests. *Facebook Messenger* is integrated into the social network and serves for real-time bilateral or group communication.

In the social network, Facebook.com offers a variety of further functionalities, e.g. a job board, an app center or event organisation.

Not only private users but also businesses, associations or business individuals can use Facebook.com to publish content in the social network to increase their reach. Publishers can create their own pages to publish content and connect with private users, e.g. via subscriptions or likes. Facebook funds its social network through online advertising offered to publishers and other businesses. The ads match a social network user's individual profile. The aim is to present users with ads that are potentially interesting to them based on their personal commercial behaviour, their interests, purchasing power and living conditions ("targeting" or "targeted advertising").

In addition, the Facebook group offers "Facebook Business Tools", a selection of free tools and products for website operators, developers, advertisers and other businesses to integrate into their own websites, apps and online offers via programming interfaces (Application Programming Interfaces, API) pre-defined by Facebook. The selection includes social plugins ("Like" or "Share" buttons), Facebook login and other analytics services (Facebook Analytics) implemented through "Facebook Pixel" or mobile "software development kits" (SDKs).

Besides Facebook.com, Facebook also offers *Instagram*, a service for sharing photos and short video clips which is often referred to as a "photo network" or "photo blogging" service. The service has been growing considerably over the last few years and is also funded through advertising. Private users have to register via the mobile app. To register, they have to enter an email address, a user name and, as an optional piece of information, a phone number. They can also upload a profile picture. They can use the Instagram camera to take pictures or record videos and edit them using filters, texts, drawings or special effects before sharing them with other users.

WhatsApp Inc. is also part of the Facebook group. In Europe it offers the mobile app *WhatsApp* via its Irish subsidiary WhatsApp Ltd. WhatsApp is a free service which was originally developed as a free internet-based alternative to short message services (SMS). Using the service, users can send and receive a multitude of media like text messages, photos, videos, documents, locations, voice messages and voice calls. While WhatsApp has not been monetised through advertising so far, the company announced that it was going to launch advertising in the "status" function in 2019.

Masquerade is another product used for editing and sharing pictures with filters and masks. Facebook also offers virtual reality headsets and software via its *Oculus* business.

Using the social network Facebook.com is conditional on the user's agreement to Facebook's terms of service upon registration, i.e. they have to agree to the terms of service to conclude the contract. The terms of service stipulate that Facebook processes personal data as specified in particular in the data and cookie policies. Pursuant to these policies, Facebook also collects data on users and their devices outside of Facebook-related activities via Facebook Business Tools integrated by advertisers, app developers and publishers. Facebook also processes user data across other Facebook companies and products and collects user and device-related data from its corporate services. As a legal basis for data processing, Facebook claims that the data are required to provide the service and to fulfil Facebook's legitimate interests.

2. Legal assessment 1. Market definition

Based on the concept of demand-side substitutability, the Bundeskartellamt defines the product market as a private social network market with private users as the relevant opposite market side.

The relevant geographic market is Germany.

In defining the market and considering the new provisions of Section 18(2a) and (3a) of the German Competition Act (GWB), the Bundeskartellamt first of all examined Facebook's business model and its special characteristics as a multi-sided network market with free services. With its service Facebook.com Facebook offers an intermediary product, which, according to the content of its services, is a combination of a network and a multi-sided market pursuant to Section 18(3a) GWB. Essentially the product is a network financed through targeted advertising, which forms a multi-sided market precisely because of this form of financing. Key user groups are private users using Facebook.com without monetary compensation on the one hand, and advertisers running targeted advertisements on the other. Indirect network effects exist between the two user groups. Facebook added further market sides to its core product. One of these market sides is publishers using Facebook.com to promote their businesses with their own Facebook pages on which they publish editorial content and connect with users. Developers represent another side of the market. They can integrate Facebook into their own websites or apps by using "Application Programming Interfaces" (APIs) to integrate Facebook Products like social plugins (e.g. "Like" button), Facebook Login or the Facebook Analytics analysis service. Indirect network effects also exist between private users and the latter two sides:

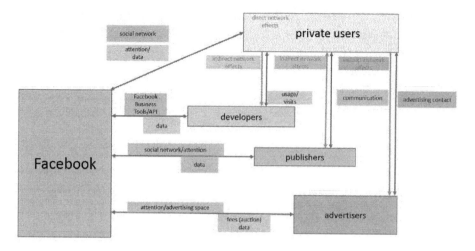

As none of the above groups of Facebook users have demands similar to the group of private users, they have to be attributed to other markets. The network has to be considered a market service pursuant to Section 18(2a) GWB despite the fact that its use is not subject to fees for private users.

The product market definition also requires an analysis of the various online services commonly referred to as "social media" and their competitive relationships. Key criteria for defining the market are the high degree of product differentiation of social media and the various overlaps of their functionalities. When defining the market, strong direct network effects are also important. The Bundeskartellamt's investigations, which included an examination of a large number of social media as well as a survey among users and competitors, and decisions by the European Commission in the *Facebook/WhatsApp* and *Microsoft/LinkedIn* cases have shown that a national market exists for social networks which essentially meet specific requirements that differ from other social media. With Google+ having disappeared from the market, this market now includes, besides Facebook, some smaller German providers of social networks. Networks like LinkedIn and Xing are designed to meet professional requirements and thus constitute a separate product market. Like the Commission in the *Facebook/WhatsApp* case, the Bundeskartellamt considers messaging services like *WhatsApp* as a separate market due to their technical characteristics and applications. The investigations have shown that although YouTube's business model has some overlaps with those of social networks, the service is not sufficiently comparable to a social network. Snapchat, whose central function is a camera that opens automatically for taking "snaps" that are deleted after a short while, is not part of the product market either. The same applies to Twitter, Pinterest and Instagram. The latter is part of the Facebook group. When defining the market the Bundeskartellamt also looks at the extent to which internet companies shaped by network effects can show flexibility in adapting the products they offer. At least as far as the services affected in this case are concerned, it is not sufficient to have a "critical mass" of users or technical, financial and personal expertise in order to be able to enter neighbouring markets and be as successful as on the original market. As the example of Google+ has shown, a service cannot expect to have the same reach when providing a different type of service, due to strong direct network effects.

The geographic market was defined as Germany-wide as a result of the investigations, based on the fact that the service was found to be used predominantly to connect with people in the users' own country, special national user habits and the lack of opportunities for supply-side substitution.

2. Market dominance

Facebook is the dominant company in the national market for social networks for private users pursuant to Section 18(1) in conjunction with (3) and (3a) GWB as, based on an overall assessment of all factors of market power, the company has a scope of action in this market that is not sufficiently controlled by competition.

First the Bundeskartellamt examined the user-based market share of Facebook on the relevant market. Facebook's user-based market share is very high, especially among daily active users, where Facebook has a market share exceeding 95%. Facebook's market share among monthly active users is above 80% and above 50% among registered users. The Bundeskartellamt considers the number of daily active users as the key indicator and relevant measurand [*sic*] for assessing the network's competitive significance and market success as a social network's success is measured by the intensity of use. Users use social networks as a virtual social space. When assessing the market share, the amount of time spent intensively using the network is an important indicator of the competitors' actual market position. The services of the Facebook group would have a combined market share far beyond the market dominance threshold pursuant to Section 18(4) GWB, even if YouTube, Snapchat, Twitter, WhatsApp, and Instagram were included in the relevant market.

A key element of the market dominance test are the strong direct network effects of Facebook's business model and the difficulties associated with switching to another social network. Facebook users connect with selected people in the social network, and it is difficult to motivate them to switch to another service as well. Competitors in the area of social networks have been experiencing a continuous decrease in user-based market shares in recent years; some of them have already left the market. Examples include StudiVZ and SchülerVZ, services which were temporarily operated by the Holtzbrinck publishing group and which were market leaders before Facebook entered the German market. Their operating company went into insolvency in 2017. The Lokalisten network, which was operated by ProSiebenSat.1, was discontinued in the autumn of 2016. Google+, the social network operated by the Google group, announced in the spring of 2018 that it would discontinue its service for private users and offer a payable service for internal business communications. In contrast to its competitors, Facebook's user figures keep rising or at least stagnate at a high level. The facts that competitors can be seen to exit the market and that there is a downward trend in the user-based market shares of the remaining competitors strongly indicate a market tipping process which will result in Facebook.com becoming a monopolist. This assessment is supported by the fact that the strong identity-based network effects lead to a lock-in effect which makes it difficult for users or prevents them from switching to another social network. Existing functionalities and interfaces do not alleviate the consequences of Facebook's incompatibility with other social networks.

Another important aspect of the examination are the indirect network effects encountered with Facebook as an advertising-funded service, which increase the barriers to market entry. Other advertising-financed platforms will find it difficult to enter the market and be successful in the long-term as all competitors would have to enter both the user market for social networks and the online advertising market.

Facebook also has excellent access to competitively relevant data. Facebook's comprehensive data sources are highly relevant for competition as a social network is driven by such personal data. In addition, these specific data facilitate highly personalised advertising. Combined with the direct and indirect network effects, this access to data constitutes another barrier to market entry for a competitor's product that can be monetised.

In its overall assessment, the Bundeskartellamt took a close look at the internet's innovative power and its significance for assessing market power. The internet's innovative power cannot be taken as a general argument against an internet company's market power. Instead, specific indications of a dynamic or disruptive process are required in each individual case. This applies in particular to the control of abuse of dominant positions which focuses on the current market situation. Against this background the Bundeskartellamt examined the recent innovations which Facebook referred to. The authority's opinion is that these developments do not go beyond responses to competition from substitutes in the case of some individual functionalities. In particular in the context of pronounced direct network effects, its responses have rather shown that Facebook has been capable of successfully fighting off competitors' innovations. As a result, there is no trend towards users withdrawing from Facebook or Facebook losing market shares to a relevant extent despite the internet's high innovative power.

3. Abusive data policy

Using and actually implementing Facebook's data policy, which allows Facebook to collect user and device-related data from sources outside of Facebook and to merge it with data collected on Facebook, constitutes an abuse of a dominant position on the social network market in the form of exploitative business terms pursuant to the general clause of Section 19(1) GWB. Taking into account the assessments under data protection law pursuant to the General Data Protection Regulation (GDPR), these are inappropriate terms to the detriment of both private users and competitors.

a) Data protection and competition law

The Bundeskartellamt holds that, being a manifestation of market power, the terms violate the stipulations of the GDPR and are abusive within the meaning of Section 19(1) GWB.

The authority bases its assessment on the case-law of the German Federal Court of Justice, which established an abuse of business terms in the *VBL-Gegenwert* and *Pechstein* cases based on the general clause of Section 19(1) GWB. In its decisions taken in the *VBL-Gegenwert* cases the Federal Court of Justice considers the agreement of contract terms abusive if terms and conditions violating Sections 307ff. of the German Civil Code are applied, in particular if the fact that such terms and conditions are applied is a manifestation of market power or superior power of the party using these terms. The Federal Court of Justice held that it was necessary to balance all interests including constitutional rights in the *Pechstein* case. Accordingly, to protect constitutional rights, Section 19 GWB must be applied in cases where one contractual party is so powerful that it is practically able to dictate the terms of the contract and the contractual autonomy of the other party is abolished. If, the Court held, in such a case a dominant company handles constitutional rights of its contractual partners, the law had to intervene to uphold the protection of such rights. Relevant legal provisions in this regard were, according to the Court, the general clauses under civil law, one of which is Section 19 GWB. The Court held that these clauses should be applied with a view to balancing the conflicting positions of the contractual parties in such a way that the constitutional rights of all parties were, as far as possible, maintained.

The Bundeskartellamt holds that as far as the appropriateness of conditions agreed in an unbalanced negotiation is concerned, these decisions of the highest court apply to all other areas of the law as well. The same applies to data protection law, the purpose of which is to counter asymmetries of power between organisations and individuals and ensure an appropriate balancing of interests between data controllers and data subjects. In order to protect the fundamental right to informational self-determination, data protection law provides the individual with the right to decide freely and without coercion on the processing of his or her personal data.

The Bundeskartellamt closely examined the relation between the competition law provisions under Section 19(1) GWB and the harmonised European data protection principles of the GDPR which are mainly enforced by data protection authorities. The authority holds that it appears to be indispensable to examine the conduct of dominant companies under competition law also in terms of their data processing procedures, as especially the conduct of online businesses is highly relevant from a competition law perspective. It is the authority's view that the European data protection regulations, which are based on constitutional rights, can or, considering the case-law of the highest German court specified above, must be considered when assessing whether data processing terms are appropriate under competition law.

The responsibility and consistency regulations in the GDPR do not rule out that the Bundeskartellamt can assess whether data processing terms infringe the GDPR. The GDPR has been in force in the Member States since May 2018. It governs the responsibility of data protection authorities and is set out to ensure a uniform level of protection and application by the national data protection authorities. For this purpose a data protection board has been set up by the Member States to decide on data protection matters in the event of disputes. The board can also instruct the national authorities accordingly. These regulations, however, do not rule out that substantive data protection law can also be applied by authorities other than the national data protection authorities. The GDPR explicitly states that data protection law can also be enforced under civil law, i.e. full consistency is not aspired to. This applies in particular to consumer protection organisations and competitors and their associations. These entities can enforce data protection based on stipulations of the Act Against Unfair Competition (UWG) or regulations on business terms linked to data protection and also based on Section 19 GWB. A large part of the ECJ's case law which data protection authorities and the data protection board have to consider has been obtained from civil law proceedings. Civil law proceedings promote rather than threaten the consistent implementation of data protection law, especially as the ECJ can be involved at an early stage as part of the preliminary ruling procedure. It is not evident that the consistency mechanism would rule out that the competition authority considers and interprets data protection law under Section 19 GWB and, at the same time, would allow a civil law enforcement of Section 19 GWB with regard to data protection law.

Also, data protection regulations do not suspend abuse control which is more specific. These regulations do not include final provisions regarding dominant companies, i.e. they only allow data processing by dominant companies to be examined by data protection authorities based on the direct data protection regulations, or the existing enforcement options under civil law (UWG or legislation on business terms). However, they do not include the prohibition of abusive practices which applies in particular to dominant companies. The GDPR does not explicitly state that its provisions are final, so it cannot be assumed that it leaves no further scope for examination by other authorities and under other aspects.

In the course of the proceeding the Bundeskartellamt maintained regular contact with data protection authorities none of which considered they had exclusive competence. The Conference of independent data protection authorities of the German Federal Government and the Länder (Konferenz der unabhängigen Datenschutzbehörden des Bundes und der Länder) expressly stated that the enforcement of data protection law must not be the sole response to violations of data protection requirements. Competition and antitrust law can, according to the conference, also be enforced. Even divestiture is mentioned as an option to punish the systematic circumvention of data protection. The Data Protection Officer for the city state of Hamburg explicitly supports the Bundeskartellamt's proceeding. The Bundeskartellamt also briefed the Irish data protection authority IDPC about the proceedings.

b) Consideration of data protection aspects

In a first step, the Bundeskartellamt examined whether the data policy is appropriate based on the data protection assessments of the GDPR. It came to the conclusion that Facebook's comprehensive processing of personal data from other corporate services and Facebook Business Tools, which enable, among other things, profiling and "device fingerprinting", violates European data protection requirements pursuant to the GDPR and is subject to the affected users' consent pursuant to data protection requirements. Facebook, which is responsible for the processing of these data, presented or substantiated hardly any justifications in the course of the proceeding. The determined facts of the case do not indicate a sufficient legal justification for the extent of data collected and merged.

There is no effective consent pursuant to Art. 6(1a) of the GDPR. The reasons for this include the fact that, in view of Facebook's dominant position in the market, users consent to Facebook's terms and conditions for the sole purpose of concluding the contract, which cannot be assessed as their free consent within the meaning of the GDPR.

Facebook does not have to process data to fulfil its contract pursuant to Art. 6(1b) GDPR. This reason for justification has to be narrowly interpreted, i.e. it has to be considered whether the unilateral determination of the contract details has to be taken into account. Particularly, it cannot be substantiated that the service has to process data to the extent that has been determined in the course of the examination for reasons of efficiency and advantages of a personalised service. If this view is taken, the company would be entitled to unlimited data processing solely on the grounds of its business model and product properties as well as the company's concept of product quality. Any kind of data processing would then have to be deemed necessary for fulfilling the contract as all data carry some information on the individual user. Processing data from third-party sources to the extent determined by Facebook in its terms and conditions is neither required for offering the social network as such nor for monetising the network through personalised advertising, as a personalised network could also be based to a large extent on the user data processed in the context of operating the social network. The latter is not a subject of the proceeding at hand. None of the stipulations of Art. 6(1c-e) GDPR apply to justify data processing for special purposes.

Even a comprehensive assessment of interests did ultimately not lead to the conclusion that Facebook's interest in processing data according to the terms and conditions it set outweighs other interests (Art. 6(1f) GDPR). This assessment is based on an evaluation of the legitimate interests Facebook brought forward, third-party interests and user interests. Criteria considered were the consequences for the affected users, taking into account the data type and the way in which it is processed, reasonable expectations of users and the respective positions of Facebook and its users. What also had to be considered pursuant to the guidelines of the data protection board was that Facebook as a dominant company has bargaining power over its users and is in a position to impose far-reaching data processing conditions, which users cannot prevent as they have no additional control mechanisms. Data processing to the extent at hand cannot be justified without the users' voluntary consent. Voluntary consent to their information being processed cannot be assumed if their consent is a prerequisite for using the Facebook.com service in the first place.

c) Manifestation of market power

The violation of data protection requirements found is a manifestation of Facebook's market power. According to the case-law it is not necessary to determine that the conduct, i.e. the violation, was only possible in the first place because of market dominance and that other market participants did not have a chance to behave in a similar way. Instead, it is sufficient to determine that the two aspects are linked by a causality which is either based on normative aspects or the outcome. Both aspects can be assumed to be fulfilled in this case.

Normative causality with regard to the violation of data protection rules exists as the restriction of the private users' right to self-determination is clearly linked to Facebook's dominant position. Data protection law considers corporate circumstances like market dominance, the concrete purpose and the amount of data processed in its justifications, i.e. Facebook's market position is significant when assessing the violation.

In addition to that there is a causality in terms of the outcome as Facebook's conduct linked to its market dominance, which was the subject of the proceedings at hand, impedes competitors because Facebook gains access to a large number of further sources by its inappropriate processing of data and their combination with Facebook accounts. It has thus gained a competitive edge over its competitors in an unlawful way and increased market entry barriers, which in turn secures Facebook's market power towards end customers.

Both data protection law and competition law consider the aspect of an unbalanced negotiation position, i.e. a weighing up of interests under competition law which could be required in addition to the examination under data protection law, and reach the same conclusions due to the largely identical considerations including market dominance. In addition, pursuant to the *Pechstein* caselaw, assessments with regard to constitutional rights have to be included in assessments of interests under competition law. Again, these assessments are largely identical with the assessments under data protection law.

As Facebook is a dominant company users cannot protect their data from being processed from a large number of sources, i.e. they cannot decide autonomously on the disclosure of their data. However, it must be ensured that the interests of the opposite market side are sufficiently considered if a provider is a dominant company which is not subject to sufficient competitive control. The terms and conditions under review have a considerable reach as Facebook's market power extends beyond its social network and consumers' data are collected whenever they use the internet. While the efficiencies of a data-driven business model for consumers are generally acknowledged, the outlined extent of data processing is to be deemed inappropriate and hence abusive.

4. Decision

Based on the above and in exercising due discretion, the Bundeskartellamt has prohibited the data processing policy Facebook imposes on its users and its corresponding implementation pursuant to Sections 19(1), 32 GWB and ordered the termination of this conduct. The prohibition refers to the terms of processing personal data as expressly stated in the terms of service and detailed in the data and cookie policies as far as they involve the collection of user and device-related data from other corporate services and Facebook Business Tools without the users' consent and their combination with Facebook data for purposes related to the social network. The Bundeskartellamt also prohibited the implementation of these terms and conditions in actual data processing procedures which Facebook performs based on its data and cookie policies. In the order to terminate the infringement Facebook is ordered to implement the necessary changes and to adapt its data and cookie policies accordingly within a period of twelve months. In addition to that Facebook has been given a deadline of four months to present an implementation road map for the adjustments. The time limits can be suspended by an emergency appeal to the Düsseldorf Higher Regional Court. Facebook has already appealed against this decision to the Düsseldorf Higher Regional Court and requested that the suspensive effect of the appeal be restored.

Notes

1.   The Bundeskartellamt's decision was suspended on appeal, with the court questioning the legal basis for making a data-protection violation a competition one. *See* https://www.d-kart.de/wp-content/uploads/2019/08/OLG-D%C3%BCsseldorf-Facebook-2019-English.pdf. The Bundeskartellamt has announced that it will appeal that suspension and seek to reinstate the effect of its decision. *See* https://www.reuters.com/article/us-facebook-germany/german-cartel-office-to-take-facebook-case-to-high-court-idUSKCN1VG1AJ.

2.   What does it mean to say that Facebook's terms were "a manifestation of market power"? If the terms are "a manifestation of market power," does that mean that this case concerns (only?) an exploitative abuse? In the discussion of single-firm conduct, consider whether exclusionary conduct is always a manifestation of power. Might a non-monopolist invest in exclusion in order to become a monopolist? Note that in the U.S. monopolization includes the "willful acquisition" of monopoly power while in Europe the offense is the abuse of (existing) dominance.

3.   Could an exploitative abuse also be an exclusionary one? Is that what the agency is indicating in saying that Facebook "has thus gained a competitive edge over its competitors in an unlawful way and increased market entry barriers, which in turn secures Facebook's market power towards end customers." Or is the exploitation of consumers the opposite of exclusionary, because it would likely make it easier for new entrants to offer better, more attractive products?

4.   What market entry barriers were increased by Facebook? Is the agency saying that those barriers were higher after the conduct than before, or that the conduct itself was a "manifestation" of barriers in that it was conduct that its competitors could not match? Is this a decision about economies of scope?

5.   Should exploitative privacy terms be treated differently from exploitative pricing terms? High prices are presumably always exploitative; is that true also for a firm's use of terms that allow it to combine personal data from a variety of sources as a condition on access to one of those sources? What evidence does the decision offer that the terms were exploitative?

6.   Should issues related to consent be issues of competition law? Is receiving consent, or not asking for it, or asking for it vaguely, "a manifestation of market power"? A manifestation of bargaining power? Are market power and bargaining power the same? If not, is bargaining power an issue for competition law?

2.2.   Exclusion

2.2.1. In General

Order (1) Granting Defendant's Motion to Dismiss with Leave to Amend, and (2) Deferring Consideration of Defendant's Special Motion to Strike
Kinderstart.com LLC v. Google, Inc.
No. C 06-2057 JF (RS) (N.D. Cal. Mar. 17, 2006)

FOGEL, J.

Defendant Google, Inc. ("Google") moves to dismiss the First Amended Complaint ("FAC") of Plaintiff Kinderstart.com LLC ("Kinderstart") pursuant to Rule 12(b)(1) and Rule 12(b)(6) of the Federal Rules of Civil Procedure. . . .

. . .

I. BACKGROUND

. . . On April 12, 2006, Kinderstart filed the operative FAC, alleging nine claims for relief: (1) Violation of Right to Free Speech under the U.S. Constitution and the California Constitution, (2) Attempted Monopolization under Section 2 of the Sherman Act, (3) Monopolization under Section 2 of the Sherman Act, (4) Violations of the Communications Act, 47 U.S.C. §§ 201, et seq., (5) Unfair Competition under California Business and Professional Code §§ 17200, et seq., (6) Price Discrimination under California Business and Professional Code § 17045, (7) Breach of the Implied Covenant of Good Faith and Fair Dealing, (8) Defamation and Libel, and (9) Negligent Interference with Prospective Economic Advantage.

Kinderstart alleges the following facts. Kinderstart operates a website, www.kinderstart.com, which is a directory and search engine for links to information and resources on subjects related to young children. At one point, Kinderstart was "one of the choicest Internet destinations for thousands of parents, caregivers, educators, nonprofit and advocacy representatives, and federal, state and local organizations and officials in the United States and worldwide to access vital information about infants and toddlers." It launched in May 2000 and at its peak was "presenting in excess of 10,000 page views to visitors on a monthly basis."

Google is the world's most widely used search engine. Google "actively invites to 'anyone with an Internet connection' worldwide to perform searches for Websites and Webpages" and presents results of its searches on a "Search Engine Results Page" or "Results Page." According to the FAC, Google "induces users, the public, and the cyberspace community at large to expect and believe that Results Pages generated from a search every single time will be objective and neutral, untrammeled by human intervention or preference and free of any arbitrariness." Google states on its "Technology Overview" page: "'There is no human involvement or manipulation of results, which is why users have come to trust Google as a source of objective information untainted by paid placement.'" . . .

Google also "has ownership and control over a computer process known as 'PageRank™', an automated, computer algorithm that generates a score as a whole number up to '10'. PageRank reflects the extent and nature of hyperlinking within the Internet to a particular Website and its web pages." Google explains: " 'Wondering whether a new website is worth your time? Use the Toolbar's format PageRank™ display to tell you how Google's algorithms assess the importance of the page you're viewing.' ' Kinderstart alleges that "PageRank is not a mere statement of opinion of the innate value or human appeal of a given Website and its web pages," but instead is "a mathematically-generated product of measuring and assessing the quantity and depth of all the hyperlinks on the Web that tie into PageRanked Website, under programmatic determination by Defendant Google." "On information and belief, PageRank as promulgated and propagated by Defendant Google throughout the Internet, has become the most widely accepted relative measure of the appeal, popularity and relevance of a Website on the Internet. As such, Defendant Google has created and now manages and controls the de facto and prevailing standard of PageRank for rating Websites throughout the United States."

. . .

According to Kinderstart, Google "does in fact monitor, manipulate and censor the output and content on Results Pages, whether programmatically through a computer or individually through the intervention and discretion of one or more human decision-makers under the employ, direction, supervision and/or oversight of Defendant Google." Google engages in the practice of "Blockage" of websites by "delisting, de-indexing and censoring" websites, including the unacknowledged practice of isolating a website from search queries, either permanently or for an unspecified probationary period. Blockage also includes "penalization," by which a site's PageRank is reduced or set to zero "presumably based on either stated or unstated 'quality guidelines.' ' Websites may experience "Blockage" at any time and may be unable to receive an explanation from Google as to why it occurred. Kinderstart alleges that although Google denies engaging in "Blockage," it has admitted engaging in the "euphemistically" named practices of " 'search quality improvement' or anti-Webspamming." Kinderstart alleges that the practice of "Blockage" is positively correlated with "the failure and/or the reduction in AdWords advertising."

In 2003, Kinderstart enrolled in Google's AdSense Program and paid for a series of sponsored links from Google. In or about August 2003, Kinderstart began placing advertisements from the Google Network onto its site and receiving payments from Google for these placements. On March 19, 2005, Kinderstart's website "suffered a cataclysmic fall of 70% or more in its monthly page views and traffic." Kinderstart eventually "realized that common key word searches on Defendant Google's search engine no longer listed KSC.com as a result with any of its past visibility." With this drop in search engine referrals, Kinderstart's "monthly AdSense revenue suffered an equally precipitous fall by over 80%." Kinderstart concludes that its website "was officially, practically and illegally Blocked by Defendant Google." Its website has been assigned a PageRank of "0" by the Google Toolbar. Kinderstart was not notified in advance that this would occur and has not been instructed as to how it can cause Google to cease the "Blockage." Kinderstart is not aware of any way in which it has violated Google's guidelines.

. . .

III. DISCUSSION

. . .

2. Attempted Monopolization Under Section 2 of the Sherman Act

Kinderstart next alleges a claim for attempted monopolization under Section 2 of the Sherman Act, 15 U.S.C. § 2, the elements of which are: (1) specific intent to control prices or destroy competition, (2) predatory or anticompetitive conduct directed toward accomplishing that purpose, (3) a dangerous probability of success and (4) causal antitrust injury. . . .

...

3. Monopolization under Section 2 of the Sherman Act

Kinderstart also asserts a claim for monopolization under Section 2 of the Sherman Act, 15 U.S.C. § 2, the elements of which are: (1) possession of monopoly power in the relevant market, (2) willful acquisition or maintenance of that power, and (3) causal antitrust injury. As with attempted monopolization, a plaintiff claiming monopolization must first define the relevant market. Kinderstart alleges monopolization of three markets: the Website Ranking Market, the Search Ad Market, and the Search Engine Market.

First, Kinderstart alleges that Google maintains monopoly power in the Website Ranking Market by "assign[ing] PageRanks of various commercial Websites and competitive Websites to induce certain behaviors or to penalize certain behaviors of such sites, all to Google's ill-conceived gain and advantage." In its present form, this allegation is too vague to state a claim under the Sherman Act. Kinderstart does not allege what behaviors are induced or discouraged, or how they affect the market.

Second, Kinderstart alleges that Google maintains monopoly power in the Search Ad Market by pressuring websites to purchase advertising in order to avoid decreased PageRank scores, and removal from Results Pages. However, because Kinderstart provides no specifics as to how Google creates this pressure, this allegation also is insufficient to state a claim under the Sherman Act.

Finally, Kinderstart alleges that Google maintains monopoly power in the Search Engine Market through false representations that its search engine Results Pages are automated and objective, when in fact they are subject to human intervention and subjective. Kinderstart argues that Google is an "essential facility" within the market, and that by manipulating its Results Pages, Google excludes competitors from this facility. Kinderstart concludes that Google is an "essential facility or essential medium" because "the indexing, linking and referrals to such content afforded by Kinderstart over the Internet are essential to the operations, Web traffic, commerce, communications, and expression of speech by Class members." However, the threshold for finding a facility "essential" in the Ninth Circuit is high: "A facility that is controlled by a single firm will be considered 'essential' only if control of the facility carries with it the power to eliminate competition in the downstream market." *Alaska Airlines, Inc. v. United Airlines, Inc.*, 948 F.2d 536, 544 (9th Cir.1991); *see also, Olympia Equipment Leasing v. Western Union Telephone Co.*, 797 F.2d 370 (7th Cir.1986) (finding no Sherman act violation where defendant obstructed plaintiff's sales efforts but did not eliminate the potential for competition).

While Kinderstart alleges that its Web traffic dropped 70%, and its ad revenue dropped 80%, it does not allege that it or similarly situated class members face elimination as a result of Google's conduct. Instead it alleges that "in spite of Defendant Google's wrongful conduct as alleged above, [Kinderstart] maintains extensive Website Content and links within its directory and index that are fully and remain actively hyperlinked throughout the Internet, and continues to generate sustainable level of traffic and PageViews from visitors." Additionally, Kinderstart alleges that class members "consistently receive significantly and relatively high rankings and referrals from other search engines such as MSN and Yahoo." Accordingly, Kinderstart has not alleged adequately that Google, or its search engine, is an "essential facility" within the Search Engine Market.

[handwritten: ANALOGY REQUIRES FACT-INTENSIVE ANALYSIS]

[handwritten margin: market]

Kinderstart argues that by refusing to remedy the alleged "Blockage" of Kinderstart's website, Google has violated Section 2 under the "refusal to deal" doctrine as set forth in *Aspen Skiing Co. v. Aspen Highlands Skiing Corp.*, 472 U.S. 585 (1985). In *Aspen*, the larger of two ski resorts with a long-standing, bilateral, cooperative and profitable arrangement to market joint ski passes later refused to deal with the smaller resort-not even allowing it to buy tickets at listed retail prices. However, as the Supreme Court has noted, "*Aspen* is at or near the outer boundary of § 2 liability." *Verizon Communications Inc. v. Law Offices of Curtis V. Trinko, LLP*, 540 U.S. 398, 399 (2004). Moreover, the facts alleged by Kinderstart are distinguishable from those in *Aspen*. Kinderstart has alleged neither that Google sold PageRanks or Results Page listings to Kinderstart or others nor that Google refused to sell these at listed prices. In fact, Kinderstart itself notes that Google denies ever selling PageRanks or listings at all. Additionally, there is no allegation that the only written agreement between the parties, the AdSense agreement, is no longer in place. *[handwritten: *but still making money from it]*

[handwritten margin: distinguishes from Aspen]

Accordingly, Kinderstart's monopolization claims under the Sherman Act will be dismissed with leave to amend. In light of this disposition, the Court need not reach Google's argument that Kinderstart's claims are precluded by the holding of *Official Airlines Guides, Inc. v. FTC*, 630 F.2d 920,[5] or because the conduct in question is protected expression.[6]

---

[5] See *Official Airline Guides, Inc. v. F.T. C.*, 630 F.2d 920 (2d Cir.1980) (upholding right of monopolist publisher of airline guides to discriminate without justification between large air carriers and commuter airlines in production of flight guide). However, in that case, the monopolist (as a publisher, rather than an airline) was not alleged to be in direct competition with the parties harmed by the conduct. Id. In the instant case, Kinderstart has alleged that it directly competes with Google in the Search Ad Market and the Search Engine Market.

[6] See *Jefferson County School Dist. No. R-1 v. Moody's Investor's Services, Inc.*, 175 F.3d 848 (10th Cir.1999). In Jefferson, a financial services company's published article stating a "negative outlook" for school district bonds was found to be protected expression. Id. Jefferson followed the Supreme Court's holding in Milkovich v. Lorain Journal Co., 497 U.S. 1 (1990) that, regarding media defendants, "a statement of opinion relating to matters of public concern which does not contain a provably false factual connotation will receive full constitutional protection." Id. at 20. Without deciding the merits of Google's argument,

[handwritten margin: 1st Amendment: expressed opinion]

. . .

8. Defamation and Libel

Kinderstart alleges claims for defamation and libel against Google based on Google's public presentation of a PageRank of '0' for Kinderstart.com. "The tort of defamation exists whenever a false and unprivileged statement which has a natural tendency to injure or which causes special damage is communicated to one or more persons who understand its defamatory meaning and its application to the injured party." To prevail on these claims, Kinderstart must allege a provably false statement.

Google argues that a PageRank is an opinion and not a factual statement. Google also contends that even if PageRank is entirely generated by an algorithm, the weights assigned to variables in programming the algorithm reflect Google's subjective opinion about the relative importance of websites such that PageRank cannot be anything but subjective. Both parties point to Google's statement promoting PageRank: "Wondering whether a new website is worth your time? Use the Toolbar's PageRank™ display to tell you how Google's algorithms assess the importance of the page you're viewing ."

As the parties' arguments suggest, whether Kinderstart can maintain a claim for defamation may turn on facts outside the pleadings. Google's statement as to whether a particular website is "worth your time" necessarily reflects its subjective judgment as to what factors make a website important. Viewed in this way, a PageRank reflects Google's opinion. However, it is possible a PageRank reasonably could be interpreted as a factual statement insofar as it purports to tell a user "how Google's algorithms assess the importance of the page you're viewing." This interpretation would be bolstered by evidence supporting Google's alleged representations that PageRank is "objective," and that a reasonable person thus might understand Google's display of a '0' PageRank for Kinderstart.com to be a statement that '0' is the (unmodified) output of Google's algorithm. If it could be shown, as Kinderstart alleges, that Google is changing that output by manual intervention, then such a statement might be provably false.

However, Kinderstart's complaint as presently framed does not explain how it is a false statement about the output of Google's algorithm regarding Kinderstart.com, as distinguished from an unfavorable opinion about Kinderstart.com's importance, that has caused injury to Kinderstart. Rather, Kinderstart makes only the conclusory assertion that Google's actions have "cause[d] irreparable harm and damage to the goodwill, value and revenue-generating capabilities of Kinderstart KSC's Website. . . ."

Accordingly, this claim will be dismissed with leave granted to amend.

---

the Court notes that Jefferson County may be distinguishable because (a) Google is not a media defendant and (b) website ranking may be of little or no public concern in comparison with municipal bond ratings.

. . .

Notes

1.   The leave to amend was to no avail. *See* Order Granting Motion to Dismiss Without Leave to Amend, Denying Special Motion Pursuant to Cal. Civ. Code § 425.16, and Denying Motion to Strike as Moot, Kinderstart.com LLC v. Google, Inc., No. C 06-2057 JF (RS) (N.D. Cal. Mar. 16, 2007).

2.   Is there really a "Website Ranking Market"? If so, who are the consumers in that market?

3.   Does it really sufficiently distinguish *Aspen Skiing* that Kinderstart "alleged neither that Google sold PageRanks or Results Page listings to Kinderstart or others nor that Google refused to sell these at listed prices"? If the claim is that Google distorted its ranking and search results, should it be sufficient to allege that it previously voluntarily and profitably had produced undistorted rankings and search results? That is, are sales the key, or is it that the monopolist had changed or avoided a profitable practice?

4.   The "opinion"/First Amendment argument is a controversial one. *Cf.* Hillary Greene, Muzzling Antitrust: Information Products, Innovation and Free Speech, 95 B.U. L. Rev. 35 (2015) *with* Eugene Volokh & Donald Falk, First Amendment Protection for Search Engine Search Results — White Paper Commissioned by Google, https://papers.ssrn.com/sol3/papers.cfm?abstract_id=2055364.

5.   In other cases as well as this one, claims have been based not on the information product at issue but on representations *about* that product. *See* Press Release, Italian Competition Authority, PS9345 - Half a million fine against Tripadvisor, December 22, 2104, https://en.agcm.it/en/media/detail?id=8492707e-c663-4cbd-9baf-2bfadf5c1d8c (fining TripAdvisor not for disseminating false reviews or reviews from improper sources but for "dissemination of misleading information about the sources of reviews"). Why might an enforcement authority or private party take that approach?

EC v. GOOGLE

European Commission — EXECUTIVE BRANCH LAW ENFORCER
Google Search (Shopping)
June 27, 2017

1.   INTRODUCTION

(1) This Decision is addressed to Google Inc. ("Google") and to Alphabet Inc. ("Alphabet").

(2) The Decision establishes that the more favourable positioning and display by Google, in its general search results pages, of its own comparison shopping service compared to competing comparison shopping services (the "Conduct") infringes Article 102 of the Treaty and Article 54 of the Agreement on the European Economic Area ("EEA Agreement").

. . .

2. GOOGLE'S BUSINESS ACTIVITIES

. . .

2.2. Overview of Google's business activities

(7) Google's business model is based on the interaction between the online products and services it offers free of charge and its online advertising services from which it generates the main source of its revenue.

2.2.1.   Google Search

(8) Google's flagship online service is its general search[7] engine, Google Search, which is accessible either through Google's main website in the US (www.google.com), or through localised websites. Google also powers the search functions of certain third party websites.

. . .

(10)   When a user enters a keyword or a string of keywords (a "query") in Google Search, Google's general search results pages return different categories of search results, including generic search results[8] (as described in section 2.2.2) and specialised search results[9] (as described in section 2.2.4). In addition, Google Search may return a third category of results, namely online search advertisements (as described in section 2.2.3).

(11)   When a user enters a query, Google's programmes essentially run two sets of algorithms: generic search algorithms and specialised search algorithms.

(12)   Google's generic search algorithms are designed to rank pages containing any possible content. Google applies these algorithms to all types of pages, including the web pages of competing specialised search services. By contrast, specialised search algorithms *are specifically optimized for*

---

[7] "General search" is also known as "online search" or "horizontal search". The term "general search" is used throughout this Decision.

[8] "Generic search results" are also known as "organic search results" or "natural search results". The term "generic search results" is used throughout this Decision.

[9] "Specialised search" is also referred to as "vertical search" or "universal search". The terms "specialised search" and "specialised search results" are used throughout this Decision.

identifying relevant results for a particular type of information", such as news, local businesses or product information.

(13)   The results of these two sets of algorithms – the generic search results and the specialised search results – appear together on Google's general search results pages.

2.2.2.   *Generic search results*

(14)   Generic search results typically appear on the left side of Google's general search results pages in the form of blue links with short excerpts ("*snippets*") in order of their "*web rank*". Generic search results can link to any page on the internet, including web pages of specialised search services competing with Google's specialised search services.

(15)   The delivery of generic search results involves three automated processes: crawling, indexing and serving. Crawling is the process by which Google discovers new and updated web pages. Indexing is the process by which web pages and their content are catalogued and added to the Google index. Serving is the process by which, when a user enters a query, Google's programmes check the index for web pages that match the query, determine their relevance to the query and "*serve*" the results to the user.

(16)   To rank generic search results in response to a query, Google uses algorithms. It relies in particular on an algorithm called PageRank, which is "*a method for rating Web pages objectively and mechanically, effectively measuring the human interest and attention devoted to them*". PageRank essentially measures the importance of a web page based on the number and quality of links to that page, the underlying assumption being that more important websites are likely to receive more links from other websites. Google applies a variety of adjustment mechanisms to the results of PageRank to improve the relevance of the generic search results on its general search results pages. PageRank and the adjustment mechanisms together determine the rank of a web page in generic search results on Google's general search results pages.

(17)   Google does not charge websites ranked in generic search results on its general search results pages and does not accept any payment that would allow websites to rank higher in these results.

2.2.3.   *Online search advertising results*

(18)   In response to a user's query on Google Search, Google's general search results pages may also return search advertisements drawn from Google's auction-based online search advertising platform, AdWords ("AdWords results").

(19)   AdWords results are not limited to specific categories of products, services or information. They typically appear on general search results pages above or below generic search results with a label informing users of their nature as advertisements (for example, "*Ads*"). AdWords results can be purchased by any advertiser and are not limited to particular categories of advertisers.

(20)   The appearance of AdWords results in response to a user's query involves two main elements. First, AdWords identifies a pool of relevant search advertisements by matching the keywords on which advertisers have associated their search advertisements with the keywords used in the query. Second, AdWords ranks the relevant search advertisements within the pool based on their "*Ad Rank*". The ranking of a search advertisement depends on two factors: the maximum price an advertiser has indicated it is willing to pay for each click on its search advertisement in a second-price auction[15] and the quality rating of that search advertisement (known as "*Quality Score*"). The Quality Score is based among other things on a search advertisement's predicted click-through rate.[16] AdWords results that appear the most visibly on Google's general search results pages are those with the highest Ad Rank scores.

(21)   When a user clicks on an AdWords result, Google receives remuneration for that click from the advertiser owning the website to which the user is directed (known as the "*pay per click*" system).

(22)   AdWords results allow advertisers to lead interested users entering queries on Google Search to their websites, including in circumstances where these websites would otherwise not rank highly in generic search results on Google's general search results pages. Specialised search services competing with services provided by Google often also purchase AdWords results.

2.2.4. *Specialised search results*

(23)   In response to a user query, Google's general search results pages may also return specialised search results from Google's specialised search services. In most instances, specialised search results are displayed with attractive graphical features, such as large scale pictures and dynamic information. Specialised search results in a particular category are positioned within sets referred to by Google as "*Universals*" or "*OneBoxes*". They are in most instances positioned above generic search results, or among the first of them.

(24)   Google operates several search services that can be described as "specialised" because they group together results for a specific category of products, services or information (for example, "Google Shopping", "Google Finance", "Google Flights", "Google Video"). In addition to the results returned in "*Universals*" or "*OneBoxes*", Google's specialised

---

[15] A second-price auction is an auction in which the bidder who submitted the highest bid is awarded the object (or service) being sold and pays a price equal to the amount bid by the second highest bidder.

[16] The predicted click-through rate represents the probability that a search advertisement will receive a click if placed for a particular query (see Google's reply to [...] the Commission's request for information [...]).

search services can also be accessed through menu-type links displayed at the top of Google's search results pages.

(25)   Certain of Google's specialised search services are based on paid inclusion. Third party websites have to enter into an agreement with Google in order to be listed in the search results of such a specialised search service. In most instances, such an agreement provides for a payment based on a pay per click system. This is the case for instance for Google Shopping (see section 2.2.5).

2.2.5.   *Google's comparison shopping service*

(26)   Google's comparison shopping service is one of Google's specialised search services. In response to queries, it returns product offers from merchant websites, enabling users to compare them.

(27)   Google launched the first version of its comparison shopping service in December 2002 in the US under the brand name "Froogle". Froogle operated as a standalone website. Merchants did not have to pay to be listed in Froogle as it was monetised by advertisements. Google launched Froogle in the United Kingdom in October 2004 and in Germany in November 2004.

(28)   In April 2007, Google renamed Froogle as "Google Product Search" and subsequently launched along the standalone Google Product Search website a dedicated "Universal" or "OneBox" for Google Product Search, referred to as the "Product Universal". Google did not, however, change the business model of its comparison shopping service: like Froogle, merchants did not have to pay to be listed in Google Product Search as it was monetised by advertisements.

(29)   The Product Universal comprised specialised search results from Google Product Search, accompanied by one or several images and additional information such as the price of the relevant items. The results within the Product Universal, including the clickable images, in most cases led the user to the standalone Google Product Search websites. There was also a header link leading to the main website of Google Product Search.

(30)   The Product Universal was launched in October 2007 in the US, in January 2008 in the United Kingdom and Germany, in October 2010 in France and in May 2011 in Italy, the Netherlands and Spain.

(31)   In May 2012, Google renamed Google Product Search as "Google Shopping" and revamped the Product Universal which was renamed first "Commercial Unit" and then "Shopping Unit". At the same time, Google also changed the business model of its comparison shopping service (both the standalone website and the Universal) to a "paid inclusion" model, in which merchants pay Google when their product is clicked on in Google Shopping, to more closely reflect the industry standard.

(32)   In the same way as the Product Universal comprised specialised search results from Google Product Search, the Shopping Unit comprises

specialised search results from Google Shopping, as illustrated by the screenshot below. Those results are commercially named "*Product Listing Ads*" – PLAs. Unlike for the Product Universal, however, the results within the Shopping Unit generally lead users directly to the pages of Google's merchant partners on which the user can purchase the relevant item.

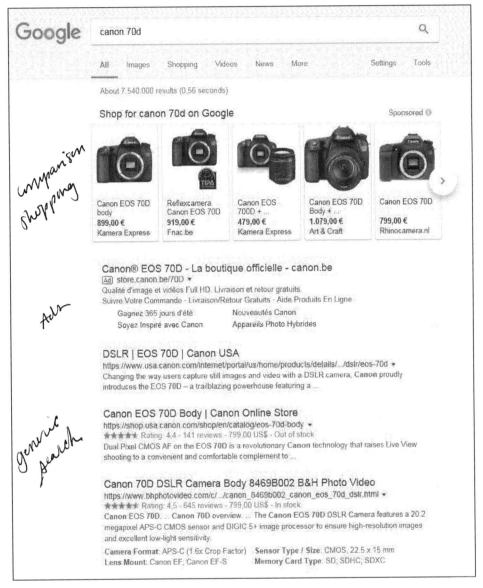

(33)   The Shopping Unit and the standalone Google Shopping website were first launched in the US in May 2012, with the transition completed by autumn 2012.

(34)   Subsequently, the Shopping Unit was launched on Google's domains in the EEA as follows: (i) in February 2013 in the Czech Republic, France, Germany, Italy, the Netherlands, Spain and the United Kingdom; and (ii)

in November 2013 in Austria, Belgium, Denmark, Norway, Poland and Sweden. Google also started running a Shopping Unit experiment in Ireland in September 2016.

(35)   As for the standalone Google Shopping website, it was launched (i) in February 2013 in the Czech Republic, France, Germany, Italy, the Netherlands, Spain and the United Kingdom; (ii) in September 2016 in Austria, Belgium, Denmark, Norway, Poland and Sweden; and (iii) in Ireland in January 2017.

. . .

5.   MARKET DEFINITION

5.1. Principles

. . .

(147)   A relevant product market comprises all those products and/or services which are regarded as interchangeable or substitutable by the consumer, by reason of the products' characteristics, their prices and their intended use.

(148)   The relevant geographic market comprises the area in which the undertakings concerned are involved in the supply and demand of products or services, in which the conditions of competition are sufficiently homogeneous and which can be distinguished from neighbouring areas because the conditions of competition are appreciably different in those areas.

(149)   Undertakings are subject to three main sources of competitive constraints: demand substitutability, supply substitutability and potential competition. From an economic point of view, for the definition of the relevant market, demand substitution constitutes the most immediate and effective disciplinary force on the suppliers of a given product.

(150)   Supply side substitutability may be taken into account in situations in which its effects are equivalent to those of demand substitution in terms of effectiveness and immediacy. There is supply side substitution when suppliers are able to switch production to the relevant products and market them in the short term without incurring significant additional costs or risks in response to small and permanent changes in relative price.

(151)   The distinctness of products or services for the purpose of an analysis under Article 102 of the Treaty has to be assessed by reference to customer demand. Factors to be taken into account include the nature and technical features of the products or services concerned, the facts observed on the market, the history of the development of the products or services concerned and also the undertaking's commercial practice.

(152)   The fact that a product or service is provided free of charge does not prevent the offering of such a service from constituting an economic activity for the purposes of the competition rules of the Treaty. This is simply a factor to be taken into account in assessing dominance.

(153)   The definition of the relevant market does not require the Commission to follow a rigid hierarchy of different sources of information or types of evidence. Rather, the Commission must make an overall assessment and can take account of a range of tools for the purposes of that assessment.

5.2. The relevant product markets

(154)   The Commission concludes that the relevant product markets for the purpose of this case are the market for general search services (section 5.2.1) and the market for comparison shopping services (section 5.2.2).

5.2.1.   The market for general search services

(155)   A number of different companies offer general search services. Some of them use their own search technology, such as Google, Microsoft (Bing) and Seznam. Others show results of a third party general search engine (often Google or Bing) with which they have an agreement. This is the case for instance, for Yahoo and America Online, both of which return Bing generic search results, and Ask, which returns Google generic search results.

(156)   The Commission concludes that the provision of general search services constitutes a distinct product market. First, the provision of general search services constitutes an economic activity (section 5.2.1.1). Second, there is limited demand side substitutability (section 5.2.1.2) and limited supply side substitutability (section 5.2.1.3) between general search services and other online services. Fourth, this conclusion does not change if general search services on static devices versus mobile devices are considered (section 5.2.1.4).

. . .

5.2.1.2. Limited demand side substitutability with other online services

(161)   General search services are not the only means by which users can explore the web. Alternative ways of discovering content include content sites, specialised search services and social networks.

(162)   For the reasons set out below, there is, however, limited demand side substitutability between general search services and other online services.

5.2.1.2.1. General search services versus content sites

(163)   There is limited substitutability between general search services and content sites.

(164)   First, the two types of services serve a different purpose. On the one hand, a general search service primarily seeks to guide users to other sites. As Google indicates on its website: *"[O]ur goal is to have people leave our website as quickly as possible"*. On the other hand, while content sites may contain references to other sites, their primary purpose is to offer directly the information, products or services users are looking for. Well-known

examples of content sites include Wikipedia, IMDb, and websites of newspapers and magazines such as The New York Times or Nature.

(165)   Second, content sites that offer sophisticated content search functionality on their websites are not substitutable for general search services. Such content search functionality remains limited to their own content or content from partners and does not allow users to search for all content over the internet, let alone all information on the web.

5.2.1.2.2. General search services versus specialised search services

(166)   There is also limited substitutability between general search services and specialised search services.

(167)   First, the nature of specialised search services and general search services is different. Specialised search services do not aim to provide all possible relevant results for queries; instead, they focus on providing specific information or purchasing options in their respective fields of specialisation. A specialised search service will also often cover a content category which is monetisable. By contrast, general search services search the entire internet and therefore generally return different, more wide-ranging results. Their services are not limited beforehand to one of several particular content categories.[95]

(168)   Second, there are a number of differences in the technical features of specialised and general search services. In the first place, specialised search services and general search services often rely on different sources of data: the main input for general search services originates from an automated process called "*web crawling*", whereas many specialised search services rely on user input or information supplied by third parties. In the second place, specialised search services are usually monetised in a different way; in addition to relying on online search advertising, they generate revenue from, for instance, paid inclusion, service fees or commissions (pay-per-acquisition fees).

(169)   Third, the facts observed in the market, the history of the development of the products concerned and Google's commercial practice further support

---

[95] By way of example, a search on https://www.google.co.uk (the website of Google's general search service in the United Kingdom) for "*Martin Luther King*" on 24 February 2015 returned 148 000 000 results, with the links on the first Google general search results page relating primarily to either historical, biographical or news-related information sources relating to Martin Luther King. By contrast, a search for "*Martin Luther King*" at virtually the same moment on https://www.google.co.uk/shopping (the website of Google's comparison shopping service Google Shopping in the United Kingdom), returned 33 pages of results (i.e. just several hundred results in total), with nearly all the links leading to commercial offerings relating to or linked with Martin Luther King (e.g. books, clothing, audio works etc.). Pages downloaded on 6 March 2015.

the conclusion that specialised search services and general search services are different.

(170) In the first place, a wide variety of specialised search services have been offered on a standalone basis for several years. Examples include services specialised in search for products such as Shopzilla, LeGuide, Idealo, Beslist, Kelkoo and Twenga, in search for local businesses such as Yelp, in search for flights such as Kayak and EasyVoyage, and in search for financial services such as MoneySupermarket or confused.com. None of these companies offers a general search service.

(171) In the second place, Google offers and describes its specialised search services as a service distinct from its general search service. Google has a help page on its website which purports to list its different products and services. The page comprises a list of Google products and services. It distinguishes between, on the one hand, *"Web Search - Search billions of web pages"*, with a link to Google's general search service, and, on the other hand *"Specialized Search"*, which comprises several different services, including for instance *"Google Shopping - Search for stuff to buy"*.

(172) Regarding specifically Google's comparison shopping service, Google offers that service as a separate standalone service, and describes its functionality and purpose differently to how it describes its general search service. For example, Google Shopping UK, Google's UK comparison shopping service, is described within Google UK's general search results pages following a query for *"Google Shopping"* as *"Google's UK price comparison service, with searches by keyword, which can then be broken down by category and ordered by price"*. There is also a dedicated information page about Google Shopping, entitled *"About Google Shopping"*. It describes Google Shopping as a distinct *"product discovery experience"*: *"Google Shopping is a new product discovery experience. The goal is to make it easy for users to research purchases, find information about different products, their features and prices, and then connect with merchants to make their purchase"*. The page then elaborates on the many search tools that are specific to Google Shopping: *"When you do a search within Google Shopping you'll see a variety of filters (like price, size, technical specifications, etc.) on the left side of the page that can help you quickly narrow down to the right product. You can also choose to display items in either a list or grid view by selecting one of these options in the top right hand corner above the results. When viewing certain apparel product detail pages (like dresses, coats and shoes), you'll also see items that are "visually similar" to the item you've selected. These are just a few of the many tools within Google Shopping and we look forward to providing more in the future"*. By contrast, Google's general search service is described within Google UK's general search results pages following a query for *"Google"* in a more general manner: *"The local version of this pre-eminent search engine, offering UK-specific pages as well as world results"*.

(173)   In the third place, reports of specialised market observers such as Nielsen and comScore distinguish between general search services and other search services.

(174)   Fourth, contrary to what Google claims, even though search results provided by a general search service may sometimes overlap with the results provided by a specialised search service, the two types of search services act as complements rather than substitutes.

(175)   In the first place, a general search service is the only online search service on which users can seek potential relevant results from all categories at the same time.

(176)   In the second place, specialised search services offer certain search functionalities that do not exist, or not to the same extent, on general search services. For instance, on search services specialised in travel, users may look for hotels with a certain number of stars, or within a certain range of a city, or they may read user reviews of these hotels. These functionalities are unavailable to the same extent on a general search service for the same queries.

(177)   In the third place, a substantial number of users reach to specialised search services only after having first entered a query in a general search service.

. . .

5.2.1.3. Limited supply side substitutability with other online services

(184)   Supply side substitutability is also limited.

(185)   In order to offer general search services, providers of other online services would need to make significant investments in terms of time and resources, particularly the initial costs associated with the development of algorithms and the costs of crawling and indexing the data. These barriers to entry are described in more detail in section 6.2.2.

. . .

5.2.2.   *The market for comparison shopping services*

(191)   Comparison shopping services are specialised search services that: (i) allow users to search for products and compare their prices and characteristics across the offers of several different online retailers (also referred to as online merchants) and merchant platforms (also referred to as online marketplaces); and (ii) provide links that lead (directly or via one or more successive intermediary pages) to the websites of such online retailers or merchant platforms.

(192)   The Commission concludes that the provision of comparison shopping services constitutes a distinct relevant product market. This is because comparison shopping services are not interchangeable with the services offered by: (i) search services specialised in different subject matters (such as flights, hotels, restaurants, or news); (ii) online search advertising

platforms; (iii) online retailers; (iv) merchant platforms; and (v) offline comparison shopping tools.

5.2.2.1. Comparison shopping services versus other specialised search services

(193)   There is limited substitutability between comparison shopping services and other specialised search services.

(194)   From the demand side perspective, each type of service focuses on providing specific information from different sources in its respective field of specialisation. Thus, comparison shopping services provide users that are looking for information on a product with a selection of existing commercial offers available on the internet for that product, as well as tools to sort and compare such offers based on various criteria. From the perspective of those users, such a service is not substitutable with that offered by search services specialised in different subject matters such as flights, hotels, locals (such as restaurants), and news.

(195)   From the supply side perspective, each specialised search service selects and ranks results through specific criteria that rely on dedicated signals and formulas designed to determine the relevance of a particular information type (e.g. price, product information, merchant rating, product popularity, stock level for comparison shopping services; freshness for news aggregators; proximity to the user for specialised search services focused e.g. on restaurants). Moreover, specialised search services mostly select content from a pool of relevant suppliers with whom they have contractual relationships and those suppliers must provide input to databases and other data infrastructure operated by specialised search service providers. Each specialised search service therefore needs to develop and maintain a dedicated data infrastructure and structured relationships with relevant suppliers. Comparison shopping services typically employ a commercial workforce whose role is to enter into agreements with online retailers, pursuant to which these retailers send them feeds of their commercial offers. These services are only partially automated and involve commercial relationships with online retailers. Likewise, flight search services use proprietary databases of content that are usually updated in real-time to ensure that they provide the most current possible information and have contractual arrangements with the booking websites, which remunerate them either by paying a commission per flight ticket booked or on a cost-per-click basis. From the supply side perspective, substitutability is therefore also limited because providers of other specialised search services are not in a position to start providing comparison shopping services in the short term and without incurring significant additional costs.

5.2.2.2. Comparison shopping services versus online search advertising platforms

(196)   There is also limited substitutability between comparison shopping services and online search advertising platforms.

(197)   From the demand side perspective, while online retailers generally promote their offers through both comparison shopping services and online search

advertising platforms, the latter do not provide services that are interchangeable from the perspectives of users and online retailers (and other advertisers).

(198)   First, users perceive comparison shopping services as a service to them and navigate – either directly (albeit to a limited extent) or (mostly) through a general search service (see section 7.2.4.1) – to a comparison shopping website (including Google Shopping) to search for a product and receive specialised search results. By contrast, users do not perceive online search advertising as a service to them and do not enter a query in a general search engine specifically in order to receive search advertising results. Indeed, Google does not offer a standalone service which users can navigate directly to in order to receive search advertising. Online search advertising is therefore not a service that users seek, but rather a compensation for the free service offered by general search engines (similar to the advertising on free-to-air TV).

(199)   Second, comparison shopping services and online search advertising platforms are also complementary and not substitutable from the perspective of online retailers and other advertisers.

(200)   In the first place, only specific subsets of advertisers (i.e. online retailers and merchant platforms) can bid to be listed in comparison shopping services whereas any advertiser can bid to be listed in online search advertising results.

(201)   In the second place, participation in comparison shopping services involves different conditions than in online search advertising results, including the provision to comparison shopping services of structured data in the form of feeds. For instance, online retailers and merchant platforms wishing to be listed in Google Shopping need to give Google dynamic access to structured information on the products that can be purchased on their websites, including dynamically adjusted information on prices, product descriptions and the number of items available in their stock (see also recital (432)).

(202)   In the third place, comparison shopping services display their results in richer formats than online search advertising results.

(203)   In the fourth place, the results of comparison shopping services are ranked based on different algorithms that take into account different parameters, tailored to the relevant specialised search category (see also recital (429)).

(204)   In the fifth place, unlike for online search advertising platforms, in order to appear in comparison shopping services such as Google Shopping, third party websites bid on products and not on keywords (see also recital (426)).

(205)   In the sixth place, when Google's own comparison shopping service appears in Google's general search results page, AdWords results may also appear, thus showing that the two services are complementary from Google's perspective.

(206)   From the supply side perspective, the functionalities and infrastructures required for the provision of comparison shopping services (see recital (195)) are different from those required for the provision of online search advertising. In particular, the provision of online search advertising services requires a company to invest in the development of a general search engine with a technology allowing users to search for keywords that can be matched with online search advertisements, as well as in a search advertisement technology to match keywords entered by users in their queries with relevant online search advertisements. According to Google, this is *"[t]he most significant task that* [a company] *wishing to provide a search advertising solution might consider undertaking [...]"*.

5.2.2.3. Comparison shopping services versus online retailers

(207)   There is also limited substitutability between comparison shopping services and online retailers.

(208)   From the demand side perspective, comparison shopping search services serve a different purpose than online retailers.

(209)   On the one hand, comparison shopping services act as intermediaries between users and online retailers. They allow users to compare offers from different online retailers in order to find the most attractive offer. They also do not offer users the possibility to purchase a product directly on their websites but rather seek to refer users to third-party websites where they can buy the relevant product. Indeed, far from being competitors, comparison shopping services consider online retailers as business partners or customers, with which they enter into contractual relationships.

(210)   On the other hand, online retailers do not allow on their websites the possibility to compare their own offers with the offers for the same or similar products on the websites of other online retailers. Online retailers also do not seek to refer users to third-party websites; rather, they want users to buy their products without leaving their own websites; accordingly, they also offer after-sale support, including product return functionality.

(211)   From the supply side perspective, the provision of comparison shopping services and online retailers requires different functionalities and infrastructures. Comparison shopping services have to retrieve the relevant information in response to each query by analysing the real-time feeds from as many online retailers as possible. By contrast, online retailers host and manage the inventory of their selected manufacturers and provide "check-out" and payment functionalities.

(212)   The limited demand side and supply side substitutability between comparison shopping services and online retailers is not called into question by Google's claims that (i) online retailers also offer product search functionalities on their websites; and (ii) many users navigate directly to the websites of online retailers to find products, thereby bypassing comparison shopping services.

(213)   First, the search functionality offered by online retailers is limited to products on their own website(s) and does not offer the possibility to compare the offers on their website with the offers for the same or similar products on the websites of other online retailers.

(214)   Second, the fact that users may navigate directly to the websites of certain online retailers indicates that the service offered by online retailers is complementary and not substitutable with comparison shopping services from the perspective of users.

(215)   On the one hand, users navigate directly to the websites of online retailers when they want to buy a product and are not particularly interested in comparing offers and prices from different sellers. On the other hand users visit a comparison shopping service when they want to search and compare offers from different online retailers in order to find the most attractive offer. As acknowledged by Google, online retailers do not offer this service, because *"they typically do not list offers from other retailers"*.

5.2.2.4. Comparison shopping services versus merchant platforms

(216)   Contrary to what Google claims, there is also limited substitutability between comparison shopping services and merchant platforms, such as Amazon Marketplace and eBay Marketplaces.

(217)   From the demand side perspective, while comparison shopping services and merchant platforms both aggregate offers from different sellers and provide a search functionality to search and filter those offers based on certain criteria, they serve a different purpose for users and for online retailers.

(218)   First, regarding the different purpose served by comparison shopping services and merchant platforms for users, on the one hand, as noted in recital (209), comparison shopping services: (i) act as intermediaries between users and online retailers/merchant platforms, allowing users to compare offers from different online retailers/merchant platforms in order to find the most attractive offer; (ii) do not offer users the possibility to purchase a product directly on their websites but rather seek to refer users to third-party websites where they can buy the relevant product; (iii) do not offer after-sale support, including product return functionality; (iv) typically list offers only from professional sellers for new products.

(219)   On the other hand, like online retailers, merchant platforms: (i) act as a place where retailers and consumers can conclude sales. Indeed, a number of merchant platforms (e.g. Amazon, Fnac, Rue Du Commerce) are online retailers that have also decided to include and sell on their websites third party products, mainly to complement their own offering; (ii) are perceived by users (and comparison shopping services) as multi-brand retailers, i.e. a final destination where users can buy products; (iii) offer after-sale support (including product return functionality and in some cases indemnification against any problem with the retailers); and (iv) list offers for second-hand products from non-professional sellers.

(220)   The different purpose served by comparison shopping services and merchant platforms for users is confirmed by the following evidence:

(1) The fact that Google itself distinguishes the different purpose and characteristics of, respectively, Google Shopping and of merchant platforms:

–   on its webpage "*About Google Shopping*", Google indicates that "*Google Shopping does not sell products directly to shoppers, instead we collect product information from participating merchants and make those products searchable for you. Our job is to find the product you want and point to the store that sells it.* […] *You can't buy products directly on www.google.com/shopping. We help you find the items you're looking for and point you to stores (both online and offline) that offer them for sale*".

–   on its webpage "*Marketplaces, Marketplace sellers and Aggregators*", Google defines "*marketplaces*" (i.e. merchant platforms) as: "*commerce sites that host items and/or websites of multiple individual sellers on the same domain* [and] *must provide a way for users to purchase the product online through either a payment service or directly from* [the merchant platforms] *website*".

(2)   The fact that Google allows merchant platforms, but not competing comparison shopping services, to participate in Google Shopping:

–   The lists of the top fifty customers of Google Shopping in the EEA based on 2015 revenues include several merchant platforms ([…]). This is true both for the whole EEA and in each of the thirteen EEA countries in which the Conduct was taking place on 3 May 2016 (Austria, Belgium, the Czech Republic, Denmark, France, Germany, Italy, the Netherlands, Norway, Poland, Spain, Sweden, and the United Kingdom). […]

–   […]

(3) The fact that a majority of comparison shopping services and merchant platforms that replied to the Commission's requests for information indicated that they are – and consider themselves as – rather business partners in a vertical relationship, not competitors.

(4) The fact that comparison shopping services list offers from merchant platforms based on the same terms and conditions applied to online retailers and that eBay and Amazon (followed by other merchant platforms) are consistently among the top online retailers in terms or revenues for many comparison shopping services.

(5) Internal Google documents indicating that Google and Amazon are business partners in a vertical relationship, not competitors . . .

(6) The responses to a survey carried out in the context of the Commission's 2014 market study on "*Comparison Tools and Third-Party Verification Schemes*" that focussed, *inter alia*, on consumers' perceptions of, respectively: (i) "*price comparison websites*" (comparison shopping services); and (ii) "*multi-trader ecommerce websites*" defined as "*online marketplaces selling products from a range of different retailers, for example Amazon, eBay, and Allegro*" (merchant platforms). On the one hand, 91% of the respondents indicated that comparison shopping services allow customers to compare prices, with 79% indicating that the price comparison aspect is by far their most valued characteristic for these services. On the other hand, "*[r]espondents also had a very specific perception of multi-trader e-commerce platforms (e.g. Amazon, eBay or Allegro)*": 62% of the respondents answered that "*these platforms were mainly dedicated to buying products*".

(221) Second, regarding the different purpose served by comparison shopping services and merchant platforms for online retailers, on the one hand, comparison shopping services offer online retailers the opportunity to promote their offerings to a large audience of users in search of a specific product. This allows online retailers both to increase brand awareness and to attract user traffic to their own websites, while retaining full control over their retail activities (including the merchandising strategy, the relationships with customers and the handling of the transactions). Comparison shopping services therefore tend to list offers from larger retailers that do not want to cede the customer interaction and data about their business and their customers to merchant platforms, such as Amazon, which they view as competitors.

(222) On the other hand, merchant platforms offer a full service to retailers that want to concentrate on sourcing and logistics only. Indeed, unlike comparison shopping services (including Google Shopping), merchant platforms also list offers from brick-and-mortar retailers which do not have their own website. Merchant platforms therefore take care of all or most of the other aspects associated with online retailing, including customer relationships, online store design, the maintenance and handling of online transactions, and customer care (including, as noted above, after-sale services and handling of complaints). Merchant platforms therefore tend to list offers mostly from certain small and medium-sized professional retailers that have limited brand awareness and/or are unable or unwilling to develop and maintain their own online stores (or even a website) or even non-professional sellers (including for second-hand products).

(223) The different purpose served by comparison shopping services and merchant platforms for online retailers is confirmed by the following evidence:

(1)   A number of internal Google documents . . . :

(2)   The reply of [...] to the Commission's request for information of [...] which confirms that out of the top [...] Google Shopping customers based on 2015 revenues in each of the thirteen EEA countries in which the Conduct takes place [...] a limited number had a registered account on [...] in 2015: [...].

(3)   The reply of [...] to the Commission's request for information [...] which indicates that out of the top [...] Google Shopping customers based on 2015 revenues in each of the thirteen EEA countries in which the Conduct takes place, [...] a limited number had an active account on [...] in 2015: [...].

(4)   The fact that in 2015, [...] listed offers from thirteen of the top fifteen online retailers in France, in terms of revenues, whereas none of these top fifteen online retailers were present on Amazon.

(5)   A comparison submitted by [...] of the top ten sellers listed by Amazon and [...] for the same product. Of the top ten sellers listed by Amazon, only three had their own standalone website and each of those websites had less than 1000 visits per month. By contrast, each of the top ten sellers listed by [...] had their own standalone website.

(6)   A study submitted by [...] conducted in November 2015 regarding how many of the top twenty online retailers of the main comparison shopping services in Germany and France (in terms of visits) were registered at that time with a merchant platform. The study indicates that, in Germany, all of the top twenty online retailers of the selected comparison shopping services were listed on at least two of the four selected comparison shopping services, whereas only three of them also listed their products on at least one marketplace, i.e. Amazon or eBay (of which, only two list products on both Amazon and eBay). The analysis for France produced equivalent results: eighteen out of the top twenty online retailers of the selected comparison shopping services were listed on at least two of the three selected comparison shopping services, whereas only two of them also listed their products on at least one marketplace, i.e. Amazon or eBay (of which, only one list products on both Amazon and eBay).

(224)   From the supply side perspective, the services provided by comparison shopping services and merchant platforms require different functionalities.

(225)   First, on the one hand, comparison shopping services collect and select the relevant information in response to each user query by analysing the real-time feeds from as many online retailers as possible and by providing users with such information. As noted (see recital (218)) they do not, however, sell the products directly on their websites but rather seek to refer users to third-party websites where they can buy the relevant product and, therefore, are not required to offer after-sale support, including product return

functionality. On the other hand, merchant platforms manage the inventory of their retailer partners and sell the products directly on their website; these activities require specific functionalities (e.g. check-out and payment functionalities) and additional services (e.g. after-sale support) and are subject to specific regulatory frameworks (e.g. concerning online payments and dispute resolution; see recital (240)).

(226)   Second, comparison shopping services and merchant platforms are generally remunerated in different ways. On the one hand, comparison shopping services are generally remunerated based on a cost-per-click model, with the retailer paying a fee for each visitor sent to its website, regardless of whether the user eventually makes a purchase. On the other hand, merchant platforms, are generally remunerated by a commission on the transaction performed on the platform or a nominal listing fee or, in case they also sell their own products, by the actual price of the products sold.

. . .

6. DOMINANT POSITION

6.1. Principles

(264)   The dominant position referred to in Article 102 of the Treaty relates to a position of economic strength enjoyed by an undertaking which enables it to prevent effective competition being maintained on the relevant market by affording it the power to behave to an appreciable extent independently of its competitors, its customers and ultimately of its consumers.

(265)   The existence of a dominant position derives in general from a combination of several factors which, taken separately, are not necessarily determinative.

(266)   One important factor is the existence of very large market shares, which are in themselves, save in exceptional circumstances, evidence of the existence of a dominant position. An undertaking which holds a very large market share for some time, without smaller competitors being able to meet rapidly the demand from those who would like to break away from that undertaking, is by virtue of that share in a position of strength which makes it an unavoidable trading partner and which, already because of this, secures for it, at the very least during relatively long periods, that freedom of action which is the special feature of a dominant position. That is the case where a company has a market share of 50% or above. Likewise, a share of between 70% and 80% is, in itself, a clear indication of the existence of a dominant position in a relevant market. The ratio between the market share held by the dominant undertaking and that of its nearest rivals is also a highly significant indicator.

(267)   In fast-growing sectors characterised by short innovation cycles, large market shares may sometimes turn out to be ephemeral and not necessarily indicative of a dominant position. However, this fact cannot preclude

application of the competition rules, in particular Article 102 of the Treaty, especially if a fast-growing market does not show signs of marked instability during the period at issue and, on the contrary, a rather stable hierarchy is established.

(268)   The fact that a service is offered free of charge is also a relevant factor to take into account in assessing dominance. In so far as users expect to receive a service free of charge, an undertaking that decides to stop innovating may run the risk of reducing its attractiveness, depending on the level of innovation on the market in question. In this respect, another relevant factor is whether there are technical or economic constraints that might prevent users from switching providers.

(269)   Another important factor when assessing dominance is the existence of barriers to entry or expansion, preventing either potential competitors from having access to the market or actual ones from expanding their activities on the market.

(270)   Such barriers may result from a number of factors, including exceptionally large capital investments that competitors would have to match, network externalities that would entail additional cost for attracting new customers, economies of scale from which newcomers to the market cannot derive any immediate benefit and the actual costs of entry incurred in penetrating the market. Switching costs are therefore only one possible type of barrier to entry and expansion.

6.2. Google's dominant position in the national markets for general search services

(271)   The Commission concludes that Google holds a dominant position in each national market for general search services since 2008, apart from in the Czech Republic, where Google holds a dominant position since 2011.

(272)   This conclusion is based on Google's market shares (section 6.2.1), the existence of barriers to expansion and entry (section 6.2.2), the infrequency of user multi-homing and the existence of brand effects (section 6.2.3) and the lack of countervailing buyer power (section 6.2.4). The conclusion holds notwithstanding the fact that general search services are offered free of charge (section 6.2.5), and regardless of whether general search on static mobile devices constitutes a distinct market from general search on mobile devices (section 6.2.6).

. . .

7.   ABUSE OF A DOMINANT POSITION

7.1. Principles

(331)   Dominant undertakings have a special responsibility not to impair, by conduct falling outside the scope of competition on the merits, genuine undistorted competition in the internal market. A system of undistorted competition can be guaranteed only if equality of opportunity is secured as

between the various economic operators. The scope of the special responsibility of the dominant undertaking has to be considered in light of the specific circumstances of the case.

(332)   Article 102 of the Treaty and Article 54 of the EEA Agreement prohibit abusive practices which may cause damage to consumers directly, but also those which harm them indirectly through their impact on an effective competition structure.

(333)   The concept of abuse is an objective concept relating to the behaviour of an undertaking in a dominant position which is such as to influence the structure of a market where, as a result of the very presence of the undertaking in question, the degree of competition is weakened and which, through recourse to methods different from those which condition normal competition on the merits, has the effect of hindering the maintenance of the degree of competition still existing in the market or the growth of that competition.

(334)   Article 102 of the Treaty and Article 54 of the EEA Agreement prohibit not only practices by an undertaking in a dominant position which tend to strengthen that position, but also the conduct of an undertaking with a dominant position in a given market that tends to extend that position to a neighbouring but separate market by distorting competition. Therefore, the fact that a dominant undertaking's abusive conduct has its adverse effects on a market distinct from the dominated one does not preclude the application of Article 102 of the Treaty or Article 54 of the EEA Agreement. It is not necessary that the dominance, the abuse and the effects of the abuse are all in the same market.

(335)   Article 102 of the Treaty and Article 54 of the EEA Agreement list a number of abusive practices. These are merely examples, not an exhaustive enumeration of the practices that may constitute abuses of dominant position prohibited by the Treaty or the EEA Agreement. For example, Article 102 of the Treaty and Article 54 of the EEA Agreement generally prohibit any abusive practice capable of limiting markets. The legal characterisation of an abusive practice does not depend on the name given to it, but on the substantive criteria used in that regard. The specific conditions to be met in order to establish the abusive nature of one form of conduct covered by Article 102 of the Treaty and Article 54 of the EEA Agreement must not necessarily also apply when assessing the abusive nature of another form of conduct covered by those articles.

(336)   In order to determine whether the undertaking in a dominant position has abused such a position, it is necessary to consider all the circumstances and to investigate whether the practice tends, for example, to bar competitors from access to the market, to apply dissimilar conditions to equivalent transactions with other trading parties, thereby placing them at a competitive disadvantage, or to strengthen the dominant position by distorting competition.

(337)   It follows from the nature of the obligations imposed by Article 102 of the Treaty and Article 54 of the EEA Agreement that, in specific circumstances, an undertaking in a dominant position must refrain from adopting a course of conduct which would be unobjectionable if adopted by non-dominant undertakings.

(338)   Similarly, the Court of Justice held that an abuse of a dominant position is prohibited under Article 102 of the Treaty and Article 54 of the EEA Agreement *"regardless of the means and procedure by which it is achieved"*, and *"irrespective of any fault"*. In the same vein, the Commission is under no obligation to establish the existence of an abusive intent on the part of the dominant undertaking in order to render Article 102 of the Treaty and Article 54 of the EEA Agreement applicable. While intent is not a necessary prerequisite to show an abuse, it is, however, one of the criteria which can be used for assessing the abusive nature of behaviour under Article 102 of the Treaty.

(339)   Concerning the effects of the dominant undertaking's conduct, Article 102 of the Treaty and Article 54 of the EEA Agreement prohibit behaviour that tends to restrict competition or is capable of having that effect, regardless of its success. This occurs not only where access to the market is made impossible for competitors, but also where the conduct of the dominant undertaking is capable of making that access more difficult, thus causing interference with the structure of competition on the market. Customers and users should have the opportunity to benefit from whatever degree of competition is possible on the market and competitors should be able to compete on the merits for the entire market and not just for a part of it. An undertaking in a dominant position may not therefore justify abusive conduct in a certain segment of a market by the fact that its competitors remain free to compete in other segments.

(340)   It is open to a dominant undertaking to provide a justification for conduct that is liable to be caught by the prohibition under Article 102 of the Treaty and Article 54 of the EEA Agreement. It may demonstrate, for that purpose, either that its conduct is objectively necessary, or that the exclusionary effect produced may be counterbalanced, outweighed even, by advantages in terms of efficiency gains that also benefit consumers.

7.2.   The abusive conduct: the more favourable positioning and display, in Google's general search results pages, of Google's own comparison shopping service compared to competing comparison shopping services

(341)   The Commission concludes that the Conduct constitutes an abuse of Google's dominant position in each of the thirteen national markets for general search services where Google either launched the Product Universal or, if the Product Universal was never launched in that market, the Shopping Unit. The Conduct is abusive because it constitutes a practice falling outside the scope of competition on the merits as it: (i) diverts traffic

in the sense that it decreases traffic from Google's general search results pages to competing comparison shopping services and increases traffic from Google's general search results pages to Google's own comparison shopping service; and (ii) is capable of having, or likely to have, anti-competitive effects in the national markets for comparison shopping services and general search services.

(342)   To demonstrate why the Conduct is abusive and falls outside the scope of competition on the merits, the Commission first describes how Google positions and displays more favourably, in its general search results pages, its own comparison shopping service compared to competing comparison shopping services (section 7.2.1). Second, it illustrates the importance of traffic for comparison shopping services (section 7.2.2) and how the Conduct diverts traffic in the sense that it decreases traffic from Google's general results pages to competing comparison shopping services and increases traffic from Google's general search results pages to Google's own comparison shopping service (section 7.2.3). Third, it shows that the generic search traffic from Google's general search results pages accounts for a large proportion of traffic for competing comparison shopping services and cannot be effectively replaced by other sources of traffic currently available to competing comparison shopping services (section 7.2.4). Fourth, it explains how the Conduct is capable of extending Google's dominant position in the national markets for general search services to the national markets for comparison shopping services (section 7.3.1), and of protecting Google's dominant position in the national markets for general search services (section 7.3.3). It also explains that, even if the alternative product market definition proposed by Google, comprising both comparison shopping services and merchant platforms, were to be followed, the Conduct would be capable of having, or likely to have, anti-competitive effects in at least the comparison shopping services segments of the possible national markets comprising both comparison shopping services and merchant platforms (section 7.3.2). Finally, it rejects Google's arguments with regard to the applicable legal test (section 7.4) and to potential objective justifications for the Conduct (section 7.5).

(343)   In summary, Google has artificially reaped the benefits of the Conduct. Google did not invent comparison shopping. Google's first comparison shopping service, Froogle, was not gaining traffic as it did not appear visibly in Google's general search results pages. It was only after Google started the Conduct in each of the thirteen national markets for general search services that traffic to Google's comparison shopping service from Google's general search results pages began to increase on a lasting basis whereas traffic to almost all competing comparison shopping services began to decrease on a lasting basis.

...

A-B Testing is not about trying to serve consumers best. It's about what can help you w/o hurting consumers

7.3. The Conduct has potential anti-competitive effects on several markets

(589)   The Commission concludes that the Conduct is capable of having, or is likely to have, anti-competitive effects in the national markets for comparison shopping services (section 7.3.1) and in the national markets for general search services (section 7.3.3).

(590)   Moreover, even if the alternative product market definition proposed by Google, comprising both comparison shopping services and merchant platforms, were to be followed, the Conduct would be capable of having, or likely to have, anticompetitive effects in at least the comparison shopping services segments of possible national markets comprising both comparison shopping services and merchant platforms (section 7.3.2).

7.3.1.   Potential anti-competitive effects in the national markets for comparison shopping services

(591)   In section 7.2.3 the Commission concluded that the Conduct decreases traffic from Google's general results pages to competing comparison shopping services and increases traffic from Google's general search results pages to Google's own comparison shopping service. In section 7.2.4 the Commission concluded that generic search traffic from Google's general search results pages accounts for a large proportion of traffic to competing comparison shopping services and cannot be effectively replaced by other sources currently available to comparison shopping services.

(592)   In light of the above (recital (591), and also for the reasons outlined in this section (recitals (593)-(607)), the Conduct is capable of having, or likely to have, anticompetitive effects, in the national markets for comparison shopping services.

(593)   First, the Conduct has the potential to foreclose competing comparison shopping services, which may lead to higher fees for merchants, higher prices for consumers, and less innovation for the reasons explained below.

(594)   In the first place, the Conduct is capable of leading competing comparison shopping services to cease providing their services. This would allow Google to impose and maintain higher fees on merchants for participation in its own comparison shopping service. These higher costs for merchants are capable of leading to higher product prices for consumers.

(595)   In the second place, the Conduct is likely to reduce the incentives of competing comparison shopping services to innovate. Competing comparison shopping services will have an incentive to invest in developing innovative services, improving the relevance of their existing services and creating new types of services, only if they can reasonably expect that their services will be able to attract a sufficient volume of user traffic to compete with Google's comparison shopping service. Moreover, even if competing comparison shopping services may try to compensate to some extent the decrease in traffic by relying more on paid sources of

traffic, this will also reduce the revenue available to invest in developing innovative services, improving the relevance of their existing services and creating new types of services.

(596)   In the third place, the Conduct is likely to reduce the incentives of Google to improve the quality of its comparison shopping service as it does not currently need to compete on the merits with competing comparison shopping services.

(597)   Second, the Conduct is likely to reduce the ability of consumers to access the most relevant comparison shopping services. This is for two reasons.

(598)   In the first place, as explained in section 7.2.3.1, users tend to consider that search results that are ranked highly in generic search results on Google's general search results pages are the most relevant for their queries and click on them irrespective of whether other results would be more relevant for their queries. For example, prior to Google beginning the Conduct in October 2007, Google's comparison shopping service was losing traffic at a pace of 21% year on year while Google's general search service was gaining 23% in the same time frame (see also recital (535)). Google started the Conduct even though as a result, it did not always show to users the most relevant results (as ranked by its generic search algorithms) at least for certain queries.

[margin handwritten: Process / Substance]

(599)   In the second place, Google did not inform users that the Product Universal was positioned and displayed in its general search results pages using different underlying mechanisms than those used to rank generic search results. As for the Shopping Unit, while the "Sponsored" label may suggest that different positioning and display mechanisms are used, that information is likely to be understandable only by the most knowledgeable users (see also recital (536)). *[handwritten: UNCLEAR INJURY*]*

[margin handwritten: NOT CLEAR THAT CONSUMERS ARE MISLED]

(600)   The Conduct therefore risks undermining the competitive structure of the national markets for comparison shopping services. The prospects of commercial success of Google's comparison shopping service are enhanced not because of the merits of that service, but because Google applies different underlying mechanisms on the basis of the advantages provided to it by its dominant position in the national markets for general search services.

(601)   Third, the Commission's conclusions are not called into question by Google's claims that (i) despite the duration of the Conduct, the Commission has not identified any competing comparison shopping service that has ceased to offer its service; and (ii) it has identified "hundreds of aggregators" from the list of the 361 SO Response Aggregators that remain active.

(602)   In the first place, the Commission is not required to prove that the Conduct has the actual effect of leading certain competing comparison shopping services to cease offering their services. Rather, it is sufficient for the

Commission to demonstrate that the Conduct is capable of having, or likely to have, such an effect.

(603)   In the second place, the absolute number of comparison shopping services that remain active is irrelevant. In the absence of the Conduct, the number of comparison shopping services that would remain active and their ability to compete might be even greater.

(604)   In the third place, a large percentage of the competing comparison services included in Google's list of 361 SO Response Aggregators have never offered, or no longer offer, comparison shopping services:

. . .

(605)   Fourth, the Commission's conclusion is not called into question by Google's claim that the Commission has failed to demonstrate, as part of its analysis of anticompetitive effects, a causal link between, on the one hand, the Conduct and the decrease in traffic to competing comparison shopping services and, on the other hand, the Conduct and the increase in traffic to Google's comparison shopping service.

(606)   In the first place, the Commission is not required to prove that the Conduct has the actual effect of decreasing traffic to competing comparison shopping services and increasing traffic to Google's comparison shopping service. Rather, it is sufficient for the Commission to demonstrate that the Conduct is capable of having, or likely to have, such effects.

(607)   In the second place, and in any event, the Commission has demonstrated by "tangible evidence" that the Conduct decreases traffic to competing comparison shopping services (section 7.2.3.2) and increases traffic to Google's own comparison shopping service (section 7.2.3.3).

7.3.2. Potential anti-competitive effects of the Conduct in possible national markets for comparison shopping services and merchant platforms

(608)   For the reasons set out in sections 5.2.2 and 7.3.1 above, the Commission concludes that comparison shopping services constitute a distinct relevant product market and that the Conduct is capable of having, or likely to have, anti-competitive effects in the national markets for comparison shopping services.

(609)   Moreover, even if the alternative product market definition proposed by Google, comprising both comparison shopping services and merchant platforms, were to be followed, the Commission concludes that the Conduct would be capable of having, or likely to have, anti-competitive effects in at least the comparison shopping services segments of the possible national markets comprising both comparison shopping services and merchant platforms.

(610)   First, contrary to what Google claims, competing comparison shopping services, and not merchant platforms, would be the closest competitors to Google's own comparison shopping service on the possible national

markets for comparison shopping services and merchant platforms. This is because, as indicated in section 5.2.2.4:

(a)   Google Shopping is a comparison shopping service;

(b)   Google distinguishes comparison shopping services (including its own comparison shopping service) from merchant platforms;

(c)   Comparison shopping services and merchant platforms are (and consider themselves as) business partners in a vertical relationship;

(d)   Comparison shopping services and merchant platforms serve different purposes from the perspective of users; and

(e)   Comparison shopping services and merchant platforms provide different services to online retailers.

(611)   Second, the Commission's conclusion is not called into question by Google's claim that, during the relevant period, certain merchant platforms have gained traffic from Google's general search results pages both in the absolute and relative to comparison shopping services. It would be unsurprising if merchant platforms have gained traffic as a result of the Conduct because:

(a)   merchant platforms are not prone to being demoted by the [...] and Panda algorithms; and

(b)   the majority of merchant platforms are eligible to be displayed in the Product Universals/Shopping Units and are in fact among Google Shopping's top customers (see section 5.2.2.4). Therefore, to the extent that their offers have been displayed in the Product Universals and/or the Shopping Units, traffic to merchant platforms have benefited from the Conduct.

(612)   Third, in reaching the conclusions set out in recitals (609)-(611), the Commission has undertaken two analyses relating to the United Kingdom, Germany, France, the Netherlands, Austria, Belgium, the Czech Republic, Denmark, Italy, Norway, Poland, Spain and Sweden, as well as to these thirteen countries in which the Conduct takes place in the aggregate, based on different sets of data and methodologies covering the period 2011-2016 (the "First Analysis" and the "Second Analysis"). The purpose of these two analyses is twofold: (i) to estimate the size of the comparison shopping services segments (including Google's own comparison shopping service and the competing comparison shopping services) of the possible national markets comprising both comparison shopping services and merchant platforms (i.e. the segments affected by the Conduct); and (ii) to analyse the evolution of traffic to Google's own comparison shopping service, the 361 SO Response Aggregators and a representative sample of merchant platforms.

(613)   Both analyses take into account the approximately 380 services that Google has identified as competing with Google Shopping, namely:

(a)   the following comparison shopping services:

      (1)   the sample of the most important comparison shopping services in the EEA included in the analysis in Section 7.2.3.2. That sample includes: […];

      (2)   the other "aggregators" listed by Google in Annex 3 to the SO Response (hereinafter, the Commission will refer to all SO Response Aggregators other than the comparison shopping services listed at point (1) as "the Other SO Response Aggregators";

      (3)   the product listing units displayed on the general search results pages of […];

      (4)   the product listing units displayed on third party websites by […], when these units are displayed in reply to a query; and

(b)   the following samples of merchant platforms: […]; […]; […].

. . .

7.3.3.   *Potential anti-competitive effects in the national markets for general search services*

(641)   The Commission concludes that the Conduct is also capable of having, or likely to have, anti-competitive effects in the national markets for general search services.

(642)   By positioning and displaying more favourably, in its general search results pages, its own comparison shopping service compared to competing comparison shopping services, Google protects the part of the revenue that it generates on its general search results pages and which serves to finance its general search service. Indeed that revenue could be channelled directly to competing comparison shopping services (therefore bypassing Google's general search service). The Conduct may therefore make it more difficult for competing comparison shopping services to reach a critical mass of users that would allow them to compete against Google.

(643)   This is confirmed by several internal Google documents:

      (1)   […]

      (2)   […] […]

      (3)   […]

      (4)   […]

. . .

7.5. Objective justification and efficiency claims

(653)   The Commission concludes that notwithstanding its arguments, Google has not demonstrated that the Conduct is either objectively necessary, or that the exclusionary effect produced may be counterbalanced, outweighed even, by advantages in terms of efficiency gains that also benefit consumers.

(654)   Google essentially provides five justifications for the Conduct.

(655)   First, Google claims that it must be entitled to apply adjustment mechanisms in order to preserve the usefulness of its generic search results: *"[...] an inability to demote low-quality sites would not serve competition or consumers [...] as it would expose Google to a flood of low-quality results [...] to the ultimate detriment of users"*.

(656)   Second, Google claims that the positioning and display of Product Universals and Shopping Units is justified because they improve the quality of Google's search service for users and advertisers. According to Google, the technologies underlying the Product Universals and the Shopping Units, their specialised ranking signals, the organisation of the structured data and their formats improve the quality of Google's general search service for consumers by *"provid[ing] users with the most relevant and useful search results possible"*.

(657)   Third, Google claims that if it were required to position and display competing comparison shopping in its general search results pages in the same way as its own comparison shopping service, this would reduce, rather than increase, competition because: (i) search services compete by showing their results, not results from other services and users do not expect search services to provide results from other services; and (ii) Google would be unable to monetise space on its general search results pages.

(658)   Fourth, Google claims that a requirement to show results from competing comparison shopping services would unduly affect its rights and freedoms under the Charter of Fundamental Rights of the European Union (CFR) to impart information (Article 11), to protect its property (Article 17), and to conduct its business (Article 16).

(659)   Fifth, Google claims that technically, it *"cannot rank results from aggregators alongside its own in a coherent way"*. Moreover, ranking offers from inventories of competing comparison shopping services would turn their results into Google Shopping results.

(660)   The Commission concludes that none of Google's five claims constitutes an objective justification for the Conduct.

(661)   First, the Commission is not preventing Google from applying adjustment mechanisms. The abuse established by this Decision concerns simply the fact that Google does not apply these mechanisms in the same way to

Google's comparison shopping service and competing comparison shopping services.

(662) Second, the Commission is not preventing Google from displaying categories of specialised search results, such as shopping results, in its general search results pages when it determines that they are likely to be relevant or useful to a query. The abuse established by this Decision concerns simply the fact that Google does not position and display in the same way results from Google's comparison shopping service and from competing comparison shopping services.

(663) Third, Google has provided no evidence to demonstrate that users do not expect search services to provide results from others. On the contrary, as indicated in recital (599), Google did not inform users that the Product Universal was positioned and displayed using different underlying mechanisms than those used to rank generic search results. Similarly, in the case of the Shopping Unit, while the "Sponsored" label may suggest that different positioning and display mechanisms are used, that information is likely to be understandable only by the most knowledgeable users.

(664) Fourth, a requirement on Google to treat competing comparison shopping services no less favourably than its own comparison shopping service within its general search services does not generally prevent it from monetising its general search results pages. Google can choose the specific measures through which it intends to comply with this Decision and the possible measures Google might take do not preclude the monetisation of its general search results pages when making this choice.

(665) Fifth, any restriction on Google's right to impart information, right to protect its property and freedom to conduct its business brought about by the Decision (i) is provided for by law; (ii) corresponds to objectives of general interest recognised by the Union; (iii) respects the essence of those rights and freedoms; and (iv) is necessary to protect the rights and freedoms of others.

(666) In the first place, the Decision is based on Article 102 of the Treaty, a provision of primary Union law that is sufficiently precise to meet the requirement that any restriction on Google's fundamental rights and freedoms resulting from a decision under Article 7 of Regulation (EC) No 1/2003 finding an infringement of Article 102 of the Treaty is "provided by law".

(667) In the second place, any restriction on Google's rights and freedoms corresponds to the objective of the Union to establish an internal market, which in accordance with Protocol No 27 on the internal market and competition, annexed to the Treaty of Lisbon, includes a system ensuring that free competition is not distorted to the detriment of the public interest, individual undertakings and consumers.

(668)   In the third place, any restriction on Google's rights and freedoms respects the essence of those rights and freedoms. In particular, any restriction does not interfere with how and what information Google can provide to users in response to a given query, including in terms of grouping together product information.

(669)   In the fourth place, any restriction on Google's rights and freedoms is necessary to protect the freedom of competing comparison shopping services and other economic operators to conduct a business consisting in returning product offers from merchant websites, enabling users to compare them. This freedom, in turn, furthers the abovementioned objective of general interest that competition is not distorted to the detriment of the public interest and consumers.

(670)   Any restriction on Google's rights and freedoms is also necessary to protect the right of users to receive information from competing comparison shopping services. As indicated in recitals (437) and (599), users are not all aware of the fact that Product Universals or the Shopping Units are subject to different underlying processes and mechanisms than competing comparison shopping services for being triggered and ranked in Google's general search results pages in response to a product query.

(671)   Sixth, Google has failed to demonstrate that it cannot use the same underlying processes and methods in deciding the positioning and display of the results of its own comparison shopping service and for those of competing comparison shopping services. Rather, the scenarios proposed and considered by Google during the commitments discussions […], […] suggests that the implementation of an equal treatment remedy is technically feasible.

. . .

12. REMEDIES

12.1.   Principles

(693)   Article 7(1) of Regulation (EC) No 1/2003 provides that where the Commission finds that there is an infringement of Article 102 of the Treaty and Article 54 of the EEA Agreement it may by decision require the undertaking concerned to bring such infringement to an end. For this purpose, it may also impose on the undertaking concerned any behavioural or structural remedies which are proportionate to the infringement committed and necessary to bring the infringement effectively to an end.

(694)   It follows that a decision pursuant to Article 7(1) of Regulation No (EC) 1/2003 may include an order to *"do certain acts or provide certain advantages which have been wrongfully withheld as well as prohibiting the continuation of certain action, practices or situations which are contrary to the Treaty"*. The Commission may

require the undertaking concerned to submit to it proposals with a view to bringing the situation into conformity with the requirements of the Treaty.

(695) The requirement that a remedy has to be effective empowers the Commission to enjoin a dominant undertaking to refrain from adopting any measures having the same or an equivalent object or effect as the conduct identified as abusive. Any remedy must also apply in relation to the infringement that has been established and be proportionate to the infringement identified.

(696) Where there is more than one way of bringing an infringement effectively to an end in conformity with the Treaty, it is for the addressee of a decision to choose between those various ways.

12.2.   Application to this case

(697) Google and Alphabet should be required to bring the infringement established by this Decision effectively to an end and henceforth refrain from any measure that has the same or an equivalent object or effect.

(698) As there is more than one way in conformity with the Treaty of bringing that infringement effectively to an end, it is for Google and Alphabet to choose between those various ways.

(699) Any measure chosen by Google and Alphabet should, however, ensure that Google treats competing comparison shopping services no less favourably than its own comparison shopping service within its general search results pages. The principles mentioned in recital (700) should apply irrespective of whether Google chooses to display a Shopping Unit or another equivalent form of grouping of links to or search results from comparison shopping services.

(700) In particular, any measure chosen by Google and Alphabet:

(a) should apply to all devices, irrespective of the type of device on which the search is performed;

(b) should apply to all users of Google situated in the thirteen EEA countries in which the Conduct takes place, irrespective of the Google domain that they use (including Google.com);

(c) should subject Google's own comparison shopping service to the same underlying processes and methods for the positioning and display in Google's general search results pages as those used for competing comparison shopping services. Such processes and methods should include all elements that have an impact on the visibility, triggering, ranking or graphical format of a search result in Google's general search results pages, including:

x processes and methods or relevance standards determining the triggering of comparison shopping services on the general search results pages in response to a query;

x   processes and methods determining the positioning and display of comparison shopping services in response to a query, including relevance standards, ranking algorithms, adjustment or demotion mechanisms and their respective conditions, parameters and signals;

x   type of landing pages for clicks on comparison shopping services;

x   visual appearance on comparison shopping services and branding possibilities;

x   type and granularity of information on the results of comparison shopping services available to users; and

x   the possibility of interaction with users.

(d)   should not lead to competing comparison shopping services being charged a fee or another form of consideration that has the same or an equivalent object or effect as the infringement established by this Decision.

(701)   Google and Alphabet should be given 90 days from the date of the notification of this Decision to implement measures that bring the infringement effectively to an end. A 90 days period is sufficient to implement such measures, considering in particular that, at the time of the discussions on commitments, Google itself offered such a deadline for the implementation of those commitments.

(702)   Google and Alphabet should be required to notify the Commission, within 60 days from the date of notification of this Decision, of the measures by means of which they intend to bring the infringement effectively to an end. That communication should be sufficiently reasoned and detailed to enable the Commission to make a preliminary assessment as to whether those measures will ensure that the infringement is brought to an end effectively and in accordance with the principles set out in recital (700). Any statements by the Commission to Google and Alphabet or silence on the part of the Commission between the 60 day deadline and 90 day deadline should not be interpreted as an indication that the intended measures communicated by Google and Alphabet will ensure that the infringement is brought to an end effectively.

(703)   The Commission is entitled to monitor the implementation by Google and Alphabet of the remedies ordered in the Decision. For those purposes, it is entitled to use the powers of investigation provided for in Regulation No (EC) 1/2003.

(704)   Considering the variety and complexity of the measures that Google and Alphabet may take to bring the infringement effectively to an end, Google and Alphabet should provide the Commission with periodic reports on the way they comply with this Decision. The first of those reports should be

sent on the day when Google and Alphabet bring the infringement effectively to an end. The next reports should be sent every four months, for a period of five years from that day.

(705)   For the same reasons set out in recital (704), the Commission may also decide to use the services of one or several external technical expert(s).

. . .

Notes

1.   What are the most fundamental differences between the U.S. *Kinderstart* decision and the EU *Google Shopping* decision?

2.   Does the *Google Shopping* decision demonstrate anticompetitive effects? In what sense?

3.   Is Google correct in claiming that "the positioning and display of Product Universals and Shopping Units is justified because they improve the quality of Google's search service for users and advertisers"? What evidence would be useful in proving or disproving this claim? *Cf.* Michael Luca et al., Is Google Degrading Search?   Consumer   Harm   from   Universal   Search, https://www.law.berkeley.edu/wp-content/uploads/2015/04/Luca-   Wu-Yelp-Is-Google-Degrading-Search-2015-4.pdf *with* Miguel de la Mano et al., Focus on the Evidence: A   Brief   Rebuttal   of   Wu,   Luca,   et   al,   Aug.   17,   2016, https://papers.ssrn.com/sol3/papers.cfm?abstract_id=2825006.

4.   Consider paragraph 609:

> Moreover, even if the alternative product market definition proposed by Google, comprising both comparison shopping services and merchant platforms, were to be followed, the Commission concludes that the Conduct would be capable of having, or likely to have, anti-competitive effects in at least the comparison shopping services segments of the possible national markets comprising both comparison shopping services and merchant platforms.

If the relevant market is "both comparison shopping services and merchant platforms," is it sufficient to find harm only in one "segment" of that market? What if there were benefits to the other segment, merchant platforms? For example, what if comparison shopping services were harmed but Amazon benefitted?

5.   A treatise on EU competition law draws this tentative conclusion: "Ultimately, the decision in *Google Search (Shopping)* may represent the necessary evolution of EU competition law to address the sorts of competition problems that are likely to arise in digital economy markets." Alison Jones, Brenda Sufrin & Niamh Dunne, EU Competition Law: Text, Cases, and Materials (7th ed. 2019). If so, in what does the evolution consist?

6.   There are a variety of different perspectives that one can take on what service a search engine like Google is actually providing. James Grimmelmann has suggested that Google is acting neither as a "conduit" nor an "editor," but as a "trusted advisor." James Grimmelmann, *Speech Engines*, 98 MINN. L. REV. 868 (2014); *see also* James Grimmelmann, "Some Skepticism About Search Neutrality," in The Next Digital Decade: Essays on the Future of the Internet (Berin Szoka & Adam Marcus, eds. 2010). Other proposals are for a theory of "information fiduciaries," *see* Jack Balkin, *Information Fiduciaries and the First Amendment*, 49 U.C. DAVIS L. REV. 1183 (2016), or that search should be a subject of government regulation. Oren Bracha & Frank Pasquale, *Federal Search Commission: Access, Fairness, and Accountability in the Law of Search*, 93 CORNELL L. REV. 1149 (2008)

7.   The search-engine market is a complicated one, particularly with respect to advertising, which was not at issue in Google Shopping. Two articles that go into some detail on how the Internet advertising market works are Damien Geradin & Dimitrios Katsifis, *An EU competition law analysis of online display advertising the programmatic age*, 15 EUR. COMP. J. 55 (2019, and Damien Geradin & Dimitrios Katsifis, 'Trust Me, I'm Fair': Analysing Google's Latest Practices in Ad Tech From the Perspective of EU Competition Law, Oct. 7, 2019, https://papers.ssrn.com/sol3/papers.cfm?abstract_id=3465780.

2.2.2. Exclusion with Intellectual Property

A Brief Outline of Relevant Patent-Law Issues

To appreciate the issues in and implications of *F.T.C. v. Qualcomm* (and to a lesser extent *Huawei v. ZTE*), some basic background information about patent law is helpful. Some of the patent issues are similar to those that might arise in connection with copyright, but patents have more antitrust implications because they generally give rise to more market power. The Supreme Court has held that there is no presumption of power from a patent, *Illinois Tool Works Inc. v. Independent Ink, Inc*, 547 U.S. 28 (2006), and certainly a new, improved, and patented mousetrap can face much competition from other mousetraps, but it is nevertheless true that many inventions will be sufficient improvements on earlier technologies to allow above-cost pricing. In contrast, it is rarer for book, music, and movies to be sufficiently significant "improvements" over prior works so as to provide significant power.

It is important to distinguish between patented inventions and the physical products in which some inventions are embodied. A patentee receives a patent for a "claim"[1] that describes an invention, and the patent gives the patentee the right to prevent others from making, using, selling, offering to sell, or importing any product that "embodies" that claim, which means that it includes all the elements of the claim. In the claim in the note, the complete trap would embody the claim, but if the ping-pong ball were removed or another kind of ball substituted, there would be no direct infringement of this claim, which requires a ping-pong ball. (There are other claims in the patent, however, that do not require that the ball be a ping-pong ball, or even require a ball.)

Having received its patent (*i.e.*, having met the requirements for a patent, as described above prior to *Actavis*), the patentee can either make and sell a product that embodies the claim, or it can license another to make and sell it. If anyone makes or sells the product without the patentee's permission, the patentee can sue for infringement. That right is limited, though, by the "exhaustion" (or "first sale") doctrine, under which an authorized sale of a product that "substantially embodies" a patented invention "exhausts" the patentee's rights. So whether the patentee sells the product itself or licenses another to make and sell it, the product can be freely resold by the purchaser. This is an important consideration in *Qualcomm*.

---

[1] Here is an example for a mousetrap, from U.S. Patent No. 5,720,125, granted in 1998:

> 1. A disposable trap functioning to capture a rodent alive, the trap comprising:
>
> > a cylinder balanced on a fulcrum which is supported on a support surface;
> >
> > said cylinder further comprising a first end having a capture module and a second bait end; and
> >
> > said capture module further comprising a rodent entrance, a ball and a pivoting locking means functioning to lock the ball in the cylinder after the rodent enters the rodent entrance, walks to the second bait end, thereby causing the cylinder to tilt to a trapped mode with the second end resting on the support surface, wherein the pivoting locking means further comprises a hinged member which urges the ball against a stop when the trap is in the trapped mode, and wherein the ball further comprises a ping pong ball, the stop further comprises a collar around the cylinder, and the hinged member further comprises a semicircular disc mounted in a slot atop the cylinder.

Some of the idiosyncratic language here—"comprising," "said," etc.—is typical of patent claims and has special significance. (This is not a humane mousetrap, at least if used according to the patent's suggestion that "mousetrap and mouse can then be put into the hazardous waste bin.")

The Standard-Essential Patent Problem

This passage from the *F.T.C. v. Qualcomm* opinion included below briefly sets out the SEP problem, which is also discussed in the IEEE business review letter above:

> Standing [*sic*] setting organizations ("SSOs") are global collaborations of industry participants that develop technical specifications for cellular standards. These specifications ensure that cellular industry participants—including modem chip suppliers, handset original equipment manufacturers ("OEMs"), infrastructure companies, and carriers—develop standard-compatible devices that can communicate with each other. Cellular standards evolve over time. Therefore, although the first generation of LTE was standardized in 2008, there have been several new LTE releases as standards contributors develop new features.
>
> Cellular standards may incorporate patented technology. Patents that are essential to a standard are called standard essential patents ("SEPs"). Because a SEP holder could prevent other industry participants from implementing a cellular standard, SSOs require patent holders to commit to license their SEPs on fair, reasonable, and nondiscriminatory ("FRAND") terms before SSOs will incorporate the patent into the cellular standard. For example, under the intellectual property policy of the Telecommunications Industry Association ("TIA"), a SSO, a SEP holder must commit to TIA that: "A license under any Essential Patent(s), the license rights which are held by the undersigned Patent Holder, will be made available to all applicants under terms and conditions that are reasonable and non-discriminatory."
>
> This promise to license SEPs on FRAND terms is generally referred to as a SEP holder's FRAND commitment. At summary judgment, the Court held that Qualcomm's FRAND commitments to SSOs, TIA and ATIS, require Qualcomm to license its modem chip SEPs to rival modem chip suppliers.

Case C-170/13,
Huawei Technologies Co. Ltd v. ZTE Corp.
Court of Justice of the European Union
July 16, 2015

1   This request for a preliminary ruling concerns the interpretation of Article 102 TFEU.

2   The request has been made in proceedings between Huawei Technologies Co. Ltd ('Huawei Technologies'), on the one hand, and ZTE Corp. and ZTE

Deutschland GmbH ('ZTE'), on the other hand, concerning an alleged infringement of a patent which is essential to a standard established by a standardisation body ('standard-essential patent' or 'SEP').

Legal context

International law

3   The Convention on the Grant of European Patents ('EPC'), which was signed in Munich on 5 October 1973 and entered into force on 7 October 1977, in the version applicable to the facts in the main proceedings, establishes, as Article 1 states, a 'system of law, common to the Contracting States, for the grant of patents for invention'.

4   Apart from common rules relating to the grant of a European patent, a European patent remains governed by the national law of each of the Contracting States for which it has been granted. In that regard, Article 2(2) of the EPC states:

> 'The European patent shall, in each of the Contracting States for which it is granted, have the effect of and be subject to the same conditions as a national patent granted by that State ...'

        . . .

EU law

6   Recitals 10, 12 and 32 of the preamble to Directive 2004/48/EC of the European Parliament and of the Council of 29 April 2004 on the enforcement of intellectual-property rights (OJ 2004 L 157, p. 45) state the following:

> '(10)   The objective of this Directive is to approximate legislative systems so as to ensure a high, equivalent and homogeneous level of protection in the Internal Market.
>
>   ...
>
> (12)   This Directive should not affect the application of the rules of competition, and in particular Articles 81 and 82 of the Treaty. The measures provided for in this Directive should not be used to restrict competition unduly in a manner contrary to the Treaty.
>
>   ...
>
> (32)   This Directive respects the fundamental rights and observes the principles recognised in particular by the Charter of Fundamental Rights of the European Union [("the Charter")]. In particular, this Directive seeks to ensure full respect for intellectual property, in accordance with Article 17(2) of th[e] Charter.'

7   Article 9 of that directive, entitled 'Provisional and precautionary measures', states, in paragraph 1:

'Member States shall ensure that the judicial authorities may, at the request of the applicant:

> (a)   issue against the alleged infringer an interlocutory injunction intended to prevent any imminent infringement of an intellectual-property right ...
>
> ...,'

...

German law

9   Under the heading 'Performance in good faith', Paragraph 242 of the German Civil Code (Bürgerliches Gesetzbuch) lays down that an obligor has a duty to perform the obligation in accordance with the requirements of good faith, with due regard for customary practice.

10   Paragraph 139(1) of the Law on Patents (Patentgesetz, BGBl. 1981 I, p. 1), as amended most recently by Paragraph 13 of the Law of 24 November 2011 (BGBl. 2011 I, p. 2302), states:

> 'The injured party may, where there is a risk of recurrence, bring an action for an injunction against any person who uses a patented invention in breach of Paragraphs 9 to 13. The injured party shall also have that right if an infringement is liable to be committed for the first time.'

11   Paragraphs 19 and 20 of the Law against Restrictions of Competition (Gesetz gegen Wettbewerbsbeschränkungen) of 26 June 2013 (BGBl. 2013 I, p. 1750) prohibit the abuse by one or more undertakings of a dominant position on a market.

The ETSI rules

12   The European Telecommunications Standards Institute ('ETSI') is a body the objective of which, according to Clause 3.1 of Annex 6 to the ETSI Rules of Procedure, which annex is entitled 'ETSI Intellectual-Property Rights Policy', is to create standards which meet the technical objectives of the European telecommunications sector and to reduce the risk to ETSI, its members and others applying ETSI standards, that investment in the preparation, adoption and application of standards could be wasted as a result of an essential intellectual-property right for those standards being unavailable. To that end, Annex 6 seeks a balance between the needs of standardisation for public use in the field of telecommunications and the rights of the owners of intellectual-property rights.

13   Clause 3.2 of that annex provides that owners of intellectual-property rights should be adequately and fairly rewarded for the use of their intellectual-property rights.

14   Under Clause 4.1 of Annex 6, each of the members of ETSI is required to use reasonable endeavours, in particular during the development of a standard

in the establishment of which it participates, to inform ETSI of that member's intellectual-property rights which are essential to that standard, in a timely fashion.

15 Clause 6.1 of Annex 6 to the ETSI Rules of Procedure provides that, when an intellectual-property right essential to a standard is brought to the attention of ETSI, the Director-General of ETSI must immediately request the owner of that right to give, within three months, an irrevocable undertaking that it is prepared to grant licences on fair, reasonable and non-discriminatory terms ('FRAND terms') in relation to that right.

16 Under Clause 6.3 of that annex, for so long as such an undertaking has not been given, ETSI is to assess whether work on the relevant parts of the standard should be suspended.

17 Clause 8.1 of Annex 6 provides that, if the owner of the intellectual-property rights refuses to give that undertaking, ETSI is to seek an alternative technology and, if no such technology exists, to stop work on the adoption of the standard in question.

18 Under Clause 14 of Annex 6 to the ETSI Rules of Procedure, any violation of the provisions of that annex by a member of ETSI is deemed to be a breach of that member's obligations to ETSI.

19 Clause 15.6 of that annex provides that an intellectual-property right is regarded as essential where, in particular, it is not possible on technical grounds to make equipment which complies with the standard without infringing the intellectual-property right ('essential patent').

20 However, ETSI does not check whether the intellectual-property right, the use of which an ETSI member has brought to its attention as being necessary, is valid or essential. Nor does Annex 6 define the concept of a 'licence on FRAND terms'.

The dispute in the main proceedings and the questions referred for a preliminary ruling

21 Huawei Technologies, a multinational company active in the telecommunications sector, is the proprietor of, inter alia, the European patent registered under the reference EP 2 090 050 B 1, bearing the title 'Method and apparatus of establishing a synchronisation signal in a communication system', granted by the Federal Republic of Germany, a Contracting State of the EPC ('patent EP 2 090 050 B 1').

22 That patent was notified to ETSI on 4 March 2009 by Huawei Technologies as a patent essential to the 'Long Term Evolution' standard. At the same time, Huawei Technologies undertook to grant licences to third parties on FRAND terms.

23 The referring court states, in the order for reference, that that patent is essential to that standard, which means that anyone using the 'Long Term Evolution' standard inevitably uses the teaching of that patent.

24 Between November 2010 and the end of March 2011, Huawei Technologies and ZTE Corp., a company belonging to a multinational group active in the telecommunications sector and which markets, in Germany, products equipped with software linked to that standard, engaged in discussions concerning, inter alia, the infringement of patent EP 2 090 050 B 1 and the possibility of concluding a licence on FRAND terms in relation to those products.

25 Huawei Technologies indicated the amount which it considered to be a reasonable royalty. For its part, ZTE Corp. sought a cross-licensing agreement. However, no offer relating to a licensing agreement was finalised.

26 None the less, ZTE markets products that operate on the basis of the 'Long Term Evolution' standard, thus using patent EP 2 090 050 B 1, without paying a royalty to Huawei Technologies or exhaustively rendering an account to Huawei Technologies in respect of past acts of use.

27 On 28 April 2011, on the basis of Article 64 of the EPC and Paragraph 139 et seq. of the German Law on Patents, as amended most recently by Paragraph 13 of the Law of 24 November 2011, Huawei Technologies brought an action for infringement against ZTE before the referring court, seeking an injunction prohibiting the infringement, the rendering of accounts, the recall of products and an award of damages.

28 That court considers that the decision on the substance in the main proceedings turns on whether the action brought by Huawei Technologies constitutes an abuse of that company's dominant position. It thus observes that it might be possible to rely on the mandatory nature of the grant of the licence in order to dismiss the action for a prohibitory injunction — in particular, on the basis of Article 102 TFEU — if, by its action, Huawei Technologies were to be regarded as abusing its dominant position. According to the referring court, the existence of that dominant position is not in dispute.

29 The referring court states, however, that different approaches may be taken in order to determine the point at which the proprietor of an SEP infringes Article 102 TFEU as a result of bringing an action for a prohibitory injunction.

30 In this connection, the referring court observes that, on the basis of Article 102 TFEU, Paragraph 20(1) of the Law of 26 June 2013 against Restrictions of Competition and Paragraph 242 of the Civil Code, the Bundesgerichtshof (Federal Court of Justice, Germany) held, in its judgment of 6 May 2009 in *Orange Book* (KZR 39/06), that, where the proprietor of a patent seeks a prohibitory injunction against a defendant which has a claim to a licence for that patent, the proprietor of the patent abuses its dominant position only in certain circumstances.

31 First, the defendant must have made the applicant an unconditional offer to conclude a licensing agreement not limited exclusively to cases of infringement, it being understood that the defendant must consider itself

bound by that offer and that the applicant is obliged to accept it where its refusal would unfairly impede the defendant or infringe the principle of non-discrimination.

32 Secondly, where the defendant uses the teachings of the patent before the applicant accepts such an offer, it must comply with the obligations that will be incumbent on it, for use of the patent, under the future licensing agreement, namely to account for acts of use and to pay the sums resulting therefrom.

33 In the light of the fact that ZTE's offers to conclude an agreement could not be regarded as 'unconditional', inasmuch as they related only to the products giving rise to the infringement, and that ZTE did not pay Huawei Technologies the amount of the royalty that it had itself calculated or provide to Huawei Technologies an exhaustive account of past acts of use, the referring court observes that it ought to preclude ZTE from being able validly to rely on the compulsory nature of the grant of the licence and, accordingly, ought to uphold Huawei Technologies' action for a prohibitory injunction.

34 However, the referring court notes that, in the press releases No IP/12/1448 and MEMO/12/1021 of 21 December 2012, concerning a Statement of Objections sent to Samsung and relating to patent-infringement proceedings brought by Samsung in the field of mobile telephony, the European Commission appears to regard the bringing of an action for a prohibitory injunction as unlawful, under Article 102 TFEU, where that action relates to an SEP, the proprietor of that SEP has indicated to a standardisation body that it is prepared to grant licences on FRAND terms and the infringer is itself willing to negotiate such a licence. Accordingly, it may be irrelevant that the parties in question cannot agree on the content of certain clauses in the licensing agreement or, in particular, on the amount of the royalty to be paid.

35 In the present case, if those criteria alone are to be applied by the referring court, the latter court observes that it ought to dismiss Huawei Technologies' action for a prohibitory injunction as constituting an abuse within the meaning of Article 102 TFEU, since it is common ground that the parties in the main proceedings were willing to negotiate.

36 The referring court takes the view that, in the case in the main proceedings, the fact that the infringer was willing to negotiate and the proprietor of patent EP 2 090 050 B 1 was prepared to grant licences to third parties ought not be sufficient to constitute an abuse of a dominant position.

37 The referring court takes the view that, in assessing whether the conduct of the proprietor of an SEP is abusive, an appropriate and fair balance has to be struck in relation to all the legitimate interests of the parties, which, it must be recognised, have equivalent bargaining power.

38 Thus, the referring court considers that the positions of the proprietor of an SEP and of the infringer ought not to make it possible for them to obtain

excessively high royalties (a 'hold-up' situation) or excessively low royalties (a 'reverse hold-up' situation), respectively. For that reason, but also on the grounds of equality of treatment between the beneficiaries of licences for, and the infringers in relation to, a given product, the proprietor of the SEP ought to be able to bring an action for a prohibitory injunction. Indeed, the exercise of a statutory right cannot, in itself, constitute an abuse of a dominant position, for characterisation as such requires other criteria to be satisfied. For that reason, it is not satisfactory to adopt, as a criterion of such an abuse, the notion of the infringer's 'willingness to negotiate', since this may give rise to numerous interpretations and provide the infringer with too wide a freedom of action. In any event, if such a notion is to be held to be relevant, certain qualitative and time requirements must be imposed in order to ensure that the applicant for the licence is acting in good faith. Accordingly, a properly formulated, acceptable, 'unconditional' request for a licence, containing all the provisions normally found in a licensing agreement, ought to be required to be submitted before the patent concerned is used. As regards, in particular, requests for a licence from operators which have already placed products using an SEP on the market, those operators must immediately comply with the obligations to render an account of use of that SEP and to pay the corresponding royalty. In addition, the referring court considers that an infringer ought, initially, to be able to provide security instead of paying the royalty directly to the proprietor of the SEP in question. The possibility of the applicant for a licence leaving the determination of a fair royalty amount to the proprietor must also be envisaged.

39 In those circumstances, the Landgericht Düsseldorf decided to stay the proceedings and to refer the following questions to the Court of Justice for a preliminary ruling:

> '(1) Does the proprietor of [an SEP] which informs a standardisation body that it is willing to grant any third party a licence on [FRAND] terms abuse its dominant market position if it brings an action for an injunction against a patent infringer even though the infringer has declared that it is willing to negotiate concerning such a licence?

> or

> Is an abuse of the dominant market position to be presumed only where the infringer has submitted to the proprietor of the [SEP] an acceptable, unconditional offer to conclude a licensing agreement which the patentee cannot refuse without unfairly impeding the infringer or breaching the prohibition of discrimination, and the infringer fulfils its contractual obligations for acts of use already performed in anticipation of the licence to be granted?

(2)   If abuse of a dominant market position is already to be presumed as a consequence of the infringer's willingness to negotiate:

Does Article 102 TFEU lay down particular qualitative and/or time requirements in relation to the willingness to negotiate? In particular, can willingness to negotiate be presumed where the patent infringer has merely stated (orally) in a general way that it is prepared to enter into negotiations, or must the infringer already have entered into negotiations by, for example, submitting specific conditions upon which it is prepared to conclude a licensing agreement?

(3)   If the submission of an acceptable, unconditional offer to conclude a licensing agreement is a prerequisite for abuse of a dominant market position:

Does Article 102 TFEU lay down particular qualitative and/or time requirements in relation to that offer? Must the offer contain all the provisions which are normally included in licensing agreements in the field of technology in question? In particular, may the offer be made subject to the condition that the [SEP] is actually used and/or is shown to be valid?

(4)   If the fulfilment of the infringer's obligations arising from the licence that is to be granted is a prerequisite for the abuse of a dominant market position:

Does Article 102 TFEU lay down particular requirements with regard to those acts of fulfilment? Is the infringer particularly required to render an account for past acts of use and/or to pay royalties? May an obligation to pay royalties be discharged, if necessary, by depositing a security?

(5)   Do the conditions under which the abuse of a dominant position by the proprietor of a[n SEP] is to be presumed apply also to an action on the ground of other claims (for rendering of accounts, recall of products, damages) arising from a patent infringement?'

Consideration of the questions referred

40 A preliminary point to note is that the present request for a preliminary ruling has arisen in the context of an action concerning infringement of a patent between two operators in the telecommunications sector, which are holders of numerous patents essential to the 'Long Term Evolution' standard established by ETSI, which standard is composed of more than 4 700 SEPs,

in respect of which those operators have undertaken to grant licences to third parties on FRAND terms.

41   In the context of that dispute, the referring court raises the question whether the action for infringement seeking an injunction prohibiting that infringement, the rendering of accounts, the recall of products and damages, brought by the proprietor of an SEP — in this case, Huawei Technologies — against the alleged infringer of that SEP — ZTE, which requested the conclusion of a licensing agreement — is to be characterised as an 'abuse of a dominant position', within the meaning of Article 102 TFEU, and, accordingly, whether the action must be dismissed.

42   For the purpose of providing an answer to the referring court and in assessing the lawfulness of such an action for infringement brought by the proprietor of an SEP against an infringer with which no licensing agreement has been concluded, the Court must strike a balance between maintaining free competition — in respect of which primary law and, in particular, Article 102 TFEU prohibit abuses of a dominant position — and the requirement to safeguard that proprietor's intellectual-property rights and its right to effective judicial protection, guaranteed by Article 17(2) and Article 47 of the Charter, respectively.

43   As the referring court states in the order for reference, the existence of a dominant position has not been contested before it by the parties to the dispute in the main proceedings. Given that the questions posed by the referring court relate only to the existence of an abuse, the analysis must be confined to the latter criterion.

Questions 1 to 4, and Question 5 in so far as that question concerns legal proceedings brought with a view to obtaining the recall of products

44   By Questions 1 to 4, and Question 5 in so far as that question concerns legal proceedings brought with a view to obtaining the recall of products, which questions it is appropriate to examine together, the referring court asks, essentially, in what circumstances the bringing of an action for infringement, by an undertaking in a dominant position and holding an SEP, which has given an undertaking to the standardisation body to grant licences to third parties on FRAND terms, seeking an injunction prohibiting the infringement of that SEP or seeking the recall of products for the manufacture of which the SEP has been used, is to be regarded as constituting an abuse contrary to Article 102 TFEU.

45   First of all, it must be recalled that the concept of an abuse of a dominant position within the meaning of Article 102 TFEU is an objective concept relating to the conduct of a dominant undertaking which, on a market where the degree of competition is already weakened precisely because of the presence of the undertaking concerned, through recourse to methods different from those governing normal competition in products or services on the basis of the transactions of commercial operators, has the effect of hindering the maintenance of the degree of competition still existing in the

market or the growth of that competition (judgments in *Hoffmann-La Roche* v *Commission*, 85/76, EU:C:1979:36, paragraph 91; *AKZO* v *Commission*, C-62/86, EU:C:1991:286, paragraph 69; and *Tomra Systems and Others* v *Commission*, C-549/10 P, EU:C:2012:221, paragraph 17).

46 It is, in this connection, settled case-law that the exercise of an exclusive right linked to an intellectual-property right — in the case in the main proceedings, namely the right to bring an action for infringement — forms part of the rights of the proprietor of an intellectual-property right, with the result that the exercise of such a right, even if it is the act of an undertaking holding a dominant position, cannot in itself constitute an abuse of a dominant position (see, to that effect, judgments in *Volvo*, 238/87, EU:C:1988:477, paragraph 8; *RTE and ITP* v *Commission*, C-241/91 P and C-242/91 P, EU:C:1995:98, paragraph 49; and *IMS Health*, C-418/01, EU:C:2004:257, paragraph 34).

47 However, it is also settled case-law that the exercise of an exclusive right linked to an intellectual-property right by the proprietor may, in exceptional circumstances, involve abusive conduct for the purposes of Article 102 TFEU (see, to that effect, judgments in *Volvo*, 238/87, EU:C:1988:477, paragraph 9; *RTE and ITP* v *Commission*, C-241/91 P and C-242/91 P, EU:C:1995:98, paragraph 50; and *IMS Health*, C-418/01, EU:C:2004:257, paragraph 35).

48 Nevertheless, it must be pointed out, as the Advocate General has observed in point 70 of his Opinion, that the particular circumstances of the case in the main proceedings distinguish that case from the cases which gave rise to the case-law cited in paragraphs 46 and 47 of the present judgment.

49 It is characterised, first, as the referring court has observed, by the fact that the patent at issue is essential to a standard established by a standardisation body, rendering its use indispensable to all competitors which envisage manufacturing products that comply with the standard to which it is linked.

50 That feature distinguishes SEPs from patents that are not essential to a standard and which normally allow third parties to manufacture competing products without recourse to the patent concerned and without compromising the essential functions of the product in question.

51 Secondly, the case in the main proceedings may be distinguished by the fact, as is apparent from paragraphs 15 to 17 and 22 of the present judgment, that the patent at issue obtained SEP status only in return for the proprietor's irrevocable undertaking, given to the standardisation body in question, that it is prepared to grant licences on FRAND terms.

52 Although the proprietor of the essential patent at issue has the right to bring an action for a prohibitory injunction or for the recall of products, the fact that that patent has obtained SEP status means that its proprietor can prevent products manufactured by competitors from appearing or remaining on the market and, thereby, reserve to itself the manufacture of the products in question.

53 In those circumstances, and having regard to the fact that an undertaking to grant licences on FRAND terms creates legitimate expectations on the part of third parties that the proprietor of the SEP will in fact grant licences on such terms, a refusal by the proprietor of the SEP to grant a licence on those terms may, in principle, constitute an abuse within the meaning of Article 102 TFEU.

54 It follows that, having regard to the legitimate expectations created, the abusive nature of such a refusal may, in principle, be raised in defence to actions for a prohibitory injunction or for the recall of products. However, under Article 102 TFEU, the proprietor of the patent is obliged only to grant a licence on FRAND terms. In the case in the main proceedings, the parties are not in agreement as to what is required by FRAND terms in the circumstances of that case.

55 In such a situation, in order to prevent an action for a prohibitory injunction or for the recall of products from being regarded as abusive, the proprietor of an SEP must comply with conditions which seek to ensure a fair balance between the interests concerned.

56 In this connection, due account must be taken of the specific legal and factual circumstances in the case (see, to that effect, judgment in *Post Danmark*, C-209/10, EU:C:2012:172, paragraph 26 and the case-law cited).

57 Thus, the need to enforce intellectual-property rights, covered by, inter alia, Directive 2004/48, which — in accordance with Article 17(2) of the Charter — provides for a range of legal remedies aimed at ensuring a high level of protection for intellectual-property rights in the internal market, and the right to effective judicial protection guaranteed by Article 47 of the Charter, comprising various elements, including the right of access to a tribunal, must be taken into consideration (see, to that effect, judgment in *Otis and Others*, C-199/11, EU:C:2012:684, paragraph 48).

58 This need for a high level of protection for intellectual-property rights means that, in principle, the proprietor may not be deprived of the right to have recourse to legal proceedings to ensure effective enforcement of his exclusive rights, and that, in principle, the user of those rights, if he is not the proprietor, is required to obtain a licence prior to any use.

59 Thus, although the irrevocable undertaking to grant licences on FRAND terms given to the standardisation body by the proprietor of an SEP cannot negate the substance of the rights guaranteed to that proprietor by Article 17(2) and Article 47 of the Charter, it does, none the less, justify the imposition on that proprietor of an obligation to comply with specific requirements when bringing actions against alleged infringers for a prohibitory injunction or for the recall of products.

60 Accordingly, the proprietor of an SEP which considers that that SEP is the subject of an infringement cannot, without infringing Article 102 TFEU, bring an action for a prohibitory injunction or for the recall of products against the alleged infringer without notice or prior consultation with the

alleged infringer, even if the SEP has already been used by the alleged infringer.

61 Prior to such proceedings, it is thus for the proprietor of the SEP in question, first, to alert the alleged infringer of the infringement complained about by designating that SEP and specifying the way in which it has been infringed.

62 As the Advocate General has observed in point 81 of his Opinion, in view of the large number of SEPs composing a standard such as that at issue in the main proceedings, it is not certain that the infringer of one of those SEPs will necessarily be aware that it is using the teaching of an SEP that is both valid and essential to a standard.

63 Secondly, after the alleged infringer has expressed its willingness to conclude a licensing agreement on FRAND terms, it is for the proprietor of the SEP to present to that alleged infringer a specific, written offer for a licence on FRAND terms, in accordance with the undertaking given to the standardisation body, specifying, in particular, the amount of the royalty and the way in which that royalty is to be calculated.

64 As the Advocate General has observed in point 86 of his Opinion, where the proprietor of an SEP has given an undertaking to the standardisation body to grant licences on FRAND terms, it can be expected that it will make such an offer. Furthermore, in the absence of a public standard licensing agreement, and where licensing agreements already concluded with other competitors are not made public, the proprietor of the SEP is better placed to check whether its offer complies with the condition of non-discrimination than is the alleged infringer.

65 By contrast, it is for the alleged infringer diligently to respond to that offer, in accordance with recognised commercial practices in the field and in good faith, a point which must be established on the basis of objective factors and which implies, in particular, that there are no delaying tactics.

66 Should the alleged infringer not accept the offer made to it, it may rely on the abusive nature of an action for a prohibitory injunction or for the recall of products only if it has submitted to the proprietor of the SEP in question, promptly and in writing, a specific counter-offer that corresponds to FRAND terms.

67 Furthermore, where the alleged infringer is using the teachings of the SEP before a licensing agreement has been concluded, it is for that alleged infringer, from the point at which its counter-offer is rejected, to provide appropriate security, in accordance with recognised commercial practices in the field, for example by providing a bank guarantee or by placing the amounts necessary on deposit. The calculation of that security must include, inter alia, the number of the past acts of use of the SEP, and the alleged infringer must be able to render an account in respect of those acts of use.

68   In addition, where no agreement is reached on the details of the FRAND terms following the counter-offer by the alleged infringer, the parties may, by common agreement, request that the amount of the royalty be determined by an independent third party, by decision without delay.

69   Lastly, having regard, first, to the fact that a standardisation body such as that which developed the standard at issue in the main proceedings does not check whether patents are valid or essential to the standard in which they are included during the standardisation procedure, and, secondly, to the right to effective judicial protection guaranteed by Article 47 of the Charter, an alleged infringer cannot be criticised either for challenging, in parallel to the negotiations relating to the grant of licences, the validity of those patents and/or the essential nature of those patents to the standard in which they are included and/or their actual use, or for reserving the right to do so in the future.

70   It is for the referring court to determine whether the abovementioned criteria are satisfied in the present case, in so far as they are relevant, in the circumstances, for the purpose of resolving the dispute in the main proceedings.

71   It follows from all the foregoing considerations that the answer to Questions 1 to 4, and to Question 5 in so far as that question concerns legal proceedings brought with a view to obtaining the recall of products, is that Article 102 TFEU must be interpreted as meaning that the proprietor of an SEP, which has given an irrevocable undertaking to a standardisation body to grant a licence to third parties on FRAND terms, does not abuse its dominant position, within the meaning of Article 102 TFEU, by bringing an action for infringement seeking an injunction prohibiting the infringement of its patent or seeking the recall of products for the manufacture of which that patent has been used, as long as:

-   prior to bringing that action, the proprietor has, first, alerted the alleged infringer of the infringement complained about by designating that patent and specifying the way in which it has been infringed, and, secondly, after the alleged infringer has expressed its willingness to conclude a licensing agreement on FRAND terms, presented to that infringer a specific, written offer for a licence on such terms, specifying, in particular, the royalty and the way in which it is to be calculated, and

-   where the alleged infringer continues to use the patent in question, the alleged infringer has not diligently responded to that offer, in accordance with recognised commercial practices in the field and in good faith, this being a matter which must be established on the basis of objective factors and which implies, in particular, that there are no delaying tactics.

Question 5, in so far as that question concerns legal proceedings brought with a view to obtaining the rendering of accounts or an award of damages

72   By Question 5, in so far as that question concerns legal proceedings brought with a view to obtaining the rendering of accounts or an award of damages, the referring court asks, in essence, whether Article 102 TFEU must be interpreted as prohibiting an undertaking in a dominant position and holding an SEP, which has given an undertaking to the standardisation body to grant licences for that patent on FRAND terms, from bringing an action for infringement against the alleged infringer of its SEP and seeking the rendering of accounts in relation to past acts of use of that SEP or an award of damages in respect of those acts of use.

73   As is apparent from paragraphs 52 and 53 above, the exercise by the proprietor of the SEP of its intellectual-property rights, by bringing actions for a prohibitory injunction or for the recall of products, may be characterised, in circumstances such as those in the main proceedings, as an abuse, where those proceedings are liable to prevent products complying with the standard in question manufactured by competitors from appearing or remaining on the market.

74   In the present case, according to the description set out in the order for reference, the actions for infringement brought by the proprietor of an SEP, seeking the rendering of accounts in relation to past acts of use of that SEP or an award of damages in respect of those acts of use, do not have a direct impact on products complying with the standard in question manufactured by competitors appearing or remaining on the market.

75   Consequently, in circumstances such as those in the main proceedings, such actions cannot be regarded as an abuse under Article 102 TFEU.

76   In the light of the foregoing considerations, the answer to Question 5, in so far as that question concerns legal proceedings brought with a view to obtaining the rendering of accounts or an award of damages, is that Article 102 TFEU must be interpreted as not prohibiting, in circumstances such as those in the main proceedings, an undertaking in a dominant position and holding an SEP, which has given an undertaking to the standardisation body to grant licences for that SEP on FRAND terms, from bringing an action for infringement against the alleged infringer of its SEP and seeking the rendering of accounts in relation to past acts of use of that SEP or an award of damages in respect of those acts of use.

. . .

Notes

1.   The CJEU states that "it is thus for the proprietor of the SEP in question, first, to alert the alleged infringer of the infringement complained about by designating that SEP and specifying the way in which it has been infringed." How would the patentee satisfy this requirement? Patentees often provide to alleged infringers "claim charts," which outline how the patentee's patent claims (which

define the scope of its right to exclude) are infringed by the alleged infringer's product. Should claim charts be required? Note that in the following Qualcomm case they were not provided.

2.   In making a FRAND offer, the patentee must "specify[], in particular, the amount of the royalty and the way in which that royalty is to be calculated." The court supports this requirement by noting that "the proprietor of the SEP is better placed to check whether its offer complies with the condition of non-discrimination than is the alleged infringer." The court also requires the alleged infringer to submit a FRAND counter-offer, though. How can the alleged infringer know whether its counter-offer is discriminatory? *See* Mark R. Patterson, "Confidentiality in Patent Dispute Resolution: Antitrust Implications," 93 Washington Law Review 827 (2018).

3.   This case leaves many issues unclear, though some have been addressed in cases both in the U.S. and in Europe. A notable example is a UK case, *Unwired Planet International Ltd. v Huawei Technologies Co. Ltd.*, [2017] EWHC 711. For example, the court in *Unwired Planet* wrote that there is only a single set of FRAND terms "in a given set of circumstances" (¶ 164), which contrasts with the approach of U.S. District Judge James Robart in *Microsoft Corp. v. Motorola, Inc.*, 963 F. Supp. 2d 1176 (W.D. Wash. 2013), who concluded there would a range of possible FRAND royalties. *See* Jorge L. Contreras, "Unwired Planct v. Huawei: An English Perspective on FRAND Royalties," Patently-O, April 10, 2017; Mark R. Patterson, "Prof Patterson: Teasing Through a Single FRAND Rate," Patently-O, April 20, 2017. The single-FRAND-rate holding of the Unwired Planet court was subsequently reversed on appeal, however. *Unwired Planet International Ltd. v Huawei Technologies Co. Ltd.*, [2018] EWCA Civ 2344, ¶121.

4.   The *Unwired Planet* court additionally held that only a global license could be FRAND, despite the fact that the proceeding was based on UK patents and that Unwired Planet had no patents at all in some countries where Huawei manufactured and sold its products. This decision was upheld on appeal with the Court of Appeal stating that "the judge found that a licensor and a licensee acting willingly and reasonably would have regarded country by country licensing as madness; and further, that no rational business would have done this if it could be avoided." *Unwired Planet International Ltd. v Huawei Technologies Co. Ltd.*, [2018] EWCA Civ 2344, ¶128.

5.   Somewhat more surprisingly, perhaps, the Court of Appeal in *Unwired Planet* also concluded that the conditions set out in *Huawei v. ZTE* were not mandatory ones, taking the view that the CJEU was only establishing what conduct would *not* violate competition law, not what conduct would be a violation. *Unwired Planet International Ltd. v Huawei Technologies Co. Ltd.*, [2018] EWCA Civ 2344, ¶269. Do you agree?

6.   Further issues from *Unwired Planet* are discussed after the following case.

F.T.C. v. Qualcomm Inc.
411 F. Supp. 3d 658
(N.D. Cal. May 21, 2019)

LUCY H. KOH, United States District Judge

Plaintiff Federal Trade Commission ("FTC") brings suit against Defendant Qualcomm Incorporated ("Qualcomm") for allegedly violating Section 5(a) of the FTC Act, 15 U.S.C. § 45(a), and seeks permanent injunctive relief. Specifically, the FTC claims that Qualcomm has harmed competition in two markets for baseband processors, also called modem chips, through a set of interrelated Qualcomm practices. The FTC Act prohibits "[u]nfair methods of competition," which include violations of the Sherman Act. The FTC asserts that Qualcomm's conduct violates (1) Section 1 of the Sherman Act, 15 U.S.C. § 1; (2) Section 2 of the Sherman Act, 15 U.S.C. § 2; and (3) Section 5 of the FTC Act, 15 U.S.C. § 45(a).

. . .

On August 30, 2018, the FTC moved for partial summary judgment on the question of whether Qualcomm's commitments to two standard setting organizations ("SSOs"), the Alliance for Telecommunications Industry Solutions ("ATIS") and the Telecommunications Industry Association ("TIA"), require Qualcomm to license to other modem chip suppliers on fair, reasonable, and nondiscriminatory terms Qualcomm's patents that are essential to practicing the ATIS and TIA standards. On November 6, 2018, the Court granted the FTC's motion for partial summary judgment.

The Court held a 10-day bench trial in this matter beginning on January 4, 2019. The parties gave closing arguments on January 29, 2019. Having considered the evidence and arguments of counsel, the relevant law, and the record in this case, the Court hereby enters the following findings of fact and conclusions of law.

I. STIPULATED FACTS

The parties stipulated to the following facts:

. . .

7. Cellular communications depend on widely distributed networks that implement cellular communications standards.

. . .

11. The Third Generation Partnership Project ("3GPP") and the Third Generation Partnership Project 2 ("3GPP2") are global collaborative partnerships of standards development/standards-setting organizations ("SDOs" or "SSOs") and other industry participants that develop technical specifications for cellular standards.

12. The current "organizational partners" of 3GPP are seven regional SSOs, specifically: the European Telecommunications Standards Institute ("ETSI"), the Alliance for Telecommunications Industry Solutions ("ATIS"), the Association of Radio Industries and Businesses, Japan ("ARIB"), the Telecommunication Technology Committee, Japan ("TTC"), the China Communications Standards Association ("CCSA"), the Telecommunications Standards Development Society, India ("TSDSI"), and the Telecommunications Technology Association, Korea ("TTA").

13. The current organizational partners of 3GPP2 are five regional SSOs, specifically: the Telecommunications Industry Association ("TIA"), ARIB, TTC, CCSA, and TTA.

14. Cellular communications standards have evolved over "generations," including second-generation ("2G"), third-generation ("3G"), and fourth-generation ("4G") standards.

15. 2G cellular standards include the Global System for Mobile ("GSM") and cdmaOne (also sometimes called "TIA/EIA/IS-95" or "IS-95").

16. ETSI adopted GSM as a cellular standard. ETSI also adopted General Packet Radio Service ("GPRS") and Enhanced Data Global Evolution ("EDGE") as improvements to GSM. These are considered 2G standards.

. . .

18. TIA adopted cdmaOne as a cellular standard. TIA also adopted IS-95A and IS-95B as improvements to cdmaOne. These are considered 2G standards.

. . .

20. 3G cellular standards include the Universal Mobile Telecommunications System ("UMTS") and CDMA2000.

21. UMTS is an umbrella term for three 3G cellular air interfaces standardized within 3GPP: UTRA-FDD, commonly called Wideband CDMA ("WCDMA"), used worldwide; UTRA-TDD High Chip Rate, having little deployment; and UTRA-TDD Low Chip Rate, commonly called Time Division-Synchronous CDMA ("TD-SCDMA"), used primarily in China.

. . .

24. In the United States, AT&T and T-Mobile have operated WCDMA networks. Verizon and Sprint have operated CDMA2000 networks.

25. All four major U.S. carriers (Verizon, AT&T, T-Mobile, and Sprint) have deployed LTE, which also encompasses the LTE Advanced, or "LTE-A" standard, as their 4G standard.

. . .

27. LTE was standardized by 3GPP.

II. BACKGROUND

The Court discusses cellular standard setting organizations ("SSOs"), Qualcomm's license agreements, Qualcomm's modem chip business, antitrust investigations into Qualcomm's licensing practices, and the credibility of many Qualcomm witnesses.

A. SSOs and FRAND

[This material is included above, prior to *Huawei v. ZTE*.]

B. Qualcomm License Agreements

Qualcomm Technology Licensing ("QTL") is the division of Qualcomm that grants licenses to Qualcomm's patent portfolio. QTL holds and licenses three broad categories of patents: (1) cellular standard essential patents ("SEPs"); (2) non-cellular SEPs; and (3) non-SEPs, which also are known as implementation patents. Cellular SEPs are patents necessary to practice a particular cellular standard. By contrast, non-cellular SEPs are necessary to the practice of a non-cellular standard. Non-SEPs are patents not necessary to the practice of any standard. Liren Chen (QTL Senior Vice President of Engineering and Legal Counsel) estimated at trial that Qualcomm held approximately 140,000 granted patents and pending patent applications as of March 2018.

Qualcomm primarily licenses its patents on a "portfolio basis," which means that a licensee pays for and receives rights to all three categories of Qualcomm patents—cellular SEPs, non-cellular SEPs, and non-SEPs. Qualcomm occasionally offers separate licenses to its SEPs. Qualcomm stated in its 2017 10-K filed with the Securities and Exchange Commission ("SEC") that SEP-only licenses "negatively impact" Qualcomm's licensing revenues because Qualcomm receives higher royalty rates for portfolio licenses than for SEP-only licenses.

In 1990, Qualcomm began licensing its CDMA patents. According to Dr. Irwin Jacobs (Qualcomm Co-Founder and former CEO), Qualcomm first licensed its patents to generate funds for continued research and development. . . .

. . .

At some point, Qualcomm stopped licensing rival modem chip suppliers and instead started licensing only OEMs at a 5% running royalty on the price of each handset sold. These licenses are called Subscriber Unit License Agreements ("SULA"). With a SULA, an OEM may sell handsets that practice Qualcomm's patents without fear of an infringement suit from Qualcomm. The parties stipulated that in a typical SULA, Qualcomm receives consideration in the form of a running royalty rate calculated as a percentage of the licensee's wholesale net selling price of the end-user device (minus applicable deductions), subject to royalty caps. An end-user device is a cellular handset, which the parties have stipulated is defined as a mobile phone.

Specifically, Qualcomm charges a 5% running royalty on handset sales for a license to Qualcomm's CDMA patent portfolio, which includes CDMA SEPs and non-SEPs. For Qualcomm's LTE portfolio, Qualcomm has historically charged a

4% running royalty rate. Qualcomm SULAs grant rights both to the relevant Qualcomm patents existing at the time of the SULA and additional relevant Qualcomm patents issued during the license term.

Qualcomm has capped the maximum royalty base or net selling price of the handset at $400. In some SULAs, Qualcomm charges an upfront fee in addition to the running royalty rate on handset sales. SULAs also require OEMs to grant cross licenses to their patents to Qualcomm, sometimes on a royalty-free basis.

Qualcomm has been forced to alter certain royalty rates and licensing practices after a 2014 investigation of Qualcomm's business practices by China's National Development and Reform Commission ("NDRC"), the government entity responsible for antitrust. The NDRC issued a "rectification plan," which requires Qualcomm to offer SEP-only licenses to Qualcomm's China patents at specified rates. The resulting agreements are Chinese Patent License Agreements ("CPLA").

In a CPLA, which is a SEP-only license, Qualcomm charges a 5% running royalty rate on sales of handsets that support multiple cellular standards and a 3.5% running royalty rate on sales of LTE-only handsets, although the CPLA charges those rates against 65% of the handset price and the rates apply only to handsets made and sold for use in China. As will be discussed further below, a presentation to a committee of the Qualcomm Board of Directors in 2015 explained that Qualcomm was able to avoid more aggressive rate cuts by making a $150 million contribution to the Chinese government.

Qualcomm now charges the same royalty rates in other SEP-only licenses regardless of whether the handsets are made and sold only for use in China.

Licensing is very profitable for Qualcomm. In 2015, David Wise (Qualcomm Senior Vice President and Treasurer) stated in a presentation shared with Alex Rogers (QTL President) that "QTL represents the vast majority of our value at $50-$70B" and that "1 point of royalty is $16-$20B." At trial, Wise agreed that QTL has historically "represented at least two thirds of the value of Qualcomm." Qualcomm's 2017 strategic plan indicates that QTL earned $7.7 billion in 2016. That figure exceeded the combined 2016 licensing revenue of twelve other patent licensors, including Ericsson, Nokia, and Interdigital. A 2012 Bain Consulting presentation that Qualcomm introduced into evidence concluded that in 2011, "Qualcomm has 25% of global patent licensing revenue" in the cellular handset space and that Qualcomm earned more than 50% of all modem chip patent licensing revenue.

C. Qualcomm Sales of Modem Chips

Next, the Court provides a general overview of Qualcomm CDMA Technologies ("QCT"), Qualcomm's modem chip supply division. Qualcomm is a "fabless" modem chip supplier, which means that QCT outsources the actual fabrication of QCT modem chips to third parties. Modem chips enable handsets to communicate with each other across cellular networks. Any OEM manufacturing a cellular handset must purchase and install a modem chip. Because the OEM must integrate the modem chip into the OEM's handset design process, OEMs may engage with potential modem chip suppliers as many as two years before the OEM plans to commercialize the handset.

Modem chips are either "single-mode" or "multimode." Whereas a single-mode modem chip supports only one cellular standard (like CDMA), a multimode modem chip supports multiple standards in one chip. For example, Qualcomm's MSM 7600 modem chip supports six different cellular standards. A multimode modem enables global roaming, as carriers in different parts of the world may support different cellular standards.

. . .

Qualcomm first sold commercial quantities of modem chips in 1996. From fiscal years 2015 to 2017, Qualcomm shipped between 804 million and 932 million modem chips each year. Although such sales are not relevant to this case, Qualcomm also sells modem chips to OEMs that manufacture items like smart cars.

As of March 2018, several other companies were selling modem chips. These companies include MediaTek; HiSilicon, a division of the OEM Huawei; Samsung LSI (also referred to as Exynos), a division of the OEM Samsung; Intel; and Unisoc (formerly known as Spreadtrum). Other modem chip suppliers exited the market between 2006 and 2016, including Freescale, Marvell, Texas Instruments, ST-Ericsson, Broadcom, and Nvidia. The Court will discuss these rivals and how Qualcomm's practices affected them in more detail below.

. . .

D. Government Investigations, Findings, and Fines

[The court discusses here government investigations in the U.S., Japan, Korea, the European Union, Taiwan, and China.]

Accordingly, Qualcomm's licensing practices have been the subject of government investigations in the United States since at least 2014 and in Asia and Europe since at least 2009.

E. Credibility Determinations

Before discussing the trial evidence in more detail, the Court observes that Qualcomm's trial presentation relied almost exclusively on trial testimony and ignored Qualcomm's own contemporaneous documents. Qualcomm introduced only 16 of its own documents at trial, as compared to the more than 125 Qualcomm documents that the FTC introduced—not counting license and supply agreements. At closing argument Qualcomm relied primarily on expert testimony and demonstratives, and largely ignored Qualcomm's own documents. Most of Qualcomm's experts did not even review Qualcomm's own documents.

The Court finds Qualcomm's internal, contemporaneous documents more persuasive than Qualcomm's trial testimony prepared specifically for this antitrust litigation. *See In re High-Tech Employee Antitrust Litig.*, 289 F.R.D. 555, 576 (N.D. Cal. 2013) (finding contemporaneous documents more persuasive than the defendants' "litigation driven" declarations).

Specifically, many Qualcomm executives' trial testimony was contradicted by these witnesses' own contemporaneous emails, handwritten notes, and recorded statements to the Internal Revenue Service ("IRS"). For example, at trial and at his deposition, Cristiano Amon (Qualcomm President) testified that he had never been informed of Qualcomm threatening to cut off chip supply:

> **Q**: You were asked, 'You have never been informed that QTL threatened to cease supplying chipsets to a customer because of a licensing dispute; is that right?' You answered 'That is correct.' That was a true statement when you said it?
>
> **A**: That is correct.

However, Amon's own handwritten notes from 2015 license negotiations with Motorola's President Rick Osterloh, entitled "12-9-15-Rick & Team-Motorola," state: "(1) Licensing > Eric [Reifschneider, QTL Senior Vice President and General Manager] constantly threatening to cut off chip supply." Thus, despite Amon's own handwriting acknowledging 2015 chip supply threats, Amon testified under oath at his deposition and trial that he was unaware of QTL threats to cutoff chip supply.

Furthermore, Cristiano Amon himself approved joint QTL and QCT plans to cut off chip supply during patent licensing disputes. For example, in November 2012, Eric Reifschneider (QTL Senior Vice President and General Manager) wrote to Amon (then QCT Co-President), Steve Mollenkopf (Qualcomm President), Derek Aberle (QTL President), and Marv Blecker (QTL Senior Vice President) regarding Chinese OEMs: "Cristiano, This summarizes the conclusions we reached regarding sales of TD-SCDMA [TD-SCDMA is a 3G standard used primarily in China] chipsets to customers that we anticipate will use them in TD-SCDMA/GSM products . . . 3. If any of these customers refuses or fails to pay royalties on any other (i.e., C2K [CDMA], UMTS, LTE) devices, we will discontinue supply to such customers as necessary." Amon replied: "This summarizes well the discussion between QMC [Qualcomm Mobile Computing, a division of QCT]/QTL and the agreed plan forward. We will start communicating the plan to the customer base." Thus, Amon not only approved the plan for QCT to cut off chip supply to Chinese OEMs who refuse to pay patent royalties to QTL, but Amon agreed to start communicating this plan to customers. Amon's trial testimony was not consistent with his contemporaneous emails and handwritten notes.

. . .

At both his deposition and at trial, Derek Aberle (QTL President in 2012) was asked about a July 2012 Qualcomm presentation to the Qualcomm Board of Directors that stated "If we cease supply of chips to current customers they may assert antitrust claims seeking damages/fines and continued supply" and listed the following strategy: "Develop a plan of communication/action that maximizes our ability to defend against the above claims while ceasing supply when necessary."

On July 2, 2012, Derek Aberle (QTL President) sent a slide from the presentation to Dr. Paul Jacobs (Qualcomm CEO), Steve Mollenkopf (Qualcomm President), and Steve Altman (Qualcomm Vice Chairman). On July 9, 2012,

Qualcomm presented the same slide—reproduced below—to the Qualcomm Board of Directors, including Dr. Irwin Jacobs (Qualcomm Co-Founder and former CEO).

At his March 2018 deposition, Derek Aberle (former Qualcomm President), who left Qualcomm in January 2018, could not answer any questions about Qualcomm's July 2012 communication plan to defend against antitrust claims: "Actually, as I read that, I don't recall it. I don't actually know what it means.".

However, at the January 2019 trial, Derek Aberle testified that the July 2012 slide reflected Qualcomm's intent to "come up with a proactive plan to make sure we could get out ahead of situations where there may be a dispute or a license renewal that needed to happen and somebody was buying chips from us." It is odd that Aberle had better recall during the January 2019 trial than nearly a year earlier at his March 2018 deposition. The Court does not find Aberle's prepared for trial testimony credible.

. . .

Fabian Gonell (QTL Legal Counsel and Senior Vice President, Licensing Strategy) also testified that Qualcomm does not cut off chip supply during license disputes:

> **Q**: What is Qualcomm's practice with respect to supplying chips to a licensee who is disputing the terms of its license?
>
> **A**: If there's a licensee that is disputing the terms of its license, then we continue to supply chips if they want them.

However, like Rogers, Gonell received the October 27, 2012 Sony email in which Eric Reifschneider (QTL Senior Vice President and General Manager) threatened Sony's chip supply. Gonell also received the November 2012 email in which Eric Reifschneider summarized the QTL and QCT plan for QCT to "discontinue supply" to Chinese OEMs who refuse to pay patent royalties to QTL Gonell also did not testify credibly when confronted by a recording of a Qualcomm meeting with the IRS, as the Court will discuss later in this order. Gonell's testimony was not consistent with his own emails and his own recorded statements to the IRS.

In addition to giving testimony under oath at trial that contradicted their contemporaneous emails, handwritten notes, and recorded statements to the IRS, some Qualcomm witnesses also lacked credibility in other ways. For example, Dr. Irwin Jacobs (Qualcomm Co-Founder), Steve Mollenkopf (Qualcomm CEO), and Dr. James Thompson (Qualcomm CTO) gave such long, fast, and practiced narratives on direct examination that Qualcomm's counsel had to tell the witnesses to slow down. For example, Qualcomm's counsel told Steve Mollenkopf (Qualcomm CEO): "Slow down just a little bit, Mr. Mollenkopf, if you will, please." Qualcomm's counsel also had to tell Irwin Jacobs to slow down: "I'm going to ask you, Dr. Jacobs, to slow down just a little bit. We're trying to take down every word." By contrast, when cross-examined by the FTC, each witness was very reluctant and slow to answer, and at times cagey.

Similarly, as CTO, James Thompson oversees engineering at Qualcomm. On direct examination, Thompson readily testified about several of Qualcomm's modem chips, identified them by their marketing codes, and discussed the standards each chip practiced:

> **Q**: Moving over to the next one, the 7600, what was that chip the first of?
>
> **A**: Okay. So that's – so I mentioned before that we had made a decision to support all modes in the world so our modems could go anywhere in the world, and that was the first chip that supported that.

However, on cross-examination, Dr. Thompson was suddenly unable to answer even basic questions about a modem chip:

> **Q**: Dr. Thompson, Qualcomm's MSM 8655 modem chip is a CDMA capable modem chip?
>
> **A**: That – the MSM 8655, I'm trying to remember. I – you know, off the top of my head, I'm trying to remember which one that is. We use internal code names, and so –
>
> **Q**: Does the second digit being a 6 tell you that this has CDMA?
>
> **A**: Honestly, I don't – I don't know the marketing codes that are used. I have kind of – I think 9 means it has LTE. But – but I'm not sure. I'm not 100 percent sure.

Similar examples exist for Dr. Irwin Jacobs (Qualcomm Co-Founder) and Steve Mollenkopf (Qualcomm CEO).

Therefore, the Court largely discounts Qualcomm's trial testimony prepared specifically for this litigation and instead relies on these witnesses' own contemporaneous emails, handwritten notes, and recorded statements to the IRS.

. . .

IV. MARKET SHARE AND MARKET POWER

The Court first addresses Qualcomm's market share and market power in the relevant antitrust markets, the market for CDMA modem chips and the market for premium LTE modem chips.

[The court concluded that Qualcomm had monopoly power in both markets.]

V. ANTICOMPETITIVE CONDUCT AND HARM

. . .

A. Legal Standard

. . .

Qualcomm argues that the FTC must also show "a causal link between the challenged conduct and the actual, significant competitive harm." However, the D.C. Circuit in *Microsoft* rejected a similar contention that "plaintiffs must present direct proof that a defendant's continued monopoly power is precisely attributable to its anticompetitive conduct." A plaintiff need not "reconstruct the hypothetical marketplace absent a defendant's anticompetitive conduct." Instead, where a government agency seeks injunctive relief—as here—courts should "infer 'causation' from the fact that a defendant has engaged in anticompetitive conduct that 'reasonably appear[s] capable of making a significant contribution to . . . maintaining monopoly power.' " A court "may infer causation when exclusionary conduct is aimed at producers of nascent competitive [products] as well as when it is aimed at producers of established substitutes." Therefore, the Court may infer causation where a defendant has maintained monopoly power and the defendant's anticompetitive conduct "reasonably appears capable" of maintaining monopoly power.

. . .

B. Anticompetitive Conduct Against OEMs and Resulting Harm

First, Qualcomm has used its monopoly power in the CDMA and premium LTE modem chip markets to engage in a wide variety of anticompetitive acts against OEMs.

In a practice that Qualcomm concedes is unique within Qualcomm and unique in the industry, Qualcomm refuses to sell modem chips to an OEM until the OEM signs a separate patent license agreement. Thus, Qualcomm refuses to sell an OEM modem chips exhaustively. Under the doctrine of patent exhaustion, "the initial authorized sale of a patented item terminates all patent rights to that item." *Quanta Comp., Inc. v. LG Elecs., Inc.*, 553 U.S. 617, 625 (2008). Thus, patent exhaustion provides that when a consumer purchases a television, the consumer does not have to separately sign a license and pay royalties for any patents practiced by the television.

To avoid exhaustion and to enforce Qualcomm's practice of requiring a separate patent license before selling modem chips, Qualcomm wields its chip monopoly power to coerce OEMs to sign patent license agreements. Specifically,

Qualcomm threatens to withhold OEMs' chip supply until OEMs sign patent license agreements on Qualcomm's preferred terms. In some cases, Qualcomm has even cut off OEMs' chip supply, although the threat of cutting off chip supply has been more than sufficient to coerce OEMs into signing Qualcomm's patent license agreements and avoiding the devastating loss of chip supply. Qualcomm has also used the "carrot" of chip incentive funds, which reduce the price of Qualcomm's chips and induce OEMs to agree to Qualcomm's licensing terms. QTL—Qualcomm's licensing division—funds these agreements even though the incentives accrue on OEMs' purchases of QCT chips. These chip incentive funds often function as de facto exclusive deals that foreclose OEMs from purchasing modem chips from Qualcomm's rivals.

In addition, Qualcomm has refused to even provide samples of Qualcomm modem chips, withheld technical support, and delayed delivery of software or threatened to require the return of software until OEMs sign Qualcomm's patent license agreements. In 2018, Qualcomm paid to extinguish Samsung's antitrust claims and to silence Samsung. Qualcomm patent license agreements also include unusual provisions that require OEMs to cross-license their patents—often royalty-free—to QCT, Qualcomm's modem chip division, in exchange for the rights to QTL's patents. Despite this host of unique arrangements, Qualcomm refuses to provide OEMs lists of Qualcomm's patents or patent claim charts during license negotiations.

Qualcomm's practice of refusing to sell modem chips until an OEM signs a patent license agreement, and Qualcomm's associated threats, generate and sustain Qualcomm's unreasonably high royalty rates. Because Qualcomm receives royalties on any handset sale, even when that handset contains a rival's modem chip, Qualcomm's unreasonably high royalty rates impose an artificial and anticompetitive surcharge on the price of rivals' modem chips. At times, Qualcomm has even charged OEMs higher royalty rates when OEMs purchase rivals' chips than when OEMs purchase Qualcomm's chips, which further harms rivals.

To provide a coherent narrative, the Court organizes its discussion of Qualcomm's anticompetitive practices in patent license negotiations around Qualcomm's conduct toward the following OEMs: (1) LGE, (2) Sony, (3) Samsung, (4) Huawei, (5) Motorola, (6) Lenovo, (7) BlackBerry, (8) Curitel, (9) BenQ, (10) Apple, (11) VIVO, (12) Wistron, (13) Pegatron, (14) ZTE, (15) Nokia, and (16) smaller Chinese OEMs.

. . .

17. Summary of Anticompetitive Conduct Against OEMs and Resulting Harm

In sum, Qualcomm has engaged in extensive anticompetitive conduct against OEMs. In practices that are unique within Qualcomm and unique in the industry, Qualcomm refuses to sell its modem chips exhaustively and to sell modem chips to an OEM until the OEM signs a separate patent license agreement. To enforce those licensing practices, Qualcomm has cut off OEMs' chip supply, threatened OEMs' chip supply, withheld sample chips, delayed software and threatened to require the return of software, withheld technical support, and refused to share patent claim charts or patent lists. In addition, Qualcomm has required OEMs to grant QCT cross-licenses (often royalty-free) to OEMs' patent portfolios and charged OEMs higher royalty rates on rivals' chips. All of these tactics ensure that OEMs will sign Qualcomm's license agreements and generally result in exclusivity.

In addition to these "sticks," Qualcomm has offered OEMs the carrot of chip incentive funds to induce OEMs to sign patent license agreements. Those chip incentive funds result in exclusivity and near-exclusivity and, by preserving Qualcomm's royalty rates, enable Qualcomm to continue to collect its unreasonably high royalty rates on rivals' chips. Lastly, in 2018, Qualcomm paid to extinguish Samsung's antitrust claims and to silence Samsung.

C. Qualcomm's Refusal to License SEPs to Rivals and Resulting Harm

Next, the Court discusses another element of Qualcomm's anticompetitive conduct, Qualcomm's practice of refusing to license its cellular SEPs to rival modem chip suppliers. This practice has promoted rivals' exit from the market, prevented rivals' entry, and delayed or hampered the entry and success of other rivals. Without a license to Qualcomm's SEPs, a rival cannot sell modem chips with any assurance that Qualcomm will not sue the rival and its customers for patent infringement. Qualcomm's refusal to license its SEPs to rivals also enables Qualcomm to demand unreasonably high royalty rates. Below, the Court discusses Qualcomm's refusal to license rivals, and how Qualcomm's practice has prevented entry, promoted rivals' entry, and hampered rivals in the market.

. . .

In sum, Qualcomm's refusal to license has prevented rivals' entry, impeded rivals' ability to sell modem chips externally or at all, promoted rivals' exit, and delayed rivals' entry. Qualcomm's refusal to license rivals has further limited OEMs' chip supply options, which has enabled Qualcomm's anticompetitive conduct toward OEMs, sustained Qualcomm's unreasonably high royalty rates, and required OEMs to spend more money on royalty payments to Qualcomm rather than on new technology and product development for consumers.

D. Qualcomm's FRAND Commitments Require Qualcomm to License its Modem Chip SEPs to Rivals

Next, the Court explains how Qualcomm's refusal to license rivals violates Qualcomm's FRAND commitments. The Court held on summary judgment that Qualcomm's FRAND commitments to two SSOs require Qualcomm to license its SEPs to rivals. Outside the context of this litigation, Qualcomm and other SEP holders have advanced the same understanding of FRAND. In addition, Qualcomm's own recorded statements to the Internal Revenue Service ("IRS") show that Qualcomm previously licensed its SEPs to rivals, but stopped doing so because Qualcomm concluded that instead licensing its SEPs to only OEMs is "humongously more lucrative." Therefore, the Court rejects as pretextual Qualcomm's justifications for refusing to license its rivals. The Court discusses these conclusions in more detail below.

1. The Court's Summary Judgment Order

On summary judgment, the Court held that under Qualcomm's FRAND commitments to two cellular SSOs, the Telecommunications Industry Association ("TIA") and Alliance for Telecommunications Industry Solutions ("ATIS"), Qualcomm is required to license its SEPs to rival modem chip suppliers.

Although standards promote interoperability, standards also "threaten to endow holders of standard-essential patents with disproportionate market power." *Microsoft Corp. v. Motorola Inc.*, 696 F.3d 872, 876 (9th Cir. 2012). As a result, the Ninth Circuit held in *Microsoft v. Motorola* that "SSOs requir[e] members who hold IP rights in standard-essential patents to agree to license those patents *to all comers* on [FRAND] terms." *Id.* (emphasis added). These SSO intellectual property policies "admit[ ] of no limitations as to who or how many applicants could receive a license." Three years later, the Ninth Circuit repeated the same principle: a "SEP holder *cannot* refuse a license to a manufacturer who commits to paying the RAND rate." *Microsoft Corp. v. Motorola Inc.*, 795 F.3d 1024, 1031 (9th Cir. 2015) (emphasis added).

For example, under the intellectual property policy of TIA, a SEP holder like Qualcomm must commit to TIA that "A license under any Essential Patent(s), the license rights which are held by the undersigned Patent Holder, will be made available to all applicants under terms and conditions that are reasonable and non-discriminatory."

Consistent with the Ninth Circuit's precedents, the Court held at summary judgment that Qualcomm's commitments to ATIS and TIA to license its SEPs on terms "free of any unfair discrimination" prohibit Qualcomm from discriminating against rival modem chip suppliers by refusing to grant them licenses. In addition, consistent with California contract law, the Court examined extrinsic evidence of the meaning of Qualcomm's FRAND commitments. The Court observed that guidelines to TIA's intellectual property policy specifically identify "a willingness to license all applicants except for competitors of the licensor" as discriminatory conduct. The Court further concluded that Qualcomm's contractual commitments to ATIS and TIA to license rivals are consistent with the purposes of SSO intellectual property policies, which require the licensing of SEPs to prevent a SEP holder from securing a monopoly based on the standardization of its technology.

2. Qualcomm Had the Same Understanding of FRAND Outside This Litigation

Outside the context of this litigation, Qualcomm expressed the same understanding of FRAND as the Court's summary judgment ruling.

In a 1999 Qualcomm email regarding an Intel request for a license, Steve Altman (then a Qualcomm lawyer, and later Qualcomm President), wrote to Lou Lupin (a Qualcomm lawyer who became Qualcomm General Counsel in 2000) and Marv Blecker (QTL Senior Vice President) that Qualcomm's "commitment to the industry to license on fair and reasonable terms free from unfair discrimination would make it difficult to argue that we have the right to refuse to license [Intel]."

Then, in 2000, Steve Altman (then a Qualcomm lawyer, and later Qualcomm President) complained in a letter to Motorola that Motorola was not licensing its modem chip SEPs *to Qualcomm* despite "Motorola's commitment to the industry to license its essential patents."

. . .

3. Qualcomm Previously Licensed Rivals and Has Received Licenses at the Modem Chip Level

Consistent with its statements about FRAND outside litigation, Qualcomm has previously licensed its modem chip SEPs to rivals and received modem chip-level (as opposed to handset-level) licenses to other patent holders' SEPs.

. . .

Qualcomm has also received chip-level licenses to others' modem chip SEPs. At trial, Fabian Gonell (QTL Legal Counsel and Senior Vice President, Licensing Strategy) conceded that Qualcomm has received modem chip licenses from other companies:

> **Q**: Qualcomm has had exhaustive chip-level licenses covering cellular standard essential patents from other companies; right?
>
> **A**: Inbound licenses?
>
> **Q**: Correct.
>
> **A**: Yes.

Specifically, Gonell conceded that Qualcomm has an existing license from Ericsson, which Christina Petersson (Ericsson Vice President of Intellectual Property) confirmed.

. . .

5. Qualcomm Now Refuses to License Rivals Because it is More Lucrative to License Only OEMs

Qualcomm stopped licensing rival modem chip suppliers not because Qualcomm's view of FRAND changed, but rather because Qualcomm determined that it was far more lucrative to license only OEMs.

For example, at the 2012 IRS meeting, Marv Blecker (QTL Senior Vice President) told the IRS that when Qualcomm licensed rival modem chip suppliers, revenue from those licenses amounted to only a tiny fraction of Qualcomm's handset royalty revenues: "[W]hen ninety-five percent of the royalties come from manufacturers of these things, and I don't know what the percentage was when we were collecting royalties, but it had to be well less than one percent came from component suppliers.". . .

Fabian Gonell (now QTL Legal Counsel and Senior Vice President, Licensing Strategy) agreed that Qualcomm stopped licensing rival modem chip suppliers because Qualcomm had to choose between licensing rivals and OEMs, and licensing OEMs is far more lucrative: "But having – having to choose between one or the other then you're right, obviously the handset is humongously more . . . lucrative for a bunch of – a bunch of reasons." At trial, Fabian Gonell again conceded that it is "absolutely correct" that licensing OEMs rather than rivals is more lucrative. Thus, Qualcomm stopped licensing its SEPs to rivals because licensing rivals could jeopardize Qualcomm's ability to charge unreasonably high royalty rates to OEMs.

. . .

7. Qualcomm's Justifications for its Refusal to License Rivals Are Pretextual

Qualcomm offers self-serving and pretextual justifications for Qualcomm's refusal to license modem chip suppliers. Qualcomm argues that refusing to license its SEPs to rivals and instead licensing only OEMs is procompetitive because the practice "reduces transaction costs, aligns royalties with the value of the licensed patents, and is much more efficient than the multi-level licensing that would be required if Qualcomm and other innovators licensed other than at the device level."

However, Qualcomm's own recorded statements to the IRS show that Qualcomm used to license rival modem chip suppliers, and that Qualcomm stopped licensing rivals because it is more lucrative to license only OEMs. Nowhere in QTL's long discussion with the IRS did any QTL executive raise concerns about multi-level licensing.

In addition, the unsupported trial testimony that Qualcomm offered to support its justification was not credible. Fabian Gonell (QTL Legal Counsel and Senior Vice President, Licensing Strategy) testified that if Qualcomm had to license modem chip suppliers, Qualcomm would have to engage in multi-level licensing because some of Qualcomm's cellular SEPs read on a handset but not on modem chips. Thus, Gonell testified, "Once you're in a world where you have to license a device anyway, it's just much more efficient to do one negotiation rather than two."

Gonell was not credible in multiple respects. First, Gonell pretended not to recall Qualcomm's 2012 IRS meeting until the FTC played a recording from the meeting with which Gonell disagreed. Second, Gonell's own recorded statements to the IRS, a U.S. government agency, contradict Gonell's prepared for trial testimony.

At trial, Fabian Gonell (QTL Legal Counsel and Senior Vice President, Licensing Strategy) initially claimed to have no memory of the IRS meeting:

> **Q**: In July 2012, you had a conversation with the Internal Revenue Service discussing Qualcomm's licensing practices. Do you recall that?
>
> **A**: No, but I've seen something that purports to be a transcript of that conversation. But I don't have a distinct recollection of that . . . . I really, at this point, don't have a, a memory of the meeting. But I have no reason to doubt that it happened.

After the FTC played a clip of Marv Blecker (then QTL Senior Vice President) speaking to the IRS, Gonell continued to claim no memory of the meeting:

Q: So do you agree with Mr. Blecker that the ASIC patent agreements that he was describing that you've just testified about were not licenses?

A: . . . That is absolutely 100 percent Marv Blecker's voice. There is no question in my mind. I don't know who the woman on the tape is, but that is absolutely Marv Blecker's voice. So he said those things, absolutely. I just don't know what he means by those things so I can't tell you whether I agree with it or not.

Q: Okay. But you agree that that is something he said?

A: That is absolutely Marv Blecker's voice. I don't know what else is said on the tape. But that is 1,000 percent, to my ears, Marv Blecker's voice.

Q: Okay. And I'd like to play another statement from Mr. Reifschneider. Actually, excuse me. Is it a true statement that Qualcomm told the IRS that its ASIC patent agreements are not license agreements in reality?

A: Well, I don't know. No, I don't know. I mean, Marv Blecker said that. I don't know what the context was, and I don't know what else was said. So I don't know the entirety of what was communicated to the IRS. But those words, whatever those words just, we just heard, Marv Blecker said for sure. But what was communicated and what was intended to be communicated, you know, I'd have to listen to the whole thing or read the transcript to try to understand.

Then, the FTC played a clip of Eric Reifschneider (then QTL Senior Vice President and General Manager) at the meeting, and Gonell continued to profess ignorance:

Q: Okay. And so that was a statement that Mr. Reifschneider made to the Internal Revenue Service on this phone – in this meeting; correct?

A: If this is – if this is a meeting of something with the Internal Revenue Service, I – and he's saying that to – that's who he's talking to, then, yes. It was clearly him talking.

Finally, the FTC played another clip of Marv Blecker (then QTL Senior Vice President) at the IRS meeting, in which Blecker said that Qualcomm could not charge unreasonably high royalty rates if Qualcomm licensed rival modem chip suppliers. Specifically, Blecker told the IRS:

Yeah, but if I would average royalty on all the handsets that we collect royalties on – I don't remember what it is anymore, I used to know the number – but if – if it were ten dollars, for example, you couldn't charge a ten-dollar royalty on a chipset that cost five dollars, or six dollars, or seven dollars.

Blecker (then QTL Senior Vice President) continued: "Yeah, and it would be hard to convince a court that that was a fair royalty also."

In court, Fabian Gonell's (QTL Legal Counsel and Senior Vice President, Licensing Strategy) memory of the call suddenly returned:

Q: Are those statements made by Mr. Blecker and yourself on this conversation, in this conversation with the IRS?

A: Yes, although the conversation continued, and I expressed my disagreement with Mr. Blecker's statement.

Q: So you recall this meeting now?

A: No. I remember – I remember reading that.

Gonell's sudden recall once the FTC played a clip with which Gonell disagreed is not credible given Gonell's prior failure to recall the IRS meeting. Previously, Gonell would only agree that he recognized Reifschneider's or Blecker's voice. Gonell's demeanor in court when feigning ignorance was also not credible.

Most importantly, Fabian Gonell's (QTL Legal Counsel and Senior Vice President, Licensing Strategy) own recorded statements to the IRS, a U.S. government agency, contradict Gonell's trial claim that Qualcomm refuses to license rivals to avoid multi-level licensing. Rather, Gonell told the IRS in 2012 that Qualcomm stopped licensing its rivals because licensing only OEMs is more lucrative: "But having – having to choose between one or the other then you're right, obviously the handset is humongously more . . . lucrative for a bunch of – a bunch of reasons." Thus, Gonell's trial testimony was not credible, and the Court rejects Qualcomm's self-serving justifications as pretextual.

Accordingly, the Court concludes that Qualcomm's FRAND commitments—consistent with Qualcomm's prior actions and statements—require Qualcomm to license its SEPs to rival modem chip suppliers.

E. Qualcomm Has an Antitrust Duty to License its SEPs to Rivals

The Court now addresses whether Qualcomm has a duty under the Sherman Act to license its SEPs to rival modem chip suppliers. The United States Supreme Court has explained that, in general, "there is no duty to aid competitors." Nonetheless, "[u]nder certain circumstances, a refusal to cooperate with rivals can constitute anticompetitive conduct and violate § 2." For the reasons explained below, the Court concludes that Qualcomm has an antitrust duty to license its SEPs to rival modem chip suppliers.

. . .

The United States Supreme Court found that the defendant in *Aspen Skiing* violated an antitrust duty to deal with its competitor. The United States Supreme Court explained the general rule that, "[i]n the absence of any purpose to create or maintain a monopoly, the [Sherman] [A]ct does not restrict the long recognized right of a" business to "exercise [its] own independent discretion as to the parties with whom [it] will deal." However, in *Aspen Skiing*, there was sufficient evidence to show that the defendant had refused to deal with the plaintiff only because of the defendant's anticompetitive intent to maintain its monopoly. Specifically, as the United States Supreme Court later explained in *Trinko*, the *Aspen Skiing* Court "found significance in the defendant's decision to cease participation in a cooperative venture." The *Aspen Skiing* defendant's "unilateral termination of a voluntary (and thus presumably profitable) course of dealing suggested a willingness to forsake short-term profits to achieve an anticompetitive end." Moreover, "the defendant's unwillingness to renew the [joint] ticket even if compensated at retail price revealed a distinctly anticompetitive bent." In those circumstances, the defendant's refusal to deal with the plaintiff violated the Sherman Act.

By contrast, the United States Supreme Court in *Trinko* held that Verizon did not have an antitrust duty to deal with its competitors. There, the Telecommunications Act of 1996 for the first time imposed on Verizon an obligation to share its telephone network with its rivals. However, Verizon did not process its rivals' requests "in a timely manner, or not at all." Among other provisions, the Telecommunications Act required Verizon to allow rivals to actually enter Verizon's property and "locate and install [the rival's] equipment on the incumbent's [Verizon's] premises."

Verizon's rivals sued Verizon and alleged that Verizon's refusal to deal was part of an anticompetitive scheme to harm its rivals and maintain Verizon's monopoly. However, the United States Supreme Court in *Trinko* held that the plaintiffs had failed to show that Verizon's conduct fell within *Aspen Skiing*'s exception to the general no-duty-to-deal rule. Specifically, the *Trinko* Court stated that the plaintiff's complaint "d[id] not allege that Verizon voluntarily engaged in a course of dealing with its rivals," or that Verizon would have ever have dealt with its rivals absent the Telecommunications Act's requirements.

Moreover, the *Trinko* Court found further significance in the fact that, unlike the lift tickets at issue in *Aspen Skiing*, the sharing of Verizon's telephone network was "not otherwise marketed or available to the public." Furthermore, elements of Verizon's telephone network "exist[ed] only deep within the bowels of Verizon" on Verizon's property and could only be shared "at considerable expense and effort" from Verizon. Thus, the *Trinko* Court "conclude[d] that Verizon's alleged insufficient assistance to the provision of service to rivals is not a recognized antitrust claim under this Court's existing refusal-to-deal precedents."

In *MetroNet Services Corp. v. Qwest Corp.*, 383 F.3d 1124, 1131 (9th Cir. 2004), the Ninth Circuit discussed *Trinko* and *Aspen Skiing* and determined that the United States Supreme Court considered three factors "significant for creating antitrust liability" in *Aspen Skiing* that were not present in *Trinko*. First, the *Aspen Skiing* defendant's "unilateral termination of a voluntary and profitable course of dealing." Second, the *Aspen Skiing* defendant's refusal to deal even if compensated at retail price, which suggested that the defendant's conduct was anticompetitive. Third, the fact that the *Aspen Skiing* defendant refused to provide its competitor a product that was "already sold in a retail market to other customers."

Therefore, *MetroNet*'s three factors "significant for creating antitrust liability" guide the Court's analysis. *See also SmithKline Beecham Corp. v. Abbott Labs.*, 2014 WL 6664226, at *4 (N.D. Cal. Nov. 24, 2014) (holding that an antitrust duty to deal exists where a defendant decided "to alter a voluntary course of dealing together with evidence of anticompetitive malice"). The Court discusses below how

Qualcomm's refusal to license rivals satisfies all three factors relevant to the antitrust duty to deal.

1. Qualcomm Terminated a Voluntary and Profitable Course of Dealing

The first factor relevant to the antitrust duty to deal is whether Qualcomm terminated a "voluntary and profitable course of dealing." For example, in *Aspen Skiing*, the defendant discontinued offering a joint lift ticket after many years of doing so. Here, because Qualcomm previously licensed its rivals, but voluntarily stopped licensing rivals even though doing so was profitable, Qualcomm terminated a voluntary and profitable course of dealing.

. . .

Thus, because Qualcomm previously licensed its rivals but voluntarily terminated that practice even though it was profitable, the Court concludes that Qualcomm voluntarily terminated a profitable course of dealing, and that the first factor relevant to the antitrust duty to deal is present in this case.

2. Qualcomm's Refusal to License Rivals is Motivated by Anticompetitive Malice

The second factor relevant to the antitrust duty to deal is whether Qualcomm's refusal to deal with its rivals is motivated by "anticompetitive malice." *SmithKline Beecham Corp.*, 2014 WL 6664226, at *4. In *Trinko*, the United States Supreme Court observed that the defendant's refusal to deal in *Aspen Skiing* "revealed a distinctly anticompetitive bent" because the defendant would not renew the joint lift ticket even if compensated at retail price. Here, Qualcomm's refusal to deal with its rivals reveals similar anticompetitive malice.

Qualcomm's own statements indicate that Qualcomm refuses to license rivals out of anticompetitive malice. For example, in 2012, Eric Reifschneider (QTL Senior Vice President and General Manager) told the IRS that QTL refuses to license rivals explicitly to avoid enabling competition to QCT, Qualcomm's chip business: "You know, we also have a big chipset business, you know, of our own, and we're also interested in protecting that, right?"

. . .

In addition, Qualcomm admits that refusing to license rivals harms its rivals in the marketplace and that Qualcomm does so intentionally. In 2009, Qualcomm refused to license MediaTek and instead entered a CDMA ASIC Agreement that permitted MediaTek to sell modem chips only to Qualcomm licensees. A Qualcomm presentation shared with Will Wyatt (QTI [Qualcomm Technologies, Inc., the Qualcomm subsidiary that operates QCT] Vice President, Finance) within days of the CDMA ASIC Agreement reveals Qualcomm's intent to reduce MediaTek's customer base and ability to invest in future products. Specifically, the presentation includes the strategy "make sure MTK can only go after customers with WCDMA SULA," with the goals to "Reduce # of MTK's 3G customers to ~50" and "Take away the $$ that MTK can invest in 3G."

Strategy Recommendations

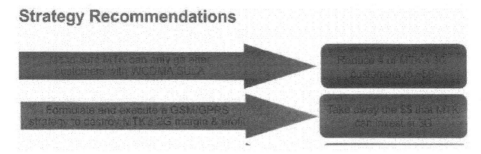

Thus, Qualcomm's contemporaneous documents and recorded statements to the IRS indicate that Qualcomm's refusal to license rivals is characterized by a "willingness to sacrifice short-term benefits"—like profitable licenses from modem chip rivals—"in order to obtain higher profits in the long run from the exclusion of competition" to QCT, Qualcomm's modem chip business. Accordingly, with Qualcomm's anticompetitive malice evident, the Court concludes that the second antitrust duty to deal factor is present in this case.

3. There is an Existing Retail Market for Licensing Modem Chip SEPs

The third factor relevant to the antitrust duty to deal is whether Qualcomm refuses to sell products "already sold at retail," such that the Court will not need to set the terms of dealing in a new market. For example, in *Trinko*, the "services allegedly withheld [were] not otherwise marketed or available to the public." Here, by contrast, because Qualcomm and other SEP holders have licensed modem chip SEPs at the chip level—as the Court explained in detail in Section V.E.—there is an existing market for modem chip SEP licenses.

. . .

H. Qualcomm's Surcharge on Rivals Bolsters Qualcomm's Monopoly Chip Market Share, Unreasonably High Royalty Rates, and Exclusivity with OEMs

Next, the Court discusses how Qualcomm's unreasonably high royalty rates impose a surcharge on rivals' modem chips. Under Qualcomm's patent license agreements with OEMs, Qualcomm charges its unreasonably high royalty rates anytime an OEM sells a handset, even when that handset contains a rival's modem chip. Thus, Qualcomm imposes an artificial surcharge on all sales of its rivals' modem chips. The surcharge increases the effective price of rivals' modem chips, reduces rivals' margins, and results in exclusivity.

For example, Brian Chong (Wistron Chief of New Technology Development and Product Planning) testified that Qualcomm's patent license restricts Wistron's ability to use rivals' modem chips because the royalty rate imposes a surcharge on rivals' chips:

> [T]here was a case that I remember in particular when we were considering introducing lower cost phones. And MTK was the chip supplier that we think best suitable for that product position in terms of price position and the spec corresponding that it offers. However, in the end we decided to stay Qualcomm for the simple reason that because Qualcomm responded that,

even if we're using non-Qualcomm chips, we would still have to pay the
onerous royalty that Qualcomm dictated in the SULA.

Chong also testified that the upfront fee Wistron had paid Qualcomm incentivized
Wistron to buy Qualcomm chips rather than rivals' chips: "So by staying with
Qualcomm we would be able to recoup that investment faster."

Practices that unfairly suppress sales of competing products "below the critical
level necessary for any rival to pose a real threat" cause anticompetitive harm
because they exclude competitors from the marketplace and thereby harm
competition in general.

The Seventh Circuit's decision in *Premier Electrical Construction Company v.
National Electrical Contractors Association*, 814 F.2d 358 (7th Cir. 1987),
demonstrates how a monopolist can use an across-the-board price increase to
impose artificial constraints that disproportionately harm the monopolist's
competitors, as Qualcomm has done.

In *Premier*, an association of electrical employers known as the National
Electrical Contractors Association ("the Association") established a fund with an
electrical workers' union ("the Union"). Association members contributed 1% of
their gross payroll into the fund to offset the cost of collective bargaining and
administrative services. However, because electrical employers who were not
Association members were "free of the 1% contribution," these electrical
employers "had lower costs of doing business" and could charge lower prices.
Electrical employers who were not Association members thus began to underbid
the Association's members for electrical contracting work.

To prevent being underbid, the Association enlisted the Union to collect the 1%
fee from non-Association electrical employers as well. In this way, the Association
"leveled" the playing field because all employers had to pay into the fund, but in so
doing the Association gave itself an advantage. "The result was higher prices to
purchasers of electrical work and higher profits for members of the Association—
both because there is more in the fund, for the Association's use, and because the
reduction in competition enabled the members to capture more of the market."
Although the Association in *Premier* charged the 1% fee directly to its rivals—
whereas Qualcomm's surcharge raises the price an OEM must pay for rivals'
modem chips—the result is substantially the same. Like the Association,
Qualcomm has "raised its rivals' costs, and thereby raised the market price to its
own advantage."

Qualcomm's unreasonably high royalty rates enable Qualcomm to control
rivals' prices because Qualcomm receives the royalty even when an OEM uses one
of Qualcomm's rival's chips. Thus, the "all-in" price of any modem chip sold by
one of Qualcomm's rivals effectively includes two components: (1) the nominal
chip price; and (2) Qualcomm's royalty surcharge.

To Qualcomm, the surcharge represents "higher profits," both because the
surcharge brings additional revenue to Qualcomm, and "because the reduction in
competition enable[s]" Qualcomm "to capture more of the [modem chip] market."
Premier, 814 F.2d at 368; *see United Shoe Mach. Corp. v. United States*, 258 U.S.

451, 457 (1922) (holding that agreements with "the practical effect" to exclude purchases of a competitor's products are anticompetitive).

Because the surcharge also raises the market price of rivals' chips, Qualcomm prevents rivals from underbidding Qualcomm, so that Qualcomm can maintain its modem chip market power. The surcharge affects demand for rivals' chips because as a matter of basic economics, regardless of whether a surcharge is imposed on OEMs or directly on Qualcomm's rivals, "the price paid by buyers rises, and the price received by sellers falls." Thus, the surcharge "places a wedge between the price that buyers pay and the price that sellers receive," and demand for such transactions decreases. Rivals see lower sales volumes and lower margins, and consumers see less advanced features as competition decreases.

The district court in *Caldera, Inc. v. Microsoft Corp.*, 87 F. Supp. 2d 1244 (D. Utah 1999), addressed how a similar royalty surcharge increased rivals' prices and promoted exclusivity. Caldera alleged that Microsoft had unlawfully maintained its monopoly in operating systems used for personal computers through several practices. In one practice, Microsoft entered multiyear licenses with OEMs that required OEMs to pay Microsoft "a royalty on every machine the OEM shipped regardless of whether the machine contained [Microsoft's operating system] or another operating system." This raised the all-in price of Caldera's operating system.

Further, Microsoft offered discounts on Microsoft's operating system if OEMs entered the license agreements, which induced OEMs to enter agreements that raised the effective price of Caldera's operating system. At summary judgment, the district court concluded that a reasonable jury could conclude that Microsoft's license agreements and discounts "resulted in an agreement with the practical effect of exclusivity" because Microsoft's surcharge increased the effective price of Caldera's operating systems. Here, too, Qualcomm's surcharge increased the effective price of rivals' modem chips and Qualcomm's agreements with OEMs result in exclusivity.

. . .

J. Qualcomm's Refusal to License Rivals Bolsters Qualcomm's Monopoly Chip Share, Unreasonably High Royalty Rates, and Exclusivity with OEMs

Qualcomm also refuses to license rivals in violation of its FRAND commitments and its antitrust duty to deal with rivals. As the Court explained in Section V.C., Qualcomm's refusal to license its modem chip SEPs to rival modem chip suppliers prevents rivals' entry, promotes rivals' exit, and hampers Qualcomm's rivals in the marketplace. Instead of licensing rivals, Qualcomm will only enter CDMA ASIC Agreements, which enable Qualcomm to control to whom its rivals sell modem chips and to require that rivals report to Qualcomm the identities of specific quantities sold to each customer.

In so doing, Qualcomm reduces its rivals' customer base and sales, which results in exclusivity. By preventing rivals from entering the market and restricting the sales of those rivals that do enter, Qualcomm entrenches its monopoly power, maintains its chip leverage over OEMs, and sustains its unreasonably high royalty rates.

Qualcomm's refusal to license rivals boxes out rivals. Scott McGregor (former Broadcom CEO) testified that Qualcomm refused to license Broadcom to prevent Broadcom from becoming a competitor: "[W]e subsequently tried to work out licensing terms with them and we didn't feel we could get reasonable licensing terms with them working on that and we felt they may be blocking us in the space."

Instead of licenses, Qualcomm enters CDMA ASIC Agreements that permit rivals to sell modem chips to only "Authorized Purchasers"—Qualcomm licensees. Qualcomm's CDMA ASIC Agreements also require rivals to report to Qualcomm "specific quantities" of modem chips sold to each Authorized Purchaser, and thus give Qualcomm sensitive business information about rivals' sales and customers. Thus, Qualcomm controls and monitors to whom its rivals sell modem chips.

Qualcomm has emphasized to OEMs that Qualcomm controls to whom its rivals sell modem chips, which bolsters Qualcomm's chip supply leverage and ability to extract unreasonably high royalty payments from OEMs. In November 2013, Ira Blumberg (Lenovo Vice President of Intellectual Property) wrote to other Lenovo executives that Qualcomm had threatened to withhold Lenovo's chip supply *and* to force MediaTek to withhold Lenovo's chip supply: "Qualcomm has threatened to stop selling its chips to Lenovo if Lenovo terminates its license. Further, Qualcomm has threatened to force its chip licensees (including MediaTek) to stop selling mobile phone chips to Lenovo if Lenovo terminates its license."

Qualcomm even boxes out its rivals through chip supply threats to OEMs. For example, in 2015, Qualcomm used the threat of chip supply cutoff to prevent VIVO from purchasing a more competitive modem chip from Qualcomm's rival MediaTek. Sanjay Mehta (QCT China Senior Vice President) told Derek Aberle (Qualcomm President) and Cristiano Amon (QCT President) in an email that QCT could secure exclusivity with VIVO if QTL permitted QCT to continue supplying chips: "What VIVO will commit to (pending QTL confirmation that if VIVO continues to negotiate with QTL in good faith, QCT will continue shipping chipsets) . . . will not launch 6755/6750 [MediaTek modem chips] based handsets (which means QCT will win significant upside in 2016)." When asked about the email, Cristiano Amon (now Qualcomm President) testified that the 6755 and 6750 modem chips were MediaTek modem chips that had "competition advantages . . . and software compatibility with whatever the incumbent chipset in VIVO was.", Qualcomm used VIVO's fear of losing chip supply to secure exclusivity with VIVO and eliminate a competitive threat from MediaTek.

Similarly, Brian Chong (Wistron Chief of New Technology Development and Product Planning) testified that Qualcomm's refusal to license rivals, and the resulting surcharge on rivals' chips, limited Wistron's ability to use a MediaTek modem chip that Wistron preferred:

> [T]here was a case that I remember in particular when we were considering introducing lower cost phones. And MTK was the chip supplier that we think best suitable for that product

position in terms of price position and the spec corresponding that it offers. However, in the end we decided to stay Qualcomm for the simple reason that because Qualcomm responded that, even if we're using non-Qualcomm chips, we would still have to pay the onerous royalty that Qualcomm dictated in the SULA.

Refusing to license rivals not only blocks rivals, but also preserves Qualcomm's ability to demand unreasonably high royalty rates from OEMs. Eric Reifschneider (QTL Senior Vice President and General Manager) told the IRS in 2012 that if Qualcomm licensed a rival, and that rival sold a modem chip to an OEM, Qualcomm could not then collect additional royalty revenues from that OEM: "[W]hen [the rival] sell[s] that chip to somebody who's going to put the chip in a cell phone, okay, the licensee's sale of that chip will exhaust our rights and then we won't be able to collect a royalty on a cell phone that's based on the price of the cellphone." Instead, Qualcomm would only charge its royalty rate against the price of a modem chip. According to an email Steve Altman (former Qualcomm President) sent in 1999, the total royalty payment per chip has been as low as $.30. That revenue pales in comparison to the $20 royalty payment per chip Qualcomm can receive when demanding a 5% royalty rate on a $400 handset.

Accordingly, when the IRS asked whether Qualcomm's decision to stop licensing its SEPs to rivals was a "business decision," Marv Blecker (QTL Senior Vice President) agreed: "Oh it's more than that, it's more than that. That's an understatement." Blecker told the IRS that to license rivals would have "the potential of threatening our entire revenue stream at the handset level."

Fabian Gonell (now QTL Legal Counsel and Senior Vice President, Licensing Strategy) also conceded to the IRS that Qualcomm stopped licensing rivals because Qualcomm had to choose between licensing rivals and OEMs, and licensing OEMs is far more lucrative: "But having – having to choose between one or the other then you're right, obviously the handset is humongously more . . . lucrative for a bunch of – a bunch of reasons."

Thus, Qualcomm's refusal to license rivals prevents entry, promotes exit, and hampers rivals in the marketplace by reducing rivals' customer base and sales. This results in exclusivity, like Qualcomm's other practices. By reducing the sales available to rivals and avoiding exhaustion claims, Qualcomm's refusal to license rivals also helps Qualcomm maintain the chip supply leverage against OEMs that sustains Qualcomm's unreasonably high royalty rates.

. . .

L. Qualcomm's Intent to Harm Competition Confirms That Qualcomm's Practices Cause Anticompetitive Harm

Qualcomm's own documents show that Qualcomm knew its licensing practices could lead to antitrust liability, knew its licensing practices violate FRAND, and knew its licensing practices harm competition, yet continued anyway—even in the face of government investigations in Japan, Korea, Taiwan, China, the European Union, and the United States. This evidence of Qualcomm's intent confirms the

Court's conclusion that Qualcomm's practices cause anticompetitive harm because "no monopolist monopolizes unconscious of what he is doing."

First, Qualcomm admitted in contemporaneous documents that its practices of avoiding patent exhaustion, requiring OEMs to sign a separate license before purchasing modem chips, and threatening to cut off OEMs' chip supply may cause antitrust liability.

For example, in a May 2012 slide deck prepared by Fabian Gonell (now QTL Legal Counsel and Senior Vice President, Licensing Strategy) and reproduced below, Qualcomm admitted that its licensing practices could lead to antitrust claims.

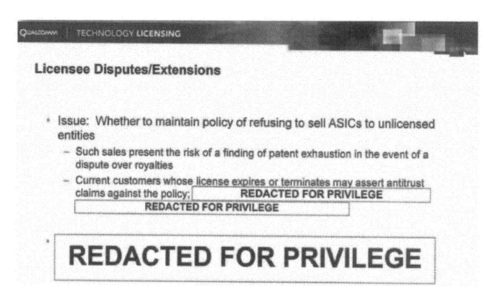

Gonell's slide was shared with Eric Reifschneider (QTL Senior Vice President and General Manager), Derek Aberle (QTL President), Marv Blecker (QTL Senior Vice President), and Lou Lupin (Qualcomm Legal Consultant). Gonell stated that selling modem chips to an unlicensed OEM could "present the risk of a finding of patent exhaustion in the event of a dispute over royalties." As a result, Qualcomm "refus[es] to sell ASICs to unlicensed entities." However, Gonell expressed the concern that "[c]urrent customers whose license expires may assert antitrust claims against the policy."

Qualcomm's internal contemporaneous documents repeatedly acknowledge that its licensing practices expose Qualcomm to antitrust claims. The following slide is contained in: (1) a July 2, 2012 QTL strategic plan presentation that Derek Aberle (QTL President) created and sent to Dr. Paul Jacobs (Qualcomm CEO), Steve Mollenkopf (Qualcomm President), and Steve Altman (Qualcomm Vice Chairman); and (2) a July 9, 2012 presentation to the Qualcomm Board of Directors, which Dr. Irwin Jacobs (Qualcomm Co-Founder) also received. Yet despite a concern about antitrust claims, Qualcomm planned to continue the anticompetitive practices and to develop a plan of communication against antitrust claims.

The slide states that Qualcomm's licensing practices may expose Qualcomm to antitrust liability: "If we cease supply of chips to current customers they may assert antitrust claims seeking damages/fines and continued supply." In response, Qualcomm planned to continue its anticompetitive practices: "Develop a plan of communication/action that maximizes our ability to defend against the above claims while ceasing supply when necessary." Thus, Qualcomm repeatedly acknowledged that its licensing practices raise antitrust claims, yet continued the licensing practices anyway.

In fact, Qualcomm's threats to OEMs' chip supply are an ongoing company practice that began with Qualcomm's co-founder, Dr. Irwin Jacobs. For example, in June 2004, Irwin Jacobs (then Qualcomm CEO) threatened LGE that unless LGE withdrew arbitration claims and paid past due royalties, Qualcomm would "stop accepting LGE purchase orders for WCDMA ASICs," "cease all shipments of WCDMA ASICs to LGE," "withdraw all of its substantial WCDMA engineering resources currently providing technical support to LGE," and require LGE to return software to Qualcomm. At trial, Irwin Jacobs testified that Qualcomm in fact did cut off LGE's chip supply: "We did not ship to them the chips that were specified here, the 500 and then 6,000 chips as far as I know at this time." Similarly, after Qualcomm presented the above July 2012 slide to the Board of Directors, Qualcomm continued to threaten OEMs' chip supply. For example, only three months after the July 2012 Board of Directors meeting, Eric Reifschneider (QTL Senior Vice President and General Manager) threatened to cut off Sony's chip supply. In an October 27, 2012 email, Eric Reifschneider told Jonathan Pearl (Sony General Counsel) that "I must report to QCT that SMC [Sony Mobile Corp.] appears unwilling to enter into a license agreement with Qualcomm," to which Reifschneider referred as "the next step in the escalation process."

In 2013, Reifschneider threatened Huawei's chip supply. In a May 1, 2013 email, Reifschneider informed Xuxin Cheng (Huawei) that "if the C2K SULA expires and has not been replaced by a new patent license agreement covering C2K products, there will be issues with Huawei's ability to continue to use C2K chipsets or QMCi's software, issues which I am sure both our companies would like to avoid."

In 2013, according to contemporaneous Lenovo documents, Qualcomm threatened to cut off chip supply to Lenovo and to force MediaTek to cut off chip supply to Lenovo: "Qualcomm has threatened to stop selling its chips to Lenovo if Lenovo terminates its license. Further, Qualcomm has threatened to force its chip licensees (including MediaTek) to stop selling mobile phone chips to Lenovo if Lenovo terminates its license."

In 2015, Cristiano Amon's (QCT President) own handwritten notes from 2015 license negotiations with Motorola's President Rick Osterloh, entitled "12-9-15-Rick & Team-Motorola," state: "(1) Licensing > Eric [Reifschneider, QTL Senior Vice President and General Manager] constantly threatening to cut off chip supply."

These chip supply threats are critical for maintaining Qualcomm's unreasonably high royalty rate. If Qualcomm sells a modem chip to an unlicensed OEM, that OEM can claim that Qualcomm's sale of the modem chip exhausted Qualcomm's patent rights, according to a 2012 QTL slide presented to the Qualcomm Board of Directors: "Such sales present the risk of a finding of patent exhaustion." If a modem chip sale exhausts Qualcomm's patent rights, Qualcomm cannot then collect its unreasonably high royalty rate from the OEM, as Eric Reifschneider (former QTL Senior Vice President and General Manager) testified: "[T]he concern for the risk to the licensing business of selling – selling chips to unlicensed customers, the – the risk of a customer making an argument of patent exhaustion and sort of undercutting the ability to license the patent portfolio."

Yet Qualcomm has recognized that Qualcomm's licensing practices and its unreasonably high royalty rates—the royalty rates that its practices are designed to sustain—violate FRAND. Marv Blecker (QTL Senior Vice President) told the IRS in 2012 that Qualcomm could not obtain the same royalty revenue through patent licenses to rival modem chip suppliers because doing so would violate FRAND. Specifically, Blecker told the IRS:

> Yeah, but if I would average royalty on all the handsets that we collect royalties on – I don't remember what it is anymore, I used to know the number – but if – if it were ten dollars, for example, you couldn't charge a ten-dollar royalty on a chipset that cost five dollars, or six dollars, or seven dollars.

Blecker (then QTL Senior Vice President) continued: "Yeah, and it would be hard to convince a court that that was a fair royalty also."

Similarly, Eric Reifschneider (QTL Senior Vice President and General Manager) told the IRS that Qualcomm's refusal to license rivals violates FRAND. Specifically, Reifschneider explained to the IRS that when Qualcomm participates in SSOs, "as part of that you often have to make commitments that you will, you know, make that technology available to people who want to make products that practice the standard." Reifschneider explained that refusing to license a rival modem chip supplier is "not a great, you know, position to be in terms of defending yourself against, you know, claims that you've broken those promises to make the technology available." Thus, Qualcomm recognizes that its licensing practices and royalty rates violate FRAND.

Moreover, Qualcomm has admitted that its monopoly chip share sustains Qualcomm's ability to receive that unreasonably high royalty rate. During Project Phoenix, David Wise (Qualcomm Senior Vice President and Treasurer) explained in an email that because there is a high correlation between Qualcomm's chip market share and the sustainability of Qualcomm's royalty rate, it is critical for Qualcomm to maintain a high modem chip share to sustain its licensing revenues:

> Notably, we are seeing in the market today that there is a high correlation between our modem (chip) share and licensing compliance and royalty rate sustainability. Where we have low chip share we are seeing challenges with compliance and maintaining the royalty rate. So in a sense, QCT has provided the 'give/get' relationship highlighted in the last point. If it's [sic] share falls, however, we lose that important element to sustaining our royalties. SO IT'S CRITICAL THAT WE MAINTAIN HIGH MODEM SHARE TO SUSTAIN LICENSING.

In short, Wise admitted that without QCT's chip market share, QTL was "seeing challenges with compliance and maintaining the royalty rate."

Because Qualcomm acknowledges that chip market share and not the value of its patents determines Qualcomm's royalty rate, Qualcomm refuses to give OEMs information about Qualcomm's patents, including even patent lists, when negotiating patent licenses with OEMs.

Nanfen Yu (Huawei Senior Legal Counsel) testified that Qualcomm has never provided patent claim charts to Huawei, but that Nokia, Ericsson, and Siemens all have. Specifically, as to Qualcomm, Yu testified:

> **Q**: [I]n all of your negotiations with Qualcomm throughout the course of your career, has Qualcomm ever provided claim charts for its patents?

> **A**: No.

Brian Chong (Wistron Chief of New Technology Development and Product Planning) testified that Qualcomm would not even provide Wistron a list of any Qualcomm patents: "I know for a fact that we asked for a list of patents and never got that."

Qualcomm not only knows that its royalty rates violate FRAND and are sustained by Qualcomm's modem chip share, but Qualcomm has also intended to harm competition via its practices.

For example, Qualcomm wielded chip supply leverage and the specter of its unreasonably high royalty rates to eliminate WiMax, a competing cellular standard supported by Intel. In the 2007 Marketing Incentive Agreement ("MIA"), Qualcomm offered Apple royalty rate rebates conditioned on (1) Apple publicly announcing that Apple had "chosen GSM technology for its phone . . . into the future with 3G and beyond"; (2) Apple not selling more than 1,000 WiMax handsets; and (3) Apple not licensing a third party to sell WiMax handsets. During MIA negotiations, Marv Blecker (QTL President) emailed Jeff Williams (Apple COO) to state that Qualcomm's first priority was eliminating WiMax: "Motivating Apple to select WCDMA to the exclusion of WiMax is our primary motivation for entering into this agreement." Irwin Jacobs (Qualcomm Co-Founder and former Qualcomm CEO) testified at trial that Qualcomm would have been behind in supplying WiMax chips had WiMax become the standard:

> **Q**: It's accurate to state, sir, that if WiMax had ended up as the standard, Qualcomm would have been far behind; is that right?
>
> **A**: That's fine.

As a result of the MIA, WiMax was eliminated. Jeff Williams (Apple COO) testified that the Qualcomm agreement ended Apple's engagement with Intel's WiMax standard:

> **Q**: And following the execution of that agreement, did Apple pursue WiMax further?
>
> **A**: No. In essence, it was killed in the cradle for us. We did not.

Similarly, Qualcomm entered an exclusive deal with Apple because doing so would eliminate competition. In an August 2010 email, Steve Mollenkopf (QCT President) told Paul Jacobs (Qualcomm CEO), Derek Aberle (QTL President), and Steve Altman (Qualcomm President) that if Qualcomm secured Apple exclusivity in the TA, Qualcomm would eliminate thin modem competitors: "[T]here are significant strategic benefits as it is unlikely that there will be enough standalone modem volume to sustain a viable competitor without that slot."

In addition, Qualcomm refused to license its rivals and restricted rivals' customer base with the intent to prevent rivals from investing in research and development, and to weaken them in the market. For example, in a 2009 pricing presentation that Qualcomm prepared within days of its CDMA ASIC Agreement with MediaTek—which limited MediaTek's sales to Qualcomm licensees only—Qualcomm stated that by reducing MediaTek's customer base, Qualcomm could "[t]ake away the $$ that MTK can invest in 3G." The slide is reproduced below:

Strategy Recommendations

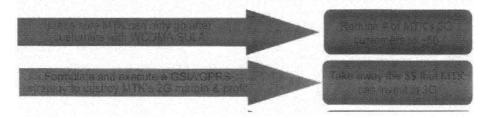

Lastly, lawyers—including Derek Aberle, Steve Altman, Eric Reifschneider, Fabian Gonell, and Lou Lupin—were the architect, implementers, and enforcers of Qualcomm's licensing practices. Lawyers explicitly stated that Qualcomm's licensing practices raised concerns about antitrust liability, but chose to continue those practices anyway, with full knowledge that Qualcomm's unreasonably high royalty rates violate FRAND and that Qualcomm's licensing practices harm rivals. That willful, conscious decision to continue Qualcomm's licensing practices is further evidence of intent to harm competition. Although intent is not dispositive, evidence of Qualcomm's intent confirms the Court's conclusion that Qualcomm's licensing practices cause antitrust harm because "no monopolist monopolizes unconscious of what he is doing."

In combination, Qualcomm's licensing practices have strangled competition in the CDMA and premium LTE modem chip markets for years, and harmed rivals, OEMs, and end consumers in the process. Qualcomm's conduct "unfairly tends to destroy competition itself." Thus, the Court concludes that Qualcomm's licensing practices are an unreasonable restraint of trade under § 1 of the Sherman Act and exclusionary conduct under § 2 of the Sherman Act. Therefore, Qualcomm's practices violate § 1 and § 2 of the Sherman Act, and that Qualcomm is liable under the FTC Act, as "unfair methods of competition" under the FTC Act include "violations of the Sherman Act."

VI. INJUNCTIVE RELIEF

In accordance with the principles above and consistent with the Court's findings of fact and conclusions of law, the Court orders the following injunctive relief:

(1) Qualcomm must not condition the supply of modem chips on a customer's patent license status and Qualcomm must negotiate or renegotiate license terms with customers in good faith under conditions free from the threat of lack of access to or discriminatory provision of modem chip supply or associated technical support or access to software.

. . .

(2) Qualcomm must make exhaustive SEP licenses available to modem-chip suppliers on fair, reasonable, and non-discriminatory ("FRAND") terms and to submit, as necessary, to arbitral or judicial dispute resolution to determine such terms.

. . .

(4) Qualcomm may not interfere with the ability of any customer to communicate with a government agency about a potential law enforcement or regulatory matter.

This remedy protects against Qualcomm's continued violation of the Sherman Act. Without the aid of market participants, a government agency may be hamstrung in pursuing a potential law enforcement or regulatory matter. Many of Qualcomm's OEM customers testified at trial in both the FTC's and Qualcomm's cases in chief. Thus, this remedy is designed to unfetter the market from anticompetitive conduct. This remedy also addresses Qualcomm's conduct in this case because Qualcomm has, even with this action in progress, interfered with the ability of its OEM customers to assist government agencies.

In January 2018, a year after the KFTC made a finding against Qualcomm in January 2017 and fined Qualcomm $927 million, and a year after the FTC filed its complaint in this case, Qualcomm entered a Settlement Agreement in which Qualcomm paid Samsung $100 million to extinguish Samsung's antitrust complaints and to silence Samsung as to any anticompetitive conduct by Qualcomm. For example, in the Settlement Agreement, Samsung specifically releases claims based on the following:

> any claim of coercion or other similar claims regarding the negotiation, execution, or terms of this Settlement Agreement, the 2018 Amendment, the CMCPCA, and/or the Collaboration Agreement . . .

> any patent licensing conduct of Qualcomm or any of its Affiliates or (b) any conduct of Qualcomm or any of its Affiliates in the Private and Regulatory Actions . . . [and]

> any claim that Qualcomm's Existing Practices violate any antitrust, competition, or similar laws of any state or territory of the United States (including federal law), Korea, or any other country or any jurisdiction, or any principle of common or civil law to similar effect including any claim based on or arising from findings or conclusions articulated in . . . (4) the ultimate decisions, settlement agreements or other dispositions of any of the cases brought against Qualcomm (or that contain counterclaims against Qualcomm) by the U.S. Federal Trade Commission ("U.S. F.T.C.") (*FTC v. Qualcomm Incorporated*, Case No. 5:17-CV-00220-LHK (N.D. Cal.))
> . . .

In addition, in the 2018 Settlement Agreement, Samsung promised to withdraw from participation in the instant action and other antitrust actions, outside of that participation required by law:

> Samsung will promptly take all actions reasonably required to withdraw all pending or accepted applications for intervention, or any other forms of substantive participation (except for any participation, including discovery or deposition, to the extent required by law), in any of the Private or Regulatory Actions and any other proceedings involving claims that

Qualcomm's Existing Practices violate antitrust, competition, or similar laws.

Moreover, Samsung promised to make the following statement to the KFTC: "[I]n any statement Samsung provides to the KFTC regarding Qualcomm's compliance with the KFTC 2017 Orders, Samsung agrees that it shall confirm that it has resolved its disputes with Qualcomm and the resolution of such dispute satisfies Samsung's demands made under the KFTC 2017 Orders." JX0122-055. Qualcomm's pursuit of this and similar releases to extinguish antitrust claims threatens to impede the government's ability to enforce the antitrust laws, and could enable future unlawful Qualcomm conduct to go unreported.

This remedy is particularly relevant given the Court's order below that Qualcomm submit to compliance and monitoring procedures. In the course of such monitoring, the FTC may seek information from OEM customers and other market participants to confirm Qualcomm's compliance with the Court's order enjoining Qualcomm's license practices. Qualcomm could frustrate such inquiries by interfering with OEM's communications to the FTC.

. . .

IT IS SO ORDERED.

Notes

1. This decision is currently on appeal, and the Department of Justice has sought and received permission from the Ninth Circuit to argue *against* the FTC. *See* Brief of the United States of America as Amicus Curiae in Support of Appellant and Vacatur (August 30, 2019).

2. The material on credibility here is included as a cautionary tale. Is it surprising, given Judge Koh's views on the credibility of the Qualcomm witnesses, that she ruled for the FTC? Can you imagine the result being otherwise? If she had decided in Qualcomm's favor, would she have included the credibility material?

3. One of the arguments made by the Justice Department is that the no-license-no-chips policy is not exclusionary, but merely exploitative of the OEMs. Consider this figure based on testimony from one of the FTC's experts:

Qualcomm Royalty Surcharge Reduces the Gains from Trade When an OEM Purchases from a Rival

- Impose royalty surcharge of $10
- Gains from trade fall to $15

- If gains from trade are split equally
  - Buyer surplus: $7.50
  - Rival margin: $7.50
  - Price of rival modem chip falls to 12.50
  - All-in price goes up to $32.50

- Rival harmed by $5
- OEM's costs rise by $5
- OEM/final consumers harmed by $5

Value = $40

Gains From Trade ($15)
Royalty Surcharge ($10)
FRAND Royalty ($10)
Rival's Cost ($5)

CDX0201-007

In this figure, the "royalty surcharge" is the license royalty that is paid to Qualcomm even if an OEM uses a rival's chip (because the Qualcomm license terms require payment of the license royalties regardless of whose chip the OEM uses). As the figure notes, under the expert's assumptions, presumably chosen for illustration only, the addition of the royalty surcharge causes the rival to be harmed by $5. Its profit margin is still $7.50, though, so one might reasonably wonder if the effect should be viewed as exclusionary. If so, why? Or, to put it another way, what would be an appropriate rule that would condemn it? Isn't it the case that the rival will not be "excluded," but only "harmed"?

If a monopolist simply lowered its price from a profit-maximizing price to a lower but still profitable price, forcing its rivals to also charge less, would that be exclusionary? Such conduct, if it makes the monopolist's rivals unprofitable, is called "limit pricing." It is not illegal under U.S. antitrust law, but it can be under the competition law of other jurisdictions. It is somewhat difficult, then, to see how Qualcomm's conduct, at least if its effects accurately represented by this figure in that the rivals remain profitable, would be illegal under U.S. law.

4. Another argument made by the Justice Department is that the refusal to deal with rivals is not a violation because that refusal was more profitable than dealing with them. Is that consistent with *Aspen Skiing*? In that case, was Ski Co.'s resistance to dealing with Highlands (such as its refusal to accept vouchers for cash) more profitable than if Ski Co. had cooperated? If not, why did Ski Co. show that resistance? Isn't the point just that Ski Co. refused profits in one product (day

skiing) in exchange for greater profits in another (destination skiing)? Did Qualcomm refuse license fees from rivals in exchange for greater profits in chip sales?

5.   The "non-discriminatory" element of FRAND was central to the court's decision. The *Unwired Planet* decisions addressed this issue extensively, distinguishing between "general" and "hard-edged" non-discrimination. The explanation of general non-discrimination by Justice Birss of the High Court was explained by the Court of Appeal: "As he explained it, a benchmark rate for what was a fair and reasonable valuation of the patents, provided that it was on offer to all potential licensees seeking the same kind of licence without reference to their size or any other characteristic, was "itself non-discriminatory." *Unwired Planet International Ltd. v Huawei Technologies Co. Ltd.*, [2018] EWCA Civ 2344, ¶177. The benchmark rate, in turn, should be "determined primarily by reference to the value of the patents being licensed." *Unwired Planet International Ltd. v Huawei Technologies Co. Ltd.*, [2017] EWHC 711, ¶175. The result was that a license at a lower rate than the benchmark rate would not be discriminatory. The prohibition of that sort of discrimination would be what Justice Birss called "hard-edged" non-discrimination, which would be "a distinct factor capable of applying to reduce a royalty rate (or adjust any licence term in any way) which would otherwise have been regarded as FRAND." *Id.*, ¶177. Both courts rejected the view that a FRAND obligation included a hard-edged non-discrimination obligation. Critically, though, both accepted if discrimination caused competitive harm, then competition law would be applicable. *See Unwired Planet International Ltd. v Huawei Technologies Co. Ltd.*, [2018] EWCA Civ 2344, ¶200. It is presumably that circumstance that exists in Qualcomm's refusal to license OEMs, though the refusal to license would presumably also violated its FRAND obligation in the first instance.

2.2.3. Exclusion by Pricing

The report below addresses the issue of online price discrimination, the charging of different prices to customers for the same product. The report focuses primarily on exploitation of consumers, as in online shopping, but it is also worth considering the exclusionary effects made possible by price discrimination. For example, if a web site charged lower prices to consumers that its data showed also went to other, competing web sites and higher prices to those that did not, should that be viewed as exclusionary? The EU has sometimes condemned similar practices of selective pricing, and they could be illegal in the U.S. as well if the pricing differences were greater than needed to meet competition.

Both the U.S. and the EU have specific provisions that in some circumstances prohibit price discrimination, or the charging of different prices to similarly positioned buyers. In the U.S., price discrimination is addressed by the Robinson-Patman Act:

> 15 U.S. Code § 13. Discrimination in price, services, or facilities
>
> It shall be unlawful for any person engaged in commerce, in the course of such commerce, either directly or indirectly, to discriminate in price between different purchasers of commodities of like grade and quality, where either or any of the purchases involved in such discrimination are in commerce, where such commodities are sold for use, consumption, or resale within the United States or any Territory thereof or the District of Columbia or any insular possession or other place under the jurisdiction of the United States, and where the effect of such discrimination may be substantially to lessen competition or tend to create a monopoly in any line of commerce, or to injure, destroy, or prevent competition with any person who either grants or knowingly receives the benefit of such discrimination, or with customers of either of them: Provided, That nothing herein contained shall prevent differentials which make only due allowance for differences in the cost of manufacture, sale, or delivery resulting from the differing methods or quantities in which such commodities are to such purchasers sold or delivered: Provided, however, That the Federal Trade Commission may, after due investigation and hearing to all interested parties, fix and establish quantity limits, and revise the same as it finds necessary, as to particular commodities or classes of commodities, where it finds that available purchasers in greater quantities are so few as to render differentials on account thereof unjustly discriminatory or promotive of monopoly in any line of commerce; and the foregoing shall then not be construed to permit differentials based on differences in quantities greater than those so fixed and established: And provided further, That nothing herein contained shall prevent persons engaged in selling goods, wares, or merchandise in commerce from selecting their own customers in bona fide transactions and not in restraint of trade: And provided further, That nothing herein contained shall prevent price changes from time to time where in response to changing conditions affecting the market for or the marketability of the goods concerned, such as but not limited to actual or imminent deterioration of perishable goods, obsolescence of seasonal goods, distress sales under court process, or sales in good faith in discontinuance of business in the goods concerned.

In recent years there have been relatively few successful Robinson-Patman Act cases, leading some commentators to suggest that law is a dead letter. Nevertheless, cases with compelling evidence of competitive harm can succeed.

Cf. Marjam Supply Co. v. Firestone Building Products Co. LLC, et al., Case No. 2:11-cv-07119 (D.N.J. 2019) with Spartan Concrete Prods. v. Argos USVI Corp., 929 F.3d 107 (3d Cir. 2019). See Theodore Banks, So Maybe the Robinson-Patman Act Isn't Dead After All, AntitrustConnect Blog, February 4, 2015, http://antitrustconnect.com/2015/02/04/so-maybe-the-robinson-patman-act-isnt-dead-after-all/; *see also* FTC, Price Discrimination: Robinson-Patman Violations, https://www.ftc.gov/tips-advice/competition-guidance/guide-antitrust-laws/price-discrimination-robinson-patman.

In the EU, the prohibition is included directly in subsection (c) of article 102:

> Any abuse by one or more undertakings of a dominant position within the internal market or in a substantial part of it shall be prohibited as incompatible with the internal market in so far as it may affect trade between Member States."

Such abuse may, in particular, consist in:

> . . .
>
> (c) applying dissimilar conditions to equivalent transactions with other trading parties, thereby placing them at a competitive disadvantage;
>
> . . .

OECD Background Note by the Secretariat
Personalised Pricing in the Digital Era
DAF/COMP(2018)13
28 November 2018

1. Introduction

1.   In the context of digitalisation and with the rise of new data-driven business models, personalised pricing is becoming an increasingly debated topic among policy makers and academics. Although this term is sometimes employed in a wide variety of circumstances, personalised pricing can essentially be seen as a form of price discrimination in which individual consumers are charged different prices based on their personal characteristics and conduct. Personalised pricing thus results in consumers paying each a different price, generally as a function of their willingness to pay, with implications for consumer welfare.

2.   From a policy perspective, personalised pricing may require policy makers to tradeoff different policy goals. On the one hand, personalised

pricing has the potential to substantially improve allocative efficiency, by enabling companies to supply to low-end consumers who would otherwise be underserved. On the other hand, personalised pricing has an unclear effect on distribution outcomes – among firms and different types of consumers – and on dynamic efficiency, since such practices can both promote innovation and rent-seeking behaviour. In some circumstances, personalised pricing can also be perceived by consumers as an unfair practice, potentially dampening trust in digital markets.

3.   In light of the ambiguous and multi-dimensional effects of personalised pricing, this background note analyses if and how competition and consumer policies can help addressing some of the risks of personalised pricing, while preserving its economic benefits. With this purpose in mind, this background note discusses whether personalised practices involving business-consumer relationships should be assessed under the scope of competition law, consumer policy, or both. It also attempts to identify some of the enforcement tools that the relevant agencies have at their disposal to address any possible risks.

      . . .

2.   What is personalised pricing?

12. This section introduces the concept of personalised pricing, framing it in the context of more traditional definitions of price discrimination and distinguishing it from other common schemes, such as dynamic pricing. The section then explains how businesses may personalise prices in practice, discussing the process of data collection, the purpose or objective of a particular personalised pricing arrangement and the mechanisms to actually implement that arrangement. Finally, it discusses the markets that might be more prone to personalised pricing, providing a few examples.

2.1. Definition and categories of personalised pricing

13.   The term personalised pricing has been used in a variety of circumstances, not always with the same meaning. Sometimes personalised pricing is used as an alternative term to price discrimination, other times it is implemented to refer exclusively to a particular form of price discrimination – such as "perfect" or "first-degree" price discrimination – and, not rarely, it is confused with other terms such as dynamic pricing. The lack of a legal definition or a generally accepted term makes it particularly important to clearly define the concept for the purpose of framing a discussion.

14.   A good starting point to understand personalised pricing is to look at the 2013 report by the former Office of Fair Trade, which defines personalised pricing as:

> "(...) the practice where businesses may use information that is observed, volunteered, inferred, or collected about individuals' conduct or characteristics, to set different prices to different

consumers (whether on an individual or group basis), based on what the business thinks they are willing to pay." (OFT, 2013)

15.   The definition proposed by the OFT has at least two important components. Firstly, it characterises personalised pricing as the practice of discriminating prices to different *consumers*, focusing thus on business-to-consumer relationships as opposed to business-to-business relations. Secondly, it specifies that the discrimination is based upon information about *personal characteristics* or *conduct*. These two components are helpful to distinguish personalised pricing from the more general concept of price discrimination – which consists in charging different prices for similar products, for reasons not related to cost (OECD, 2016).

16.   Considering this definition, it appears to be the case that personalised pricing can take the form of alternative categories of price discrimination (Box 1). While most often personalised pricing is associated to "perfect" or first-degree price discrimination, there is no reason to exclude from the definition more realistic pricing schemes where consumers are only charged a proportional share (not necessarily the total value) of their willingness to pay. Likewise, when data available is limited, it is also possible that personalised pricing discriminates groups instead of individuals, thus resulting in third-degree price discrimination. In digital markets where offers tend to be highly customised, it is also plausible that firms tailor both prices and products to consumers, resulting in a very granular second-degree price discrimination (or "versioning").

Box 1. Categories of price discrimination

The economic literature usually defines three traditional categories of price discrimination (Pigou, 1920):

- **First-degree price discrimination** (or perfect price discrimination): theoretical form of price discrimination where each consumer is charged his or her full willingness to pay. It is considered a benchmark of price discrimination (EC, 2018) or an unattainable ideal (Odlyzko, 2004), as it requires the firm to perfectly observe all relevant heterogeneity among consumers and to price discriminate them accordingly (OFT, 2013).

- **Second-degree price discrimination** (versioning): price discrimination where the seller offers a number of versions of the same product at different prices, leaving for the consumers the decision of choosing a version according to his or her preferences. It is an indirect form of discrimination, as it does not rely on information about consumers (EC, 2018).

- **Third-degree price discrimination** (group pricing): practice of setting different prices to different groups of consumers, which are partitioned according to their observed characteristics. As the seller does not perfectly observe heterogeneity among consumers, the pricing is based on known group characteristics instead of individual characteristics (OFT, 2013).

17.   In light of these considerations, this background note adopts a broad definition of personalised pricing, which is herein defined as *any practice of price discriminating final consumers based on their personal characteristics and conduct, resulting in prices being set as an increasing function of consumers' willingness to pay* (Figure 1). The range of practices contained within this definition deserves special attention in the context of digital markets, where the amount and variety of data collected online may enable firms to estimate more accurately consumers' willingness to pay, as compared to brick-and-mortar markets. Moreover,

the fact that personalised pricing often involves a granular discrimination of consumers may lead to strong economic effects (see section 3).

18.   It is important to distinguish personalised pricing from dynamic pricing, as these two terms are often used interchangeably despite having different meanings. While personalised pricing involves charging a different price to consumers based on their personal characteristics, dynamic pricing involves adjusting prices to changes in demand and supply, often in real time, not implying any kind of discrimination between consumers. Therefore, from a policy perspective, dynamic pricing tends to pose fewer concerns, enabling price mechanisms to operate more effectively without implying any form of discrimination.

19.   It is equally important not to confuse personalised pricing with other forms of online personalisation, such as:

- **A/B testing**: practice of setting multiple prices for the same product in order to test how consumers react to different price points.

- **Targeted advertising**: marketing practice of tailoring personalised adverts to consumers based on their preferences and behaviour, in order to increase the probability of acquiring the costumer.

- **Price steering** (also known as personalised offers or search discrimination): manipulation of search results according to consumers' preferences and behaviour, in order to display more expensive products to consumers with higher willingness to pay (Mikians et al., 2012).

Figure 1. Illustration of personalised pricing

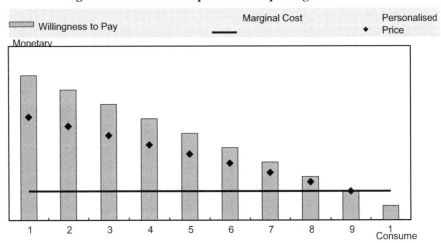

Note: Under personalised pricing, the price charged to each consumer varies according to an estimation of his or her willingness to pay.

2.2. The mechanisms behind personalised pricing

20.   Once established the meaning of personalised pricing, the natural question that follows is how firms can personalise prices in practice as part of their business strategy. Naturally, there is not a single answer for this question, as the process may vary substantially across firms and change over time with the rapid evolution of digital markets and the development of better technologies. The fact that these practices are relatively new and not necessarily implemented in a transparent way makes it more challenging to understand them, though it is still possible to identify some common principles used by firms to personalise prices.

21.   There are at least three important steps that any firm must follow in order to implement personalised pricing. First, the firm must collect data concerning consumers' personal characteristics and conduct. Second, the firm must use the data gathered to estimate consumers' willingness to pay. Third, based on the estimated willingness to pay, the firm must choose the optimal price for each consumer and decide how to implement personalised pricing. Each of these steps will be discussed in turn.

22.   The data collection process is particularly resource-intensive, and potentially the most critical one for the successful implementation of personalised pricing. It involves identifying the variables that affect buying decisions, which can be classified in three broad categories: (1) data volunteered by consumers; (2) data directly observed by the firm; and (3) data inferred from consumer behaviour (Table 1). For each of these categories, the firm must set a different mechanism to collect data, such as requiring consumers to fill an online form (volunteered data), installing cookies in consumers' personal devices (observed data) and using advanced data analytics or machine learning to infer certain consumer characteristics (inferred data).

Table 1. Categories of personal data collected online

Volunteered data	Observed data	Inferred data
Name	IP address	Income
Phone number	Operating system	Health status
Email address	Past purchases	Risk profile
Date of birth	Website visits	Responsiveness to ads
Address for delivery	Speed of click through	Consumer loyalty
Responses to surveys	User's location	Political ideology
Professional occupation	Search history	Behavioural bias
Level of education	"Likes" in social networks	Hobbies

Note: The categories of volunteered, observed and inferred data are discussed in previous OECD work on data-driven innovation (OECD, 2015). Some of the examples in the table were extracted from other reports (OFT, 2013) (EOP, 2015).

23.   An important effect of digitalisation is that, with the development of sensor-equipped smart devices and advanced data analytics, businesses can increasingly rely on both observed and inferred data, unlike pre-digitalisation times when most business models would fundamentally rely on data volunteered by consumers (OECD, 2015). This shift has key implications, enabling firms not only to personalise prices more effectively, but also to potentially do so without the awareness and consent of consumers, who may not be aware of the fact that firms keep detailed profiles about them. Concerns about privacy are well illustrated in a few anecdotal cases, such as the finding that the company Target was estimating "pregnancy scores" and sending coupons of baby products to clients with high probability of being pregnant (Hill, 2012).

24.   Once detailed personal data is available, the following step is to estimate how consumer's willingness to pay is explained by their personal characteristics, such as their professional occupation, past purchases and hobbies. The main challenge at this point is the fact that willingness to pay is not an observed variable that can be collected and run in a traditional regression model. Instead, what firms observe is whether a consumer visiting the company website decided or not to purchase a product at a given price. This information can be used to estimate consumers' willingness to pay as a function of personal characteristics, by implementing more advanced regression techniques such as discrete choice models.

25.   Lastly, after estimating consumers' willingness to pay, firms are faced with the decision of setting prices to maximise profits. While it is

[handwritten margin note: risk reduction constrained by competition]

often assumed in the literature on personalised pricing that firms would charge consumers the full value of their willingness to pay, in reality there are several reasons why this may not be the case. Firstly, since estimations are imperfect by nature, firms might set lower prices in order to reduce the risk of losing consumers whose willingness to pay was overestimated. Secondly, the existence of some level of competition may constrain the ability of firms to charge the full willingness to pay, as suggested by some research in experimental economics (Box 2).

Box 2. Natural experiment in personalised pricing

Recent research in experimental economics has looked at the behaviour of everyday consumers that were invited to play the role of sellers setting personalised prices, under simulated competing conditions (Vulkan, N. and Shem-Tov, Y., 2015).

Methodology

The study consisted in two independent online experiments involving respectively 128 and 122 individuals recruited through a social science laboratory pool from a UK University. In the first experiment, the subjects were asked to simultaneously set prices for a product sold to six fictional consumers with different (publicly-known) willingness to pay. The subjects were further informed that they were competing in groups of two and that each consumer would purchase a unit of product from the seller who offered the cheapest price, as long as the price would not exceed the willingness to pay. The second experiment was similar, but it included three different rounds where the subjects were organised in groups of two, three and four sellers competing for the same consumers. At the end of both experiments, some of the subjects were randomly selected and awarded their total earnings in Amazon vouchers.

Results

As expected, the price setting behaviour of individuals was different under uniform and personalised pricing:

- When required to set a uniform price to all consumers, the subjects set prices well above marginal costs. In

> average, prices were lower in the rounds where there
> were more sellers competing for the same consumers.
>
> • When allowed personalised pricing, the subjects set
>   prices as a fixed share (and not the full value) of
>   consumers' willingness to pay. A curious finding was
>   that the fraction charged was around 64% of the
>   willingness to pay across all experiments, therefore
>   not varying with the number of sellers competing
>   against each other.

2.3. Market conditions for personalised pricing

26.   Another relevant question that should be addressed refers to the circumstances under which personalised pricing is more likely to be observed. The OECD has identified three necessary conditions for price discrimination in general to occur (OECD, 2016), which also apply to personalised pricing:

- **Identification of consumer's valuation**: The first fundamental condition is that businesses have a mechanism to measure consumer's willingness to pay. This requires the firm to have good computational resources and access to a large volume and variety of data, as *"big data has lowered the costs of collecting customer-level information, making it easier for sellers to identify new customer segments and to target those populations with customized marketing and pricing plans"* (Council of Economic Advisers, 2015). Accordingly personalised pricing might more easily be observed in online markets where data assets are highly concentrated, for instance due to network effects, economies of scale and economies of scope.

- **Absence of arbitrage**: Personalised pricing can only be effective if arbitrage is not possible, that is, if consumers with low valuation cannot resell the product to consumers with high valuation. This is easy to guarantee for the sale of services for offline consumption (such as booking of hotels, flights, concerts, museums, etc.), as tickets are often non-transferrable. Arbitrage may also be prevented in the sale of digital content such as movies, e-books, online courses or journal subscriptions, by guaranteeing that the content can only be accessed using a personal device or account. On the other hand, it might be harder to prevent arbitrage in the sale of tangible durable goods such as computer equipment, cosmetics or clothing, as compared to perishable or less expensive tangible goods for which arbitrage would be less feasible.

- **Element of market power**: Personalised pricing requires a minimum level of market power, as in perfectly competitive markets prices go down to marginal costs for all consumers. This means that personalised pricing may be particularly feasible in markets with some degree of economies of scale, economies of scope, network effects, entry costs or switching costs, enabling firms to exert some market power by differentiating prices above the marginal cost curve.

27.   Out of the three conditions identified, the one that appears to have increased the most in recent years is the ability of firms to measure consumers' valuations, explaining the growing concerns about the risk of personalised pricing. Nowadays, the vast majority of businesses have a website or home page, and around half of them are using social media (Figure 2), enabling them to collect information on IP addresses, webpage visits, historical purchases or number of "likes" of a product or service, through the use of cookies and other automated data collection tools. A smaller but still noteworthy number of businesses are performing big data analysis or using Customer Relationship Management software, which may further assist companies personalising services and discriminating prices to consumers on an individual basis.

Figure 2. Use of information & communication technologies (ICTs) in OECD countries

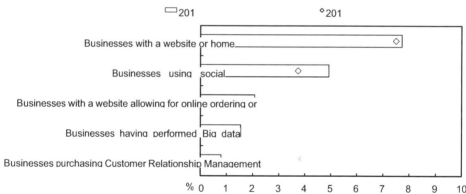

Note: All indicators are calculated for a sample of at least 21 OECD countries. When data is not available for 2014 and 2017, data for the closest year is used.
Source: OECD (2018), *Improving Online Disclosures with Behavioural Insight*, OECD Publishing, Paris, www.oecd.org/sti/consumer/policy-note-improving-online-disclosures-behavioural-insights.pdf.

28.   Moreover, the fact that personalised pricing requires some element of market power and a mechanism to prevent arbitrage may provide some hints about the type of firms that are more likely to engage in these practices. The most obvious candidates are online platforms and giant online retailers that sell services for offline consumption, digital content and

less expensive tangible goods, particularly in markets with some level of entry costs and switching costs. Personalised pricing might also be observed among brick-and-mortar businesses, such as big supermarket chains with fidelity cards, or even utility service providers (e.g. telecom, energy) that keep close track of consumer behaviour. Naturally this list is non exhaustive, as personalised pricing may be also observed in other industries.

2.4. Empirical evidence of personalised pricing

29.   Although the basic conditions for personalised pricing are satisfied in several markets, it is still hard to find evidence of actual cases reported in the literature. This may be due to different reasons. On the one hand, it is possible that most businesses are still reluctant to engage in personalised pricing, due to fears of losing reputation or of triggering a negative reaction by consumers (Council of Economic Advisers, 2015). On the other hand, it is also plausible that firms are already personalising prices, but chose to do so in a non-transparent way, for the same reasons previously stated. Either way, detecting personalised pricing is a complex task, as the "*technical possibilities for online personalisation have become much more advanced and hard to capture/measure*" (EC,

2018).

30.   Even though existing evidence is relatively limited, there is some data showing that personalised pricing is already occurring, at least to some extent. A recent survey by Deloitte involving over 500 companies (Hogan, 2018) found that, among all retailers that have adopted artificial intelligence (AI) to personalise consumer experience, 40% of them used AI with the specific purpose of tailoring pricing and promotions in real time (Figure 3). In addition, the consumer survey of the European Commission revealed that between 12% to 20% of consumers have had bad experiences related to personalised pricing (Figure 4). Another study used the accounts and cookies of over 300 real-world users in order to test for the presence of price discrimination in 16 popular e-commerce websites, of which 9 were found to have some element of personalisation (Box 3) (Hannak et al., 2014).

31.   Further evidence of personalised pricing has been uncovered by some journals that identified companies setting personalised prices based on consumer information. A Wall Street Journal investigation in 2012 detected that the retailers Staples and Home Depot, the education technology company Rosetta Stone and the financial company Discover Financial Services have personalised prices based on different consumer characteristics, such as their geolocation, income level, browsing history and proximity to rival's stores, among others (Valentino-DeVries, Singer-Vine and Soltani, 2012). In the same year, the New York Times also found evidence of personalised pricing undergoing in the supermarket chains Safeway and Kroger, with prices being set higher for loyal consumers and lower to those consumers that alternate between competing brands (Clifford, 2012).

Figure 3. How brands use artificial intelligence (AI) to personalise the consumer experience

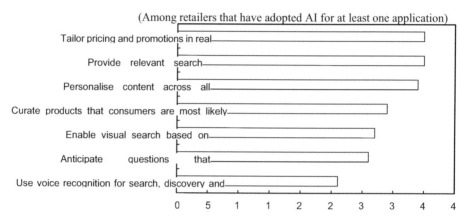

(Among retailers that have adopted AI for at least one application)

Tailor pricing and promotions in real

Provide relevant search

Personalise content across all

Curate products that consumers are most likely

Enable visual search based on

Anticipate questions that

Use voice recognition for search, discovery and

%

Note: "Based on a survey to more than 500 traditional retail, pure play, consumer goods, and branded manufacturing leaders from around the world."
Source: Hogan, K. (2018), Consumer Experience in the Retail Renaissance: How Leading Brands Build a Bedrock with Data, https://www.deloittedigital.com/us/en/blog-list/2018/consumer-experience-in-the-retailrenaissance--how-leading-brand.html.

Figure 4. Consumers who had bad experiences related to personalised pricing in the EU

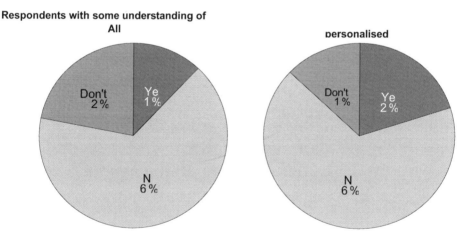

Respondents with some understanding of

All   personalised

Note: Based on a 2018 consumer survey to 21 734 respondents (of which 9 798 respondents have some understanding of personalised pricing).
Source: EC (2018), Consumer market study on online market segmentation through personalised pricing/offers in the European Union, European Commission, https://ec.europa.eu/info/sites/info/files/aid_development_cooperation_fundamental_rights/aid_and_develop
ment_by_topic/documents/synthesis_report_online_personalisation_study_final_0.pdf.

Box 3. A methodology to measure personalised pricing in e-commerce websites

Researchers from Northeastern University have proposed a new methodology to measure the extent to which personalised pricing is taking place online (Hannak et al., 2014). The methodology was applied to 16 leading e-commerce websites of two categories: general e-commerce retailers and travel retailers.

Methodology

The authors wrote HTML programs specifically designed to automatically extract price information from the results of search pages of 16 e-commerce websites, which were accessed using 300 real-world user accounts, as well as synthetically generated fake accounts. Real and fake users varied in attributes such as tracking cookies, browser, operating system and IP address, which are all a potential source of price personalisation. However, because price differences can be observed at the same instant of time for reasons other than personalisation (for instance if firms are testing different pricing points), the authors attempted to eliminate any noise in price differences by running, as a control, the same programs through many identical user accounts.

Results

After applying this methodology to the 16 e-commerce websites, the authors found that some form of personalisation takes place within 9 of them, namely 4 general retailers and 5 travel websites. The results provide evidence of both price steering (that is, the practice of personalising search results in order to display more expensive products to some consumers) as well as price discrimination, which appears to be based on consumer attributes such as membership, history of clicks and past purchases. It is worth noting that the study did not account for price differences resulting from discounts or coupons, which may be an additional important mechanism that reinforces personalised pricing.

---

32. There are also some anecdotal cases where consumers themselves uncovered potential personalised pricing practices, though many of the companies involved have rejected such claims. The first case goes back to 2000, when a consumer found out that Amazon was selling products – including DVDs – to regular consumers at higher prices, and that deleting the cookies on the computer would cause those prices to drop. In light of the negative consumer reaction at the time, Amazon stated that the

differences in prices were a random price test and refunded all consumers who overpaid (Abnett, 2015). Since then, several other anecdotal cases have emerged:

- In 2015, the online employment marketplace ZipRecruiter did an experiment with algorithmic pricing based on customer data that resulted in an 85% increase in profits (Wallheimer, 2018).

- In 2016, the online platform Coupons.com was reported to use proprietary data on consumer behaviour to target digital coupons to consumers (Ezrachi and Stucke, 2016).

- In 2017, the airline AirAsia Bhd has started testing personalised baggage pricing in order to increase revenues, "using data and machine-learning to better understand what passengers were prepared to pay" (Reuters, 2017).

- In 2018, some consumers have realised that Uber charges sometimes different prices for rides involving the same route at the same moment (Box 4).

Box 4. Personalised pricing in Uber

Uber Technologies Inc., the ride-sourcing and ride-sharing US company currently operating in hundreds metropolitan areas worldwide, has been implementing a new pricing system that seems to fit the category of personalised pricing. In an interview with Bloomberg, the head of product Daniel Graf said that "*the company applies machine-learning techniques to estimate how much groups of customers are willing to shell out for a ride*" (Newcomer, 2017). For that, the company partitions consumers according to the particular route and time of the day they travel, eventually charging more to individuals commuting between wealthy neighbourhoods.

It is still unclear the extent to which Uber is using other personal data to discriminate prices on an individual basis. A consumer has reported identifying price differences, for instance, when interchanging between his personal credit card and the corporate credit card. It has also been hypothesised that prices may be based on observables such as the ride history, the brand of the phone or even the battery level of the phone, which could significantly affect the consumer's willingness to pay (Mahdawi, 2018). Nonetheless, so far it appears that Uber's personalised pricing system is confined to group-level data (third-degree price discrimination), as suggested by an Uber spokesman: "*We may price routes differently based on our understanding of demand patterns, not individual riders*" (Mahdawi, 2018).

> The new "routed-based pricing" has led to different reactions among the public. On the one hand, drivers and riders are the ones that are more likely to have a negative response to a potential increase in the difference between rider fares and driver pay. The Microsoft researcher Glen Weyl commented that Uber "could really lose the trust of the riders", while some drivers have complained that the new pricing system is unethical (Newcomer, 2017). On the other hand, Glen Weyl also recognises good economic reasons for the new pricing system, and the MIT Professor Chris Knittel suggests that *Society is more willing to accept wealthy people paying higher fares*". In particular, this could be a mechanism for Uber to become profitable without sacrificing the quality of the service.

33. Naturally, the existence of some anecdotal cases does not provide enough evidence to conclude that personalised pricing is a generalised practice in the digital world. In the future it would be useful to engage in more comprehensive studies that can better quantify these practices. The existing evidence suggests, however, that at the very least it is worth understanding the economic effects of personalised pricing and its implications for competition and consumer policy.

3. Economic effects of personalised pricing

34. In light of the concerns that have been recently raised, this section attempts to analyse the economic effects of personalised pricing, which tend to be similar but somewhat stronger than those of more traditional price discrimination. Firstly, this section discusses the potential of personalised pricing to improve static efficiency, by leading to an output expansion. Secondly, it shows that personalised pricing may have either a positive or negative impact on distribution outcomes. Thirdly, it discusses the impact on dynamic efficiency depending on the particular characteristics of the market. Lastly, the section addresses questions about fairness and market trust that are often raised within the context of personalised pricing.

35. For the purpose of illustration, the analysis in this section assumes that personalised pricing is set as a linear function of consumers' willingness to pay, as portrayed in Figure 5. Although in reality firms may not always have enough data to implement personalised price at the individual consumer level – opting instead for classifying consumers in multiple disaggregated groups – this simplification is useful to illustrate the potential effects of personalised pricing at its best conditions. Naturally, changing this assumption may alter the magnitude of the effects identified.

Figure 5. Illustration of uniform pricing vs personalised pricing

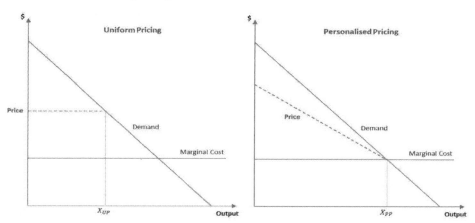

Note: With uniform pricing (on the left), each consumer pays the same price for each unit. With personalised pricing (on the right), each consumer pays a different price for each unit, as a linear function of the willingness to pay.

36.   It should be also pointed out that the economic effects of personalised pricing may differ significantly from those reported in this section if the pricing scheme is implemented with a different purpose than charging consumers according to their willingness to pay. For instance, firms could hypothetically use their ability to personalise price to undercut rivals' costumers with a predatory motive – also known as selective pricing. While this would likely harm the competitive process and have negative effects overall, it is not the purpose of this paper to analyse in detail such predatory strategies, whose effects and antitrust treatment are well established in the literature.

3.1. Impact on static efficiency

37.   Personalised pricing has the potential to increase static (allocative) efficiency, by creating an incentive for firms to reduce prices to low-end consumers – who would otherwise be underserved – while preserving the profitability of high-end consumers. The impact of personalised pricing on static efficiency can be measured by changes in "social welfare" (also commonly known as total welfare or economic surplus), which is defined as the sum of consumers' and producers' surplus (Varian, 1985). In other words, the social welfare corresponds to the difference between consumers' willingness to pay and producers' willingness to sell – generally the marginal cost – for each unit of product transacted.

38.   The effects of traditional price discrimination on social welfare are well established in the empirical economic literature, which tends to identify a positive link between the two in several industries, including in the UK intermediary brick market (Beckert, Smith and Takahashi, 2015), the US market for coronary stents (Grennan, 2013), the US market for ready-to-eat breakfast cereals (Nevo and Wolfram, 2002) and in a Las

Vegas hotel and casino (Cuddeford-Jones, 2013). However, traditional price discrimination does not inevitably lead to greater social welfare, as "*a necessary condition for price discrimination to increase social welfare (...) is that output increase*" (Schwartz, 1990) (Varian, 1985).

39.   While empirical studies about personalised pricing are still scarce or even nonexistent, economic theory suggests that personalised pricing can improve static efficiency beyond the level of traditional price discrimination, potentially maximising the output transacted. The intuition for this result is that, as long as firms are able to tailor prices to consumers' valuations, and assuming that arbitrage is not possible, it is always optimal to serve each and every consumer whose willingness to pay exceeds the marginal cost of production, as that will not affect the profitability of other units sold.

40.   The potential of personalised pricing to maximise social welfare is illustrated in Figure 6. Under uniform pricing (on the left), firms with a certain level of market power sustain prices above marginal cost, thereby restricting the total output transacted below the social optimum. In opposition, under personalised pricing (on the right), firms can always profitably serve all consumers, increasing social welfare to its maximum. It is important to note that this conclusion holds for any personalised pricing curve comprised between the demand and marginal cost curves, and not exclusively for scenarios of perfect price discrimination.

Figure 6. Impact of personalised pricing on social welfare

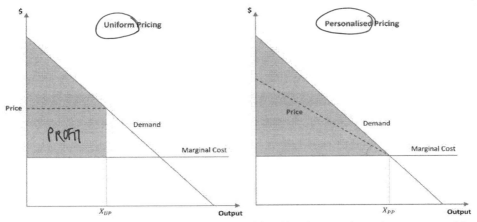

Note: Personalised pricing can increase social welfare / economic surplus, as measured by the blue area.

3.2. Impact on distribution outcomes

41.   While personalised pricing has the potential to improve static efficiency by boosting social welfare to its maximum level, it also affects the way surplus is distributed among different agents, potentially leaving

some individuals worse-off. Firstly, personalised pricing is likely to create a transfer of surplus from consumers with high willingness to pay, who are charged higher prices, to consumers with lower willingness to pay. Secondly, it may also affect the distribution of surplus between consumers and producers. This last effect is of particular concern for competition and consumer protection authorities, who usually have as legal standard the promotion of consumer welfare, often measured as the excess of consumer valuation of product over the price actually paid (OECD, 1993).

42.   The empirical evidence about the impact of traditional price discrimination on the distribution of surplus among consumers and producers is mixed. Some studies find that price discrimination reduces average prices, increasing thereby consumer welfare (Beckert, Smith and Takahashi, 2015) (Grennan, 2013) (Nevo and Wolfram, 2002). Other studies show that in some industries price discrimination can also lead to higher average prices, potentially resulting in a loss of consumer welfare – at least if the higher prices are not compensated by the output expansion (Cuddeford-Jones, 2013) (Shiller, 2014) (Shiller and Waldfogel, 2011).

43.   Just like traditional price discrimination, personalised pricing also creates redistribution effects that may either benefit or harm consumers, though the magnitude of the effect can be much stronger. In theory, if personalised pricing resulted in perfect or first degree price discrimination, the economic surplus would be entirely captured by the producer, reducing consumer welfare to zero. In opposition, if the degree of personalisation is small and prices are set at a level close to costs, almost the entire surplus would be captured by the consumer. So the potential outcomes of personalised pricing can theoretically range from maximising consumer welfare to a scenario where consumer welfare drops to zero.

44.   Figure 7 illustrates the ambiguous impact of personalised pricing on the level of consumer surplus (blue area) and producer surplus (light grey). As seen, even though the total surplus is higher under personalised pricing, it is not clear how the total surplus is redistributed among consumers and firms, as that will fundamentally depend on the slope of the personalised pricing curve. Rotating the personalised pricing curve upwards in the direction of the demand curve would bring additional surplus to the firm, whereas rotating the personalised pricing curve downwards towards the marginal cost curve would increase consumer welfare.

45.   Ultimately the impact of personalised pricing on consumer welfare is likely to depend on the competition conditions of the market. Indeed, if personalised pricing is implemented within a monopolistic market where little price competition is observed, firms may have a greater ability to use their knowledge about consumers' valuations to charge higher prices. Yet, in more competitive markets, personalised pricing may actually result in firms competing more aggressively for each individual consumer, potentially increasing the incentive of firms to cut down prices. Some academic work suggests that personalised pricing may, in fact, lead to more

aggressive price competition even in duopoly markets, though perfect price discrimination can still be observed under some conditions (Chen, Choe and Matsushima, 2018).

Figure 7. Impact of personalised pricing on consumer and producer surplus

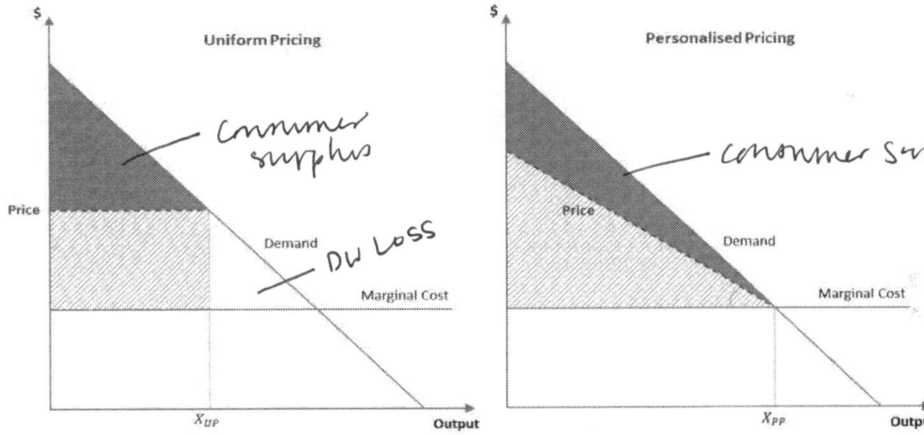

Note: Consumer surplus is represented by the blue area and producer surplus is represented by the stripped grey area. The impact of personalised pricing on consumer and producer surplus depends on the slope of the personalised pricing line between the demand and the marginal cost curves.

46.   Another important consideration is that personalised pricing decreases the ability of firms to engage in concerted practices to fix prices, making it substantially harder to agree on a common policy and to monitor the agreement, especially if personalised pricing is implemented through secret discounts that are not observed by competitors. This effect may be particularly relevant when there is a substantial risk of algorithmic tacit collusion (OECD, 2017). Personalised pricing also renders agreements to restrict output useless, because when firms can discriminate each consumer individually it is in their interest to expand output, not to reduce it.

47.   In conclusion, while personalised pricing has ambiguous distributional effects, the risk of a loss in consumer surplus is smaller when companies engage in aggressive price competition to acquire each individual consumer. In opposition, if firms have substantial market power, there is a greater risk that personalised pricing approaches perfect or first-degree price discrimination.

3.3. Impact on dynamic efficiency

48.   Another potential effect of personalised pricing that is less frequently addressed in the literature relates to its impact on dynamic efficiency. By creating a mechanism for firms to raise revenues without sacrificing sales, personalised pricing can encourage firms to innovate and to differentiate themselves (OECD, 2016), but in other instances it may also

promote rent-seeking activities that can reduce social welfare (Ezrachi and Stucke, 2016). The overall effect on dynamics efficiency may depend on the particular market conditions observed.

49.   In dynamic and highly innovative markets where firms can obtain market power through means of innovation and differentiation – as it is often the case of digital markets – personalised pricing is more likely to improve dynamic efficiency, as it increases the reward from any future innovation. Moreover, as long as market power is temporary and not preserved through anti-competitive means, new entry would imply that dynamic efficiency gains would be passed through to consumers over time.

50.   The potential of personalised pricing to increase dynamic efficiency under certain conditions is shown in Figure 8, which portrays the effect of a product innovation as an upward shift in demand, reflecting the higher consumers' willingness to pay for the new product. As illustrated, under uniform pricing (on the left), a firm with market power can only capture a part of the value of the innovation, as it is forced to restrict total output in order to keep prices high. Yet, under personalised pricing (on the right), the firm can capture the entire value of the innovation, by charging to each consumer the additional willingness to pay for the new product. The additional profit incentives for the firm mean, in turn, that the innovation has greater probability of actually taking place.

51.   Apart from its potential to increase incentives for innovation, personalised pricing may also affect the risk of rent-seeking activities. This effect is more likely to be observed in regulated industries – such as utilities, communication, transport, professional services and, in some cases, retail – where firms may engage in lobbying activities and political action to convince governments to introduce regulations that protect incumbents from competition, in what is often called regulatory incumbency.

52.   However, even in heavily regulated industries the effect of personalised pricing on rent-seeking activities is ambiguous and may depend on the degree of market power that firms hold. While in highly monopolised markets personalised pricing may increase profits and enhance incentives for rent-seeking behaviour, in more competitive markets it can actually foster competition and reduce rent-seeking conduct. This is illustrated in Figure 9, where the total profits lost due to rent-seeking behaviour (yellow area) ultimately depends on the slope of the personalised pricing line.

Figure 8. Impact of personalised pricing on incentives for innovation

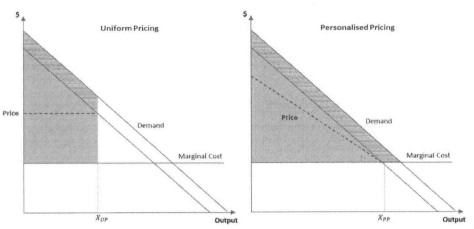

Note: The light blue area represents social welfare before the innovation takes place, while the striped green area represents the surplus generated by the innovation.

Figure 9. Impact of personalised pricing on rent-seeking activities

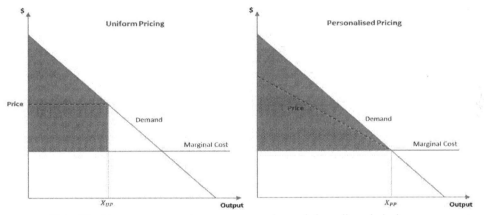

Note: The blue area represents consumer surplus and the yellow dashed area represents deadweight loss through rent-seeking activities by firms. The impact of personalised pricing on deadweight loss due to rent-seeking activities depends on the slope of the personalised pricing line between the demand and the marginal cost curves.

53.   In conclusion, personalised pricing can in general create incentives for innovation and differentiation, but in some occasions it may also promote rent-seeking behaviour by firms. The overall effect on dynamic efficiency depends thus on the specific market conditions and is more likely to be negative in highly regulated industries where firms have a certain degree of market power.

    . . .

4.   Competition policy approach to personalised pricing

61.   The potential risks of personalised pricing can be addressed through different policies and legal instruments, of which competition law is one. To the best of the OECD Secretariat's knowledge, to date there is no case law where personalised pricing – strictly defined as a form of price discriminating *final consumers* based on their personal characteristics – was established as an infringement of competition law. Yet, as these practices become more common, it is possible that some competition authorities decide to open investigations in the future and tackle some forms of personalised pricing, using the antitrust tools they have in their arsenal.

62.   This section focus on how personalised pricing can be assessed as a potential abuse of dominance, whenever the conduct is implemented by a dominant firm and has the effect of harming consumers, by forcing some of them to pay higher prices than they otherwise would. For that, the section firstly summarises the current law and practice on abuse of dominance. Then it discusses the circumstances under which personalised pricing may qualify as an abuse, as well as the different enforcement procedures that competition authorities may consider.

4.1. Law and practice on abuse of dominance

63.   Abuse of dominance is one of the fundamental infringements of competition law, consisting in any "*anticompetitive business practices in which a dominant firm may engage in order to maintain or increase its position in the market*" (OECD, 1993). In most jurisdictions, qualifying a conduct as an abuse of dominance requires three fundamental conditions to be met: (1) the offender must be dominant in the relevant market; (2) the conduct must fit a generally accepted category of abuse; and (3) the conduct must be shown to have anti-competitive effects that are not counter-balanced by efficiencies. These three conditions are discussed in turn.

64.   Firstly, the fact that provisions on abuse of dominance only apply to dominant firms is consistent with the idea that, for a firm to be able to unilaterally harm the competitive process, it must have a degree of market power in the relevant market. Secondly, as dominance is in itself not unlawful, but only its abuse, it is necessary to identify an anticompetitive conduct in order to establish an infringement. There are several types of anticompetitive conduct that can amount to an abuse of dominance, and which are often distinguished in two broad categories, exclusionary and exploitative:

> "*'[E]xclusionary' abuses refer to those practices of a dominant undertaking which seek to harm the competitive position of its competitors or to exclude them from the market, whereas 'exploitative' abuses can be defined as attempts by a dominant undertaking to use the opportunities provided by its market strength in order to harm customers directly.*" (Akman, 2008)

65.   While exclusionary abuses, such as refusal to supply and predatory pricing, are at the core of competition law enforcement, exploitative abuses are rarely prosecuted in most OECD jurisdictions. In some countries in the North and Latin America, including the US, Canada and Mexico, exploitative abuses are not contemplated within competition rules. In other countries, such as Brazil and Japan, competition law covers exploitative practices but the respective authorities have not found any exploitative conduct to amount to an antitrust infringement to date. In opposition, exploitative abuse cases have been occasionally investigated in Europe (Figure 12) and also in other OECD countries, such as Australia, Korea and Turkey.

Figure 12. Categories of abuse of dominance enforced by the EC between 2000 and 2017

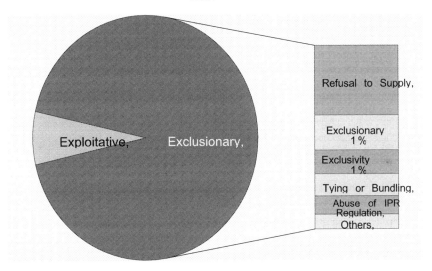

Note: Exploitative abuses include excessive pricing, price discrimination, and unfair commercial terms and conditions.

Source: Adapted from Dethmers, F. and J. Blondeel (2017), "EU Enforcement Policy on Abuse of Dominance:
Some Statistics and Facts", European Competition Law Review, Vol. 38/4, https://awards.concurrences.com/IMG/pdf/eu_enforcement_policy_on_abuse_of_dominance_some_statistics_and_facts_f_dethmers_and_j_blondeel.pdf.

66.   Thirdly, provisions on abuse of dominance are generally subject to the so-called effects-based approach, which is currently endorsed by most competition authorities. This approach implies that if a dominant firm engages in a behaviour that fits any potential category of abuse, such conduct does not automatically amount to a *per se* infringement, but it must be assessed on a case-by-case basis and subject to a "rule of reason". The conduct will then be qualified as unlawful only if the potential anti-competitive effects exceed any countervailing efficiencies.

4.2. Qualifying personalised pricing as an abuse

67.   In order to understand whether personalised pricing may potentially qualify as an abuse of dominance, and therefore amount to an antitrust violation, one must consider whether such conduct is an acceptable category of abuse that is likely to be investigated by competition authorities. This question remains largely unanswered, because competition provisions in many countries appear to *explicitly* forbid only the discrimination of business trading partners, and not final consumers, as in the case of the EU (Maggiolino, 2017). Moreover, the question of whether personalised pricing amounts to a competition law infringement can hardly be answered by the scarce case law on price discrimination, as so far competition authorities have not investigated cases where price discrimination directly targets final consumers.

68.   Despite the legal uncertainty and lack of case law in this area, hypothetically it may be possible to treat personalised pricing as an exploitative abuse, at least in jurisdictions where exploitative practices are covered by competition law. For that it would be necessary to prove that personalise pricing is a form of excessive or unfair pricing, under the rational that some consumers are charged higher prices for reasons not related to costs. A similar approach could be observed in Japan, where exploitative price discrimination is regulated as an abuse of superior bargaining position (although there are no cases to date). Still, none of these options appears to be a clear cut case for competition enforcement.

69.   In some circumstances it might also be possible to qualify personalised pricing as an exclusionary abuse, specifically whenever firms use their pricing strategies to target lower prices to rivals' customers, in an attempt to foreclose the market. This strategy is known as selective pricing and has been investigated in a few cases by the Commission, including the 1996 case against Compagnie Maritime Belge Transports (C-395/96 P) and the 1999 case against Irish Sugar (T-228/97). Nonetheless, such infringement can only be established where some form of predation takes place, not addressing the more general concerns about personalised pricing as a mechanism to exploit consumers.

70.   In the event that personalised pricing fits an existing or even a new category of abuse, it matters then to identify the circumstances under which a particular instance of personalised pricing is anti-competitive. The effects-based approach to abuse of dominance appears to play a particularly important role in the context of personalised pricing, whose effects are often ambiguous. Therefore, even though in practice competition authorities sometimes establish an infringement based on presumed effects of a conduct (Dethmers and Blondeel, 2017), personalised pricing should not be assumed to be harmful and its effects on competition should be analysed on a case-by-case basis:

> *"The welfare effects of personalised pricing are a priori ambiguous. As we have shown, the economic literature emphasises*

that price discrimination is not necessarily detrimental to welfare or consumer surplus, and that it can increase welfare and/or consumer surplus in comparison to uniform pricing. From an economic viewpoint, there is therefore no rationale for banning personalised pricing per se (as there is no rationale for banning price discrimination)." (Bourreau, Streel and Graef, 2017)

71.   It is important to note that the effects-based analysis of personalised pricing may depend on the legal standard or general mission of the competition law in a specific jurisdiction. According to a survey by the ICN, in 89% of the jurisdictions consumer welfare is *the* primary goal or one of the goals of competition law (Figure 13), but there are other countries where the standard is total welfare, such as Australia, Canada, New Zealand, Norway and South Africa. Also, among those countries where consumer welfare is one of the goals, some also have the institutional role of promoting efficiency (not necessarily passed through to consumers), potentially requiring the respective competition authorities to balance a trade-off between total and consumer welfare.

72.   In general, competition authorities that prioritise the promotion of consumer welfare are more likely to find instances where personalised pricing can be harmful and, hence, to establish an infringement of competition law. Naturally, as personalised pricing can always favour some consumers while leaving others worse-off, the analysis of the effects should be based on consumer welfare as a whole, and not on the harm imposed on a subgroup of individuals.

Figure 13. The role of consumer welfare in competition law enforcement

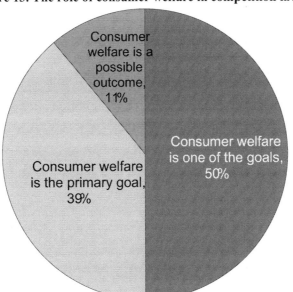

Note: Results based on the answers of 56 competition authorities. A common alternative or complementary goal is total welfare.
Source: ICN (2011), "Competition Enforcement and Consumer Welfare – Setting the Agenda", *International Competition Network*, Conference 17-20 May 2011, The Hague, http://www.internationalcompetitionnetwork.org/uploads/library/doc857.pdf.

73.   In opposition, competition authorities that give more weight to total welfare may find personalised pricing to be harmful in a narrower range of circumstances, given that the effects on static and dynamic efficiency are often positive. An exception is when there is evidence that personalised pricing actually promotes rent-seeking activities, for instance in highly regulated industries, case in which efficiency could potentially drop. It is interesting to note that this trade-off between consumer welfare and total welfare is very specific to personalised pricing (as well as merger review), not being commonly observed in other types of abuse that generally affect consumer welfare and total welfare in a similar way.

74.   In conclusion, it seems possible to address some of the risks of personalised pricing through competition law, particularly in jurisdictions that investigate exploitative abuses and apply a consumer welfare standard (Box 5 proposes a step-by-step enforcement framework). At the same time, competition law has also clear limitations, due to the fact that provisions on abuse of dominance only apply to dominant firms, while the vast majority of online businesses have little to no market power. This is not, however, necessarily problematic, as the risk that personalised pricing results in consumer exploitation tends to be notably higher when firms have substantial market power, as already discussed in section 3.

Box 5. A step-by-step framework to analyse personalised pricing

When faced with an allegation of personalised pricing, competition authorities may consider following the next steps in order to determine whether such conduct is abusive.

- **Step 1: Identify price differences not based on costs.** Identifying price differences across consumers is not a sufficient condition to establish that a practice is discriminatory, as those price differences may reflect different marginal costs of serving different consumers. Thus, in order to infer that discrimination has occurred, differences in prices should not be cost-based.

- **Step 2: Establish dominance**. While personalised pricing can be observed in markets that are relatively competitive (Levine, 2012), there is a higher risk of exploitation when a firm has substantial market power in the relevant market. Also, establishing dominance is a legal requirement in most jurisdictions to apply rules on abuse of dominance.

- **Step 3: Analyse effects on consumer welfare and efficiency**. As the effects of personalised pricing are ambiguous, an infringement should only be established if there is evidence of harm. The analysis may give a different weight to consumer welfare and total welfare, depending on the antitrust standard of a particular jurisdiction.

- **Step 4: Assess the persistency of the effects**. Even if personalised pricing harms consumers by increasing average prices, this does not necessarily merit an antitrust intervention, as those effects may be temporary and likely to be resolved by the market. In opposition, an intervention may be preferable when the existence of barriers to entry or switching costs may extend the negative effects over time.

- **Step 5: Identify the source of discrimination**. Discrimination can be facilitated by many factors, such as business strategies to partition the market, consumer inertia, lack of price transparency, data collection and even regulations. Identifying the source of the discrimination can be useful to define the appropriate remedies.

Source: OECD (2016), Price   Discrimination - Background note by the Secretariat, https://one.oecd.org/document/DAF/COMP(2016)15/en/pdf.

. . .

6.1. Privacy and data protection

101.   Privacy and data protection policy plays an increasingly important role in a digital world where firms may engage in many personalising strategies – including personalised pricing – that are dependent on the collection and use of consumer data. Although it is not within the reach of

privacy and data protection laws to directly regulate businesses pricing decisions, these laws can still govern some of the means required to implement personalised pricing, namely the collection, storing and processing of personal data.

102.   Privacy laws in most OECD countries are consistent with the OECD Privacy Guidelines principles that require the disclosure of the purposes for which personal data is collected and typically a consumer's consent to those uses (OECD, 1980). The use of personal data to determine the price to be charged would fall within those requirements and provide an independent legal basis for demanding transparency around the data use. This and other privacy and data protection laws may help insuring that personalised pricing practices are transparent and fully understood by consumers.

103.   A relevant example of privacy and data protection laws that may apply to personalised pricing are rules related to *profiling*, which have gained particular importance in the EU with the release of the General Data Protection Regulation (GDPR), where profiling is defined as:

> *"Any form of automated processing of personal data consisting of the use of personal data to evaluate certain personal aspects relating to a natural person, in particular to analyse or predict aspects concerning that natural person's performance at work, economic situation, health, personal preferences, interests, reliability, behaviour, location or movements."*

104.   Under the new GDPR, businesses are only allowed to carry out profiling in instances where this is either necessary for the activity of the business, authorised by law, or based on the consent of the individual. Other requirements include providing individuals with information about the profiling process, and giving them the right to change or request a review of their profiles. Box 6 provides a checklist with the conditions under which profiling and automated individual decision-making comply with the GDPR.

Box 6. Checklist for profiling and automated individual decision-making

"To comply with the GDPR . . .

☐   *We have a lawful basis to carry out profiling and/or automated decisionmaking and document this in our data protection policy.*

- ☐ *We send individuals a link to our privacy statement when we have obtained their personal data indirectly.*

- ☐ *We explain how people can access details of the information we used to create their profile.*

- ☐ *We tell people who provide us with their personal data how they can object to profiling, including profiling for marketing purposes.*

- ☐ *We have procedures for customers to access the personal data input into the profiles so they can review and edit for any accuracy issues.*

- ☐ *We have additional checks in place for our profiling/automated decisionmaking systems to protect any vulnerable groups (including children).*

- ☐ *We only collect the minimum amount of data needed and have a clear retention policy for the profiles we create.*

As a model of best practice . . .

- ☐ *We carry out a DPIA to consider and address the risks before we start any new automated decision-making or profiling.*

- ☐ *We tell our customers about the profiling and automated decision-making we carry out, what information we use to create the profiles and where we get this information from.*

- ☐ *We use anonymised data in our profiling activities."*

Source: ICO (2018), Guide to the General Data Protection Regulation (GDPR), Information Commissioner's Office, https://ico.org.uk/media/for-organisations/guide-to-the-general-data-protectionregulation-gdpr-1-0.pdf.

may not have to make it illegal → just make it impossible . . .

Notes

1.   If price discrimination typically has the effect of charging less to those with a lower willingness to pay, perhaps because they have less money, and more to those who will pay more, should preventing it be a priority?

2.   The use of the term "deadweight loss" in Figure 9 is not the typical one. The term is usually used to refer to the loss that results from sales not made that would have provided surplus (profits) to both seller and buyer; in the left-hand figure, that would be the white triangle to the right of the lightly shaded area, not the lightly shaded area itself. Therefore, there is no area in the right-hand figure that is typical deadweight loss. But if "profits" are all dissipated by wasteful effort—rent-seeking—to obtain them, then we could view them as deadweight loss, as the figure apparently does.

3.   One problem with price discrimination is that if done imperfectly by the seller, it can result in lower output (though perhaps greater profits) than would be produced with a single price, as in the figure below.

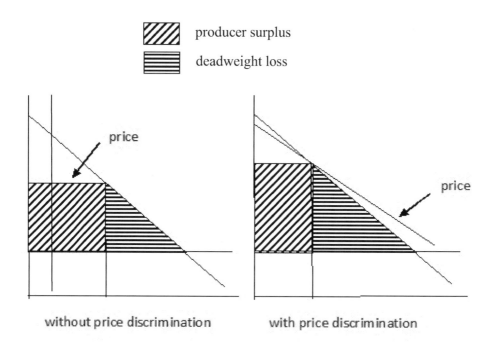

Note that output is lower and deadweight loss is greater with (this) price discrimination, despite the fact that prices are fairly close to demand. Producer surplus is similar in the two cases, though, and whether the producer would respond to the lower output by adjusting prices is therefore not clear. If output is to be used as a determinant of anticompetitive effect, which party should bear the burden of proof on that issue?

4. There is considerable disagreement regarding whether "fairness" should be a consideration for competition law (as well as considerable disagreement regarding what "fairness" is). Is price discrimination an issue of fairness or competition or both? Or something else? Is consumer protection a better remedy, or will new protections be necessary if the "problem" is to be addressed?

3. Vertical Agreements

3.1.   Exclusive Dealing

Exclusive-dealing agreements have been at issue in a number of technology cases, including both the U.S. and EU *Microsoft* cases, at least one of which is usually considered in a traditional antitrust course. A variation on exclusive dealing, the most-favored-nation (MFN) clause, was also at issue in the *Apple* case above, though that case turned largely on the existence of a horizontal agreement.

Purely vertical MFN clauses have been a focus of enforcement on both sides of the Atlantic as well, though. In the U.S., much of the enforcement effort has taken place in the health-care industry. *See* U.S. v. Blue Cross Blue Shield of Michigan, 809 F. Supp. 2d 665 (E.D. Mich. 2011); United States v. Delta Dental of Rhode Island, 943 F. Supp. 172 (D.R.I. 1996). In Europe, though, there have been a number of enforcement actions against Internet sales platforms like booking.com that demand MFN treatment from the suppliers of the services that they sell. Most of these cases have resulted in commitment decisions (settlements), but the Bundeskartellamt successfully pursued the following case.

Bundeskartellamt
HRS-Hotel Reservation Service
9th Decision Division, B 9 - 66/10
20 December 2013

I.

1. It is herewith found that the 'best price' clauses (most favoured customer clauses [MFN clauses]) agreed between the party concerned and its hotel partners on the basis of No. 5 a) to d) and No. 18 (i) of the general terms and conditions which have been applicable since 1 March 2012, or in individual contracts with corresponding content, are in infringement of competition law as far as they affect hotels in Germany.

2. The party concerned is herewith prohibited from continuing to implement such clauses as far as they affect hotels in Germany.

3. The party concerned is herewith ordered to delete the MFN clauses

from the contracts, and from the general terms and conditions underlying these contracts, by 1 March 2014, as far as they affect hotels in Germany.

4.   The requirement in No. 3 shall also be satisfied in the case of individual contracts by timely changes in the contracts at the next possible date, even if these do not become effective until the deadline has expired.

. . .

Statment of reasons:

A.   Summary

1 HRS-Hotel Reservation Service Robert Ragge GmbH, Cologne, (hereafter: "HRS") is infringing valid competition law by means of the MFN (most favoured customer) clause which it has agreed with its hotel partners. The relevant product market is the market for the sale of hotel rooms via hotel portals (hotel portal market), which in geographic terms should be defined to cover all of Germany. . . . In view of the fact that HRS has had a market share of more than 30% in the past four years, the MFN clauses are not exempted in accordance with the Vertical Restraints Block Exemption Regulation. It can thus be left open whether the MFN clauses are a non-exemptible hardcore restriction. The MFN clauses also do not satisfy the requirements for an individual exemption. . . .

2 The service agreements concluded between hotels and HRS provide for the hotels to be included in the HRS hotel reservation system. HRS does not buy room contingents, but sells (the German term used in this context is "vermitteln") single hotel rooms and receives a standard commission from the hotel for each booking that is made, currently amounting to 15% of the final hotel room price.

3 There is also a contractual relationship between hotel customers and HRS: via the HRS reservation system, the hotel customer can make direct bookings at the current hotel prices which are displayed on the portal. HRS does not charge the hotel customers any direct costs for the service, and the customers only pay the displayed room price to the hotel. The displayed hotel price as a rule includes the commission which the hotel is to pay to HRS.

4 The MFN clauses are contained in contracts between HRS (including its subsidiaries Tiscover and Hotel.de) and the hotels and in the general terms and conditions underlying these contracts. The general terms and conditions were most recently agreed in the

version of 1 March 2012. HRS has agreed MFN clauses with its hotel partners in various countries since 2006. The wording of the MFN clauses is largely identical. HRS has continued to systematically monitor compliance with the MFN clauses until October 2013, and, most recently only in isolated cases, has threatened the hotels with sanctions should they fail to comply. HRS has enforced sanctions, in particular in form of booking deactivation and contract termination.

5 The product market for the sale of hotel rooms via hotel portals (hotel portal market) is not a substitute for offline sales, for instance via travel agencies or sales at the hotel reception desk. Because hotel portals offer hotel customers the functions "search, comparison and booking" in a bundle of services which customers find convenient, the own website of the hotel and specialised portals, like e.g. city portals, do not belong to the hotel portal market. Online travel agencies and tour operator portals as a rule do not have any direct contractual ties with the hotels, and hence operate at another level of the distribution chain. This also applies to meta search engines, which regularly only offer a price comparison function and establish contact between the connected hotel portals (and in some cases major hotels and hotel chains) and the hotel customers.

6 By contrast, the corporate customer business of HRS is just as much part of the relevant product market as is private customer business. At best, travel management, which consists of a comprehensive bundle of services for corporate customers going beyond the sale of hotel rooms should be treated as being separate from private customer business. HRS, however, does not offer this service.

7 In geographic terms, one may assume a market for hotel portals which covers the whole of Germany. The hotel portals are Internet platforms which are technically accessible to customers from anywhere in the world. Nonetheless, the hotel portal market is neither a worldwide market nor a European market because the hotel portals operating on it have a regional focus, especially as to the local presence of the staff and as to the services offered on the portal (e.g. concerning destinations and advertising).

8 The MFN agreements between HRS and its hotel partners are likely to affect trade between Member States within the European Union. The agreements are within the scope of both the German and of the European bans on anti-competitive agreements. This is neither contradicted by the status of HRS, which HRS considers to be that of a "genuine agent", nor are the MFN clauses mere ancillary

agreements implementing contracts which are neutral in terms of competition law. The MFN clauses bring about a restraint of competition, in particular they are a competitive restraint between the hotel portals and between the hotels; it can be left open whether competition is restrained by object, as well.

9 There are significant restraints of competition by effect. The MFN clauses remove the economic incentives for the hotel portals to offer lower commissions to the hotels or to face up to competition by adopting new sales strategies. Market entries by new competitors are made more difficult and opportunities open to hotels are considerably restricted. Hotels cannot use different hotel portals and other sales channels in order to make offers at different prices and conditions. Moreover, the MFN clauses of the two other major hotel portals operating in Germany, namely Booking and Expedia, strengthen the restraints of competition which are brought about by the MFN clauses of HRS.

10 The MFN clauses are not exempt from the application of the ban on anti-competitive agreements. The MFN clauses are vertical restraints, which as a matter of principle may fall under the exemption of the Vertical Restraints Block Exemption Regulation; this, however, does not apply in the present case. The market share of HRS was above 30%, not only in the past year 2012, but for at least four years. It can thus be left open whether the MFN clauses are hardcore restrictions within the meaning of the Vertical Restraints Block Exemption Regulation.

11 An individual exemption of the MFN clauses is not possible in the present case because the possible positive effects of the MFN clauses do not outweigh the anti-competitive effects. The potential efficiency impact of the MFN clauses solving a free riding problem, if there is such a problem at all, is slight at best; the restraint of competition which is brought about as a result of the MFN clauses is not indispensable, and it does not allow consumers a fair share of the benefit. It is hence left open whether the MFN clauses lead to the elimination of competition in respect to a "substantial part of the products", even though there is much to suggest that they do.

12 The implementation of the MFN clauses constitutes an unfair hindrance of the small and medium-sized hotel partners which are dependent on HRS.

13 The Decision Division decided that the infringement that has been identified is to be brought to an end. As a further measure, HRS

is instructed to remove the MFN clauses from the contracts and from the general terms and conditions by 1 March 2014.

14 By contrast, the Decision Division does not consider the time-limited commitments recently offered by HRS, as adequate alternative. Time-limited commitments would not permanently eliminate the serious concerns of the Decision Division with regard to the MFN clauses. Moreover, a precedence effect for other cases only emanates from an explicit finding of the infringement. The prohibition order at hand is an effective and enforceable remedy for removing the MFN clauses in the interest of creating legal certainty for all contracting partners of HRS.

15 The withdrawal of the benefit of the relevant block exemption, which the Decision Division initially considered, cannot be carried out because of the current results of the investigation in this case. The market share of HRS remains above 30% according to the current findings of the Decision Division. Therefore HRS, at least currently, does not enjoy the benefit of the Vertical Restraints Block Exemption Regulation.

B.   Statement of facts

1.   HRS and other hotel portals

16 HRS operates a worldwide electronic hotel portal[17] for business and private travellers on the basis of a database of more than 250,000 hotels in all price categories in Germany, Europe and worldwide. HRS is one of the leading hotel portals in Germany.

. . .

18 HRS provides services both for its hotel partners and for their customers who book hotel rooms via the portal:

19 According to the contracts between HRS and the hotels HRS receives a standard commission of currently 15% of the accommodation price for each individual booking that is made; the commission is billed on a monthly basis. Furthermore, the contracts regulate questions on the quality and on the prices for the accommodation as well as the data maintenance of the hotels and the booking and cancellation conditions. The ranking of the hotels on the HRS portal

---

[17] The definition of "hotel portal" used here includes online portals which act as an intermediary on the basis of direct contracts with hotels both with regard to individual accommodation in hotels and where appropriate other travel services (cf. for details of this Section D.1.2.2).

depends on categories and criteria individually selected by the customers, such as the most favourable price, "HRS recommends!", discounts, evaluations and "HRS stars".

20 According to the "General Terms and Conditions for Reservations", which apply in the relationship between HRS and the hotel customers, customers are not billed for the portal service of HRS; they only pay the displayed room price to the selected hotel. Further clauses of the general terms and conditions refer to bookings and cancellation, as well as to the various prices that are offered by the hotels (e.g. daily, last minute, seasonal or weekend prices).

21 The HRS system allows direct bookings to be made at the current prices. For users with German IP addresses, the bookings are made via the hotel portals hrs.de and hrs.com, and can also be made on mobile devices.

22 HRS offers booking information in more than 30 languages, and hence also targets hotel customers abroad. The hotel selection is made easier by a large number of filters, on deals and offers, theme hotels, business travel and groups, as well as by providing detailed hotel descriptions, hotel videos and roughly 2.5 million evaluations by hotel guests. For many years HRS operated the only well-known hotel portal, Hrs.de, in Germany, until two hotel portals, which are to some degree better known abroad, also gained a clearly visible presence on the German hotel market after the turn of the millennium. These are, firstly, Booking.com (below: "Booking"), the Dutch leading hotel portal in Europe, and Expedia.com, which belongs to the US online travel agency Expedia, Inc. (below: "Expedia"), which concentrates its operations on the U.S.A. and on Canada.

23 The worldwide turnover of HRS from commissions and, to a small extent, from advertising was approx. […] € in 2012, of which approx. […] € in Europe and approx. […] € in Germany. Of the more than […] million hotel guests in Europe who booked hotels via HRS, [the lion's share] came from Germany.

24 Booking, which belongs to the US Priceline Group, is the only enterprise which, on a scale comparable to HRS, concentrates exclusively on the sale of hotel rooms in Germany as well as in other EU Member States. The sale takes place via the booking.com portal and the domains which redirect to booking.com, such as booking.de. Other hotel and travel sites operated by the Priceline

Group focus their services on the U.S.A. (priceline.com for hotel accommodation, flights, hire cars, package tours and cruises) and on Asia (agoda.com for hotel accommodation).

25 Expedia, the portal which currently has the third-largest turnover in Germany, sells single hotel rooms (also referred to below as "hotel-only") and travel products via its portals expedia.com and hotwire.com (discount), as well as hotel rooms only via the hotels.com portal, which is owned by its UK subsidiary Hotels.com, L.P. and via the venere.com portal, which is owned by its Italian subsidiary Venere Net S.p.A. (hereinafter: "Venere").

26 In addition to the service offered by HRS, Booking and Expedia, there are other portals which as a rule sell hotel rooms in Germany as well as travel products, flights, hire cars and other items, but have not yet become as significant for German hotels as HRS, Booking and Expedia. . . .

27 Hotel rooms in Germany have also been sold via mobile hotel portals in form of Apps on smartphones or tablet PCs since 2012 at the latest. In addition to the HRS "Hotels Now" App, these include "JustBook" and "BookitNow!", as well as Booking's "Tonight" App, the US "Hotel Tonight" and the "BlinkBooking" App.

2. The MFN clauses of HRS

28 MFN clauses[27] have been a part of the contracts between HRS and its hotel partners worldwide since 2006. The scope of the MFN clauses which have been applied since 1 March 2010 was expanded with effect as per 1 March 2012. The proceedings pending in the present case were initiated by a complaint against HRS in January 2010. The 2010 MFN clauses, the transition to the 2012 MFN clauses and the most recent clauses, which are currently still applicable, are therefore described below. HRS has continued the practice of enforcing the MFN clauses by applying pressure, as was the case prior to the amendment of the MFN clauses.

2.1 MFN Clauses 2010

29 The 2010 MFN clauses of HRS are contained in Nos. 4 and 5 sentence 1 and No. 21 (h) of the general terms and conditions which have been applicable between HRS and its hotel partners since 1 March

---

[27] The term "MFN clauses" used here and below refers to all booking and cancellation conditions, as well as to room availability.

2010, and read as follows.

30 "4. Best-price and availability guarantee

    a.   In principle, HRS expects its partner hotels to offer HRS the lowest room rates available including all taxes and other fees (so-called end prices). The hotel guarantees that the HRS price is at least as low as the cheapest rate offered by or for the hotel on other booking and travel platforms on the Internet or on offers on the hotel's own Web pages (the so-called parity rate). In this respect, the hotel also pledges to hold its other sales partners (e.g. tour operators) to this guarantee or to ensure that, if it is bookable at a cheaper rate elsewhere on the Internet, this price will definitely be available to HRS customers.

    b.   Furthermore, the hotel guarantees not to treat HRS unfairly vis-à-vis other online sales channels with regard to availability. Therefore, if rooms are available on other online sales channels, they must also be made available on HRS.

    c.   The hotel guarantees not to treat HRS unfairly vis-à-vis other online sales channels with regard to the booking and cancellation conditions for customers. Therefore, better conditions that the hotel offers online on other booking and travel platforms must also apply on HRS."

31 It also says in No. 5 sentence 1 of the general terms and conditions: "The hotel is obliged to notify HRS without delay about all current temporary price reductions and to make these bookable through HRS."

32 According to No. 21 (h) of the Contractual Terms and Conditions 2010, "HRS may bar the hotel immediately or temporarily prevent it from receiving further bookings" in case of "uncooperative behaviour, e.g. quoting unfair market prices or entering higher prices on the HRS system than those charged to persons "walking in" as well as breaches of the best-price guarantee or parity with availability or booking conditions as per Section 4".

33 Prior to the amendment of its general terms and conditions, HRS explained the new conditions to its hotel partners in writing. The Bundeskartellamt has at its disposal a letter from HRS to its hotel partners of 4 September 2009 and a letter of 13 January 2010.

34 Referring to the MFN clauses existing at that time, the letter of

September 2009 states the following as the reason for the transition: "[...]. HRS has developed a system which monitors the rates offered on our site and compares them on a daily basis with those of our competitors and of the hotels' own websites. [...] This routine monitoring has revealed rates in various online portals which were originally meant for tour operators to put together package tours. Some of these rates were far below the HRS guaranteed best prices, and also below those being offered on the hotels' own websites. [...] Against this background, we have called on all of you, our hotel partners [...] to provide HRS with [...] parity rates. [...]" All in all, this concerned roughly 100 hotels from various hotel chains and other hotels. The majority of the hotels in question reacted directly, and immediately restored rate parity. Where our demand was, however, not met, we have removed the hotels from sales until the prices are adjusted. This meant that roughly 40 hotels could no longer be booked via our site for a certain time. We are now able to state that, with the exception of two hotels, all partner hotels can now be booked via HRS once more, since the appropriate corrections have been carried out. [...]

35 In an intensive discussion that was provoked by HRS, a sectoral solution [was] developed which [...] ensures that operator rates can no longer [...] be passed into the portal world. Rate parity has thus been restored, and we can keep the promise which we make to our customers, and we can guarantee to offer them the best price."

36 HRS explained the content of the new general terms and conditions in the letter of 13 January 2010 as follows:

37 "As is the customary practice in cooperation between hotels and online sales channels, we will be expanding the existing, generally recognised best price guarantee to include availability and booking conditions. [...] If you therefore also sell a room on other online portals, we would like to be able to continue to offer your hotel. [...] As one of your strongest and most advantageous sales channels, we presume that, where you still have free capacities which are offered via other portals, you can also be booked via HRS. Moreover, HRS is also not to be placed at a disadvantage over other Internet sales channels with regard to the reservation and cancellation conditions. [...] Should you object to the changes [...], this is deemed as cancellation of your HRS contract with effect as per 1 March 2010, so that it will no longer be possible to book your hotel via HRS from that time onwards."

2.2   MFN Clauses 2012

38 By letter of 17 January 2012, HRS informed its hotel partners of a change in its contractual terms and conditions from 1 March 2012 and pointed out that the opposition of a hotel to the changes would be regarded as constituting termination of the contract with effect from the date of the changes. Major changes relate to the tightening up of the MFN clauses (expansion of price and condition parity to cover all sales channels) as well as the increased commission, inter alia for individual bookings from a previous level of 13 to 15%.

39 The general terms and conditions in the version of 1 March 2012 now apply exclusively between HRS (including its subsidiaries Tiscover and Hotel.de) and its hotel partners.

40 No. 5 of the general terms and conditions reads as follows:

"Best price guarantee and availability guarantee

In principle, HRS expects its hotel partners to offer the lowest room rates available including all taxes and other fees (so-called end prices) and the maximum possible availability. The hotel is therefore obliged to

a. guarantee that HRS always receives a price (hereinafter referred to jointly as "price" or "rate") at least as low as the cheapest rate offered by or for the hotel on other booking and travel platforms on the Internet or on offers through the hotel's own sales channels (so-called parity rate). The hotel is obliged in this context to also hold its other sales partners (e.g. tour operators) to this guarantee or to ensure that, if it is bookable at a cheaper rate elsewhere, this price will definitely be available to HRS customers.

b. A successful claim by a HRS customer resulting from the breach of the best price guarantee must be settled when invoicing the guest. In addition, the Hotel will modify the HRS price accordingly without delay.

c. Furthermore, the Hotel guarantees not to treat HRS unfairly vis-à-vis other distribution channels with regard to availability. Therefore, if rooms are available on other sales channels, they must also be made available on HRS.

d. The Hotel guarantees not to treat HRS unfairly vis-à-vis other distribution channels with regard to the booking and cancellation conditions for customers. Therefore, better conditions that the hotel or a third party acting on behalf of the hotel offers online or offline on other booking and travel platforms must also apply on HRS."

41 In accordance with No. 18 (i) of the new contractual terms and conditions, an "infringement against the best price guarantee or parity for availability or booking terms" authorises HRS to "directly and temporarily block the hotel from receiving any additional bookings".

42 HRS has supported the impact of these clauses by means of a price guarantee which applies to the customers of its hotel partners. The price guarantee reads as follows:

43 "With the HRS best price guarantee, you can be certain that you will always receive the best offer for your hotel reservation from HRS. If a hotel offers its rooms more cheaply via a different Internet service with the same booking conditions, HRS will also only charge you the lower price. We guarantee this! [...] Within best the price guarantee, after we have checked the alternative offer, we will send you a new booking confirmation with the cheaper room price."

44 HRS continued until September 2013 the practice which it had already exercised in the past, namely of routinely monitoring rates and threatening to impose sanctions (in particular booking deactivations and issuing contract terminations) in the event of non- compliance with rate parity.

45 HRS also agreed clauses in individual contracts with its hotel partners the content of which, according to its own information, is similar with the MFN clauses in No. 5 of the currently applicable terms and conditions.

2.3 "Top Quality Hotel" seal

46 By letter of 1 October 2012, HRS informed the Decision Division of the introduction of the "Top Quality Hotel" seal from November 2012 onwards. Since then, it has been possible for HRS hotel partners to conclude an additional agreement with HRS containing the conditions for the award of the seal. These conditions include a high level of customer satisfaction, flexible booking conditions and "objectively advantageous prices". [...] The seal is withdrawn if the hotel that was awarded the "Top Quality Hotel" seal no longer meets the requirements of the quality seal (No. 2 of the additional agreement). The participating hotel appears on the HRS portal with the "Top Quality Hotel" seal [...]. HRS informed the Decision Division by e-mail of 9 December 2013 that the Top

Quality Hotel is now shown with […] hotels in Germany. Hence, fewer than […] of the approx. […] hotel partners of HRS in Germany have currently been awarded the seal.

47 The Decision Division decided not to make the HRS "Top Quality Hotel" seal part of its prohibition order in these proceedings. Nonetheless, the Decision Division will continue to precisely observe whether the use of the seal by HRS results in an impact on the market which is similar to the impact of the MFN clauses contained in the terms and conditions and in individual contracts. Looking at the impact on competition it is crucial whether HRS combines the "Top Quality Hotel" seal with further services for hotels, e.g. in form of better ranking or lower commissions, and to what degree hotels use the seal.

3.   MFN clauses of other portals

48 Just like HRS, the other major portals in Germany, such as Booking and Expedia, introduced MFN clauses some years ago.

. . .

D. Legal assessment

68 HRS is in infringement of applicable competition law by virtue of the MFN clauses agreed with its hotel partners. These clauses certainly bring about a significant restraint of competition between the hotel portals and between the hotels within the meaning of section 1 GWB/Art. 101 (1) TFEU (cf. on this section D.3) on the relevant market for the sale of hotel rooms via hotel portals (cf. on this section D.1), which, in geographic terms, is to be defined to cover all parts of Germany (cf. on this section D.2). The criteria for an exemption in accordance with section 2 (1) GWB/Art. 101 (3) TFEU in conjunction with Art. 2 of the Vertical Restraints Block Exemption Regulation would not be satisfied if the MFN clauses of HRS were a hardcore restriction within the meaning of Art. 4 a) of the Vertical Restraints Block Exemption Regulation. Whether this is the case may, however, remain open since the HRS market share was above 30%, at least from 2009 to 2012 (cf. on this section D.4.3). The criteria for an individual exemption in accordance with section 2 (1) GWB/Art. 101 (3) TFEU are not satisfied (cf. on this section D.5); an exemption in accordance with section 3 GWB cannot be considered in the present case (cf. on this section D.6). By applying the MFN clauses, HRS has acted in violation of section 20 (1) in conjunction with section 19 (1) and (2) No. 1 GWB (cf. on this section D.7).

1.   The relevant product market

69 The relevant product market is the market for the sale of hotel rooms via hotel portals (hereinafter referred to as "hotel portal market"). The relevant product market encompasses all goods or services which have a substitute function in the view of the customer as to their characteristics, economic purpose and prices. The purpose of market definition is to identify and define the area with regard to a specific set of proceedings in which companies compete with one another, i.e. the purpose is to identify competitors that are capable of constraining the behaviour of companies and of preventing them from behaving independently of effective competitive pressure.\

1.1   The pleading of HRS

70 HRS submits that hotel portals belong to a broad product market which, in addition to the providers of the typical bundle of services of a hotel portal ("search, comparison and booking"), also includes all providers of services possibly leading to a booking. It was hence not necessary to distinguish between online and offline services. . . .

1.2   The market definition of the Decision Division

71 The Decision Division does not share the view held by HRS according to which hotel portals belong to a broad product market including both providers of the typical bundle of services of a hotel portal ("search, comparison and booking"), and all providers of single services. The present case relates to the market for the sale of hotel rooms via hotel portals. In particular, there is a need to distinguish between the various sales channels and the sales-relevant services specified by HRS since there are considerable differences here. Relevant points are, in particular, whether services are offered as a bundle or individually and whether the service is offered at the same level of the distribution chain. Furthermore, the orientation and the range of services offered by the channels need to be considered. The Decision Division, like HRS, looks at both sides of the market but focuses on the view of the hotels. The meaning and purpose of the market definition under competition law is to include competition relationships between market players whose relationships are the focus of the investigation in a specific case. This case relates to the MFN clauses that are agreed by contract between HRS and the hotels. It is vital for the hotels to define who provides the service and subject to what contractually-agreed conditions. In the view of the hotels only those

channels are substitutes, and hence to be included in the same market, via which substitute services are provided. This is not the case for the providers and services mentioned by HRS from Google to offline travel agencies and to offline sales by the hotels.

72 The Decision Division has also investigated the perspective of the hotel customer in the market definition. It should be taken into account that, even where hotel customers consider a certain degree of substitution to exist between the various channels, hotels might have a different perspective. From their point of view specific channels may not be substitutes, but complement one another.

. . .

79 The approach taken by some hotel customers, as described by HRS, namely "looking on the Web, sorting out questions in a travel agency and then booking"[101], may well apply to complex travel services comprising accommodation, flights, hire cars, travel insurance and tourist attractions, but hardly to individual hotel stays. General experience suggests that a change from online to offline sales in any case does not take place with a simple hotel room search. According to a market survey of the European Commission travel customers who do not get the information from one online provider typically continue their search with another online provider, but they do not continue their search offline.

. . .

1.2.2.1   Hotel portals

81 The relevant product market includes the services of all portals which relate to the sale of hotel rooms ("hotel-only"), this also being the case if the portals additionally offer other travel services. Hotel portals either display the information provided by the hotels via the respective central booking system of the hotel chains (CRS) or a technical interface (e.g. Pegasus), or they process and complete the information provided by hotels by including photographs and videos, editing and translating the descriptions and evaluating the hotels, and they finally post this information on their websites (in the case of HRS via the so-called extranet). The hotel portal market is a two-sided market. The customers that hotel portals connect are the hotels on one side and the hotel customers on the other side. A typical feature of two-sided markets is the network effect: the more intensive use of a portal by one side of the market triggers greater use of the portal by the other side. The larger the network, the more comprehensive the services can be. In some cases hotel

portals charge standard commissions for their services, in other cases for different reasons, they impose highly differentiated commissions (e.g. higher commissions in large cities). The hotels are, however, left to shoulder the room occupancy risk.

. . .

86   An indication of the special status, in particular of the major hotel portals, such as HRS, is the reaction of the German hotels to HRS increasing its commission from 13% to 15% (from 12% to 15% for the Hotel.de hotel portal which belongs to HRS) and to the tightening up of the MFN clauses in March 2012. General experience suggests that, were sales via HRS actually a substitute for all other online sales channels, the cumulative price increase by more than 15% at HRS and by more than 25% at Hotel.de, as well as the additional tightening up of the MFN clauses, should have led to large numbers of cancellations and to the hotels changing to other channels which compete with HRS. The action of HRS did lead to vociferous public protest in the German hotel market, but there were few cancellations. HRS confirmed that with only fifty cancellations from hotels only a very low resonance to the tightening up of the conditions had been recorded. The lack of competitive pressure on the part of the providers of other sales channels is a clear indication that HRS and other hotel portals, such as Booking and Expedia, constitute a separate product market. This is also made clear by the fact that the major portals are managing to use MFN clauses, which influence price setting for hotel rooms on the other sales channels.

87 The view expressed by HRS according to which the joint designation of hotel portals, tour operator portals, online travel agencies and travel evaluation portals (e.g. holidaycheck.de) in some studies, and in the self-evaluation of some of the companies surveyed by the Decision Division, as "competitors" already proves that these companies are actually operating on one and the same product market, does not hold true. The designation of other companies as "competitors" depends on what service a study is investigating or on the designation that is offered by the companies surveyed. The designation as "competitors" does not answer the question of whether the functions offered in each case are substitutes from the point of view of the customers. The term "competitors" is, rather, used in a non-technical manner in such studies. The providers which only offer single functions of the hotel portals or other product bundles exert very little or no competitive pressure on the hotel portals.

1.2.2.2   Hotels' own websites

88 The websites of the hotels offering real-time booking are not part of the same product market as hotel portals. They are not substitutes for hotel portals because they do not offer the same bundle of services for hotel customers that hotel portals do. They only offer customers the possibility of booking a room in a specific hotel or hotel chain. appropriate overview is offered only by hotel portals, and not by the hotels' own websites.

. . .

1.2.2.3   Specialised portals

91 Specialised portals, such as city portals or ebay, are not part of the same relevant product market as hotel portals. Specialised portals do not concentrate on the sale of hotel rooms and they display a much narrower range of hotels on the website. Where specialised portals only redirect hotel customers to other portals – and not directly to the websites of the hotels –, they operate on another level of the distribution chain than hotel portals do, and for this reason they belong to another market.

. . .

1.2.2.4   Online travel agencies

93 Online travel agencies do not belong to the same product market as hotel portals. They target a different category of customers, overlapping only slightly with that of the hotel portals, and hence operate on another level of the distribution chain. With its comprehensive range of services, including lastminute travel products, package tours and holiday apartments as well as flights, railway tickets and hire cars, the service offered by online travel agencies, such as Opodo, primarily addresses holiday travellers but not individuals who initially only wish to book a hotel room. Unlike hotel portals, they do not have contractual ties with a large number of hotels, but sell hotel rooms of other portals or of wholesalers. Accordingly, online travel agencies do not receive a fee for the sale of hotel rooms from the hotels, but from other portals and wholesalers. Online travel agencies are less a "sales channel of the hotels" than a sales channel for other portals and for wholesalers. According to information from Hotel.de, for instance, some of the bookings made on Opodo were carried out via its Hotel.de portal.

. . .

3.   Violation of section 1 GWB/Art. 101 (1) TFEU

137   The MFN clauses implemented by HRS violate section 1
      GWB/Art. 101 (1) TFEU. This provision prohibits agreements
      between companies which prevent or restrict competition, either
      by object or by effect.

      Even though it is arguable whether the MFN agreements between
      HRS and its hotel partners bring about significant restraints of
      competition by object, they certainly do so by effect. The economic
      incentive for hotel portals to offer lower commissions to the hotels
      or the incentive to face up to competition by adopting new sales
      strategies is taken away; it is made more difficult for new
      competitors to enter the market. The possibilities open to the
      hotels to submit offers on various hotel portals and other sales
      channels at different   prices and conditions are considerably
      restricted. The restraints of competition caused by the MFN clauses
      of HRS are strengthened by the MFN clauses of the two other
      major portals in Germany, namely Booking and Expedia.

138   The MFN agreements between HRS and its hotel partners are
      agreements between companies (cf. on this section 3.1 below) which
      can impact trade between Member States of the European Union
      (cf. on this section 3.2). The agreements fall within the scope of
      section 1 GWB/Art. 101 (1) TFEU (cf. on this section 3.3). The
      MFN clauses restrain competition (cf. on this section 3.4). The
      restraints of competition are significant (cf. on this section 3.5).

      3.1   Agreements within the meaning of section 1 GWB/Art. 101
               (1) TFEU

139   The MFN clauses used by HRS are agreements within the meaning
      of section 1 GWB/Art. 101 (1) TFEU. Agreements are reached by
      congruent statements of intent of the parties to engage in a certain
      market conduct. Agreements also cover expressions of will which
      provide for or authorise a company to adopt unilateral conduct
      which is binding on the other company. The agreements here in
      question fall within this definition.

      . . .

      3.2   Scope of section 1 GWB/Art. 101 (1) TFEU

144   The MFN clause of HRS falls within the scope of section 1
      GWB/Art. 101 TFEU. HRS is neither a genuine agent who might
      be permitted to agree such a clause (cf. on this section 3.3.1), nor are

the MFN clauses only ancillary agreements in contracts which are otherwise neutral in terms of competition law (cf. on this section 3.3.2).

3.3.1   Agent

145   With regard to the sale of hotel rooms, HRS does not operate as a genuine, and hence dependent agent within the meaning of competition law. Competition law therefore applies.

146   Where agents do not bear any economic risk of their own with regard to their contract services, and are therefore largely dependent on the instructions of the principal, the ban on anti-competitive agreements only applies to a limited degree to legal relations between the principal and the genuine agent. Restraints of competition committed by the principal vis-à-vis the agent are only allowed if the principal takes the risks and determines the commercial strategy, such as restrictions as to the sales area, the customers or the prices and conditions at which the agent must buy or re-sell the goods or services.

147   HRS does not act as a genuine agent with regard to the sale of hotel rooms. HRS cannot qualify as a genuine agent because the MFN clauses do not bring about any restraints of competition which emerge from a principal - in this case the hotel partners -, but from the agent HRS. As described in section B.2, HRS has amended the general terms and conditions which apply between HRS and its hotel partners. It is HRS which has unilaterally decided to amend the general terms and conditions. The hotel partners do not exert influence on the activities of HRS: They do not make demands on HRS either relating to the sales area or to the customers, nor do they influence further activities of HRS. The activities of HRS do not depend on the hotel partners of HRS. The MFN clauses do not restrict the conduct of the alleged agent, but rather that of the alleged principal.

148   HRS is not a dependent agent since HRS bears its own financial and economic risk. HRS does not dispute its extensive commercial activities and the economic risks. Examples are the HRS investment in advertising the HRS "brand", the establishment of a contractual network with a large number of hotels and cooperation partners (e.g. major travel companies, such as DB AG, AirBerlin, Germanwings and public clients, such as the

Bundeswehr), as well as the establishment and ongoing technical refinement and development of the content of the HRS website, and cooperation with major Internet providers, such as Amadeus, Google, Facebook, Twitter and TravelTainment.

149   The European Court of Justice has ruled that the ban on anti-competitive agreements is to be applied to travel agents which sell tourist services, including hotel rooms. Accordingly, travel agents are not genuine (dependent) agents, but are to be regarded as independent providers of services for a large number of tour operators. The activities of HRS are similar. HRS does not act in the interest of a single principal. Rather, HRS sells hotel rooms for more than 250,000 different hotels worldwide. It is ultimately not relevant for HRS which hotels are booked.

3.3.2   Ancillary agreement

150   The MFN clauses are not ancillary agreements which are required to safeguard the main purpose of a contract which does not violate competition law. The clauses are therefore not exempt from the scope of the ban on anti-competitive agreements.

151   In particular, the MFN clauses are not required for avoiding free riding on the information and advertising services provided by HRS (more detail on this in section 5.2.1).

The MFN clauses are not necessary because a large number of competitors in the market apply them. Where MFN clauses of other market players constitute a restraint of competition, the HRS MFN clauses contribute to further strengthening the restraints of competition already existing on the German market.

3.4   Restraint of competition by object and by effect

152   Even though it may be arguable that the MFN clauses of HRS do not bring about restraints of competition by object, they do at least bring them about by effect. The restriction of freedom to compete is regarded to be intentional if it is objectively suited to do so, if it is part of the contractual obligations of the parties in question and if the fulfilment of the contractual obligations is indeed enforced. When examining whether an agreement contains a restraint of competition "by object", the ECJ also looks at the goals pursued by the agreement and the economic and legal context.

153   The HRS MFN clauses are objectively suited to directly restrict the freedom of price setting of the hotel partners of HRS on the other sales channels, since the hotel partners may not offer their hotel rooms at lower prices and better conditions via the other sales channels. The hotel partners of HRS can freely set the price

for the hotel rooms on the portal of HRS, but they may not have a different price on other portals. Because of the transparency which is inherent to online sales, HRS can effectively monitor compliance with the MFN clauses and impose sanctions. HRS further expanded the area of application of its previous MFN clauses with effect as per 1 March 2012 (concerning parity of availability and conditions to include all sales channels), and enforces these clauses by an automatic price monitoring system and by threatening and implementing booking deactivations and by the termination of contracts. The MFN clauses are suited and indeed intended to restrain competition between the hotel portals and to make it difficult to enter the market (cf. on this in detail section 3.4.1); they also restrain competition between the hotels (cf. on this section 3.4.2).

154 Whether the HRS clauses are genuine or typical MFN clauses (in the sense of direct pricing) is ultimately not relevant. The effect of the MFN clauses is anti-competitive even taking account the problem of free riding and the possible reduction of the search costs for hotel customers.

3.4.1   Restraint of competition between the hotel portals

155 The restraint of competition between the hotel portals relates to competition for the lowest booking commissions (cf. on this section 3.4.1.1), aggressive competition for the best conditions (cf. on this section 3.4.1.2) and the market entry of new competitors (cf. on this section 3.4.1.3). Anti-competitive effects of the MFN clauses are strengthened by the application of MFN clauses by the other major portals in Germany Booking and Expedia (cf. on this section 3.4.1.4).

3.4.1.1 Booking Fees

156 The MFN clauses of HRS remove the economic incentive for hotel portals to offer lower commissions to the hotel partners of HRS in order to have in turn rooms provided at lower prices and at more favourable conditions. The MFN clauses thus restrain intra-brand competition when selling hotel rooms and hence also restrain inter-brand-competition between the hotels. The significance attached by hotel portals, and by HRS in particular, to low room prices and to favourable booking and cancellation conditions is proven by the application of MFN clauses: They are to ensure that no other hotel portal offers better conditions.

157   The economic effect of the MFN clauses is similar to direct collusion between the hotel portals, namely concerted behaviour regarding the sale of a specific hotel room at a specific minimum price. Hotel portals which provide the same or at least similar hotel rooms as HRS are prevented from selling hotel rooms at lower prices or at more favourable conditions than HRS. In turn, HRS can increase its commissions without having to fear that its hotel partners will pass on the increase in the commission to hotel customers. The room price on the HRS portal is a central competition factor. Therefore the MFN clauses have strong anti-competitive effects and HRS profits from them.

3.4.1.2   Competitive advances

158   The MFN clauses also prevent competitive advances by other portals. New sales strategies are negatively affected. HRS confirmed that it removed forty of its partner hotels from the HRS reservation system because these hotel partners had permitted that hotel rooms which had originally been offered by tour operators within package tours were offered in various other portals at prices that were lower than those of HRS.

159   HRS also barred the "deal of the day" offered by Unister in 2011. In each "deal", a discount is granted against the nominal amount of the voucher. HRS invoked its MFN clauses to exclude hotel partners from the HRS booking system in cases where the hotel partners did not offer the "deal of the day" to HRS. Thus special offers from hotel portals which could have intensified competition and increased price pressure did not succeed.

3.4.1.3   Market entry

160   The MFN clauses furthermore impede the market access of new competitors. If a hotel portal is prevented from gaining access to cheaper rooms by charging lower commissions or through a new sales strategy, market access will be difficult.

161   There is less economic incentive for HRS hotel partners to take up the services of another hotel portal if they cannot pass on the lower commissions of this portal to their hotel customers or use new sales strategies to the advantage of their customers. Ultimately, the use of MFN clauses by HRS is particularly damaging for competition, because it protects an established enterprise against innovative offers from newcomers. A specific example is the market introduction of mobile hotel portals, such as JustBook and BookitNow!. Hotels had to grant to the portals discounts of 30%

or more on the daily rate for last minute offers. Both JustBook and BookitNow! have initiated proceedings targeting the MFN clauses of HRS.

162   MFN clauses even prevent market access by competitors if the latter are particularly efficient. A new hotel portal can only achieve a prominent status among the hotel customers if the hotels presented on the portal can satisfy the demand of the customers. The hotels approached by JustBook referred to the MFN clauses of HRS and refused to offer hotel rooms to JustBook. A new competitor who is de facto refused access to the market cannot demonstrate that he is an efficient competitor.

3.4.1.4   Strengthening of the anti-competitive effect through the application of MFN clauses by other hotel portals

163   The anti-competitive effects of the MFN clauses of HRS on competition between the hotel portals are strengthened by the application of MFN clauses by other portals. Looking at commissions earned, Booking has a larger market share than HRS ([40-50]% of the total volume). Booking has, agreed MFN clauses with its hotel partners, and it is in a position to enforce the clauses. Expedia, the third-largest market player with a value-based market share of [10-20]%, obliges hotels to implement parity of room rates and room availabilities, as well as parity of booking and cancellation conditions. HRS, Booking and Expedia together reached a market share of roughly 90% on the German hotel portal market. The MFN agreements of HRS, Booking and Expedia cover almost the entire market. Hotel portals cannot compete by using different booking commissions on the portals or different sales strategies. Market entry by new competitors is not impossible but much more difficult.

. . .

3.4.2   Restraint of competition between the hotels

164   The MFN clauses have negative effects on competition between the hotel partners of HRS and other hotels. Competition between the hotels for the best prices of rooms is particularly affected (cf. on this section 3.4.2.1). Competition is restrained for all channels which the hotels use for selling hotel rooms (cf. on this section 3.4.2.2). Anti-competitive effects of the MFN clauses on competition between the hotels are strengthened by MFN clauses which other major portals in Germany, like Booking and Expedia, apply (cf. on this section 3.4.2.3).

3.4.2.1 Hotel room prices

165 The MFN clauses of HRS prevent hotels from directly passing on lower commissions to their customers. Thus the hotels may attract a smaller number of customers. If the hotels cannot charge differential prices, they cannot effectively cover their costs. The hotels are prevented from adapting to specific market situations ("yield management").

166 The hotel partners of HRS are not free to set prices when it comes to pricing special offers (e.g. accommodation with or without breakfast). Since the MFN clauses do not only include booking and cancellation conditions, but also "prices and price conditions", hotels have to apply the MFN clauses, when they make special offers. In this case, the hotels must put HRS in a position to post the new offer on its portal, as well. Competition between the hotels for the best room offer ("inter-brand" competition) is thus restricted.

167 It is irrelevant whether, in the interest of "branding", major brand hotels might prefer one and the same hotel room price in any case, or whether smaller hotels might do so in order to achieve a simpler (price) management. Freedom of price setting can only strengthen competition if the price setting is not restricted. Hotels are prevented from granting discounts on other hotel portals by the MFN clauses of HRS since these clauses cover "prices and price conditions", and hence discounts, too. Price setting should always be decided by the hotels since they bear the sales risk. The hotels may therefore not be obliged by means of the MFN clauses to offer the same price on different sales channels.

168 There has been little price differentiation by hotels across the various sales channels in the past few years. This shows how emphatically the hotel portals enforce rate parity. According to the information that is available to the Bundeskartellamt, HRS automatically checks 80% of all hotels in the system for breaches of rate parity. Just like the other hotel portals, HRS uses "crawlers" which search the Internet several times a day for rates. HRS staff approaches hotels orally and in writing in order to enforce rate parity and threatens to expel hotels from the HRS portal, at least this was the case until October of this year.

3.4.2.2 The sales channels concerned

169 The MFN clauses restrain competition between the hotels on the various Internet sales channels, but also outside the Internet. HRS has extended parity requirements for the booking and cancellation

conditions in accordance with No 5 d) of its general terms and conditions to include offline sales channels.

170   From the point of view of major hotels, which largely sell their rooms via their own websites, the MFN clauses particularly restrict the opportunity to design these websites and to offer accommodation at more favourable conditions for specific periods. Since hotels do not pay commissions if bookings are made via their own websites, they could as a matter of principle sell rooms here at a lower price than via third-party channels. The accommodation services posted on the hotels´ own websites are theoretically allowed to differ from those on the HRS portal, if they cannot be presented on the HRS portal. The Decision Division is, however, not aware of any practical examples.

171   Because the MFN clauses cover the availability of rooms, the hotels cannot offer the remaining contingents on portals which have more visitors. HRS submits that it does not demand "last room availability" from its hotel partners. This is, however, not explicitly incorporated in the contractual terms applicable between HRS and its hotel partners; rather, in No. 5 c) the MFN clauses extend the availability parity for the hotel rooms to all "other sales channels", and hence at least in terms of the wording, to the own websites of the hotels.

172   The MFN clauses restrict the price setting on hotel rooms across the entire Internet, even when third parties sell the hotel rooms without the influence of the hotels. According to No. 5 (a) of the general terms and conditions which are applicable between HRS and its hotel partners the MFN clauses relate to prices and price conditions which customers can find on other platforms. They oblige hotel partners to ensure that the same price is available to HRS even if the price on the other channels was set by the sales partner (e.g. a tour operator) and not by the hotels.

173   HRS brings about a further restriction of competition between the hotels by extending the application of the MFN clauses to bookings over the counter. Hotels can no longer sell off remaining rooms at particularly good conditions at the hotel reception desk.

3.4.2.3 Strengthening of the anti-competitive effect through the application of MFN clauses by other hotel portals

174The anti-competitive effect of the MFN clauses between the hotels is strengthened by the application of MFN clauses by the other major portals like Booking and Expedia. German hotels are frequently hotel partners of all three major hotel portals or partners of at least one of these portals. Thus the German hotel portal market is nearly completely covered by MFN clauses and the vast majority of the hotels in Germany are obliged to apply MFN clauses. There is practically no way for hotels to use the services of a hotel portal which does not apply MFN clauses. Competition between the hotel partners of the various hotel portals is significantly restricted.

3.5   Significance of the restriction

175   An agreement restraints competition significantly if it affects the possibility for the companies involved to exert influence on the market conditions. The case-law decides on the question of significance of the restraint by looking at the number of market players and their market shares.

176   As stated above, the relevant market is the German market for hotel portals. Only a small number of large market players are operating on this market, like HRS, Booking and Expedia; the market share of other market players which sell hotel rooms in Germany on any larger scale is [0-5]% each. HRS is one of the leading hotel portals, with a market share of more than 30% (2012). HRS enforces the MFN clauses by continually checking on its hotel partners and in case of a breach of the clause deactivating them for further bookings or permanently removing the hotels from the HRS portal. The anti- competitive impact of the MFN clauses is strengthened by the application of MFN clauses by Booking and Expedia. Since HRS, Booking and Expedia together achieve a market share of roughly 90%, the restraints of competition are significant.

4.   No exemption in accordance with section 2 (2) GWB/Art. 101 (3) TFEU in conjunction with the Vertical Restraints Block Exemption Regulation

177   The MFN clauses are not exempt from the application of section 1 GWB/Art. 101 (1) TFEU in accordance with section 2 (2) GWB/Art. 101 (3) TFEU in conjunction with Art. 2 (1) of the Vertical Restraints Block Exemption Regulation. In accordance with Art. 2 (1) of the Vertical Restraints Block Exemption Regulation, the ban on anti-competitive agreements contained in Art. 101 (1) TFEU does not apply to the vertical restrictions contained in vertical agreements, but this exemption only applies if the share of the provider and of the purchaser on the relevant market is not more than 30% each (Art. 3 (1) of the Vertical

Restraints Block Exemption Regulation). The exemption does not apply to agreements containing hardcore restrictions (Art. 4 of the Vertical Restraints Block Exemption Regulation).

. . .

5.   No individual exemption in accordance with section 2 (1) GWB/Art. 101 (3) TFEU

196   The MFN clauses are not exempted in accordance with section 2 (1) GWB/Art. 101 (3) TFEU. Vertical agreements are only exempt from the prohibition contained in section 1 GWB/Art. 101 (1) TFEU if the positive competition effects outweigh the anti-competitive effects. In accordance with section 2 (1) GWB/Art. 101 (3) TFEU, this is the case if the agreements allow consumers a fair share of the resulting benefit and contribute to improving the production or distribution of goods or to promoting technical or economic progress; restrictions being imposed on the companies may not be indispensable to the attainment of these objectives or eliminate competition in respect to a "substantial part of the products".

197   The MFN clauses restrict price and quality competition between the hotel portals and between the hotels. The first three criteria for an individual exemption from a ban on anti-competitive agreements in accordance with section 2 GWB/Art. 101 (3) TFEU are not fulfilled. Where, as the market continues to grow, the remaining competition has nonetheless led to shifts in the market share between the two largest hotel portals, it is not clear whether the fourth criterion for exemption contained in section 2 GWB/Art. 101 (3) TFEU, namely no possibility of "eliminating competition in respect of a substantial part of the products", is fulfilled. This question can remain open since at least the other criteria for exemption are not fulfilled.

198   The potential positive efficiency impact of the MFN clauses, namely avoiding free riding, is at best very small (cf. on this section 5.1), and the restraints of competition brought about by the MFN clauses are at least not indispensable for the achievement of such efficiency (cf. on this section 5.2). Consumers are not granted a fair share of the resulting benefit with regard to efficiencies of the MFN clauses (cf. on this section 5.3). Whether the last criterion for exemption contained in section 2 (1) GWB/Art. 101 (3) TFEU, namely that there be no possibility of "eliminating competition in respect of a substantial part of the products" is fulfilled is ultimately not relevant (cf. on this section 5.4).

5.1 Efficiency gains

199   HRS claims that the efficiency gains brought about by the MFN clauses include the elimination of free riding, a positive impact on the quality of the services provided by the portals and intense competition on quality between portals. There could be a free riding problem in this context (cf. on this section 5.1.1). However, since quality competition plays an important role in the hotel portal market (cf. on this section 5.1.2), the efficiency gains of the MFN clauses in terms of better quality of the service offered by the portals are at best limited (cf. on this section 5.1.3).

5.1.1   Occurrence and scope of the free riding problem

200   In the present case, there are hardly adequate indications that any free riding problem exists at all.

201   The essence of the free riding problem in the present case is the danger that differences in the room prices might have a negative effect on the incentives for investments made by hotel portals and thus on the quality of their services they provide, as well as on the competition on quality between the portals. This is the case when investments in the quality of the portal can only be recovered to an unsatisfactory degree as a result of the lower room prices on lower-quality hotel portals (or via other sales channels). The investments would not be compensated for by adequate booking commissions, and hence by adequate commission earnings.

202   There is a danger of reducing incentives for investments in the quality of the service offered by portals when the investments of the portal are contract-specific and long term so that they cannot be recovered in the short term. In the present case, investments are to be regarded as contract-specific if they arise on the basis of the contractual relationship between the hotel portals and a specific hotel and if they cannot be used for the service offered to other hotels.

203   As a matter of principle, the free riding problem could also have a negative impact on the incentive of hotel portals for carrying out investments on the overall quality of the services offered to all hotel partners (e.g. investments in improving the functionalities and in the content of the platform). Thus, because of the competitive pressure from other portals (and possibly from other sales channels) which might only make limited investment in the quality of their services, the overall incentive to carry out investments could be reduced. Without restricting price competition

by means of MFN clauses the customer could ultimately receive a worse price/quality ratio.

204 The investments of HRS in the quality of its website are largely not contract-specific. HRS states a total amount of approx. […] € for online-advertising in 2012 and an amount of approx. […] € for offline-advertising, almost all of which was carried out in Germany. The total advertising expenditure of HRS was hence almost […]% of its worldwide turnover and almost […] of its turnover in Germany. This adds to the contractually- agreed, and thus contract-specific, investments carried out by HRS for hotel partners that are connected via the extranet (photographs, text editing, etc.). Taking as a basis the expenditure stated by HRS for the approx. […] hotels in Germany that are connected via the extranet ([…]), this results in a total amount of almost […] €. If one relates the expenditure for each single hotel (almost […] € during the first year) to the average annual commission income that HRS earns with German hotels which are connected via the extranet (almost […] €), the contract-specific investments of HRS are small. They are less than […]% of the average annual commission income per hotel. Contract-specific investments can be recovered after one year.

205 When HRS carries out non-contract-specific investments in the quality of its portal, these serve to improve the general image of the portal, and are therefore not lost as a result of free riding. Against the background of the structure of the German hotel market, there is a small probability that the hotels listed on a portal will exploit the advertising effect of the portal on a large scale in order to directly attract the booking to their own (commission- free) websites by means of lower prices (so called "billboard effect"). In supporting its argument, HRS exclusively relies on studies that mostly relate to the U.S. market, which in turn is primarily characterized by large branded hotels. Unlike in the U.S. in Germany there are far more independent small and medium-sized hotels which use their own website as pure and simple information pages. They have a reservation form on the website but do not offer continually-updated prices and the possibility of real-time bookings. Bookings without real-time confirmation are, however, not as convenient for the customer. Since the customer does usually not incur in any directly-invoiced costs when booking via a hotel portal, there is no good reason why he should give up the convenience of real-time bookings provided by the hotel portal and book via reservation forms. When it comes

to branded hotel chains, it should be taken into account that they are well known and customers frequently have direct access to rooms presented on the websites of these hotels.

5.1.2   The significance of quality competition in comparison to price competition

206   The quality of a hotel portal is very important to its position on the market. The MFN clauses cover major qualitative aspects of the service offered by hotels and portals, and thus restrain quality competition.

207   The weight the customer attaches to "price" and "quality" must be assessed in order to determine to what extent, the restriction of price competition between competing hotel portals (and any alternative sales channel) may positively impact the range of services and the intensity of quality competition by means of MFN clauses. If the criterion "quality" is anyways highly important to customers, the potentially positive impact of a restriction of price competition on product quality and on the intensity of quality competition will be limited. The scope for competing hotel portals (and any other sales channel) to compensate for low investment in the quality of the service by means of lower prices would be limited. Because of the relevance of the parameter "quality" for portals competition between portals is sufficient to guarantee a high level of quality to the benefit of the customers without restricting price competition.

208   Vertical restraints in the hotel portal market do not have particularly strong effects on quality because, in any case, only prices and quantity are agreed between suppliers and buyers. The success of a portal depends on the range of services available on the portal, the booking and cancellation conditions and the presentation and the ranking of hotels on the portal, as well as on the technical equipment and popularity of the portal. Price parity is less important. HRS stresses that the genuine services provided by a portal (search, comparison and booking) are essential for attracting customers. Currently, HRS installs new filters and thus tries to improve the quality of its portal. The MFN clauses do not only cover prices, but also the other conditions on offers (e.g. "deal of the day"), as well as booking and cancellation conditions. Hence they contribute to standardize major quality aspects of the services offered by the portals and thus even restrict quality competition.

5.1.3   Specific connection identified between the restriction of price competition and the scope of quality competition

209   The MFN clauses are not needed to achieve greater booking volume for HRS, and to make its investment in the quality of the portal pay off. The connection between the restriction of price competition brought about by the MFN clauses and the quality of the service is at best weak.

210   In order to underpin its argument, HRS has investigated the relationship between MFN clauses and the conversion rate ("look to book ratio"). For the analysis HRS compared for the period of […] weekly prices of approx. […] hotels on the HRS portal with the prices on three other major hotel portals (booking.com, expedia.com and venere.com). HRS estimated that the abolition of the MFN clauses would cause a reduction of its total turnover by approx. […]%.

211   The Bundeskartellamt has examined and evaluated the analysis on the conversion rate as well as the raw data underlying the analysis. The results of the analysis show that the conversion rate for HRS may be higher if hotel rooms that are offered on the HRS portal are not more expensive than similar rooms presented on other portals. Price deviations have a statistically significant impact on the conversion rate. The analysis, however, shows that the price deviations alone do not explain all the variance in the conversion rate. Other variables, in particular destination and the hotel category, have a stronger effect on the conversion rate. The analysis shows that customers both in the low-price segment and in the high-price segment ("1 star" and "5 star" hotels) tend to book immediately on HRS, and that the MFN clause is unlikely to have a significant influence on these customers. These results make clear that price sensitive customers attach considerable importance to the factors quality and service. The incentive of portals to invest in the quality of its services is high, even without a restriction of price competition. The MFN clause has a small efficieny [sic] effect, if at all.

5.2   The indispensability of the restraints of competition

212   The restraints of competition imposed on the hotel partners of HRS are at least not indispensable.

213   Restraints of competition are indispensable if they are necessary for obtaining the efficiency gains. Ultimately, greater efficiency gains must be achieved with the restraint of competition than

without it. Restraints of competition are indispensable if alternatives which are less restrictive would be significantly less efficient.

214   In the case of the MFN clauses of HRS, at best low efficiency gains can be identified (cf. on this section 5.2.1). Alternative business models without MFN clauses exist and HRS would not (necessarily) have to suffer considerable efficiency losses by applying them (cf. on this section 5.2.2).

. . .

5.3   Allowing consumers a fair share of the resulting benefit

223   The Decision Division cannot find any fair share of the resulting benefit for consumers with regard to the efficiency gains brought about by the MFN clauses. The MFN clauses are not suited to further stimulate quality competition between the hotel portals since. Quality competition is already strong. The HRS commission model which includes the MFN clauses is neither a particularly low-risk and low-cost business model (cf. on this section 5.3.1), nor do the MFN clauses increase market transparency (cf. on this section 5.3.2) or reduce search costs for hotel customers (cf. on this section 5.3.3).

5.3.1   Low-risk and low-cost business model

224   The commission model currently used by HRS with MFN clauses does not allow consumers a fair share of the resulting benefit only because this model involves low risks and low costs for consumers in comparison with other models which do not make use of MFN clauses.

225   Within the business model currently operated by HRS, the commission costs are only incurred for hotels if the customer makes a booking. Hotels which do not receive a booking do not contribute to the costs, but nonetheless benefit from the advertising services of HRS. If HRS wished to avoid unilaterally burdening hotels whose rooms are booked other business models would make more sense than those which exclusively rely upon booking fees as a source of income.

226   The standard commissions charged by HRS on the basis of its current business model are not lower than the standard commissions charged by other hotel portals. In fact, HRS increased its commissions in March 2012 from 13% to 15% for individual bookings and from 10% to 13% for group bookings.

The MFN clauses do not lead to lower prices for hotel customers, either. In the view of the extensive application of MFN clauses in the German hotel portal market, hotel portals have no incentive to reduce their commissions, and the hotel partners of HRS have no incentive to offer their hotel rooms at lower prices on the other portals.

5.3.2   Market transparency

227   The MFN clauses and the possibility of a more efficient hotel search do not allow consumers a share of the resulting benefits in form of improved market transparency. Hotel customers who rely on the MFN clauses are less likely to compare identical or similar offers on other portals, and will hence not compare various hotel rooms, because they believe that, in any case, they have been presented with the "best offer" on the HRS portal. The price guarantee offered by HRS may influence the behaviour of the hotel customers in the sense that they would not bother comparing offers on other hotel portals. Only in a small number of cases, hotel customers have complained about hotels not keeping the best price promise of HRS. If customers do not look for hotel rooms in other hotel portals than HRS, they do not take up other offers which might be better adapted to their specific needs. Thus, not only "intra-brand" competition, that is competition between the hotel portals when selling the same or similar rooms of the same hotel, but also "inter- brand competition", that is competition between the different hotels, is restrained. Hotel customers are offered an illusion of transparency.

5.3.3   Search costs

228   Consumers will not be allowed a fair share of the resulting benefit in form of lower search costs. In any case, it is not the hotel customers but the hotels which pay for the search of hotel rooms on the Internet. Customers do not incur costs in form of financial expenditure. Meta search engines which are available on the Internet, such as Google, and meta search engines which specialise in travel products and hotel rooms, such as trivago and Kayak, help reduce the time needed for search. Additionally, hotel portals are present on meta search engines (e.g. HRS and Booking on trivago), and they profit themselves from the transparency that meta search engines offer.

. . .

Notes

1. For a U.S. analysis, see Jonathan B. Baker, *Vertical Restraints with Horizontal Consequences: Competitive Effects of 'Most-Favored-Customer' Clauses*, 64 ANTITRUST LAW JOURNAL 517 (1996).

2. As a consumer, would you prefer that each distribution channel sell at the same price, or would you rather they all choose their prices independently? What are the "horizontal consequences referred to in the title of Professor Baker's article cited above?

3. In this respect, is it significant that, for example, Booking Holdings Inc. owns and operates Booking.com, Priceline.com, Agoda.com, Kayak.com, Cheapflights, Rentalcars.com, Momondo, and OpenTable. What effect does common ownership like this have on the value of shopping around? Would it be better if each of Booking's websites were required to disclose the common ownership? Would it be better if another firm provided information about prices available at different outlets? Is that what Kayak purports to do?

3.2.   Tying Arrangements

Although U.S. law regarding tying arrangements focuses on tying "agreements" under section 1 of the Sherman Act, European cases challenging such agreements (and also exclusive-dealing arrangements) are generally pursued under article 102 of the TFEU. To some extent the European approach makes more sense, in that the agreements at issue in such cases are typically imposed by powerful firms on their customers. An earlier EU tying case concerning technology markets was the EU Microsoft decision, Case T- 201/04 Microsoft Corp. v. Commission [2007] ECR II-3601.

European Commission
Summary of Commission Decision of 18 July 2018
Google Android
(2019/C 402/08)

On 18 July 2018, the Commission adopted a decision relating to a proceeding under Article 102 of the Treaty on the Functioning of the European Union and Article 54 of the EEA agreement. In accordance with the provisions of Article 30 of Council Regulation (EC) No 1/2003, the Commission herewith publishes the

names of the parties and the main content of the decision, including any penalties
imposed, having regard to the legitimate interest of undertakings in the protection
of their business secrets.

1. Introduction

(1) The Decision establishes that conduct by Google LLC ('Google') with regard
to certain conditions in agreements associated with the use of Google's
smart mobile operating system, Android, and certain proprietary mobile
applications ('app's) and services, constitutes a single and continuous
infringement of Article 102 of the Treaty on the Functioning of the
European Union ('TFEU') and Article 54 of the EEA Agreement.

(2) This Decision also establishes that Google's conduct constitutes four separate
infringements of Article 102 TFEU and Article 54 of the EEA Agreement,
each of which is also part of the single and continuous infringement.

(3) The Decision orders Google and its parent company Alphabet Inc. ('Alphabet')
to bring the infringement effectively to an end, and imposes a fine on
Google and Alphabet for the abusive conduct for the period 1 January 2011
to date. *July 2018*

(4) On 6 July 2018 and 17 July 2018, the Advisory Committee on Restrictive
Practices and Dominant Positions issued favourable opinions on the
Decision pursuant to Article 7 of Regulation (EC) No 1/2003 and on the
fine imposed on Google and Alphabet.

2. Market definition

(5) The Decision concludes that the relevant product markets for the purpose
of this case are:

    (a)   the worldwide market (excluding China) for the licensing
of smart mobile operating systems ('OS's);

    (b)   the worldwide market (excluding China) for Android app
stores;

    (c)   the national markets for general search services; and

    (d)   the worldwide market for non OS-specific mobile web
browsers.

3. Dominance

(6) The Decision concludes that since 2011, Google holds a dominant position in:
(i) the worldwide market (excluding China) for the licensing of smart
mobile OSs; (ii) the worldwide market (excluding China) for Android app
stores; and (iii) each of the national markets for general search services in
the EEA.

(7) The conclusion that Google holds a dominant position in the worldwide market (excluding China) for the licensing of smart mobile OSs is based on Google's market share, the existence of barriers to entry and expansion, the lack of countervailing buyer power and the insufficient indirect constraint from non-licensable smart mobile OSs (such as Apple's iOS).

(8) The conclusion that Google holds a dominant position in the worldwide market (excluding China) for Android app stores is based on Google's market share, the quantity and popularity of apps available on the Google Play Store, the automatic update functionalities of the Play Store, the fact that the only way for original equipment manufacturers ('OEM's) to obtain Google Play Services is to obtain the Play Store, the existence of barriers to entry and expansion, the lack of countervailing buyer power of OEMs and the insufficient constraint from app stores for non-licensable smart mobile OSs (such as Apple's AppStore).

(9) The conclusion that Google holds a dominant position in each of the national markets for general search services in the EEA is based on Google's market shares, the existence of barriers to entry and expansion, the infrequency of user multi-homing and the existence of brand effects and the lack of countervailing buyer power. 4. Abuse of a dominant position

Tying of the Google Search app

(10) Since at least 1 January 2011, Google has tied the Google Search app with the Play Store. The Commission concludes that this conduct constitutes an abuse of Google's dominant position in the worldwide market (excluding China) for Android app stores.

(11) First, the Decision demonstrates that: (i) the Play Store and the Google Search app are distinct products; (ii) Google is dominant in the market for the tying product (worldwide market (excluding China) for Android app stores); and (iii) the tying product (Play Store) cannot be obtained without the tied product (the Google Search app).

(12) Second, the Decision concludes that the tying of the Google Search app with the Play Store is capable of restricting competition. This is because: (i) the tying provides Google with a significant competitive advantage that competing general search service providers cannot offset; and (ii) the tying helps to maintain and strengthen Google's dominant position in each national market for general search services, increases barriers to entry, deters innovation and tends to harm, directly or indirectly, consumers.

(13) Third, the Decision concludes that Google has not demonstrated the existence of any objective justification for the tying of the Google Search app with the Play Store.

Tying of Google Chrome

(14)   Since 1 August 2012, Google has tied Google Chrome with the Play Store and the Google Search app. The Commission concludes that this conduct constitutes an abuse of Google's dominant position in the worldwide market (excluding China) for Android app stores and the national markets for general search services.

(15)   First, the Decision demonstrates that: (i) Google Chrome is a distinct product from the Play Store and the Google Search app; (ii) Google is dominant in the markets for the tying products (worldwide market (excluding China) for Android app stores and national markets for general search services); and (iii) the tying products (the Play Store and the Google Search app) cannot be obtained without the tied product (Google Chrome).

(16)   Second, the Decision concludes that the tying of Google Chrome with the Play Store and the Google Search app is capable of restricting competition. This is because: (i) the tying provides Google with a significant advantage that competing non OS-specific mobile browsers cannot offset; and (ii) the tying deters innovation, tends to harm, directly or indirectly, consumers of mobile web browsers and helps to maintain and strengthen Google's dominant position in each national market for general search services.

(17)   Third, the Decision concludes that Google has not demonstrated the existence of any objective justification for the tying of Google Chrome with the Play Store and the Google Search app.

The licensing of the Play Store and the Google Search app conditional on the anti-fragmentation obligations in the AFAs

(18)   Since at least 1 January 2011, Google makes the licensing of the Play Store and the Google Search app conditional on hardware manufacturers agreeing to the anti-fragmentation obligations in the AFAs. The Commission concludes that this conduct constitutes an abuse of Google's dominant positions in the worldwide market (excluding China) for Android app stores and the national markets for general search services.

(19)   First, the Decision demonstrates that entering into the anti-fragmentation obligations is unrelated to the licensing of the Play Store and the Google Search app, that Google is dominant in the worldwide market (excluding China) for Android app stores and in the national markets for general search services, and that the Play Store and the Google Search app cannot be obtained without entering into the anti-fragmentation obligations.

(20)   Second, the Decision establishes that the anti-fragmentation obligations are capable of restricting competition. This is because: (i) Android forks constitute a credible competitive threat to Google; (ii) Google actively monitors compliance with, and enforces, the anti-fragmentation obligations; (iii) the anti-fragmentation obligations hinder the development of Android forks; (iv) compatible forks do not constitute a credible competitive threat to Google; (v) the capability of the anti-fragmentation obligations to restrict competition is reinforced by the unavailability of Google's proprietary APIs to fork developers; and (vi) Google's conduct

helps to maintain and strengthen Google's dominant position in each national market for general search services, deters innovation, and tends to harm, directly or indirectly, consumers.

(21)   Third, the Decision concludes that Google has not demonstrated the existence of any objective justification for making the licensing of the Play Store and Google Search conditional on the anti-fragmentation obligations.

Portfolio-based revenue share payments conditional on the pre-installation of no competing general search service

(22)   Between at least 1 January 2011 and 31 March 2014, Google granted payments to OEMs and mobile network operators ('MNO's) on condition that they pre-installed no competing general search service on any device within an agreed portfolio. The Decision concludes that this conduct constituted an abuse of Google's dominant position in the national markets for general search services.

(23)   First, the Decision concludes that Google's portfolio-based revenue share payments constituted exclusivity payments.

(24)   Second, the Decision concludes that Google's portfolio-based revenue share payments were capable of restricting competition. This is because Google's portfolio-based revenue share payments: (i) reduced the incentives of OEMs and MNOs to pre-install competing general search services; (ii) made access to the national markets for general search services more difficult; and (iii) deterred innovation.

(25)   Third, the Decision concludes that Google has not demonstrated the existence of any objective justification for the grant of portfolio-based revenue share payments.

Single and continuous infringement

(26)   The Decision concludes that the four different forms of conduct described above constitute a single and continuous infringement of Article 102 TFEU and Article 54 of the EEA Agreement.

(27)   First, the four different forms of conduct all pursue an identical objective of protecting and strengthening Google's dominant position in general search services and thus its revenues via search advertisements.

(28)   Second, the four different forms of conduct are complementary in that Google creates an interlocking interdependence between them.

5. Jurisdiction

(29)   The Decision concludes that the Commission has jurisdiction to apply Article 102 TFEU and Article 54 of the EEA Agreement to Google's conduct, since it is implemented in the EEA and is capable of having substantial, immediate and foreseeable effects in the EEA.

6. Effect on trade

(30)   The Decision concludes that Google's conduct has an appreciable effect on trade between Member States within the meaning of Article 102 TFEU and between the EEA Contracting Parties within the meaning of Article 54 of the EEA Agreement.

7. Remedies and Fines

(31)   The Decision requires Google and Alphabet to bring effectively to an end the single and continuous infringement and each of the four separate infringements, within 90 days of notification of the Decision, insofar as they have not already done so, and to refrain from adopting any act or conduct having the same or equivalent object or effect. The Decision indicates that if Google and Alphabet fail to comply with the requirements of the Decision, the Commission imposes a daily periodic penalty payment of 5 % of Alphabet's average daily turnover in the preceding business year.

(32)   The fine imposed on Google and Alphabet for the infringements is calculated on the basis of the principles laid out in the 2006 Guidelines on the method of setting fines imposed pursuant to Article 23(2)(a) of Regulation (EC) No 1/2003. For the single and continuous infringement consisting of four separate infringements, the Decision imposes a fine of EUR 4 342 865 000 on Google, of which EUR 1 921 666 000 jointly and severally with Alphabet.

Notes

1.   Are consumers who have preferences regarding search engines or browsers likely to be capable of switching to the one they prefer? If so, should the focus be on obstacles to switching rather than on initial tying?

2.   Is the Commission's concern really with consumers who do *not* have strong preferences regarding search engines or browsers? Do such consumers really want to have a choice? If not, will another market actor make the choice for them? If the choice is made by phone manufacturers, why is that better than Google making the choice?

3.   What is "fragmentation"? Is it another word for competition?

3.3.   Other Vertical Restraints

As discussed in the introductory readings above, the issue of platform competition is central to the new economy. The U.S. Supreme Court takes up that issue below, citing extensively Filistrucchi et al., *Market Definition in Two-Sided Markets: Theory and Practice*, 10 J. COMPETITION L. & ECON. 293, 297 (2014). There is now an extensive economic literature regarding platform markets, in which one of the leading pieces is Jean-Charles Rochet & Jean Tirole, *Platform Competition in Two-sided Markets*, 1 JOURNAL OF THE EUROPEAN ECONOMIC ASSOCIATION 990 (2003). In 2014, Jean Tirole received the Nobel Prize in Economics "for his analysis of market power and regulation."

Ohio v. American Express Co.
585 U.S. ___ (2018)

JUSTICE THOMAS delivered the opinion of the Court.

American Express Company and American Express Travel Related Services Company (collectively, Amex) provide credit-card services to both merchants and cardholders. When a cardholder buys something from a merchant who accepts Amex credit cards, Amex processes the transaction through its network, promptly pays the merchant, and subtracts a fee. If a merchant wants to accept Amex credit cards—and attract Amex cardholders to its business—Amex requires the merchant to agree to an antisteering contractual provision. The antisteering provision prohibits merchants from discouraging customers from using their Amex card after they have already entered the store and are about to buy something, thereby avoiding Amex's fee. In this case, we must decide whether Amex's antisteering provisions violate federal antitrust law. We conclude they do not.

I

A

Credit cards have become a primary way that consumers in the United States purchase goods and services. When a cardholder uses a credit card to buy something from a merchant, the transaction is facilitated by a credit-card network. The network provides separate but inter- related services to both cardholders and merchants. For cardholders, the network extends them credit, which allows them to make purchases without cash and to defer payment until later. Cardholders also can receive rewards based on the amount of money they spend, such as airline miles, points for travel, or cash back. For merchants, the network allows them to avoid the cost of processing transactions and offers them quick, guaranteed payment. This saves merchants the trouble and risk of extending credit to customers, and it increases the number and value of sales that they can make.

By providing these services to cardholders and merchants, credit-card companies bring these parties together, and therefore operate what economists call a "two-sided platform." As the name implies, a two-sided platform offers different products or services to two different groups who both depend on the platform to intermediate between them. For credit cards, that interaction is a transaction. Thus, credit-card networks are a special type of two-sided platform known as a "transaction" platform. The key feature of transaction platforms is that they cannot make a sale to one side of the platform without simultaneously making a sale to the other. For example, no credit-card transaction can occur unless both the merchant and the cardholder simultaneously agree to use the same credit-card network.

Two-sided platforms differ from traditional markets in important ways. Most relevant here, two-sided platforms often exhibit what economists call "indirect network effects." Indirect network effects exist where the value of the two-sided platform to one group of participants depends on how many members of a different group participate. In other words, the value of the services that a two-sided platform provides increases as the number of participants on both sides of the platform increases. A credit card, for example, is more valuable to cardholders when more merchants accept it, and is more valuable to merchants when more cardholders use it. To ensure sufficient participation, two-sided platforms must be sensitive to the prices that they charge each side. Raising the price on side A risks losing participation on that side, which decreases the value of the platform to side B. If participants on side B leave due to this loss in value, then the platform has even less value to side A—risking a feedback loop of declining demand. Two-sided platforms therefore must take these indirect network effects into account before making a change in price on either side.[1]

Sometimes indirect network effects require two-sided platforms to charge one side much more than the other. For two-sided platforms, "'the [relative] price structure matters, and platforms must design it so as to bring both sides on board.' The optimal price might require charging the side with more elastic demand a below-cost (or even negative) price. With credit cards, for example, networks often charge cardholders a lower fee than merchants because cardholders are more price sensitive. In fact, the network might well *lose* money on the cardholder side by offering rewards such as cash back, airline miles, or gift cards. The network can do this because increasing the number of cardholders increases the value of accepting the card to merchants and, thus, increases the number of merchants who accept it. Networks can then charge those merchants a fee for every transaction (typically a percentage of the purchase price). Striking the optimal balance of the prices charged on each side of the platform is essential for two-sided platforms to maximize the value of their services and to compete with their rivals.

B

. . .

Amex competes with Visa and MasterCard by using a different business model. While Visa and MasterCard earn half of their revenue by collecting interest from their cardholders, Amex does not. Amex instead earns most of its revenue from merchant fees. Amex's business model thus focuses on cardholder spending rather than card-holder lending. To encourage cardholder spending, Amex provides better

---

[1] In a competitive market, indirect network effects also encourage companies to take increased profits from a price increase on side A and spend them on side B to ensure more robust participation on that side and to stem the impact of indirect network effects. Indirect network effects thus limit the platform's ability to raise overall prices and impose a check on its market power.

rewards than other networks. Due to its superior rewards, Amex tends to attract cardholders who are wealthier and spend more money. Merchants place a higher value on these cardholders, and Amex uses this advantage to recruit merchants.

Amex's business model has significantly influenced the credit-card market. To compete for the valuable cardholders that Amex attracts, both Visa and MasterCard have introduced premium cards that, like Amex, charge merchants higher fees and offer cardholders better rewards. To maintain their lower merchant fees, Visa and MasterCard have created a sliding scale for their various cards— charging merchants less for low-reward cards and more for high-reward cards. This differs from Amex's strategy, which is to charge merchants the same fee no matter the rewards that its card offers. Another way that Amex has influenced the credit-card market is by making banking and card-payment services available to low-income individuals, who otherwise could not qualify for a credit card and could not afford the fees that traditional banks charge. In sum, Amex's business model has stimulated competitive innovations in the credit-card market, increasing the volume of transactions and improving the quality of the services.

Despite these improvements, Amex's business model sometimes causes friction with merchants. To maintain the loyalty of its cardholders, Amex must continually invest in its rewards program. But, to fund those investments, Amex must charge merchants higher fees than its rivals. Even though Amex's investments benefit merchants by encouraging cardholders to spend more money, merchants would prefer not to pay the higher fees. One way that merchants try to avoid them, while still enticing Amex's cardholders to shop at their stores, is by dissuading cardholders from using Amex at the point of sale. This practice is known as "steering."

Amex has prohibited steering since the 1950s by placing antisteering provisions in its contracts with merchants. These antisteering provisions prohibit merchants from implying a preference for non-Amex cards; dissuading customers from using Amex cards; persuading customers to use other cards; imposing any special restrictions, conditions, disadvantages, or fees on Amex cards; or promoting other cards more than Amex. The antisteering provisions do not, however, prevent merchants from steering customers toward debit cards, checks, or cash.

C

In October 2010, the United States and several States (collectively, plaintiffs) sued Amex, claiming that its antisteering provisions violate §1 of the Sherman Act, 15 U. S. C. §1.[5] After a 7-week trial, the District Court agreed that Amex's antisteering provisions violate §1. It found that the credit-card market should be treated as two separate markets—one for merchants and one for cardholders. Evaluating the effects on the merchant side of the market, the District Court found

---

[5] Plaintiffs also sued Visa and MasterCard, claiming that their antisteering provisions violated §1. But Visa and MasterCard voluntarily revoked their antisteering provisions and are no longer parties to this case.

that Amex's antisteering provisions are anticompetitive because they result in higher merchant fees.

The Court of Appeals for the Second Circuit reversed. It concluded that the credit-card market is one market, not two. Evaluating the credit-card market as a whole, the Second Circuit concluded that Amex's antisteering provisions were not anticompetitive and did not violate §1.

We granted certiorari and now affirm.

II

. . .

In this case, both sides correctly acknowledge that Amex's antisteering provisions are vertical restraints— *i.e.,* restraints "imposed by agreement between firms at different levels of distribution." The parties also correctly acknowledge that, like nearly every other vertical restraint, the anti- steering provisions should be assessed under the rule of reason.

To determine whether a restraint violates the rule of reason, the parties agree that a three-step, burden-shifting framework applies. . . .

Here, the parties ask us to decide whether the plaintiffs have carried their initial burden of proving that Amex's antisteering provisions have an anticompetitive effect. The plaintiffs can make this showing directly or indirectly. Direct evidence of anticompetitive effects would be "'proof of actual detrimental effects [on competition],'" *FTC* v. *Indiana Federation of Dentists*, 476 U. S. 447, 460 (1986), such as reduced output, increased prices, or decreased quality in the relevant market. Indirect evidence would be proof of market power plus some evidence that the challenged restraint harms competition.

Here, the plaintiffs rely exclusively on direct evidence to prove that Amex's antisteering provisions have caused anticompetitive effects in the credit-card market. To assess this evidence, we must first define the relevant market. Once defined, it becomes clear that the plaintiffs' evidence is insufficient to carry their burden.

A

Because "[l]egal presumptions that rest on formalistic distinctions rather than actual market realities are generally disfavored in antitrust law," courts usually cannot properly apply the rule of reason without an accurate definition of the relevant market.[7] "Without a definition of [the] market there is no way to measure

---

[7] The plaintiffs argue that we need not define the relevant market in this case because they have offered actual evidence of adverse effects on competition—namely, increased merchant fees. See Brief for United States 40–41 (citing *FTC* v. *Indiana Federation of Dentists*, 476 U. S. 447 (1986), and *Catalano, Inc.* v. *Target Sales, Inc.*, 446 U. S. 643 (1980) (*per curiam*)). We disagree. The cases that the plaintiffs cite for this proposition evaluated whether horizontal restraints had an adverse effect on competition. See *Indiana Federation of Dentists, supra,* at 450–451, 459 (agreement between competing

[the defendant's] ability to lessen or destroy competition." *Walker Process Equipment, Inc.* v. *Food Machinery & Chemical Corp.*, 382 U. S. 172, 177 (1965). Thus, the relevant market is defined as "the area of effective competition." Typically this is the "arena within which significant substitution in consumption or production occurs." Areeda & Hovenkamp §5.02; *United States* v. *Grinnell Corp.*, 384 U. S. 563, 571 (1966). But courts should "combin[e]" different products or services into "a single market" when "that combination reflects commercial realities." *Id.,* at 572; see also *Brown Shoe Co.* v. *United States*, 370 U. S. 294, 336–337 (1962) (pointing out that "the definition of the relevant market" must "'correspond to the commercial realities' of the industry").

As explained, credit-card networks are two-sided platforms. Due to indirect network effects, two-sided platforms cannot raise prices on one side without risking a feedback loop of declining demand. And the fact that two-sided platforms charge one side a price that is below or above cost reflects differences in the two sides' demand elasticity, not market power or anticompetitive pricing. Price increases on one side of the platform likewise do not suggest anticompetitive effects without some evidence that they have increased the overall cost of the platform's services. Thus, courts must include both sides of the platform—merchants and cardholders—when defining the credit-card market.

To be sure, it is not always necessary to consider both sides of a two-sided platform. A market should be treated as one sided when the impacts of indirect network effects and relative pricing in that market are minor. Newspapers that sell advertisements, for example, arguably operate a two-sided platform because the value of an advertisement increases as more people read the newspaper. But in the newspaper-advertisement market, the indirect networks effects operate in only one direction; newspaper readers are largely indifferent to the amount of advertising that a newspaper contains. Because of these weak indirect network effects, the market for newspaper advertising behaves much like a one-sided market and should be analyzed as such. But two-sided transaction platforms, like the credit-card market, are different. These platforms facilitate a single, simultaneous transaction between participants. For credit cards, the network can sell its services only if a

---

dentists not to share X rays with insurance companies); *Catalano, supra,* at 644–645, 650 (agreement among competing wholesalers not to compete on extending credit to retailers). Given that horizontal restraints involve agreements between competitors not to compete in some way, this Court concluded that it did not need to precisely define the relevant market to conclude that these agreements were anticompetitive. See *Indiana Federation of Dentists, supra,* at 460–461; *Catalano, supra,* at 648–649. But vertical restraints are different. See Arizona v. Maricopa County Medical Soc., 457 U. S. 332, 348, n. 18 (1982); Leegin Creative Leather Products, Inc. v. PSKS, Inc., 551 U. S. 877, 888 (2007). Vertical restraints often pose no risk to competition unless the entity imposing them has market power, which cannot be evaluated unless the Court first defines the relevant market. See *id.,* at 898 (noting that a vertical restraint "may not be a serious concern unless the relevant entity has market power"); Easterbrook, Vertical Arrangements and the Rule of Reason, 53 Antitrust L. J. 135, 160 (1984) ("[T]he possibly anticompetitive manifestations of vertical arrangements can occur only if there is market power").

merchant and cardholder both simultaneously choose to use the network. Thus, whenever a credit-card network sells one transaction's worth of card-acceptance services to a merchant it also must sell one transaction's worth of card-payment services to a cardholder. It cannot sell transaction services to either cardholders or merchants individually. To optimize sales, the network must find the balance of pricing that encourages the greatest number of matches between cardholders and merchants.

Because they cannot make a sale unless both sides of the platform simultaneously agree to use their services, two-sided transaction platforms exhibit more pronounced indirect network effects and interconnected pricing and demand. Transaction platforms are thus better understood as "suppl[ying] only one product"—transactions. In the credit-card market, these transactions "are jointly consumed by a cardholder, who uses the payment card to make a transaction, and a merchant, who accepts the payment card as a method of payment." *Ibid.* Tellingly, credit cards determine their market share by measuring the volume of transactions they have sold.

Evaluating both sides of a two-sided transaction platform is also necessary to accurately assess competition. Only other two-sided platforms can compete with a two-sided platform for transactions. A credit-card company that processed transactions for merchants, but that had no cardholders willing to use its card, could not compete with Amex. Only a company that had both cardholders and merchants willing to use its network could sell transactions and compete in the credit-card market. Similarly, if a merchant accepts the four major credit cards, but a cardholder only uses Visa or Amex, only those two cards can compete for the particular transaction. Thus, competition cannot be accurately assessed by looking at only one side of the platform in isolation.[9]

For all these reasons, "[i]n two-sided transaction markets, only one market should be defined." Any other analysis would lead to """"mistaken inferences"""" of the kind that could """"chill the very conduct the antitrust laws are designed to protect."""" *Brooke Group Ltd.* v. *Brown & Williamson Tobacco Corp.*, 509 U. S. 209, 226 (1993); see also *Matsushita Elec. Industrial Co.* v. *Zenith Radio Corp.*, 475 U. S. 574, 594 (1986) ("'[W]e must be concerned lest a rule or precedent that authorizes a search for a particular type of undesirable pricing behavior end up by discouraging legitimate price competition'"); *Leegin*, 551 U. S., at 895 (noting that courts should avoid "increas[ing] the total cost of the antitrust system by prohibiting procompetitive conduct the antitrust laws should encourage"). Accordingly, we will analyze the two-sided market for credit-card transactions as a whole to determine whether the plaintiffs have shown that Amex's antisteering provisions have anticompetitive effects.

---

[9] Nontransaction platforms, by contrast, often do compete with companies that do not operate on both sides of their platform. A newspaper that sells advertising, for example, might have to compete with a television network, even though the two do not meaningfully compete for viewers.

B

The plaintiffs have not carried their burden to prove anticompetitive effects in the relevant market. The plaintiffs stake their entire case on proving that Amex's agreements increase merchant fees. We find this argument unpersuasive.

As an initial matter, the plaintiffs' argument about merchant fees wrongly focuses on only one side of the two-sided credit-card market. As explained, the credit-card market must be defined to include both merchants and cardholders. Focusing on merchant fees alone misses the mark because the product that credit-card companies sell is transactions, not services to merchants, and the competitive effects of a restraint on transactions cannot be judged by looking at merchants alone. Evidence of a price increase on one side of a two-sided transaction platform cannot by itself demonstrate an anticompetitive exercise of market power. To demonstrate anticompetitive effects on the two-sided credit-card market as a whole, the plaintiffs must prove that Amex's antisteering provisions increased the cost of credit-card transactions above a competitive level, reduced the number of credit-card transactions, or otherwise stifled competition in the credit-card market. They failed to do so.

1

The plaintiffs did not offer any evidence that the price of credit-card transactions was higher than the price one would expect to find in a competitive market. As the District Court found, the plaintiffs failed to offer any reliable measure of Amex's transaction price or profit margins. And the evidence about whether Amex charges more than its competitors was ultimately inconclusive.

Amex's increased merchant fees reflect increases in the value of its services and the cost of its transactions, not an ability to charge above a competitive price. Amex began raising its merchant fees in 2005 after Visa and MasterCard raised their fees in the early 2000s. As explained, Amex has historically charged higher merchant fees than these competitors because it delivers wealthier cardholders who spend more money. Amex's higher merchant fees are based on a careful study of how much additional value its cardholders offer merchants. On the other side of the market, Amex uses its higher merchant fees to offer its cardholders a more robust rewards program, which is necessary to maintain cardholder loyalty and encourage the level of spending that makes Amex valuable to merchants. That Amex allocates prices between merchants and cardholders differently from Visa and MasterCard is simply not evidence that it wields market power to achieve anticompetitive ends.

In addition, the evidence that does exist cuts against the plaintiffs' view that Amex's antisteering provisions are the cause of any increases in merchant fees. Visa and MasterCard's merchant fees have continued to increase, even at merchant locations where Amex is not accepted and, thus, Amex's antisteering provisions do not apply. This suggests that the cause of increased merchant fees is not Amex's antisteering provisions, but rather increased competition for cardholders and a corresponding marketwide adjustment in the relative price charged to merchants.

2

The plaintiffs did offer evidence that Amex increased the percentage of the purchase price that it charges merchants by an average of 0.09% between 2005 and 2010 and that this increase was not entirely spent on cardholder rewards. The plaintiffs believe that this evidence shows that the price of Amex's transactions increased.

Even assuming the plaintiffs are correct, this evidence does not prove that Amex's antisteering provisions gave it the power to charge anticompetitive prices. "Market power is the ability to raise price profitably *by restricting output*." Areeda & Hovenkamp §5.01 (emphasis added); accord, *Kodak*, 504 U. S., at 464; *Business Electronics*, 485 U. S., at 723. This Court will "not infer competitive injury from price and output data absent some evidence that tends to prove that output was restricted or prices were above a competitive level." *Brooke Group Ltd.*, 509 U. S., at 237. There is no such evidence in this case. The output of credit-card transactions grew dramatically from 2008 to 2013, increasing 30%. "Where . . . output is expanding at the same time prices are increasing, rising prices are equally consistent with growing product demand." *Brooke Group Ltd.*, *supra,* at 237. And, as previously explained, the plaintiffs did not show that Amex charged more than its competitors.

3

The plaintiffs also failed to prove that Amex's antisteering provisions have stifled competition among credit-card companies. To the contrary, while these agreements have been in place, the credit-card market experienced expanding output and improved quality. Amex's business model spurred Visa and MasterCard to offer new premium card categories with higher rewards. And it has increased the availability of card services, including free banking and card-payment services for low-income customers who otherwise would not be served. Indeed, between 1970 and 2001, the percentage of households with credit cards more than quadrupled, and the proportion of households in the bottom-income quintile with credit cards grew from just 2% to over 38%.

Nor have Amex's antisteering provisions ended competition between credit-card networks with respect to merchant fees. Instead, fierce competition between networks has constrained Amex's ability to raise these fees and has, at times, forced Amex to lower them. For instance, when Amex raised its merchant prices between 2005 and 2010, some merchants chose to leave its network. And when its remaining merchants complained, Amex stopped raising its merchant prices. In another instance in the late 1980s and early 1990s, competition forced Amex to offer lower merchant fees to "everyday spend" merchants—supermarkets, gas stations, pharmacies, and the like—to persuade them to accept Amex.

In addition, Amex's competitors have exploited its higher merchant fees to their advantage. By charging lower merchant fees, Visa, MasterCard, and Discover have achieved broader merchant acceptance—approximately 3 million more locations than Amex. This broader merchant acceptance is a major advantage for these networks and a significant challenge for Amex, since consumers prefer cards that will be accepted everywhere. And to compete even further with Amex, Visa and MasterCard charge different merchant fees for different types of cards to maintain their comparatively lower merchant fees and broader acceptance. Over the long run, this competition has created a trend of declining merchant fees in the credit-card market. In fact, since the first credit card was introduced in the 1950s, merchant fees— including Amex's merchant fees—have decreased by more than half.

Lastly, there is nothing inherently anticompetitive about Amex's antisteering provisions. These agreements actually stem negative externalities in the credit-card market and promote interbrand competition. When merchants steer cardholders away from Amex at the point of sale, it undermines the cardholder's expectation of "welcome acceptance"—the promise of a frictionless transaction. A lack of welcome acceptance at one merchant makes a cardholder less likely to use Amex at all other merchants. This externality endangers the viability of the entire Amex network. And it undermines the investments that Amex has made to encourage increased cardholder spending, which discourages investments in rewards and ultimately harms both cardholders and merchants. Cf. *Leegin*, 551 U. S., at 890–891 (recognizing that vertical restraints can prevent retailers from free riding and thus increase the availability of "tangible or intangible services or promotional efforts" that enhance competition and consumer welfare). Perhaps most importantly, antisteering provisions do not prevent Visa, MasterCard, or Discover from competing against Amex by offering lower merchant fees or promoting their broader merchant acceptance.

In sum, the plaintiffs have not satisfied the first step of the rule of reason. They have not carried their burden of proving that Amex's antisteering provisions have anticompetitive effects. Amex's business model has spurred robust interbrand competition and has increased the quality and quantity of credit-card transactions. And it is "[t]he promotion of interbrand competition," after all, that "is . . . 'the primary purpose of the antitrust laws.'"

* * *

Because Amex's antisteering provisions do not unreasonably restrain trade, we affirm the judgment of the Court of Appeals.

It is so ordered.

JUSTICE BREYER, with whom JUSTICE GINSBURG, JUSTICE SOTOMAYOR, and JUSTICE KAGAN join, dissenting.

For more than 120 years, the American economy has prospered by charting a middle path between pure *laissez-faire* and state capitalism, governed by an antitrust law "dedicated to the principle that *markets*, not individual firms and certainly not political power, produce the optimal mixture of goods and services." 1 P. Areeda & H. Hovenkamp, Antitrust Law ¶100b, p. 4 (4th ed. 2013) (Areeda & Hovenkamp). By means of a strong antitrust law, the United States has sought to avoid the danger of monopoly capitalism. Long gone, we hope, are the days when the great trusts presided unfettered by competition over the American economy.

This lawsuit is emblematic of the American approach. Many governments around the world have responded to concerns about the high fees that credit-card companies often charge merchants by regulating such fees directly. The United States has not followed that approach. The Government instead filed this lawsuit, which seeks to restore market competition over credit-card merchant fees by eliminating a contractual barrier with anticompetitive effects. The majority rejects that effort. But because the challenged contractual term clearly has serious anticompetitive effects, I dissent.

. . .

II

. . .

C

In 2010 the United States and 17 States brought this antitrust case against American Express. They claimed that the "nondiscrimination provisions" in its contracts with merchants created an unreasonable restraint of trade. (Initially Visa and MasterCard were also defendants, but they entered into consent judgments, dropping similar provisions from their contracts with merchants). After a 7-week bench trial, the District Court entered judgment for the Government, setting forth its findings of fact and conclusions of law in a 97-page opinion

Because the majority devotes little attention to the District Court's detailed factual findings, I will summarize some of the more significant ones here. Among other things, the District Court found that beginning in 2005 and during the next five years, American Express raised the prices it charged merchants on 20 separate occasions. In doing so, American Express did not take account of the possibility that large merchants would respond to the price increases by encouraging shoppers to use a different credit card because the nondiscrimination provisions prohibited any such steering. The District Court pointed to merchants' testimony stating that, had it not been for those provisions, the large merchants would have responded to the price increases by encouraging customers to use other, less-expensive cards.

The District Court also found that even though American Express raised its merchant prices 20 times in this 5year period, it did not lose the business of any large merchant. Nor did American Express increase benefits (or cut credit-card prices) to American Express cardholders in tandem with the merchant price increases. Even had there been no direct evidence of injury to competition, American Express' ability to raise merchant prices without losing any meaningful market share, in the District Court's view, showed that American Express possessed power in the relevant market.

The District Court also found that, in the absence of the provisions, prices to merchants would likely have been lower. It wrote that in the late 1990's, Discover, one of American Express' competitors, had tried to develop a business model that involved charging lower prices to merchants than the other companies charged. Discover then invited each "merchant to save money by shifting volume to Discover," while simultaneously offering merchants additional discounts "if they would steer customers to Discover." The court determined that these efforts failed because of American Express' (and the other card companies') "nondiscrimination provisions." These provisions, the court found, "denied merchants the ability to express a preference for Discover or to employ any other tool by which they might steer share to Discover's lower-priced network." Because the provisions eliminated any advantage that lower prices might produce, Discover "abandoned its low-price business model" and raised its merchant fees to match those of its competitors. This series of events, the court concluded was "emblematic of the harm done to the competitive process" by the "nondiscrimination provisions."

The District Court added that it found no offsetting procompetitive benefit to shoppers. Indeed, it found no offsetting benefit of any kind.

American Express appealed, and the U. S. Court of Appeals for the Second Circuit held in its favor. The Court of Appeals did not reject any fact found by the District Court as "clearly erroneous." See Fed. Rule Civ. Proc. 52(a)(6). Rather, it concluded that the District Court had erred in step 1 of its rule-of-reason analysis by failing to account for what the Second Circuit called the credit-card business's "two-sided market" (or "two-sided platform").

III

The majority, like the Court of Appeals, reaches only step 1 in its "rule of reason" analysis. To repeat, that step consists of determining whether the challenged "nondiscrimination provisions" have had, or are likely to have, anticompetitive effects. See *Indiana Federation of Dentists*, 476 U. S., at 459. Do those provisions tend to impede competition? And if so, does American Express, which imposed that restraint as a condition of doing business with its merchant customers, have sufficient economic or commercial power for the provision to make a negative difference?

A

Here the District Court found that the challenged provisions have had significant anticompetitive effects. In particular, it found that the provisions have limited or prevented price competition among credit-card firms for the business of merchants. That conclusion makes sense: In the provisions, American Express required the merchants to agree not to encourage customers to use American Express' competitors' credit cards, even cards from those competitors, such as Discover, that intended to charge the merchants lower prices. By doing so, American Express has "disrupt[ed] the normal price-setting mechanism" in the market. As a result of the provisions, the District Court found, American Express was able to raise merchant prices repeatedly without any significant loss of business, because merchants were unable to respond to such price increases by encouraging shoppers to pay with other cards. The provisions also meant that competitors like Discover had little incentive to lower their merchant prices, because doing so did not lead to any additional market share. The provisions thereby "suppress[ed] [American Express'] . . . competitors' incentives to offer lower prices . . . resulting in higher profit-maximizing prices across the network services market." Consumers throughout the economy paid higher retail prices as a result, and they were denied the opportunity to accept incentives that merchants might otherwise have offered to use less-expensive cards. I should think that, considering step 1 alone, there is little more that need be said.

The majority, like the Court of Appeals, says that the District Court should have looked not only at the market for the card companies' merchant-related services but also at the market for the card companies' shopper-related services, and that it should have combined them, treating them as a single market. But I am not aware of any support for that view in antitrust law. Indeed, this Court has held to the contrary.

In *Times-Picayune Publishing Co.* v. *United States*, 345 U. S. 594, 610 (1953), the Court held that an antitrust court should begin its definition of a relevant market by focusing narrowly on the good or service directly affected by a challenged restraint. The Government in that case claimed that a newspaper's advertising policy violated the Sherman Act's "rule of reason." In support of that argument, the Government pointed out, and the District Court had held, that the newspaper dominated the market for the sales of newspapers to readers in New Orleans, where it was the sole morning daily newspaper. But this Court reversed. We explained that "every newspaper is a dual trader in separate though interdependent markets; it sells the paper's news and advertising content to its readers; in effect that readership is in turn sold to the buyers of advertising space." We then added:

> "This case concerns solely one of those markets. The Publishing Company stands accused not of tying sales to its readers but only to buyers of general and classified space in its papers. For this reason, dominance in the advertising market, not in readership, must be decisive in gauging the legality of the Company's unit plan."

Here, American Express stands accused not of limiting or harming competition for shopper-related card services, but only of merchant-related card services, because the challenged contract provisions appear only in American Express' contracts with merchants. That is why the District Court was correct in considering, at step 1, simply whether the agreement had diminished competition in merchant-related services.

B

The District Court did refer to market definition, and the majority does the same. And I recognize that properly defining a market is often a complex business. Once a court has identified the good or service directly restrained, as *Times-Picayune Publishing Co.* requires, it will sometimes add to the relevant market what economists call "substitutes": other goods or services that are reasonably substitutable for that good or service. See, *e.g., United States* v. *E. I. du Pont de Nemours & Co.*, 351 U. S. 377, 395–396 (1956) (explaining that cellophane market includes other, substitutable flexible wrapping materials as well). The reason that substitutes are included in the relevant market is that they restrain a firm's ability to profitably raise prices, because customers will switch to the substitutes rather than pay the higher prices.

But while the market includes substitutes, it does not include what economists call complements: goods or services that are used together with the restrained product, but that cannot be substituted for that product. An example of complements is gasoline and tires. A driver needs both gasoline and tires to drive, but they are not substitutes for each other, and so the sale price of tires does not check the ability of a gasoline firm (say a gasoline monopolist) to raise the price of gasoline above competitive levels. As a treatise on the subject states: "Grouping complementary goods into the same market" is "economic nonsense," and would "undermin[e] the rationale for the policy against monopolization or collusion in the first place."

Here, the relationship between merchant-related card services and shopper-related card services is primarily that of complements, not substitutes. Like gasoline and tires, both must be purchased for either to have value. Merchants upset about a price increase for merchant-related services cannot avoid that price increase by becoming cardholders, in the way that, say, a buyer of newspaper advertising can switch to television advertising or direct mail in response to a newspaper's advertising price increase. The two categories of services serve fundamentally different purposes. And so, also like gasoline and tires, it is difficult to see any way in which the price of shopper-related services could act as a check on the card firm's sale price of merchant-related services. If anything, a lower price of shopper-related card services is likely to cause more shoppers to use the card, and increased shopper popularity should make it *easier* for a card firm to raise prices to merchants, not *harder*, as would be the case if the services were substitutes. Thus, unless there is something unusual about this case—a possibility I discuss below—there is no justification for treating shopper-related services and merchant-related services as if they were part of a single market, at least not at step 1 of the "rule of reason."

C

Regardless, a discussion of market definition was legally unnecessary at step 1. That is because the District Court found strong *direct* evidence of anticompetitive effects flowing from the challenged restraint. As I said, supra, this evidence included Discover's efforts to break into the credit-card business by charging lower prices for merchant-related services, only to find that the "nondiscrimination provisions," by preventing merchants from encouraging shoppers to use Discover cards, meant that lower merchant prices did not result in any additional transactions using Discover credit cards. The direct evidence also included the fact that American Express raised its merchant prices 20 times in five years without losing any appreciable market share. It also included the testimony of numerous merchants that they would have steered shoppers away from American Express cards in response to merchant price increases (thereby checking the ability of American Express to raise prices) had it not been for the nondiscrimination provisions. It included the factual finding that American Express "did not even account for the possibility that [large] merchants would respond to its price increases by attempting to shift share to a competitor's network" because the nondiscrimination provisions prohibited steering. It included the District Court's ultimate finding of fact, not overturned by the Court of Appeals, that the challenged provisions "were integral to" American Express' "[price] increases and thereby caused merchants to pay higher prices."

As I explained above, this Court has stated that "[s]ince the purpose of the inquiries into market definition and market power is to determine whether an arrangement has the potential for genuine adverse effects on competition, proof of actual detrimental effects . . . can obviate the need for" those inquiries. *Indiana Federation of Dentists*, 476 U. S., at 460–461 (internal quotation marks omitted). That statement is fully applicable here. Doubts about the District Court's market-definition analysis are beside the point in the face of the District Court's findings of actual anticompetitive harm.

The majority disagrees that market definition is irrelevant. The majority explains that market definition is necessary because the nondiscrimination provisions are "vertical restraints" and "[v]ertical restraints often pose no risk to competition unless the entity imposing them has market power, which cannot be evaluated unless the Court first determines the relevant market." *Ante,* n. 7. The majority thus, in a footnote, seems categorically to exempt vertical restraints from the ordinary "rule of reason" analysis that has applied to them since the Sherman Act's enactment in 1890. The majority's only support for this novel exemption is *Leegin Creative Leather Products, Inc.* v. *PSKS, Inc.*, 551 U. S. 877 (2007). But *Leegin* held that the "rule of reason" *applied* to the vertical restraint at issue in that case. It said nothing to suggest that vertical restraints are not subject to the usual "rule of reason" analysis.

One critical point that the majority's argument ignores is that proof of actual adverse effects on competition *is, a fortiori,* proof of market power. Without such power, the restraints could not have brought about the anticompetitive effects that the plaintiff proved. See *Indiana Federation of Dentists, supra,* at 460 ("[T]he purpose of the inquiries into market definition and market power is to determine *whether an arrangement has the potential for* genuine adverse effects on competition" (emphasis added)). The District Court's findings of actual anticompetitive harm from the nondiscrimination provisions thus showed that, whatever the relevant market might be, American Express had enough power in that market to cause that harm. There is no reason to require a separate showing of market definition and market power under such circumstances. And so the majority's extensive discussion of market definition is legally unnecessary.

D

The majority's discussion of market definition is also wrong. Without raising any objection in general with the longstanding approach I describe above, the majority agrees with the Court of Appeals that the market for American Express' card services is special because it is a "two-sided transaction platform." The majority explains that credit-card firms connect two distinct groups of customers: First, merchants who accept credit cards, and second, shoppers who use the cards. The majority adds that "no credit-card transaction can occur unless both the merchant and the cardholder simultaneously agree to use to the same credit-card network." And it explains that the credit-card market involves "indirect network effects," by which it means that shoppers want a card that many merchants will accept and merchants want to accept those cards that many customers have and use. From this, the majority concludes that "courts must include both sides of the platform—merchants and cardholders—when defining the credit-card market."

1

Missing from the majority's analysis is any explanation as to *why*, given the purposes that market definition serves in antitrust law, the fact that a credit-card firm can be said to operate a "two-sided transaction platform" means that its merchant-related and shopper-related services should be combined into a single market. The phrase "two-sided transaction platform" is not one of antitrust art—I can find no case from this Court using those words. The majority defines the phrase as covering a business that "offers different products or services to two different groups who both depend on the platform to intermediate between them," where the business "cannot make a sale to one side of the platform without simultaneously making a sale to the other" side of the platform. I take from that definition that there are four relevant features of such businesses on the majority's account: they (1) offer different products or services, (2) to different groups of customers, (3) whom the "platform" connects, (4) in simultaneous transactions. What is it about businesses with those four features that the majority thinks justifies a special market-definition approach for them? It cannot be the first two features—that the company sells different products to different groups of customers. Companies that sell multiple products to multiple types of customers are commonplace. A firm might mine for gold, which it refines and sells both to dentists in the form of fillings and to investors in the form of ingots. Or, a firm might drill for both oil and natural gas. Or a firm might make both ignition switches inserted into auto bodies and tires used for cars. I have already explained that, ordinarily, antitrust law will not group the two nonsubstitutable products together for step 1 purposes.

Neither should it normally matter whether a company sells related, or complementary, products, *i.e.*, products which must both be purchased to have any function, such as ignition switches and tires, or cameras and film. It is well established that an antitrust court in such cases looks at the product where the attacked restraint has an anticompetitive effect. The court does not combine the customers for the separate, nonsubstitutable goods and see if "overall" the restraint has a negative effect. That is because, as I have explained, the complementary relationship between the products is irrelevant to the purposes of market-definition.

The majority disputes my characterization of merchant-related and shopper-related services as "complements." The majority relies on an academic article which devotes one sentence to the question, saying that "a two-sided market [is] different from markets for complementary products [*e.g.*, tires and gas], in which both products are bought by the same buyers, who, in their buying decisions, can therefore be expected to take into account both prices." Filistrucchi, Geradin, Van Damme, & Affeldt, Market Definition in Two-Sided Markets: Theory and Practice, 10 J. Competition L. & Econ. 293, 297 (2014) (Filistrucchi). I agree that two-sided platforms—at least as some academics define them—may be distinct from some types of complements in the respect the majority mentions (even though the services resemble complements because they must be used together for either to have value). But the distinction the majority mentions has nothing to do with the relevant question. The relevant question is whether merchant-related and shopper-related services are *substitutes*, one for the other, so that customers can respond to a price increase for one service by switching to the other service. As I have explained, the two types of services are not substitutes in this way. And so the question remains, just as before: What is it about the economic relationship between merchant-related and shopper-related services that would justify the majority's novel approach to market definition?

What about the last two features—that the company connects the two groups of customers to each other, in simultaneous transactions? That, too, is commonplace. Consider a farmers' market. It brings local farmers and local shoppers together, and transactions will occur only if a farmer and a shopper simultaneously agree to engage in one. Should courts abandon their ordinary step 1 inquiry if several competing farmers' markets in a city agree that only certain kinds of farmers can participate, or if a farmers' market charges a higher fee than its competitors do and prohibits participating farmers from raising their prices to cover it? Why? If farmers' markets are special, what about travel agents that connect airlines and passengers? What about internet retailers, who, in addition to selling their own goods, allow (for a fee) other goods-producers to sell over their networks? Each of those businesses seems to meet the majority's four-prong definition.

Apparently as its justification for applying a special market-definition rule to "two-sided transaction platforms," the majority explains that such platforms "often exhibit" what it calls "indirect network effects." By this, the majority means that sales of merchant-related card services and (different) shopper-related card services are interconnected, in that increased merchant-buyers mean increased shopper-buyers (the more stores in the card's network, the more customers likely to use the card), and vice versa. But this, too, is commonplace. Consider, again, a farmers' market. The more farmers that participate (within physical and esthetic limits), the more customers the market will likely attract, and vice versa. So too with travel agents: the more airlines whose tickets a travel agent sells, the more potential passengers will likely use that travel agent, and the more potential passengers that use the travel agent, the easier it will likely be to convince airlines to sell through the travel agent. And so forth. Nothing in antitrust law, to my knowledge, suggests that a court, when presented with an agreement that restricts competition in any one of the markets my examples suggest, should abandon traditional market-definition approaches and include in the relevant market services that are complements, not substitutes, of the restrained good.

2

To justify special treatment for "two-sided transaction platforms," the majority relies on the Court's decision in *United States* v. *Grinnell Corp.*, 384 U. S. 563, 571–572 (1966). In *Grinnell*, the Court treated as a single market several different "central station services," including burglar alarm services and fire alarm services. It did so even though, for *consumers*, "burglar alarm services are not interchangeable with fire alarm services." But that is because, for *producers*, the services were indeed interchangeable: A company that offered one could easily offer the other, because they all involve "a single basic service—the protection of property through use of a central service station." Thus, the "commercial realit[y]" that the *Grinnell* Court relied on was that the services being grouped were what economists call "producer substitutes." And the law is clear that "two products produced interchangeably from the same production facilities are presumptively in the same market," even if they are not "close substitutes for each other on the demand side." *Ibid.* That is because a firm that produces one such product can, in response to a price increase in the other, easily shift its production and thereby limit its competitor's power to impose the higher price.

Unlike the various types of central station services at issue in *Grinnell Corp.*, however, the shopper-related and merchant-related services that American Express provides are not "producer substitutes" any more than they are traditional substitutes. For producers as for consumers, the services are instead complements. Credit card companies must sell them together for them to be useful. As a result, the credit-card companies cannot respond to, say, merchant-related price increases by shifting production away from shopper-related services to merchant-related services. The relevant "commercial realities" in this case are thus completely different from those in *Grinnell Corp.* (The majority also cites *Brown Shoe Co.* v. *United States*, 370 U. S. 294, 336–337 (1962), for this point, but the "commercial realities" considered in that case were that "shoe stores in the outskirts of cities compete effectively with stores in central downtown areas," and thus are part of the same market. Here, merchant-related services do not, as I have said, compete with shopper-related services, and so *Brown Shoe Co.* does not support the majority's position.) Thus, our precedent provides no support for the majority's special approach to defining markets involving "two-sided transaction platforms."

3

What about the academic articles the majority cites? The first thing to note is that the majority defines "two-sided transaction platforms" much more broadly than the economists do. As the economists who coined the term explain, if a "two-sided market" meant simply that a firm connects two different groups of customers via a platform, then "pretty much any market would be two-sided, since buyers and sellers need to be brought together for markets to exist and gains from trade to be realized." Rochet & Tirole, Two-Sided Markets: A Progress Report, 37 RAND J. Econ. 645, 646 (2006). The defining feature of a "two-sided market," according to these economists, is that "the platform can affect the volume of transactions by charging more to one side of the market and reducing the price paid by the other side by an equal amount. That requirement appears nowhere in the majority's definition. By failing to limit its definition to platforms that economists would recognize as "two sided" in the relevant respect, the majority carves out a much broader exception to the ordinary antitrust rules than the academic articles it relies on could possibly support.

Even as limited to the narrower definition that economists use, however, the academic articles the majority cites do not support the majority's flat rule that firms operating "two-sided transaction platforms" should always be treated as part of a single market for all antitrust purposes. Rather, the academics explain that for market-definition purposes, "[i]n some cases, the fact that a business can be thought of as two-sided may be irrelevant," including because "nothing in the analysis of the practices [at issue] really hinges on the linkages between the demands of participating groups." Evans & Schmalensee, Markets With Two-Sided Platforms, 1 Issues in Competition L. & Pol'y 667, 689 (2008). "In other cases, the fact that a business is two-sided will prove important both by identifying the real dimensions of competition and focusing on sources of constraints." That flexible approach, however, is precisely the one the District Court followed in this case, by considering the effects of "[t]he two-sided nature of the . . . card industry" throughout its analysis. Neither the majority nor the academic articles it cites offer any explanation for why the features of a "two-sided transaction platform" justify always treating it as a single antitrust market, rather than accounting for its economic features in other ways, as the District Court did. The article that the majority repeatedly quotes as saying that "'[i]n two-sided transaction markets, only one market   should be defined,'" *ante* (quoting Filistrucchi 302), justifies that conclusion only for purposes of assessing the effects of a merger. In such a case, the article explains, "[e]veryone would probably agree that a payment card company such as American Express is either in the relevant market on both sides or on neither side . . . . The analysis of a merger between two payment card platforms should thus consider . . . both sides of the market." In a merger case this makes sense, but is also meaningless, because, whether there is one market or two, a reviewing court will consider both sides, because it must examine the effects of the merger in each affected market and submarket. See *Brown Shoe Co.*, 370 U. S., at 325. As for a nonmerger case, the article offers only *United States* v. *Grinnell* as a justification, and as I have already explained, *Grinnell* does not support this proposition.

E

Put all of those substantial problems with the majority's reasoning aside, though. Even if the majority were right to say that market definition was relevant, and even if the majority were right to further say that the District Court should have defined the market in this case to include shopper-related services as well as merchant-related services, that *still* would not justify the majority in affirming the Court of Appeals. That is because, as the majority is forced to admit, the plaintiffs *made* the factual showing that the majority thinks is required.

Recall why it is that the majority says that market definition matters: because if the relevant market includes both merchant-related services and card-related services, then the plaintiffs had the burden to show that as a result of the nondiscrimination provisions, "the price of credit-card transactions"—considering both fees charged to merchants and rewards paid to cardholders—"was higher than the price one would expect to find in a competitive market." This mirrors the Court of Appeals' holding that the Government had to show that the "nondiscrimination provisions" had "made *all* [American Express] customers on both sides of the platform—*i.e.*, both merchants and cardholders—worse off overall."

The problem with this reasoning, aside from it being wrong, is that the majority admits that the plaintiffs *did* show this: they "offer[ed] evidence" that American Express "increased the percentage of the purchase price that it charges merchants . . . and that this increase was not entirely spent on cardholder rewards." Indeed, the plaintiffs did not merely "offer evidence" of this—they persuaded the District Court, which made an unchallenged factual finding that the merchant price increases that resulted from the nondiscrimination provisions "were not wholly offset by additional rewards expenditures or otherwise passed through to cardholders, and *resulted in a higher net price.*"

In the face of this problem, the majority retreats to saying that even net price increases do not matter after all, absent a showing of lower output, because if output is increasing, "'rising prices are equally consistent with growing product demand.'" *Ante,* at 18 (quoting *Brooke Group Ltd.* v. *Brown & Williamson Tobacco Corp.,* 509 U. S. 209, 237 (1993)). This argument, unlike the price argument, has nothing to do with the credit-card market being a "two-sided transaction platform," so if this is the basis for the majority's holding, then nearly all of the opinion is dicta. The argument is also wrong. It is true as an economic matter that a firm exercises market power by restricting output in order to raise prices. But the relevant restriction of output is as compared with a hypothetical world in which the restraint was not present and prices were lower. The fact that credit-card use in general has grown over the last decade, as the majority says, says nothing about whether such use would have grown more or less without the nondiscrimination provisions. And because the relevant question is a comparison between reality and a hypothetical state of affairs, to require actual proof of reduced output is often to require the impossible—tantamount to saying that the Sherman Act does not apply at all.

In any event, there are features of the credit-card market that may tend to limit the usual relationship between price and output. In particular, merchants generally spread the costs of credit-card acceptance across all their customers (whatever payment method they may use), while the benefits of card use go only to the cardholders. Thus, higher credit-card merchant fees may have only a limited effect on credit-card transaction volume, even as they disrupt the marketplace by extracting anticompetitive profits.

IV

A

For the reasons I have stated, the Second Circuit was wrong to lump together the two different services sold, *at step 1.* But I recognize that the Court of Appeals has not yet considered whether the relationship between the two services might make a difference at steps 2 and 3. That is to say, American Express might wish to argue that the nondiscrimination provisions, while anticompetitive in respect to merchant-related services, nonetheless have an adequate offsetting procompetitive benefit in respect to its shopper-related services. I believe that American Express should have an opportunity to ask the Court of Appeals to consider that matter.

American Express might face an uphill battle. A Sherman Act §1 defendant can rarely, if ever, show that a procompetitive benefit in the market for one product offsets an anticompetitive harm in the market for another. In *United States* v. *Topco Associates, Inc.*, 405 U. S. 596, 611 (1972), this Court wrote:

> "If a decision is to be made to sacrifice competition in one portion of the economy for greater competition in another portion, this . . . is a decision that must be made by Congress and not by private forces or by the courts. Private forces are too keenly aware of their own interests in making such decisions and courts are ill-equipped and ill-situated for such decisionmaking."

American Express, pointing to vertical price-fixing cases like our decision in *Leegin*, argues that comparing competition-related pros and cons is more common than I have just suggested. But *Leegin* held only that vertical price fixing is subject to the "rule of reason" instead of being *per se* unlawful; the "rule of reason" still applies to vertical agreements just as it applies to horizontal agreements. Moreover, the procompetitive justifications for vertical price-fixing agreements are not apparently applicable to the distinct types of restraints at issue in this case. A vertically imposed price-fixing agreement typically involves a manufacturer controlling the terms of sale for its own product. A television-set manufacturer, for example, will insist that its dealers not cut prices for the manufacturer's own televisions below a particular level. Why might a manufacturer want its dealers to refrain from price competition in the manufacturer's own products? Perhaps because, for example, the manufacturer wants to encourage the dealers to develop the market for the manufacturer's brand, thereby increasing *interbrand* competition for the same ultimate product, namely a television set. This type of reasoning does not appear to apply to American Express' nondiscrimination provisions, which seek to control the terms on which merchants accept *other brands'* cards, not merely American Express' own. Regardless, I would not now hold that an agreement such as the one before us can never be justified by procompetitive benefits of some kind. But the Court of Appeals would properly consider procompetitive justifications not at step 1, but at steps 2 and 3 of the "rule of reason" inquiry. American Express would need to show just how this particular anticompetitive merchant-related agreement has procompetitive benefits in the shopper-related market. In doing so, American Express would need to overcome the District Court's factual findings that the agreement had no such effects.

B

The majority charts a different path. Notwithstanding its purported acceptance of the three-step, burden-shifting framework I have described, the majority addresses American Express' procompetitive justifications now, at step 1 of the analysis. And in doing so, the majority inexplicably ignores the District Court's factual findings on the subject.

The majority reasons that the challenged nondiscrimination provisions "stem negative externalities in the credit-card market and promote interbrand competition." The "negative externality" the majority has in mind is this: If one merchant persuades a shopper not to use his American Express card at that merchant's store, that shopper becomes less likely to use his American Express card at other merchants' stores. The majority worries that this "endangers the viability of the entire [American Express] network," but if so that is simply a consequence of American Express' merchant fees being higher than a competitive market will support. "The antitrust laws were enacted for 'the protection of *competition,* not *competitors.'" Atlantic Richfield Co.* v. *USA Petroleum Co.*, 495 U. S. 328, 338 (1990). If American Express' merchant fees are so high that merchants successfully induce their customers to use other cards, American Express can remedy that problem by lowering those fees or by spending more on cardholder rewards so that cardholders decline such requests. What it may not do is demand contractual protection from price competition. In any event, the majority ignores the fact that the District Court, in addition to saying what I have just said, also rejected this argument on independent factual grounds. It explained that American Express "presented no expert testimony, financial analysis, or other direct evidence establishing that without its [nondiscrimination provisions] it will, in fact, be unable to adapt its business to a more competitive market." It further explained that the testimony that was provided on the topic "was notably inconsistent," with some of American Express' witnesses saying only that invalidation of the provisions "would require American Express to adapt its current business model." After an extensive discussion of the record, the District Court found that "American Express possesses the flexibility and expertise necessary to adapt its business model to suit a market in which it is required to compete on both the cardholder and merchant sides of the [credit-card] platform." majority evidently rejects these factual findings, even though no one has challenged them as clearly erroneous. Similarly, the majority refers to the nondiscrimination provisions as preventing "free riding" on American Express' "investments in rewards" for cardholders. But as the District Court explained, "[p]lainly ... investments tied to card use (such as Membership Rewards points, purchase protection, and the like) are not subject to free-riding, since the network does not incur any cost if the cardholder is successfully steered away from using his or her American Express card." This, I should think, is an unassailable conclusion: American Express pays rewards to cardholders only for transactions in which cardholders use their American Express cards, so if a steering effort succeeds, no rewards are paid. As for concerns about free riding on American Express' fixed expenses, including its investments in its brand, the District Court acknowledged that free-riding was in theory possible, but explained that American Express "ma[de] no effort to identify the fixed expenses to which its experts referred or to explain how they are subject to free riding." The majority does not even acknowledge, much less reject, these factual findings, despite coming to the contrary conclusion.

Finally, the majority reasons that the nondiscrimination provisions "do not prevent Visa, MasterCard, or Discover from competing against [American Express] by offering lower merchant fees or promoting their broader merchant acceptance." But again, the District Court's factual findings were to the contrary. As I laid out above, the District Court found that the nondiscrimination provisions *in fact did prevent* Discover from pursuing a low-merchant-fee business model, by "den[ying] merchants the ability to express a preference for Discover or to employ any other tool by which they might steer share to Discover's lower-priced network." The majority's statements that the nondiscrimination provisions are procompetitive are directly contradicted by this and other factual findings.

* * *

For the reasons I have explained, the majority's decision in this case is contrary to basic principles of antitrust law, and it ignores and contradicts the District Court's detailed factual findings, which were based on an extensive trial record. I respectfully dissent.

Notes

1.   Is a manufacturer that buys an input from an upstream seller, processes it, and sells the resulting product to a downstream buyer also a two-sided transaction platform? Why not? Because the manufacturer enters into two separate transactions, one on each side, rather than facilitating a transaction between the two sides? Because the usual manufacturing situation does not typically involve indirect network effects?

2.   The dissent responds to the majority's negative-externality argument by characterizing it as based on price: "If American Express' merchant fees are so high that merchants successfully induce their customers to use other cards, American Express can remedy that problem by lowering those fees or by spending more on cardholder rewards so that cardholders decline such requests." Is that fair? Why isn't a merchant that posts its acceptance of American Express but then tries to steer customers to other cards engaging in a "bait and switch" strategy? Consider the following section from the FTC's "Guides Against Bait Advertising":

§238.3   Discouragement of purchase of advertised merchandise.

No act or practice should be engaged in by an advertiser to discourage the purchase of the advertised merchandise as part of a bait scheme to sell other merchandise. Among acts or practices which will be considered in determining if an advertisement is a bona fide offer are:

(a) The refusal to show, demonstrate, or sell the product offered in accordance with the terms of the offer,

(b) The disparagement by acts or words of the advertised product or the disparagement of the guarantee, credit terms, availability of service, repairs or parts, or in any other respect, in connection with it,

(c) The failure to have available at all outlets listed in the advertisement a sufficient quantity of the advertised product to meet reasonably anticipated demands, unless the advertisement clearly and adequately discloses that supply is limited and/or the merchandise is available only at designated outlets,

(d) The refusal to take orders for the advertised merchandise to be delivered within a reasonable period of time,

(e) The showing or demonstrating of a product which is defective, unusable or impractical for the purpose represented or implied in the advertisement,

(f) Use of a sales plan or method of compensation for salesmen or penalizing salesmen, designed to prevent or discourage them from selling the advertised product.

16 C.F.R. § 238.3.

3.   Is the majority's approach similar to, but more extreme than, the one rejected by the Court in *Kodak*? Recall that Kodak argued that its high market share in the parts market was not sufficient to withstand a summary judgment challenge because it was constrained by conditions in the equipment market. The Court rejected that argument, saying that any constraint imposed by the equipment market was a fact question. Is the majority here holding that proof of conditions in the customer side of the market are insufficient to meet the plaintiffs' burden because of constraints on the merchant side? Is the difference that the majority is saying that the district court did not perform the factual inquiry described in *Kodak*?

4.   The *American Express* decision has been the subject of considerable controversy. *Cf.* Herbert J. Hovenkamp, "Platforms and the Rule of Reason: The *American Express* Case." 2019 Colum. Bus. L. Rev. 35 (2019); Tim Wu, The *American Express* opinion, the rule of reason, and tech platforms, 7 J. of Antitrust Enforcement 117 (2019) *with* Geoffrey A. Manne, In defence of the Supreme Court's 'single market' definition in *Ohio v American Express*, 7 J. of Antitrust Enforcement 104 (2019); Mark McCarthy, Ohio v. American Express is sensible antitrust policy, Aug. 7, 2018, https://www.cio.com/article/3295539/ohio-v-american-express-is-sensible-antitrust-policy.html.

4. Proof of Agreement

Firms' use of algorithms for pricing can fall with a broad range of conduct often described as "facilitating practices": practices that are not, strictly speaking, agreements on price but that facilitate parallel pricing. Such practices are sometimes pursued under antitrust law, but there is no standard treatment of them and results are fact-specific. See United States v. Socony-Vacuum Oil Co., 310 U.S. 150 (1940); In re Ethyl Corp., *101* F.T.C. 425, 470 (1983). *rev'd sub nom.*, E.I. DuPont De Nemours & Co. v. FTC, 729 F.2d 128, 134(2d Cir. 1984); see also Joseph J. Simons, *Fixing Price with Your Victim: Efficiency and Collusion with Competitor-Based Formula Pricing Clauses*, 17 HOFSTRA L. REV. 599 (1989).

UK Competition & Markets Authority
Pricing Algorithms
Economic working paper on the use of algorithms
to facilitate collusion and personalised pricing
8 October 2018

. . .

1. Introduction

1.1   This research project focuses on identifying the conditions under which algorithmic pricing could cause harm to consumers. We have analysed how algorithms might facilitate collusive agreements, how they could result in tacit coordination, and whether there are particular features that make this form of coordination more likely. We have also investigated the use of algorithms to drive personalised pricing, and the interaction between this and collusion.

1.2   Algorithms are increasingly used by firms for a wide range of business decisions. This paper focuses on the use of algorithms in firms' pricing decisions, such as setting the market-wide price or offering personalised prices to individual consumers.

1.3   Understanding how markets work is an important part of the CMA's duty to promote effective competition for the benefit of consumers. Algorithms and data-based decision making which does not require human involvement are becoming more prevalent. These approaches will continue to develop as access to Big Data and computing power improves.

1.4   Algorithms have brought many benefits to consumers and competition in the form of lower costs for suppliers, better service, better product availability, and an improved customer experience. However, it is important for the CMA to understand if and when the use of algorithms might lead to consumer harm.

1.5   The analysis in this paper draws on four main sources of evidence:

(a)   First, we have reviewed the growing competition policy and economic literature which is concerned that the use of algorithms may distort or diminish competition by facilitating explicit collusion or causing tacit coordination;

(b)   Second, we have contacted a small number of commercial algorithm providers to understand how they operate, and what role pricing algorithms play in market competition.

(c)   Third, we have spoken to other competition authorities to understand their experience of investigating the use of algorithms.

(d)   Fourth, we have carried out some pilot tests for the presence of personalised pricing using the CMA internet lab. (See Annex 1 for further detail.)

1.6   The aim of the paper is to draw together this evidence and start to identify features of markets and types of algorithms that might raise potential competition concerns. These factors could help provide a means of preliminary prioritisation for considering future complaints or calls for intervention.

1.7   The paper focuses on economic evidence and analysis. It does not seek to assess the lawfulness or otherwise of a given use of pricing algorithms. Nor does it cover broader legal issues such as whether, or in what circumstances, tacit coordination resulting from pricing algorithms could lead to an infringement of competition law.

1.8   The remainder of the paper is structured as follows:

(a)   First, we define what we mean by pricing algorithms, outline how they are currently used by firms, and discuss some of the efficiency benefits flowing from the use of algorithms.

(b)   Second, we outline the theories of harm by which pricing algorithms might lead to or facilitate collusive outcomes. We describe the conditions under which collusion might be more or less likely to occur. We also summarise some of the literature simulating the possible outcomes of pricing algorithms.

(c)   Third, we consider the use of algorithms to target personalised pricing offers at individual customers or groups of customers. We focus particularly on the relationship between personalised pricing and the coordination theories of harm, and consider whether coordination and personalised pricing could co-exist in the same market.

    (d)   Fourth, we summarise some of the market features that might raise particular concerns about the use of pricing algorithms either in relation to tacit coordination or personalised pricing.

    (e)   Fifth, we suggest some possible next steps.

2.   What are pricing algorithms?

2.1   Algorithms are used for calculation, data processing and automated reasoning. There is not one precise definition of an algorithm that has been universally adopted. Instead there are numerous formal and informal definitions that have been included within the literature. For the purposes of this paper, we adopt the following informal definition:

> An algorithm is any well-defined computational procedure that takes some value, or set of values, as input and produces some value, or set of values as output.

2.2   Algorithms can be specified in English, as a computer program, or even using hardware. The only requirement is that they must be specified using a precise description of the computational steps to be used.

2.3   Algorithms have been developed to solve a wide range of practical applications. This includes algorithms that complete simple tasks such as ordering a series of unordered numbers, to complex algorithms that enable digital encryption, internet communication, and the management of scarce resources.

2.4   The focus of this research paper is on pricing algorithms, and their real and potential effects on how online and offline markets work. Within the broad definition of an algorithm, we define a pricing algorithm as an algorithm that uses price as an input, and/or uses a computational procedure to determine price as an output.

2.5   This definition includes price monitoring algorithms, price recommendation algorithms, and price-setting algorithms. We also consider ranking algorithms, which produce a list of items in an order which is influenced by some training data.

Different levels of sophistication

2.6   Algorithms can be created to address a variety of problems or tasks, from simple to very sophisticated. Pricing algorithms similarly fall on a spectrum of complexity.

Business rules and simple pricing algorithms

2.7   Firms have long applied business rules to their operations, including rules on pricing and discounts. Some of these rules can be easily converted into algorithms.

2.8   Some pricing algorithms have been designed to follow simple rules such as matching the lowest competitor's price, or remaining within the lowest quartile of prices. For example, Amazon offers a "Match Low Price" feature to third-party sellers on their platform. This allows sellers to match the lowest price offered by competitors, and allows them to choose which competitors to match based on a combination of listing condition, fulfilment method, customer feedback rating, and handling time.[2] Automated information collection and pricing could mean that the response to a rival's price change could occur within minutes whereas without an algorithm the response could have taken a few days.

2.9   An example is what happened to the price of the book "The Making of a Fly" on Amazon in 2011. This textbook on developmental biology reached a peak price of $23 million. This price was the result of two sellers' pricing algorithms. The first algorithm automatically set the price of the first seller for 1.27059 times the price of the second seller. The second algorithm automatically set the price of the second seller at 0.9983 times the price of the first seller. This resulted in the price spiralling upwards until one of the sellers spotted the mistake and repriced their offer to $106.23. This example appears to have been the result of a lack of "sanity checks" within the algorithms, rather than any anti-competitive intent. However, it demonstrates how the lack of human intervention in algorithmic pricing may lead to unintended results.

Machine learning

2.10   Alternatively, a more advanced algorithm could be left to decide what data it considers is most relevant to meeting its objective (such as profit maximising). The algorithm would then act as a "black box" so that even the employees who instruct the algorithm would not know which variables it was using to set a particular price, and may not be aware of whether any increase in profit was due to attracting additional customers, charging higher prices to loyal customers, or tacit coordination. Such complexities may increase when many of the other firms in the market are also using the same or similar algorithms to set their pricing.

2.11   Machine learning algorithms can solve more complex problems. These kinds of algorithms do not have to be explicitly programmed to solve a problem, but can iteratively change and improve by themselves, and therefore they are more flexible than regular hard-coded algorithms.

2.12   Machine learning is a very broad field, with many different approaches. A full overview is beyond the scope of this paper. However, it is common to describe machine learning algorithms in terms of three broad categories, depending on the nature of the feedback available to the algorithm:

> *(a)*   Supervised learning – the algorithm is provided with a training set of inputs paired with the correct output ('labels', or 'true'

---

[2] See Amazon's Match Low Price Help Page.

values), and its goal is to work out a function that maps inputs to outputs. The performance of the algorithm can be measured by comparing the predictions of the function when it is applied to a dataset that was not used for training (e.g. cross-validation).

(b)   Unsupervised learning – the algorithm is provided with data but no labels or examples, and its goal is to find an appropriate function that describes the structure of data (e.g. clustering).

(c)   Reinforcement learning - in contrast to supervised and unsupervised learning, in which the algorithm is presented with a static dataset (often using historic data, and sometimes referred to as an 'offline' learning), reinforcement learning algorithms iteratively interacts with a dynamic environment. Using the feedback that it gets from the environment, the algorithm tries to work out which actions in the environment will maximise some objective (such as profit).

2.13   An early and simple machine learning algorithm developed to set prices is a 'Win-Continue Lose-Reverse' rule, and it commonly serves as a benchmark against which other more sophisticated algorithms are tested. This adaptive algorithm adjusts prices incrementally in one direction and evaluates what happens to revenue. If revenue increases, it continues to make similar changes to price. If not, it makes an incremental change in the opposite direction. The algorithm make small changes to price in order to learn about market demand, and requires very limited computational resources and no data at all on customers.

2.14   Q-learning appears to be a common approach to algorithmic pricing problems. Q-learning attempts to maximises sand-error' to interact with its environment to learn the optimal pricing policy. It is well suited to pricing because it does not require a model of the environment, such as the demand and competitors' costs functions. It continuously trades-off between 'exploiting' its current knowledge by selecting the action which provides the highest learned payoff, and 'exploring' to expand its knowledge by selecting other actions. However, one prominent drawback with Q-learning methods is that it treats the environment as stationary, but the presence of other competitors who are also learning makes the environment non-stationary.

Artificial Neural Networks

2.15   One approach to machine learning that has gained recent prominence is Artificial Neural Networks (ANNs), which has been used in applications such as AlphaGo and AlphaZero. ANNs are based on collections of connected units ('artificial neurons') that receive, process, and transmit signals to other connected neurons. These connections each have a 'weight' that determines the strength of signals in the connection. The network 'learns' as the weights are adjusted based on its performance.[9]

2.16 The simplest ANNs have a single 'layer' (or level) of neurons, which receives inputs and generates outputs. Deep learning refers to more complex ANNs which have multiple (two or more) layers of neurons, with each layer using the output from the previous layer as input (see Figure 1).

Figure 1: A Deep Learning ANN

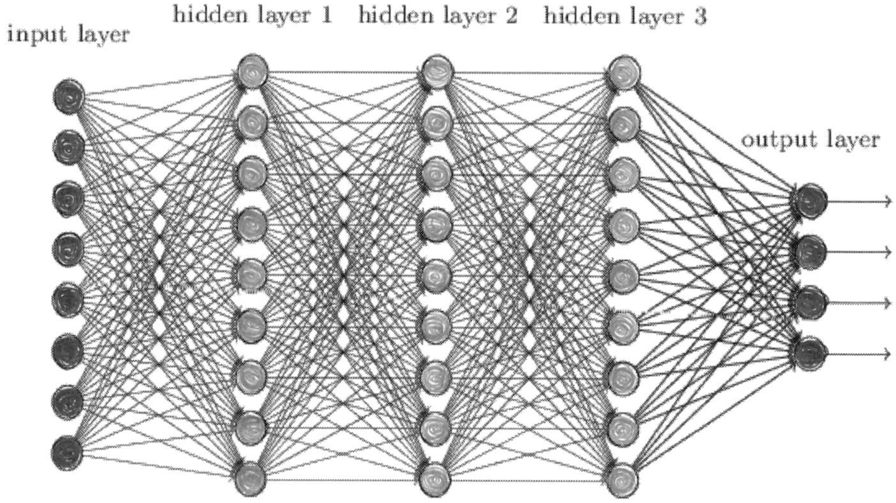

Source: Nielsen (2017)

2.17   With sufficiently intricate and layered design, deep learning algorithms can be very flexible in their application, and could lead to very nuanced decisions even in complex environments like real-world markets.

2.18   Firms can use neural networks to estimate market demand. In contrast with econometric demand models, which usually require some assumption about the functional form of demand, a neural network approach would not need to make any assumptions about demand in advance.

---

[9] This is done by minimising some suitably chosen 'cost function', and using methods like gradient descent and backpropagation to overcome the curse of dimensionality created by the high number of weights to be optimised. For our purposes, it is not necessary to explain the details for these methods, but the underlying intuition behind these methods will be familiar to economists who have worked on multivariable optimisation problems. Readers who are interested in these methods may find it helpful to read Nielsen (2017), *Neural Networks and Deep Learning*.

2.19   However, deep learning neural networks are also more difficult to understand and it can be hard to tell what is happening in the many layers, creating a 'black box' so that firms using such networks (and regulators) may not be able to tell the underlying causes of the network's output.

2.20   Some companies that sell repricing algorithms claim to use machine learning techniques to improve on simple re-pricing rules. One example of this is an Amazon marketplace algorithmic re-pricer which the CMA contacted (although it is not clear whether they are using a neural network). The firm providing pricing services claims to use the Amazon seller's past pricing/profit/revenue data, competing firms' prices, and market information such as competitors' stock levels, to determine the optimal price to charge consumers. Its algorithm also takes into account competitors' publicly-available pricing information and customer feedback. Whereas simple re-pricers often charge the lowest price amongst competitors, this machine learning re-pricer maximises profits through optimising the trade-off between higher prices and lower sales. It adapts to specific business goals such as meeting sales targets, or capturing a specific share of the 'Buy Box' sales (which is the 'default' seller for a product on Amazon).[12]

The relationship between "Big Data" and algorithms

. . .

2.27   Although Big Data and algorithms are closely related and discussed together, we focus primarily on the latter in this paper. Therefore, we do not examine whether Big Data, or extensive user data collected and used by incumbents, could be a barrier to entry, create strong network effects, or (in the extreme) whether data could be an 'essential facility'.

3.   The use of pricing algorithms in practice

3.1   There has been a considerable increase in the sources, types, and volume of data collected by businesses. Ninety percent of the digital data in the world today has been created in the past two years alone. With the growth of Big Data, more businesses are purchasing data analysis services. Worldwide revenue for Big Data and business analytics is predicted to grow from $130 billion in 2016 to more than $200 billion in 2020.

3.2   Pricing algorithms generally fall into two categories:

   (a)   Algorithms which are developed by businesses to set the prices for products which they produce and sell to consumers.

---

[12] As explained in the Annex 1 on firms selling re-pricers, the Buy Box lists the default retailer for any product listed on Amazon. Most customers do not review the individual sellers and just purchase from the default in the Buy Box if one is listed.

Generally, they are produced by larger companies with the resources and expertise to develop them.

(b)   Algorithms which are developed by specialist algorithm development firms. They do not specifically tailor their algorithm to one product or market, and instead license their algorithms for other companies to use. These are sometimes bundled with a broader suite of "business intelligence" services.

3.3   Both of these approaches could in principle apply in either online or offline markets, as set out below.

Pricing algorithms in online markets

3.4   Pricing algorithms have become prevalent within some online retail markets. Even more than four years ago, in December 2013, Amazon implemented more than 2.5 million price changes every day, a 10-fold increase on the number of price changes in December 2012. This is compared to just 52,956 price changes made by Best Buy and 54,633 changes made by Walmart during November 2013.

3.5   Not only are large retailers such as Amazon taking advantage of algorithms to re-price their goods, but so are smaller online retailers. A research paper[18] developed a methodology to detect whether Amazon third-party sellers are using pricing algorithms to re-price their goods. Analysing the pricing history of the top 1,641 best-selling products, and approximately 30,000 sellers, they predicted that 500 sellers were using algorithmic pricing strategies. These sellers received more feedback and won the Buy Box[20] more frequently than non-algorithmic sellers, suggesting higher sales volumes and more revenue. The researchers found that some sellers changed the prices of products tens or even hundreds of times a day. These kinds of price changes would be impossible for a human to replicate, and indicate that algorithms are necessary for sellers to keep pace with the repricing behaviours of their competitors. However, this paper could not conclude whether algorithmic repricing led to higher profits overall, nor how it impacted consumer welfare.

3.6   A number of these third-party sellers use algorithmic pricing software developed by specialist algorithm suppliers. In conversations with

---

[20] Amazon on the Buy Box: "The Buy Box is the box on a product detail page where customers can begin the purchasing process by adding items to their shopping carts. A key feature of the Amazon website is that multiple sellers can offer the same product. If more than one eligible seller offers a product, they may compete for the Buy Box for that product. To give customers the best possible shopping experience, sellers must meet performance-based requirements to be eligible to compete for Buy Box placement. For many sellers, Buy Box placement can lead to increased sales." (See Amazon's page on How the Buy Box Works.)

these sellers, they have indicated that for large Amazon sellers (more than $1,000,000 in annual revenue), having automatic repricing software is necessary in order to be able to handle their large numbers of products. Further, they have stated that Amazon products can be fiercely competitive markets, and so dynamically responding to changes in competitors' prices is necessary to remain competitive. However, we are not aware of any empirical analysis of what size firms utilise algorithmic re-pricing software.

3.7   As part of our research we spoke to two firms that sell pricing algorithm services. One of the firms supplied 'off-the-shelf' pricing algorithms to third party sellers on Amazon Marketplace. The other manages clients' Amazon marketplace pricing on their behalf. We are also aware of other firms that provide bespoke pricing algorithms to individual clients.

3.8   The two firms appear to vary in their sophistication, with one offering relatively simple automated business rules and the other claiming to implement more sophisticated machine learning techniques. Both firms aim to help their clients to respond quickly and efficiently to competition and to improve sales. The firms also outline how it can be useful to understand the pricing strategy of competitors and how price rises at times of the day with low sales volume may reduce competitive pressure.

Pricing algorithms in offline markets

3.9   Algorithms are not necessarily constrained to digital or online markets. Algorithms are defined as a procedure that takes inputs and follows a series of well-defined steps to produce an output, and therefore can be implemented without the use of code. Many business rules and processes are simply algorithms. However, the use of data-scraping methods allows for real-time data collection on consumers and competitors which makes it easier to implement algorithmic pricing strategies.

3.10   Algorithmic pricing strategies are typically difficult to use in traditional brick-and-mortar retail settings. This is because data, such as competitors' prices, must be collected manually. It is more difficult to collect and store. Re-pricing the products requires manual human intervention in order to physically change the price on offer.

3.11   There have been moves to adopt electronic price tags in retail shops. Some major UK retailers, such as Tesco, Sainsbury's and Morrisons are trialling electronic price tags within their shops. These tags allow them to change prices on in-store goods more quickly and frequently in response to fluctuations in demand or to cheaply sell off excess stock. This would make it easier to implement algorithmic pricing strategies.

3.12   Algorithmic pricing strategies have been observed in some offline markets. For example, there have been a number of press reports and academic studies that allege that retail petrol providers have used algorithms to facilitate tacit coordination and improve their profit margins. Although retail petrol is not an 'online' market, there are online websites or services that monitor petrol prices, and individual sites can adjust their prices quickly at almost zero cost.

4.   Possible pro-competitive effects of algorithms

4.1   In many cases the introduction of algorithms (both pricing algorithms and others) is likely to have positive impacts on consumers and on competition. In this section, we briefly discuss the positive impacts that all algorithms could have on markets by increasing supply-side and demand-side efficiencies. In addition to the direct benefits on the market, algorithms can also assist regulators and competition authorities. One example of this is the cartel screening tool that the CMA has developed to help public bodies and others running procurement.

Supply-side efficiencies

4.2   In general, the use of Artificial Intelligence (AI) can significantly reduce labour costs if it is able to replace human workers. For example, one recent survey of machine learning researchers predicts that AI will outperform humans in many activities in the next ten years, such as translating languages (by 2024), driving a truck (by 2027), and working as a surgeon (by 2053). However, AI and algorithms are less likely to be able to perform jobs that require intuition, abstract thinking, or complex physical movements.

4.3   There are further potential efficiencies and cost-savings if algorithms can improve the efficiency of human workers. Mass data collection and algorithmic processing promises to assist managers in making more, faster and better decisions. Where the decision making is also automated, robo-sellers promise still more cost savings.

4.4   More specifically, pricing algorithms may be expected to make markets more efficient and clear faster, as prices become more responsive to changes in supply and demand. Thus perishable goods like groceries or airline tickets are less likely to go to waste, where the remaining stock has no value to the seller but would have some value to buyers. Related to this, pricing algorithms may also enable or facilitate improved inventory management, particularly for perishable goods like hotel rooms and flights.

Demand-side efficiencies

4.5   A wide variety of algorithms help consumers make decisions in market transactions. Some offer consumers information that is relevant to their choices. For example, third-party price monitoring tools like CamelCamelCamel help consumers on the Amazon platform purchase products when they are at their lowest price by alerting them when the price for a specific product reaches a certain level.

CHAPTER 4 PROOF OF AGREEMENT

4.6   More sophisticated algorithms use price forecasting to suggest to the consumer whether they should purchase products immediately or wait for an expected decrease in price. An example is the flight price aggregator Kayak, which uses data on previous flight price trends to suggest whether to purchase flights or wait. However, the effectiveness of this algorithm has been shown to be mixed. An article showed that for a sample of 15 routes, if a customer were to follow the algorithm's suggestions they would have paid 2% more than if they had instead simply bought the tickets on a random day. It concludes this is likely statistically insignificant.

4.7   With a considerable increase in the complexity of algorithms, consumers could completely outsource their purchasing decisions. Digital agents could use data to predict consumer preferences, optimally choose the most suitable product and services, negotiate and execute the transaction, and potentially form consumer coalitions ('buyer groups') to obtain the best terms and conditions. This would significantly reduce search and transaction costs, allow for more sophisticated and rational choices, and even strengthen buyer power.

4.8   Both search and comparison services (in the form of digital comparison tools) and collective buying services (such as Groupon, LivingSocial and Google Offers) already exist. There is speculation that digital personal assistants (like Amazon's Alexa, Apple's Siri and Google's Google Assistant) could go beyond what is currently available. For instance, it may be that digital personal assistants can collect and process enough information about users and encourage enough user uptake (e.g. through a better or more seamless user interface), to be able to co-ordinate purchases across a much wider range of users and products than what is currently available.

5.   Algorithms and coordination

5.1   In spite of the benefits of algorithms outlined above, there is a growing competition policy literature raising concerns about the potential for algorithms to lead to consumer harm. One of the main theories of harm relates to the possibility that pricing algorithms might lead to collusive outcomes, with consumers paying higher prices than in a competitive market.

5.2   In practice, the concern about collusion covers a broad spectrum of different potential issues. It is important to distinguish between:

(a)   the use of algorithms to monitor and enforce an existing coordinated strategy; and

(b)   theories of harm under which pricing algorithms might lead to coordinated outcomes even when each firm is using the pricing algorithm to make unilateral pricing decisions.

5.3   The section below discusses each of these theories of harm in turn.

The use of algorithms to facilitate explicit agreements

5.4   Algorithms may be used as a tool to implement explicit collusion. Below, we give detail on recent cases where algorithms have been used to implement collusive agreements. We then discuss the circumstances in which pricing algorithms could increase the stability of a collusive agreement.

Example of a cartel case involving algorithms

5.5   In the CMA's *Trod Ltd/GB eye Ltd* case, the two parties agreed a 'classic' horizontal price-fixing cartel for posters and frames sold on Amazon's UK website. They implemented this agreement using automated repricing software which automatically monitored and adjusted their prices to make sure neither was undercutting the other. The parties kept in contact with each other through regular means to ensure the arrangement was working, and to deal with issues regarding the operation of the re-pricing software. Because there was a clear anti-competitive agreement made between humans, the CMA was able to demonstrate that the parties infringed the Chapter I prohibition.

Figure 2: Explicit coordination implemented or facilitated by algorithms

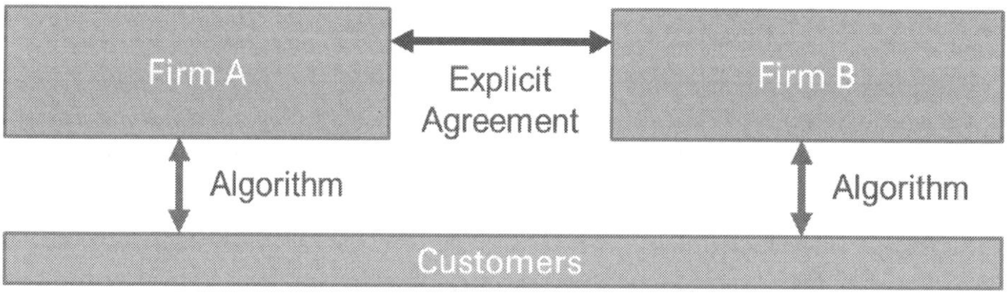

Source: CMA

Mechanisms by which algorithms might facilitate collusion

5.6   From an economic perspective, algorithms may make explicitly collusive agreements more stable for a number of reasons:

(a)   it is easier to detect and respond to deviations;

(b)   it reduces the chance of errors or accidental deviations; and (c) it reduces agency slack.

Detecting deviations

5.7   Collusive agreements are only stable if the firms can detect when their partners have deviated from the collusive price. Without detection, one of the firms would be able to lower its price, increase its sales and therefore increase its profits. This results in the collusive agreement breaking down.

5.8   If firms are able to detect a deviation, they are then able to 'punish' the deviating firm by lowering their prices even further. This means that the deviating firm is able to enjoy higher profits in the period before 'punishment', but once they have been undercut, their profits fall to below the collusive level. Therefore, the speed at which a deviation is detected and punished influences the incentive for the firms to deviate. The faster the deviation is detected, the lower the expected profits from deviation, and therefore the cartel is more stable.

5.9   Pricing algorithms make the detection of deviation quicker and less costly. This is due to the greater availability of pricing data, both in terms of speed at which it is communicated and the volume of available data. This makes it easier for competitors, even without the use of algorithms, to monitor prices. The likely impact depends to some extent on where in the supply chain the firms operate. At the retail level, it is simple for firms to collect pricing data because prices are typically transparent. With intermediate products, however, prices may not be transparently advertised and therefore pricing algorithms may have little to no effect on how deviations are detected.

Reducing chance of errors

5.10   One way in which a cartel can break down is due to 'noisy price information'. This occurs when firms in the agreement do not receive perfect information about what their co-conspirators are charging. This might then lead, for example, to a seller confusing a period of unusually low demand, and hence low sales, with cheating by its cartel partner.

5.11   Algorithms could make explicitly collusive agreements more stable by making errors such as these less likely. The increased ease and availability of mass data collection makes it easier for firms to accurately understand how their competitors are pricing. Effectively, an algorithm could function similarly to a resale price maintenance agreement, where an upstream cartel is certain that their agreed-upon prices are being followed.

Reducing agency slack

5.12   Another feature that reduces the stability of cartels in traditional economic models is "agency slack". This occurs when, although a collusive agreement has been agreed on between senior managers within a firm, salespeople and other non-management employees may have incentives to undermine the cartel. They may do this if they favour immediate payoffs rather than the long-term benefits of maintaining a cartel; or there may be intra-firm competition for promotions or sales-linked salary rewards. For these reasons, they may choose to undercut the collusive price.

5.13   Using algorithmic pricing could reduce the possibility that agency slack will lead to the cartel breaking down. This is because there is less scope for individuals within an organisation to take pricing decisions themselves which might go against the collusive agreement.

Could algorithms result in tacit coordination or conscious parallelism?

5.14   In addition to facilitating explicit collusion, some commentators have expressed concerns that pricing algorithms could lead to tacit coordination. This section considers theories of harm under which pricing algorithms might lead to coordinated outcomes even when each firm is using the pricing algorithm to make unilateral pricing decisions.

Alternative theories of harm

5.15   Ezrachi and Stucke (2015) describe three main ways in which algorithms could result in the formation of a tacit coordinated pricing outcome: hub-and-spoke; predictable agent; and autonomous machine.

Hub-and-spoke

5.16   The first way in which algorithms may lead to a tacitly-collusive outcome is when sellers use the same algorithm or data pool to determine price.

5.17   If multiple competitors use the same pricing algorithm, this may lead the competitors to react in a similar way to external events, such as changes in input costs or demand. Furthermore, if the competitors are aware or able to infer that they are using the same or similar pricing algorithms, firms would be better able to predict their competitors' responses to price changes, and this might help firms to better interpret the logic or intention behind competitors' price setting behaviour. Widespread knowledge and use of common pricing algorithms may therefore have a similar effect to information exchange in reducing strategic uncertainty, which may help sustain (but not necessarily lead to) a tacitly coordinated outcome.

5.18   There are some caveats to this theory of harm:

(a)   First, the mere fact that firms use the same pricing algorithm is not, by itself, sufficient to establish a tacitly coordinated outcome. There must still be some intention on the part of competitors to acquiesce to the tacit suppression of rivalry. This is because if firms using the same pricing algorithm can reach a collusive outcome in which prices are higher than the competitive level, they still need to decide to maintain their strategy and resist the temptation to modify their algorithm or switch strategy to undercut the collusive price and earn higher (short-term) profits. It is not obvious how common pricing algorithms, by themselves, can help firms to overcome this central problem of maintaining collusion, particularly if firms can change or modify their pricing algorithms as easily as they can change individual prices – albeit that algorithms can accelerate the learning process, because price setting is much more rapid.

(b)   Second, how would a firm know that its rivals are using the same algorithms? In a real-world market, many factors could be influencing firms' pricing behaviour, and it may not be possible to fully deduce or reverse engineer a competitors' pricing algorithm. Those seeking to coordinate prices may need to explicitly announce or communicate the details of their pricing algorithm to rivals, which would be akin to explicit coordination.

Figure 3: 'Tacit' coordination due to common pricing algorithms

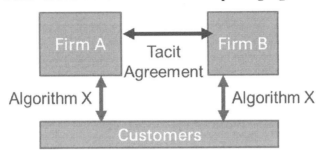

Source: CMA

5.19   Arguably a more serious situation is if competitors decide, instead of using their own data and algorithms, that it is more effective to delegate their pricing decisions to a common intermediary which provides algorithmic pricing services. This may result in a hub-and-spoke-like framework emerging, even though competitors are not expressly fixing the price.

5.20   Relevant considerations for this theory of harm include:

(a)   The proportion of the relevant market that has delegated its pricing to a common intermediary's pricing algorithms.

(b)   Whether the common intermediary's pricing algorithm makes use of nonpublic information or data from multiple clients (competitors) when determining prices for each client.

(c)   Whether the objective function of the pricing algorithm is to maximise the total joint profit of all the common intermediary's clients, perhaps because the common intermediary's remuneration is calculated as a proportion of all its clients' sales.

5.21   If a sufficiently large proportion of an industry uses a single algorithm to set prices, this could result in a hub-and-spoke structure that may have the ability and incentive to increase prices. In this scenario, existing competition law analysis of hub-and-spoke could be sufficient to address competition concerns if certain criteria can be established.

Figure 4: 'Tacit' coordination due to common intermediary

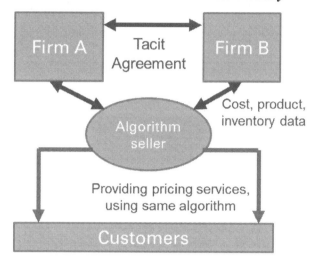

Source: CMA

Predictable agent

5.22   The second category is that of a predictable agent. Here, humans unilaterally design pricing algorithms which react to external factors in a predictable way. Again, this would have the effect of reducing strategic uncertainty, which may help sustain (but not necessarily lead to) a tacitly coordinated outcome. The algorithms can be programmed to monitor the market prices, rationally follow price leadership, and punish deviations from a tacit agreement.

5.23   In the absence of explicit communication, tacit coordination appears to be more likely to be a concern if the price-setting algorithms leads firms to adopt very simple, transparent, and predictable pricing behaviour (like price matching, or price cycles), which can be recognised by other firms.

Figure 5: Tacit coordination without agreement due to algorithms

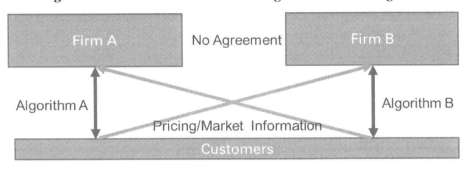

Source: CMA

Autonomous machine

> 5.24   The third category is that of the autonomous machine. Here, competitors unilaterally design an algorithm to reach a pre-set target, such as the maximisation of profit. If the algorithm is sufficiently complex, it can learn by itself and experiment with the optimal pricing strategy. There is the possibility that the algorithms may find the optimal strategy is to enhance market transparency and tacitly collude. The important difference with the Predictable Agent model is that the algorithm is not explicitly designed to tacitly collude, but does so itself through self-learning. It is similar to the Predictable Agent model in that it would appear difficult to categorise this as falling within Article 101. The algorithms are not just sustaining existing coordination but generating this coordination themselves.

Reasons why tacit coordination may be more likely as a result of algorithmic pricing

> 5.25   Tacit coordination refers to an anti-competitive market outcome which is achieved without the need for explicit communication between competitors. Below, we consider the reasons why algorithmic pricing may make tacit coordination more likely.

Market Transparency

> 5.26   A paper by the OECD details how the prevalence of algorithmic pricing may result in greater market transparency. It argues that in order for a firm to adopt algorithmic pricing, it must first collect detailed real-time data on its competitors. Therefore, they have an incentive to develop automated methods to collect and store data without human intervention. Once some market players invest in the systems needed to benefit from algorithmic pricing, the remaining firms have a stronger competitive incentive to do the same. The result of this is an industry where all firms collect real-time data on each other and on market characteristics. This

transparent market would not have occurred without the incentive of gaining an 'algorithmic competitive advantage'.

Frequency of interaction

5.27   Price adjustments, and the detection of price adjustments, require a significant amount of time and resources in brick-and-mortar retailers. With the use of algorithmic pricing, firms can reprice their products many thousands of times per day. As described earlier, even back in 2013, Amazon has implemented millions of price changes per day, whereas Best Buy and Walmart were only able to adjust prices approximately 50,000 times during a month. As a result, when firms are tacitly colluding using algorithmic pricing, they will be able to detect and respond to deviations from collusion almost immediately.

5.28   In the extreme case if there is no delay before punishment then there is no benefit to deviation and coordination can be established regardless of the discount rate.

Calculation of optimal price

5.29   A further reason why algorithms may make tacit coordination more likely is that they may be more capable or efficient at calculating the profit-maximising tacit coordination price in the absence of an explicit agreement. As Mehra (2016) notes, there may be 'instances in which humans would be cognitively incapable of assessing their competitors' responses.' In some cases, an algorithm may be better able to calculate the profit-maximising price, taking into account the predicted responses of their competitors.

Incentive compatibility and choice of pricing algorithm

5.30   Anticipating the discussion on pricing algorithm simulations, we know that it is possible for firms using simple pricing algorithms to reach and sustain collusive outcomes, at least in simple, highly stylised market environments. The algorithms do not even have to be highly complex. Simple 'win-continue lose-reverse' algorithms and 'match low price' (tit-for-tat) algorithms have been shown to be capable of sustaining collusion. (in fact, complex deep learning algorithms often fail to collude, especially when competing against humans as well as algorithms. However, these collusive outcomes are vulnerable to disruption, if there is uncertainty ('noise') in the observed prices or changes in the market (e.g. firms' costs and demand conditions).

5.31   The deeper question is whether firms would find it in their interest to implement and stick to such a pricing algorithm. It is not at all clear that simply replacing a human price-setter with a pricing algorithm would solve the central problem that businesses seeking to coordinate prices face (i.e. that it is in their short-term interest to 'cheat' on the coordinated price, while in their longer term interest to maintain coordination), in the wider game where firms are choosing pricing algorithms (i.e. deciding whether to sacrifice short-term profits by giving up control of their prices to an algorithm that keeps prices high).

5.32   Salcedo (2016) explicitly models this wider game. In his model, firms simultaneously and independently commit to a pricing algorithm in the short run, and compete in a product market in which customers with unit demand arrive randomly over time. Firms must commit to a pricing policy in the short term because it takes time to revise an algorithm, but over time firms get (stochastic) opportunities to a) successfully infer or 'decode' others' pricing algorithms and b) revise their own pricing algorithm.

5.33   Salcedo finds that, if customers arrive frequently, and revision opportunities are infrequent, then any equilibrium of his model will have long-run industry profits that will be arbitrarily close to the monopolist level.

5.34   Salcedo's result is underpinned by very strong assumptions. These include perfect ex post observability, not only of all market outcomes (prices, sales, customer arrivals), but also of rivals' algorithms, including information on how that algorithm would respond to hypothetical outcomes that haven't yet been observed in the market. This is because, for the result to hold, firms need to be able to interpret 'proposals' to raise prices embedded within rivals' algorithms, such as a feature to match price increases from particular competitors. It is not clear that these assumptions would be satisfied in real markets, particularly where firms are using machine learning pricing algorithms that are effective "black boxes", or where there is opaque and personalised pricing. Furthermore, it could be argued that this process of decoding rivals' pricing algorithms could be understood as more akin to a form of explicit private communication between the firms (or as a public announcement of pricing intentions, if customers could also 'decode' pricing algorithms), rather than a model of tacit coordination.

Conclusions on likelihood of tacit coordination

5.35   Of the theories of harm outlined above, we consider that the hub-and-spoke model is likely to present the most immediate risk. This is because it simply requires firms to adopt the same algorithmic pricing model. Additionally, third party providers of pricing algorithm services may be a natural (and potentially 'unwitting') 'hub' for hub-and-spoke collusion.

5.36   The predictable agent and autonomous machine models of coordination could also occur if the pricing algorithms were sufficiently technologically advanced and in widespread use. It is unclear how likely they are to materialise at this point. However, these concerns may become more important in the future.

5.37   Anticipating our discussion in section 8 on risk factors for coordination, we think that algorithmic pricing is more likely to facilitate collusion in markets which are already susceptible to coordination. For these 'marginal' markets, the increasing use of data and algorithmic pricing may be the 'last piece of the puzzle' that could allow suppliers to move to a coordinated equilibrium. However, in our tentative view, it seems less likely than not that the increasing use of data and algorithms would be so impactful that they could enable sustained collusion in markets that are currently highly competitive, or those with very differentiated products, many competitors, and low barriers to entry and expansion.

. . .

8.   Features which might raise competition concerns

8.1   This section draws together some tentative conclusions on what features of the market or of the algorithms themselves might lead to greater concern about algorithmic pricing.

8.2   We first outline risk factors which might raise concerns about algorithmic pricing leading to coordinated outcomes. We then discuss risk factors relating to personalised pricing.

Risk factors for coordination

8.3   Below, we list some traditional risk factors for price co-ordination, with details regarding how algorithmic pricing and online markets in general could result in these creating more risk of harm to consumers.

(a)   **Concentrated markets**. Because of algorithmic pricing, both explicit and tacit co-ordination could occur in less concentrated markets. This is because algorithms can collect information about more competitors at a faster rate than humans. Therefore, deviations can be detected from more firms and punishment strategies could be implemented more rapidly.

(b)   **Market Transparency**. Increasing availability of data and use of pricing algorithms can increase market transparency (especially online), even if there are many products with complex offers. This is because algorithms can scrape data from many websites more quickly than humans would be able to. Therefore, price deviations can be detected more quickly. Not only do algorithms lead to Greater information on competitors' actions and customers but they can lead to simpler and more predictable pricing behaviours.

(c)   **Frequency of interaction and price setting**. Pricing algorithms allow firms to set their prices automatically. This means that whenever a price change occurs, competitors can respond by undercutting or matching very quickly with low or zero menu cost. Therefore, the short-term return for a firm that lowers its price below the market price may be very small, which would discourage price wars. Further to this, an algorithm could allow firms to test their competitors' responses to changes in price during periods of low demand, because price feedback is so quick and multiple rounds of price change can occur very quickly even when there are no customers present in the market. Although the firm that has been undercut in this price war would not face a real punishment, because little to no sales have been made, the algorithm would learn about the likely effects of future price competition and may be discouraged from engaging in price wars at busier periods.

(d)   **Low buyer power or small regular purchases.** Online markets operate 24 hours a day, and sometimes internationally, therefore there can be a high frequency of purchase with low buyer power. However, as described previously, there may be opportunities for customers to use algorithms to form buying groups, increasing their buyer power.

8.4   Algorithms could potentially increase the chance that tacit coordination occurs in ways that go beyond traditional risk factors:

(a)   An algorithm could monitor prices, introduce parallel conduct (e.g. follow the price leader), signal to competitors about intentions or just learn to coordinate.

(b)   An algorithm could increase the stability of a cartel by increasing barriers to entry, if it is able to identify and quickly target customers who are most likely to buy from a new entrant (a form of personalised pricing).

(c)   Firms using the same algorithm or the same data set (which means the algorithm learns/adapts in the same way) may act in parallel.

8.5   The mechanisms by which algorithms could have an additional impact beyond 'traditional' risk factors are quite speculative and are likely to be difficult to evidence. Instead, the main impact of increasing use of data and algorithms appear to be that it can exacerbate 'traditional' risk factors, such as transparency and the speed of price setting.

8.6   Algorithmic pricing is more likely to facilitate collusion in markets which are already susceptible to (human) coordination. For these "marginal" markets, the increasing use of data and algorithmic pricing may be the 'last piece of the puzzle' that could allow suppliers to move to a coordinated equilibrium.

8.7   Factors which could give competition authorities an indication of whether a price-setting algorithm may result in tacit coordination include:

(a)   **The time horizon of a reinforcement learning algorithm's objective function**. It is plausible that if the objective function is very short-term or places a large weight on short-term profits (e.g. maximise profit just on one sale) then a reinforcement

learning algorithm is less likely to engage in stable coordination. For stable tacit coordination to take place, the firm must be willing to sacrifice short term profits in favour of a longer-term, more profitable outcome. However, we note that this is may not be a reliably useful indicator of potential harm, as even simple Win-Continue Lose-Reverse algorithms, which aim myopically to maximise revenue in just the current period, could give rise to a collusive outcome in favourable conditions (e.g. other competitors using similar strategies, underlying market conditions like costs and demand are stable, etc.).

(b)   **Whether all/many competitors are using the same algorithm/objective function**. In the case of markets where intermediaries provide algorithmic price services to several competitors (a 'hub and spoke' scenario), this is closely related to how much of the market the intermediaries cover.

(c)   **What data the algorithm is using**, and in particular whether the algorithm makes use of information or data from multiple competitors, which may be a particular risk in markets where intermediaries receive data from multiple clients that are competitors.

   . . .

9.   Further Work

9.1   We consider that there could be value in further economic research exploring the topics discussed in this paper. Some specific areas for further research could include:

(a)   **Auditing algorithms** – deep learning algorithms are often described as "black boxes", but there is a small and emerging research community dedicated to auditing algorithms, mainly in the context of detecting discrimination based on protected characteristics (like race, sex, etc.). It may be useful to take insights from this field and apply them to auditing pricing algorithms. From an enforcement and regulatory perspective, it would be beneficial to understand further whether and if a firm could know that its algorithm is implementing a collusive outcome. For instance, if a firm observes that its profits have risen since it implemented algorithmic pricing, would it be able to determine whether this is because the algorithm has attracted new customers, increased sales to existing customers, raised prices to loyal customers, or engaged in collusion? There may be little difference between collusion and raising prices on some products that are considered less elastic for other reasons (such as loyal customers).

(b)   **Algorithmic decision rules that should be presumed to be anticompetitive** – in the case of simpler algorithms, are there certain kinds of decision rules which have no plausible rationale other than to facilitate an anti-competitive outcome? For instance, one might argue that there are no pro-competitive reasons to have decision rule in an algorithm that raises price in response to a competitor's price increase, or a decision rule that never undercuts a competitor's price. However, for both of these examples, these decision rules are consistent with competitive firms trying to maximise profit, and it may be too interventionist and damage the competitive process to restrict firms' ability to set its own prices.

(c)   **Secret offers and masking** – consumers may not be helpless in response to collusion and personalised pricing, and they may be able to use countermeasures.

In the case of collusion, to what extent can customers request (potentially using an algorithm or 'shopbot' in an online context) secret offers from suppliers in order to undermine collusion? To what extent could customers build up and exercise buyer power through joint purchasing? From the perspective of implementing a cartel, are competitors able to gather data or monitor for deviations by pretending to be a customer?

In the case of personalised pricing, to what extent can customers hide information that firms are using to set personalised prices? Alternatively, could consumer groups, price comparison services, regulators, or the government develop a tool which allows consumers to compare the price that they are quoted with a price based on a 'clean' profile?

. . .

Notes

1.   The *Trod Ltd.* case described in paragraph 5.5 followed a U.S. criminal case, *U.S. v. Topkins*, Case No. CR-15-00201-WHO (N.D. Cal. filed Apr. 6, 2015), based on similar facts. In that case, Topkins, the founder of a poster retailer, pled guilty to price-fixing. Plea Agreement, U.S. v. Topkins, Case No. CR-15-00201-WHO (N.D. Cal. filed Apr. 30, 2015), https://www.justice.gov/atr/case-document/file/628891/download. Subsequently, Trod and one of its executives also pled guilty in the U.S. *See* Plea Agreement, *U.S. v. Trod Ltd.*, Case No. CR-15-0419-WHO (N.D. Cal. filed Aug. 11, 2016.

2.   If a group of firms using algorithmic pricing charge the same high prices, where is the agreement? Is there only an agreement if the firms agree to use the same algorithm? Is there an agreement even if the firms use different algorithms, but they produce the same result? Is there an agreement if the firms agree to use algorithms but do not agree on the algorithm?

3. An oft-quoted statement has it that "no monopolist monopolizes unconscious of what he is doing." United States v. Aluminum Co. of Am., 148 F.2d 416, 432 (1945). Can price-fixers price-fix unconscious of what they are doing? That is, if firms independently adopt algorithms that result in high prices, would the firms' employees lack of knowledge about what is happening, or how it was happening, mean they are not liable? One of the reasons that antitrust law does not condemn simple parallel pricing is that firms must set prices and often the only sensible, or at least the profit-maximizing, price will the one charged by other firms. If a firm's employees find that adoption of an algorithm for price-setting results in higher prices and profits, must it stop using the algorithm to avoid liability?

5. Mergers

5.1. Horizontal Mergers

The novel issues that arise in the online environment regarding horizontal mergers are primarily those involving relevant markets. In this area, the enforcement agencies have won some and lost some.

One win was the Department of Justice's challenge to the merger of Bazaarvoice, "the unquestioned market leading provider of Ratings and Reviews platforms," and PowerReviews, "its primary competitor." Memorandum Opinion, United States v. Bazaarvoice, Inc., Case No. 13-cv-00133-WHO (N.D. Cal. filed Jan. 8, 2014). In its opinion condemning the merger, the court explained the significance of ratings and review (R & R) platforms:

    5.   R&R platforms are one of many social commerce tools. "Social commerce" is "a very broad term" that refers generally to the engagement or interaction of consumers as part of their shopping or buying process, typically in a digital medium such as a website. To determine the appropriate product market and understand the effect of the merger, one must first understand what R&R platforms are and how they fit into the social commerce tools industry.

    6.   The software component of a R&R platform provides a user interface and review form for the collection and display of user-generated content on the product page of a commercial website where the product can be purchased. Most review forms prompt consumers to rate a product on a five-star scale and offer consumers an option to write an open-ended review of the product. Other forms also allow consumers to rate products along several dimensions (e.g., product appearance, ease of assembly, value). There are various features offered by R&R software and social commerce suppliers such as syndication, moderation, attribute ratings, and data analytics. R&R platforms vary in their level of sophistication, features offered, and other available capabilities that may be bundled with the platform or sold separately.

    7.   R&R platforms increase the likelihood a consumer will purchase a R&R customer's product on the customer's website. Consumers find R&R useful because it provides authentic information regarding another consumer's experience with a particular product. Feedback from other consumers can help a prospective buyer make a more informed purchasing decision. Even negative reviews have a positive impact on sales because they confirm the authenticity of all R&R.

8.   In addition to the basic ratings and reviews components of R&R platforms, sophisticated R&R platforms also allow manufacturers to share, or "syndicate," ratings and reviews with their retail partners. Through the syndication network, retailers can display user-generated content that was originally collected by a product's manufacturer. For example, a retailer's website, such as Staples.com, can display ratings and reviews for a product, such as a Canon printer, that were collected by Canon on Canon.com. Syndication is an important selling feature for any R&R platform provider. Syndication is of particular interest to manufacturers (also referred to as "brands") and is increasingly popular among retailers because it allows them to obtain more content than they could independently.

9.   Although each R&R customer has unique interests and priorities, as a general proposition, manufacturers and retailers both benefit from the ability to display more reviews at the point of sale. The increase in R&R content helps retailers sell more products and further reduce return of products. Because R&R increases conversion rates, manufacturers also see a benefit in the form of increased sales of their products through retailers.

10.   Moderation is another key R&R feature. After receiving a review, but before the review is posted on the manufacturer's or retailer's website. the R&R platform provider applies software algorithms to scan the submission for inappropriate or fraudulent content. After the automated scan, a human moderator (either provided by the R&R provider, a third party, or in-house personnel) examines each submission to ensure that it complies with a particular customer's moderation standards. Moderation ensures that the R&R is credible, not offensive, and otherwise complies with the company's business rules.

11.   Some R&R platforms also include analytics software that manufacturers and retailers use to analyze information collected from R&R. With these tools, manufacturers and retailers can track and analyze real-time consumer sentiment. Manufacturers and retailers can use this information to identify product design defects, make product design decisions, or identify consumers for targeted marketing efforts. R&R provides valuable data about consumer preferences and behavior, which retailers and manufacturers can use to make inventory purchasing or product design decisions.

The court then explained that R&R platforms are a relevant antitrust market, noting that "[w]itness after witness testified to the effect that R&R is considered 'critical' to the business of many online retailers and that it is unlikely that most online retailers would ever eliminate R&R entirely, as consumers now expect ratings and reviews to be a part of their online shopping experience." Both parties to the proposed merger, the court said, "recognized that R&R platforms comprise a distinct market." The case thus illustrates the novel circumstances of the online economy, though the sort of evidence on which the court relied were not significantly different from those in other merger cases.

On the other hand, online markets can present new challenges to merger analysis. In a surprising recent case, involving the proposed merger of Sabre and Farelogix, two firms that provide airline booking information to travel agents, the U.S. and the UK reached different conclusions in the same week. A U.S. court rejected the Department of Justice's challenge to the merger, but the UK Competition and Markets Authority (CMA) blocked it, despite Farelogix's limited presence in the UK. The CMA's decision was based in large part on Farelogix's role in a new approach to the market:

> In 2012, the International Air Transport Association (IATA) –a trade association for airlines –launched the New Distribution Capability (NDC) standard to address the industry's current limitations. The NDC standard is a computer messaging standard. Farelogix, among others, was instrumental in its development. Retailing and distribution solutions compatible with the NDC standard (NDC solutions) allow for dynamic, personalised offers to be created by airlines and for this rich content to be communicated and accessed by travel agents in real-time.

Competition and Markets Authority, Final Report, Anticipated acquisition by Sabre Corporation of Farelogix Inc., Apr. 9, 2020, https://assets.publishing.service.gov.uk/ media/5e8f17e4d3bf7f4120cb1881/Final_Report_-_Sabre_Farelogix.pdf, ¶22. The CMA stated that Sabre and other services had been much slower than Farelogix to take advantage of the NDC approach, so that the merger would likely slow innovation.

In contrast, the District Court of Delaware relied on the Supreme Court's decision in *Ohio v. American Express* in stating that "as a matter of antitrust law, Sabre and Farelogix do not compete in a relevant market." Opinion, United States v. Sabre Corp., C.A. No. 19-1548-LPS (D. Del. Apr. 7, 2020), https://www.ded.uscourts.gov/sites/ded/files/opinions/19-1548_0.pdf, at 69. That is so, the court said, because Sabre is a two-sided market but Farelogix is not. In effect, Farelogix provides services to airlines that let them deliver information directly to travel agents, thus circumventing services like Sabre that sit between airlines and travel agents. It is true, therefore, that Farelogix does not provide the same services that Sabre does and does not compete with them in that sense. But what Farelogix does is provide an alternative that poses a competitive threat to Sabre. Surely the *American Express* decision should not be read to hold that a merger between firms that compete directly but in different ways cannot injure competition.

5.2. Vertical Mergers

Vertical mergers, particularly those in the media industry, have received considerable recent publicity. Several, such as AT&T/Time Warner and Comcast/NBC Universal, have been completed despite agency concerns, and, in the case of AT&T/Time Warner, court challenges.

The traditional concern regarding vertical mergers has been one of foreclosure: that either merging firm could use denial of the goods or services of the other to injure competitors. In AT&T/Time Warner, for example, this concern would be that the merged entity might deny Time Warner content to competitors of AT&T. The foreclosure concern also has a pricing counterpart in that the threat of foreclosure could cause competitors to pay supracompetitive prices for the goods or service that the merged entity could deny. Another concern is that the merged entity could use information about that it acquired before the merger about competitors of either merging entity to disadvantage those competitors.

A possible procompetitive effect, on the other hand, is the elimination of double marginalization as a result of the fact that a single firm with power in two vertically related markets will typically charge less for the downstream product than would be charged if the components of the firm in the two markets were separately owned. But see Steven C. Salop, Invigorating Vertical Merger Enforcement, 127 Yale L.J. 1962 (2018) (arguing that this effect is more often claimed than applicable).

Presumably because of the increased importance of vertical mergers, and with the age of the agencies' last guidance, which came in 1984, they have issued a new set of draft guidelines on their vertical merger enforcement practices, excerpts of which follow.

U.S. Department of Justice and Federal Trade Commission
Draft Vertical Merger Guidelines
January 10, 2020

1.   OVERVIEW

These Guidelines outline the principal analytical techniques, practices and enforcement policy of the Department of Justice and the Federal Trade Commission (the "Agencies") with respect to vertical mergers and acquisitions ("vertical mergers") under the federal antitrust laws. The relevant statutory provisions include Section 7 of the Clayton Act, 15 U.S.C. § 18, Sections 1 and 2 of the Sherman Act, 15 U.S.C. §§ 1–2, and Section 5 of the Federal Trade Commission Act, 15 U.S.C. § 45. Most particularly, Section 7 of the Clayton Act prohibits mergers if "in any line of commerce or in any activity affecting commerce in any section of the country, the effect of such acquisition may be substantially to lessen competition, or to tend to create a monopoly." This provision applies to vertical mergers, as Congress made plain in the 1950 amendments to the Clayton Act.

These Guidelines should be read in conjunction with the Horizontal Merger Guidelines. The principles and analytical frameworks used to assess horizontal mergers apply to vertical mergers. . . .

These Guidelines are intended to assist the business community and antitrust practitioners by increasing the transparency of the analytical process underlying the Agencies' enforcement decisions. They may also assist the courts in developing an appropriate framework for interpreting and applying the antitrust laws in the vertical merger context.

2.   MARKET DEFINITION AND RELATED PRODUCTS

In any merger enforcement action involving a vertical merger, the Agencies will normally identify one or more relevant markets in which the merger may substantially lessen competition. Many of the general purposes and limitations of market definition described in Section 4 of the Horizontal Merger Guidelines are also relevant when the Agencies define markets for vertical mergers, and the Agencies use the methodology set forth in Sections 4.1 and 4.2 of the Horizontal Merger Guidelines to define relevant markets for vertical mergers.

When the Agencies identify a potential competitive concern in a relevant market, they will also specify one or more related products. A related product is a product or service that is supplied by the merged firm, is vertically related to the products and services in the relevant market, and to which access by the merged firm's rivals affects competition in the relevant market. A related product could be, for example, an input, a means of distribution, or access to a set of customers.

> *Example 1: A retail chain buys a manufacturer of cleaning products. In this example, the Agencies may identify two relevant markets. The first potential relevant market is the supply of cleaning products to retail customers in a given geographic area. For this relevant market, the related product is the supply of the cleaning products by the manufacturer to retailers in the geographic area. The second potential relevant market is the supply of cleaning products to retailers in a given geographic area. For this relevant market, the related product is the purchase or distribution of that manufacturer's cleaning products to sell to retail customers in the geographic area.*

3.   MARKET PARTICIPANTS, MARKET SHARES, AND MARKET CONCENTRATION

The Agencies may consider measures of market shares and market concentration in a relevant market as part of their evaluation of competitive effects. The Agencies evaluate market shares and concentration in conjunction with other reasonably available and reliable evidence for the ultimate purpose of determining whether a merger may substantially lessen competition.

The Agencies use the methodology set out in Sections 5.1, 5.2 and 5.3 of the Horizontal Merger Guidelines to measure shares and concentration in a relevant market, but do not rely on changes in concentration as a screen for or indicator of competitive effects from vertical theories of harm.

The Agencies may also consider measures of the competitive significance of the related products as part of their evaluation of competitive effects in a relevant market. One such measure may be the share of the output in a relevant market that uses the related products. If the related products are used in a smaller share of sales in the relevant market the merged firm's control of the related products may be less likely to have substantial effects on competition in the relevant market.

> *Example 2: Company A is a wholesale supplier of orange juice. It seeks to acquire Company B, an owner of orange orchards. The Agencies may consider whether the merger would lessen competition in the wholesale supply of orange juice in region X (the relevant market). The Agencies may identify Company B's supply of oranges as the related product. Company B's oranges are used in fifteen percent of the sales in the relevant market for wholesale supply of orange juice. The Agencies may consider the share of fifteen percent as one indicator of the competitive significance of the related product to participants in the relevant market.*

The Agencies are unlikely to challenge a vertical merger where the parties to the merger have a share in the relevant market of less than 20 percent, and the related product is used in less than 20 percent of the relevant market.

In some circumstances, mergers with shares below the thresholds can give rise to competitive concerns. For example, the share of the relevant market that uses the related product may understate the scope for material effects if the related product is relatively new, and its share of use in the relevant market is rapidly growing. Moreover, a share of 20 percent or more in the relevant market or a related products' share of use in the relevant market of 20 percent or more, or both, does not, on its own, support an inference that the vertical merger is likely to substantially lessen competition. The purpose of these thresholds is not to provide a rigid screen to separate competitively benign mergers from anticompetitive ones. Rather, they provide one way to identify some mergers unlikely to raise competitive concerns and some others for which it is particularly important to examine other competitive factors to arrive at a determination of likely competitive effects.

4.   EVIDENCE OF ADVERSE COMPETITIVE EFFECTS

The Agencies consider any reasonably available and reliable evidence to address the central question of whether a vertical merger may substantially lessen competition. . . .

5.   UNILATERAL EFFECTS

A vertical merger may diminish competition between one merging firm and rivals that trade with, or could trade with, the other merging firm. Whether the elimination of double marginalization resulting from the merger, or cognizable efficiencies, are likely to reduce or reverse the adverse unilateral effects, is addressed in Sections 6 and 8.

This section discusses common types of unilateral effects arising from vertical mergers. Section (a) discusses foreclosure and raising rivals' costs. Section (b) discusses competitively sensitive information. These effects do not exhaust the types of possible unilateral effects.

    a. Foreclosure and Raising Rivals' Costs

A vertical merger may diminish competition by allowing the merged firm to profitably weaken or remove the competitive constraint from one or more of its actual or potential rivals in the relevant market by changing the terms of those rivals' access to one or more related products. For example, the merged firm may be able to raise its rivals' costs by charging a higher price for the related products or by lowering service or product quality. The merged firm could also refuse to supply rivals with the related products altogether ("foreclosure").

. . .

A vertical merger may diminish competition by making it profitable for the merged firm to foreclose rivals in the relevant market by denying them access to a related product. Alternatively, the merger may increase the incentive or ability of the merged firm to raise its rivals' costs or decrease the quality of their rivals' products or services, thereby reducing the competitive constraints imposed by those rival firms. In identifying whether a vertical merger is likely to result in unilateral harm to competition through foreclosure or raising rivals' costs, the Agencies may consider whether:

> (1)   The merged firm's foreclosure of, or raising costs of, one or more rivals would cause those rivals to lose sales (for example, if they are forced out of the market, if they are deterred from innovating, entering or expanding, or cannot finance these activities, or if they have incentives to pass on higher costs through higher prices), or to otherwise compete less aggressively for customers' business;

> (2)   The merged firm's business in the relevant market would benefit (for example if some portion of those lost sales would be diverted to the merged firm);

> (3)   Capturing this benefit through merger may make foreclosure, or raising rivals' costs, profitable even though it would not have been profitable prior to the merger; and,

> (4)   The magnitude of likely foreclosure or raising rivals' costs is not *de minimis* such that it would substantially lessen competition.

Mergers for which each of these conditions are met potentially raise significant competitive concerns and often warrant scrutiny. The next paragraphs provide illustrative examples of the application of this general framework to different settings.

> *Example 3: In Example 2, the merged firm may be able to profitably stop supplying oranges (the related product) to rival orange juice suppliers (in the relevant market). The merged firm will lose the margin on the foregone sales of oranges but may benefit from increased sales of orange juice if foreclosed rivals would lose sales, and some of those sales were diverted to the merged firm. If the benefits outweighed the costs, the merged firm would find it profitable to foreclose. If the likely effect of the foreclosure were to substantially lessen competition in the orange juice market, the merger potentially raises significant competitive concerns and may warrant scrutiny.*

> *Example 4: Company A supplies a component (the related product) to Companies B and C, which each use to make final products in a downstream market (the relevant market). Companies A and B merge. When the merged firm bargains with Company C over the price of the related product, it may be more willing to hold out for higher prices compared to an unintegrated Company A because losing (or delaying) sales of the related product to Company C may be more costly for standalone Company A than for the merged firm. Higher prices paid by Company C for the related product may lead to higher downstream prices.*

> *Example 5: Company A is the sole supplier of an active ingredient (the related product) for a pharmaceutical drug made by Company B (the relevant market). Company C is considering entering the relevant market. If Company B buys Company A, the merged firm may find it profitable to refuse to supply the ingredient to any rivals or potential rivals if doing so would deter Company C from entering, or prevent it from financing entry, by requiring it to start producing both the active ingredient and the drug at the same time (two stage entry). If refusing to supply entrants was profitable for the merged firm, and if the likely result was that competition in the relevant market would be substantially lessened compared to the level that would have obtained absent the merger, the merger potentially raises significant concerns and may warrant scrutiny.*

> *Example 6: Company A distributes wholesale consumer cleaning products to retailers (the relevant market). It buys Company B, which makes one of the brands that Company A distributes. The merged firm may find it profitable to raise the price of wholesale distribution of rival brands (the related products) after the merger, even if the price rise was not profitable for the unintegrated Company A. As a result of the merger, the merged firm captures the upstream margin on any sales that are diverted from rival brands to Company B's brand. If the merged firm has a sufficiently*

important position in the relevant market, and the price rise it imposes on the wholesale distribution of rival brands is sufficiently high, competition may be substantially lessened compared to the level that would have obtained absent the merger, the merger potentially raises significant concerns and may warrant scrutiny.

b. Access to Competitively Sensitive Information

In a vertical merger, the combined firm may, through the acquisition, gain access to and control of sensitive business information about its upstream or downstream rivals that was unavailable to it before the merger. For example, a downstream rival to the merged firm may have been a premerger customer of the upstream firm. Post-merger, the downstream component of the merged firm could now have access to its rival's sensitive business information. Access to a rival's competitively sensitive information can, in some circumstances, be used by the merged firm to moderate its competitive response to its rival's competitive actions, for example it may preempt or react quickly to a rival's procompetitive business actions. Under such conditions, rivals may see less competitive value in taking procompetitive actions. Relatedly, rivals may refrain from doing business with the merged firm rather than risk that the merged firm would use their competitively sensitive business information as described above. They may become less effective competitors if they are forced to rely on less preferred trading partners, or if they pay higher prices because they have fewer competing options.

6. ELIMINATION OF DOUBLE MARGINALIZATION

Elimination of double marginalization can occur when two vertically related firms that individually charge a profit-maximizing margin on their products choose to merge. Absent the merger, the downstream merging firm would ignore any benefit to the upstream merging firm from setting a lower downstream price and making higher sales. But if the two merge, the resulting firm will benefit from both margins on any additional sales, and capturing the upstream margin, through merger, may make the price reduction profitable even though it would not have been profitable prior to the merger. Elimination of double marginalization may thus benefit both the merged firm and buyers of the downstream product or service.

The agencies generally rely on the parties to identify and demonstrate whether and how the merger eliminates double marginalization. There will be no elimination of double marginalization if the downstream firm cannot use the inputs from the upstream one, for example, because it uses an incompatible technology. The effects of the elimination of double marginalization may be lower if, prior to the merger, the merging parties already engaged in contracting that aligned their incentives, for example by using a two-part tariff with a fixed fee and low unit prices that incorporate no, or a small, margin. The effects of the elimination of double marginalization in the downstream market may also be offset by a change in pricing incentives working in the opposite direction: if the merged firm raises its price in the downstream market, downstream rivals may increase their sales, which could increase their demand for inputs from the merged firm's upstream business.

Capturing this benefit through merger may make the downstream price increase more profitable.

The Agencies will not challenge a merger if the net effect of elimination of double marginalization means that the merger is unlikely to be anticompetitive in any relevant market.

7.   COORDINATED EFFECTS

In some cases, a vertical merger may diminish competition by enabling or encouraging postmerger coordinated interaction among firms in the relevant market that harms customers. Section 7 of the Horizontal Merger Guidelines describes how the Agencies evaluate coordinated effects. . . .

A vertical merger may enhance the market's vulnerability to coordination by eliminating or hobbling a maverick firm that otherwise plays or would play an important role in preventing or limiting anticompetitive coordination in the relevant market. For example, the merged firm could use its power over a product or service in a related product to harm the ability of a non-merging maverick in the relevant market to compete, thereby increasing the likelihood of coordinated interaction among the merged firm and rivals participating in that market.

Coordinated effects may also arise in other ways, including when changes in market structure or the merged firm's access to confidential information facilitate (a) reaching a tacit agreement among market participants, (b) detecting cheating on such an agreement, or (c) punishing cheating firms.

> *Example 7: The merger brings together a manufacturer of components and a maker of final products. If the component manufacturer supplies rival makers of final products, it will have information about how much they are making, and will be better able to detect cheating on a tacit agreement to limit supplies. As a result the merger may make the tacit agreement more effective.*

Some effects of a vertical merger may make the market less vulnerable to coordination. For example, a vertical merger's elimination of double marginalization (see Section 6) may increase the merged firm's incentive to cheat on a tacit agreement, thereby reducing the risk of coordinated effects.

8.   EFFICIENCIES

Because vertical mergers combine complementary economic functions and eliminate contracting frictions, they have the potential to create cognizable efficiencies that benefit competition and consumers. Vertical mergers bring together assets used at different levels in the supply chain to make a final product. A single firm able to coordinate how these assets are used may be able to streamline production, inventory management, or distribution, or create innovative products in ways that would have been hard to achieve though arm's length contracts.

The Agencies will evaluate efficiency claims by the parties using the approach set forth in Section 10 of the Horizontal Merger Guidelines. The Agencies do not challenge a merger if cognizable efficiencies are of a character and magnitude such that the merger is unlikely to be anticompetitive in any relevant market.

Notes

1.   The American Bar Association's Section of Antitrust Law has submitted comments on these guidelines. The Section objects to a possible contrast between the statement that "[t]he Agencies are unlikely to challenge a vertical merger when the parties to the merger have a share in the relevant market of less than 20 percent, and the related product is used in less than 20 percent of the relevant market" and the statement that "[t]he purpose of these thresholds is not to provide a rigid screen to separate competitively benign mergers from anticompetitive ones." The comments note that the Horizontal Merger Guidelines state that "[m]ergers involving an increase in the HHI of less than 100 points are unlikely to have adverse competitive effects and ordinarily require no further analysis."

The Section suggests that "the Agencies should adopt a higher relevant market share threshold and provide clearer guidance to business about the circumstances in which the Agencies will deviate from a screen." Is that point well-taken, or is the problem that the effects of vertical mergers are simply more variable and less well understood? Even if they are, could the increased certainty that the Section prefers still be preferable? Do you think the Section bolsters its argument with the additional suggestion that "[i]ncrease the 20 percent quasi-safe harbor to a number in the range of 30 to 40 percent," or does that simply suggest that the real goal is less scrutiny of vertical mergers?

In contrast to the Antitrust Section's suggestion, Steven Salop, who has been an advocate of more vigorous vertical merger enforcement, joined with others to provide this description of a situation in which the 20 percent threshold for related products does not, they say, capture the problem:

> Consider the acquisition by an automobile original equipment manufacturer ("OEM") of one of the only two manufacturers of mechanisms to control convertible tops. Assume further that the two competing mechanisms are very close substitutes, which leads to pre-merger prices that are very close to marginal cost. The competitive effects problem involves input foreclosure, with convertible automobiles as the relevant downstream market and mechanisms as the upstream related product.

> Suppose that the merging mechanism manufacturer has a share of (just under) 20%, while the other mechanism manufacturer has a share of (just over) 80%. Suppose the acquiring automobile OEM has share of convertibles of (just under) 20%, and that convertibles are a relevant output market. This vertical merger would fall within the 20-20 safe harbor.

If the merged firm raises the price of its mechanisms to other convertible automobile manufacturers, the competing mechanism firm would gain the power to raise its mechanism prices to the other convertible OEMs. As a result, there would be diversion to the downstream merging firm and convertible prices likely would rise. The 20-20 safe harbor entirely misses the competitive problem here because it does not account for concentration in the supply of the related product. Note that the harm from this input foreclosure does not require the downstream merging firm to have a high share or for there to be high concentration in the convertible automobile market.

Jonathan B. Baker et al., Recommendations and Comments on the Draft Vertical Merger Guidelines [hereafter, "Recommendations and Comments"], Feb. 24, 2020, https://media.justice.gov/vod/atr/comments-draft-vmg/dvmg-0017.pdf, at 13-14.

Is that criticism well-taken, or is that why the draft guidelines propose a safe-ish, not a safe, harbor? Are the commenters correct that the 20% threshold unwisely neglect other aspects of the structure of the market for the related product?

2.   The ABA Antitrust Section also has suggestions regarding the "related product" concept:

Clarify the analysis for defining "related product" markets. For example, specify whether there are situations under which a full market definition is required; the required degree of direct or indirect "relatedness;" and when transactions that do not involve adjacent, linearly-related firms may fall within the provision.

Given that the draft Guidelines introduce the "related product" concept, are those suggestions well-taken? Are the "related product" concept and the guidelines description of how it will be applied an end-run around the usual requirements of market definition and analysis? If so, is that an appropriate response to the recent push toward more direct focus on effects and less focus on market definition? On this point, the Recommendations and Comments quoted above have this to say:

The agencies do not explain how output is measured. We would expect the agencies to use a share of output measure that best captures the foreclosure threat, in order to tie the measure to the competitive effects concerns set forth later. For example, it is not made clear whether the agencies will measure the "units" in the numerator and denominator in terms of volume or revenue, which could make a substantial difference if inputs or outputs are differentiated.

Recommendations and Comments, at 9.

3.   In section 5.a of the draft guidelines, one of the conditions for foreclosure is stated as "[c]apturing this benefit [of foreclosure] through merger may make foreclosure, or raising rivals' costs, profitable even though it would not have been profitable prior to the merger." Often the "benefits" of foreclosure could be obtained by contract as well as by merger. For example, the party that would benefit could pay the vertically related to engage in the exclusionary conduct. Do the draft

guidelines require a challenger of a vertical merger to prove that this sort of contractual foreclosure would have been impossible or unprofitable? Would it require them to do so even if merger would make the exclusionary conduct more likely?

should it matter that you are engaging with an antitrust violator?

6. Standing and Procedural Issues

6.1. Standing Issues

Antitrust law in the U.S. has a number of standing and standing-related doctrines that determine whether private plaintiffs may bring suit to challenge particular conduct. Among those doctrines are those that address "antitrust injury," indirect purchasers from the defendants, and a more general standing test. *See* Brunswick Corp. v. Pueblo Bowl-O-Mat, Inc., 429 U.S. 477 (1977) (antitrust injury); Atlantic Richfield v. USA Petroleum, 495 U.S. 328 (1990) (same); Hanover Shoe, Inc. v. United Shoe Machinery Corp., 392 U.S. 481 (1968) (indirect purchaser); Illinois Brick Co. v. Illinois, 431 U.S. 720 (1977) (same); Associated Gen. Contractors v. California State Council of Carpenters, 459 U.S. 519 (1983) (standing); Blue Shield of Virginia v. McCready, 457 U.S. 465 (1982) (same). The following case takes up the indirect-purchaser issue in the context of Apple's App Store.

Apple Inc. v. Pepper
5~~87~~ U.S. ___ (2019)

[handwritten margin note: This is a probably a two-sided platform, so it is unclear why Ohio or. Am Ex not mentioned/discussed]

[handwritten note: "This is clearly not a case of pass-on"]

JUSTICE KAVANAUGH delivered the opinion of the Court.

In 2007, Apple started selling iPhones. The next year, Apple launched the retail App Store, an electronic store where iPhone owners can purchase iPhone applications from Apple. Those "apps" enable iPhone owners to send messages, take photos, watch videos, buy clothes, order food, arrange transportation, purchase concert tickets, donate to charities, and the list goes on. "There's an app for that" has become part of the 21st-century American lexicon.

In this case, however, several consumers contend that Apple charges too much for apps. The consumers argue, in particular, that Apple has monopolized the retail market for the sale of apps and has unlawfully used its monopolistic power to charge consumers higher-than-competitive prices.

A claim that a monopolistic retailer (here, Apple) has used its monopoly to overcharge consumers is a classic antitrust claim. But Apple asserts that the consumer plaintiffs in this case may not sue Apple because they supposedly were not "direct purchasers" from Apple under our decision in *Illinois Brick Co.* v. *Illinois*, 431 U. S. 720, 745–746 (1977). We disagree. The plaintiffs purchased apps directly from Apple and therefore are direct purchasers under *Illinois Brick*. At this early pleadings stage of the litigation, we do not assess the merits of the plaintiffs' antitrust claims against Apple, nor do we consider any other defenses Apple might have. We merely hold that the *Illinois Brick* direct-purchaser rule does not bar these plaintiffs from suing Apple under the antitrust laws. We affirm the judgment of the U. S. Court of Appeals for the Ninth Circuit.

I

. . . By contract and through technological limitations, the App Store is the only place where iPhone owners may lawfully buy apps.

For the most part, Apple does not itself create apps. Rather, independent app developers create apps. Those independent app developers then contract with Apple to make the apps available to iPhone owners in the App Store.

Through the App Store, Apple sells the apps directly to iPhone owners. To sell an app in the App Store, app developers must pay Apple a $99 annual membership fee. Apple requires that the retail sales price end in $0.99, but otherwise allows the app developers to set the retail price. Apple keeps 30 percent of the sales price, no matter what the sales price might be. In other words, Apple pockets a 30 percent commission on every app sale.

In 2011, four iPhone owners sued Apple. They allege that Apple has unlawfully monopolized "the iPhone apps aftermarket." The plaintiffs allege that, via the App Store, Apple locks iPhone owners "into buying apps only from Apple and paying Apple's 30% fee, even if " the iPhone owners wish "to buy apps elsewhere or pay less." According to the complaint, that 30 percent commission is "pure profit" for Apple and, in a competitive environment with other retailers, "Apple would be under considerable pressure to substantially lower its 30% profit margin." plaintiffs allege that in a competitive market, they would be able to "choose between Apple's high-priced App Store and less costly alternatives." And they allege that they have "paid more for their iPhone apps than they would have paid in a competitive market."

Apple moved to dismiss the complaint, arguing that the iPhone owners were not direct purchasers from Apple and therefore may not sue. In *Illinois Brick*, this Court held that direct purchasers may sue antitrust violators, but also ruled that indirect purchasers may not sue. The District Court agreed with Apple and dismissed the complaint. According to the District Court, the iPhone owners were not direct purchasers from Apple because the app developers, not Apple, set the consumers' purchase price. The Ninth Circuit reversed. The Ninth Circuit concluded that the iPhone owners were direct purchasers under *Illinois Brick* because the iPhone owners purchased apps directly from Apple. According to the Ninth Circuit, *Illinois Brick* means that a consumer may not sue an alleged monopolist who is two or more steps removed from the consumer in a vertical distribution chain. Here, however, the consumers purchased directly from Apple, the alleged monopolist. Therefore, the Ninth Circuit held that the iPhone owners could sue Apple for allegedly monopolizing the sale of iPhone apps and charging higher-than-competitive prices. We granted certiorari.

II

A

The plaintiffs' allegations boil down to one straightforward claim: that Apple exercises monopoly power in the retail market for the sale of apps and has unlawfully used its monopoly power to force iPhone owners to pay Apple higher-than-competitive prices for apps. According to the plaintiffs, when iPhone owners want to purchase an app, they have only two options: (1) buy the app from Apple's App Store at a higher-than-competitive price or (2) do not buy the app at all. Any iPhone owners who are dissatisfied with the selection of apps available in the App Store or with the price of the apps available in the App Store are out of luck, or so the plaintiffs allege.

The sole question presented at this early stage of the case is whether these consumers are proper plaintiffs for this kind of antitrust suit—in particular, our precedents ask, whether the consumers were "direct purchasers" from Apple. It is undisputed that the iPhone owners bought the apps directly from Apple. Therefore, under *Illinois Brick*, the iPhone owners were direct purchasers who may sue Apple for alleged monopolization.

That straightforward conclusion follows from the text of the antitrust laws and from our precedents.

First is text: Section 2 of the Sherman Act makes it unlawful for any person to "monopolize, or attempt to monopolize, or combine or conspire with any other person or persons, to monopolize any part of the trade or commerce among the several States, or with foreign nations." Section 4 of the Clayton Act in turn provides that "*any person* who shall be injured in his business or property by reason of anything forbidden in the antitrust laws may sue . . . the defendant . . . and shall recover threefold the damages by him sustained, and the cost of suit, including a reasonable attorney's fee." 15 U. S. C. §15(a) (emphasis added). The broad text of §4—"any person" who has been "injured" by an antitrust violator may sue—readily covers consumers who purchase goods or services at higher-than-competitive prices from an allegedly monopolistic retailer.

Second is precedent: Applying §4, we have consistently stated that "the immediate buyers from the alleged antitrust violators" may maintain a suit against the antitrust violators. *Kansas* v. *UtiliCorp United Inc.*, 497 U. S. 199, 207 (1990); see also *Illinois Brick*, 431 U. S., at 745–746. At the same time, incorporating principles of proximate cause into §4, we have ruled that *indirect* purchasers who are two or more steps removed from the violator in a distribution chain may not sue. Our decision in *Illinois Brick* established a bright-line rule that authorizes suits by *direct* purchasers but bars suits by *indirect* purchasers.

The facts of *Illinois Brick* illustrate the rule. Illinois Brick Company manufactured and distributed concrete blocks. Illinois Brick sold the blocks primarily to masonry contractors, and those contractors in turn sold masonry structures to general contractors. Those general contractors in turn sold their services for larger construction projects to the State of Illinois, the ultimate consumer of the blocks.

The consumer State of Illinois sued the manufacturer Illinois Brick. The State alleged that Illinois Brick had engaged in a conspiracy to fix the price of concrete blocks. According to the complaint, the State paid more for the concrete blocks than it would have paid absent the price-fixing conspiracy. The monopoly overcharge allegedly flowed all the way down the distribution chain to the ultimate consumer, who was the State of Illinois.

This Court ruled that the State could not bring an antitrust action against Illinois Brick, the alleged violator, because the State had not purchased concrete blocks directly from Illinois Brick. The proper plaintiff to bring that claim against Illinois Brick, the Court stated, would be an entity that had purchased directly from Illinois Brick. *Ibid.*

The bright-line rule of *Illinois Brick*, as articulated in that case and as we reiterated in *UtiliCorp*, means that indirect purchasers who are two or more steps removed from the antitrust violator in a distribution chain may not sue. By contrast, direct purchasers—that is, those who are "the immediate buyers from the alleged antitrust violators"—may sue. *UtiliCorp*, 497 U. S., at 207.

For example, if manufacturer A sells to retailer B, and retailer B sells to consumer C, then C may not sue A. But B may sue A if A is an antitrust violator. And C may sue B if B is an antitrust violator. That is the straightforward rule of *Illinois Brick*. In this case, unlike in *Illinois Brick*, the iPhone owners are not consumers at the bottom of a vertical distribution chain who are attempting to sue manufacturers at the top of the chain. There is no intermediary in the distribution chain between Apple and the consumer. The iPhone owners purchase apps directly from the retailer Apple, who is the alleged antitrust violator. The iPhone owners pay the alleged overcharge directly to Apple. The absence of an intermediary is dispositive. Under *Illinois Brick*, the iPhone owners are direct purchasers from Apple and are proper plaintiffs to maintain this antitrust suit.

B

All of that seems simple enough. But Apple argues strenuously against that seemingly simple conclusion, and we address its arguments carefully. For this kind of retailer case, Apple's theory is that *Illinois Brick* allows consumers to sue only the party who sets the retail price, whether or not that party sells the good or service directly to the complaining party. Apple says that its theory accords with the economics of the transaction. Here, Apple argues that the app developers, not Apple, set the retail price charged to consumers, which according to Apple means that the consumers may not sue Apple. We see three main problems with Apple's "who sets the price" theory.

First, Apple's theory contradicts statutory text and precedent. As we explained above, the text of §4 broadly affords injured parties a right to sue under the antitrust laws. And our precedent in *Illinois Brick* established a bright-line rule where direct purchasers such as the consumers here may sue antitrust violators from whom they purchased a good or service. *Illinois Brick*, as we read the opinion, was not based on an economic theory about who set the price. Rather, *Illinois Brick* sought to ensure an effective and efficient litigation scheme in antitrust cases. To do so, the

Court drew a bright line that allowed direct purchasers to sue but barred indirect purchasers from suing. When there is no intermediary between the purchaser and the antitrust violator, the purchaser may sue. The *Illinois Brick* bright-line rule is grounded on the "belief that simplified administration improves antitrust enforcement." Apple's theory would require us to rewrite the rationale of *Illinois Brick* and to gut the longstanding bright-line rule.

To the extent that *Illinois Brick* leaves any ambiguity about whether a direct purchaser may sue an antitrust violator, we should resolve that ambiguity in the direction of the statutory text. And under the text, direct purchasers from monopolistic retailers are proper plaintiffs to sue those retailers.

Second, in addition to deviating from statutory text and precedent, Apple's proposed rule is not persuasive economically or legally. Apple's effort to transform *Illinois Brick* from a direct-purchaser rule to a "who sets the price" rule would draw an arbitrary and unprincipled line among retailers based on retailers' financial arrangements with their manufacturers or suppliers.

In the retail context, the price charged by a retailer to a consumer is often a result (at least in part) of the price charged by the manufacturer or supplier to the retailer, or of negotiations between the manufacturer or supplier and the retailer. Those agreements between manufacturer or supplier and retailer may take myriad forms, including for example a markup pricing model or a commission pricing model. In a traditional markup pricing model, a hypothetical monopolistic retailer might pay $6 to the manufacturer and then sell the product for $10, keeping $4 for itself. In a commission pricing model, the retailer might pay nothing to the manufacturer; agree with the manufacturer that the retailer will sell the product for $10 and keep 40 percent of the sales price; and then sell the product for $10, send $6 back to the manufacturer, and keep $4. In those two different pricing scenarios, everything turns out to be economically the same for the manufacturer, retailer, and consumer.

Yet Apple's proposed rule would allow a consumer to sue the monopolistic retailer in the former situation but not the latter. In other words, under Apple's rule a consumer could sue a monopolistic retailer when the retailer set the retail price by marking up the price it had paid the manufacturer or supplier for the good or service. But a consumer could not sue a monopolistic retailer when the manufacturer or supplier set the retail price and the retailer took a commission on each sale.

Apple's line-drawing does not make a lot of sense, other than as a way to gerrymander Apple out of this and similar lawsuits. In particular, we fail to see why the form of the upstream arrangement between the manufacturer or supplier and the retailer should determine whether a monopolistic retailer can be sued by a downstream consumer who has purchased a good or service directly from the retailer and has paid a higher-than-competitive price because of the retailer's unlawful monopolistic conduct. As the Court of Appeals aptly stated, "the distinction between a markup and a commission is immaterial." A leading antitrust treatise likewise states: "Denying standing because 'title' never passes to a broker is an overly lawyered approach that ignores the reality that a distribution system that relies on brokerage is economically indistinguishable from one that relies on purchaser-resellers." If a retailer has engaged in unlawful monopolistic conduct that has caused consumers to pay higher-than-competitive prices, it does not matter how the retailer structured its relationship with an upstream manufacturer or supplier— whether, for example, the retailer employed a markup or kept a commission.

To be sure, if the monopolistic retailer's conduct has not caused the consumer to pay a higher-than-competitive price, then the plaintiff's damages will be zero. Here, for example, if the competitive commission rate were 10 percent rather than 30 percent but Apple could prove that app developers in a 10 percent commission system would always set a higher price such that consumers would pay the same retail price regardless of whether Apple's commission was 10 percent or 30 percent, then the consumers' damages would presumably be zero. But we cannot assume in all cases—as Apple would necessarily have us do—that a monopolistic retailer who keeps a commission does not ever cause the consumer to pay a higher-than-competitive price. We find no persuasive legal or economic basis for such a blanket assertion.

In short, we do not understand the relevance of the upstream market structure in deciding whether a downstream consumer may sue a monopolistic retailer. Apple's rule would elevate form (what is the precise arrangement between manufacturers or suppliers and retailers?) over substance (is the consumer paying a higher price because of the monopolistic retailer's actions?). If the retailer's unlawful monopolistic conduct caused a consumer to pay the retailer a higher-than-competitive price, the consumer is entitled to sue the retailer under the antitrust laws.

Third, if accepted, Apple's theory would provide a roadmap for monopolistic retailers to structure transactions with manufacturers or suppliers so as to evade antitrust claims by consumers and thereby thwart effective antitrust enforcement.

Consider a traditional supplier-retailer relationship, in which the retailer purchases a product from the supplier and sells the product with a markup to consumers. Under Apple's proposed rule, a retailer, instead of buying the product from the supplier, could arrange to sell the product for the supplier without purchasing it from the supplier. In other words, rather than paying the supplier a certain price for the product and then marking up the price to sell the product to consumers, the retailer could collect the price of the product from consumers and remit only a fraction of that price to the supplier.

That restructuring would allow a monopolistic retailer to insulate itself from antitrust suits by consumers, even in situations where a monopolistic retailer is using its monopoly to charge higher-than-competitive prices to consumers. We decline to green-light monopolistic retailers to exploit their market position in that way. We refuse to rubber-stamp such a blatant evasion of statutory text and judicial precedent.

In sum, Apple's theory would disregard statutory text and precedent, create an unprincipled and economically senseless distinction among monopolistic retailers, and furnish monopolistic retailers with a how-to guide for evasion of the antitrust laws.

C

In arguing that the Court should transform the direct-purchaser rule into a "who sets the price" rule, Apple insists that the three reasons that the Court identified in *Illinois Brick* for adopting the direct-purchaser rule apply to this case—even though the consumers here (unlike in *Illinois Brick*) were direct purchasers from the alleged monopolist. The *Illinois Brick* Court listed three reasons for barring indirect-purchaser suits: (1) facilitating more effective enforcement of antitrust laws; (2) avoiding complicated damages calculations; and (3) eliminating duplicative damages against antitrust defendants. As we said in *UtiliCorp*, however, the bright-line rule of *Illinois Brick* means that there is no reason to ask whether the rationales of *Illinois Brick* "apply with equal force" in every individual case. 497 U. S., at 216. We should not engage in "an unwarranted and counterproductive exercise to litigate a series of exceptions." *Id.,* at 217.

But even if we engage with this argument, we conclude that the three *Illinois Brick* rationales—whether considered individually or together—cut strongly in the plaintiffs' favor here, not Apple's.

First, Apple argues that barring the iPhone owners from suing Apple will better promote effective enforcement of the antitrust laws. Apple posits that allowing only the upstream app developers—and not the downstream consumers—to sue Apple would mean more effective enforcement of the antitrust laws. We do not agree. Leaving consumers at the mercy of monopolistic retailers simply because upstream suppliers could *also* sue the retailers makes little sense and would directly contradict the longstanding goal of effective private enforcement and consumer protection in antitrust cases.

Second, Apple warns that calculating the damages in successful consumer antitrust suits against monopolistic retailers might be complicated. It is true that it may be hard to determine what the retailer would have charged in a competitive market. Expert testimony will often be necessary. But that is hardly unusual in antitrust cases. *Illinois Brick* is not a get-out-of-court-free card for monopolistic retailers to play any time that a damages calculation might be complicated. *Illinois Brick* surely did not wipe out consumer antitrust suits against monopolistic retailers from whom the consumers purchased goods or services at higher-than-competitive prices. Moreover, the damages calculation may be just as complicated in a retailer markup case as it is in a retailer commission case. Yet Apple apparently accepts consumers suing monopolistic retailers in a retailer markup case. If Apple accepts that kind of suit, then Apple should also accept consumers suing monopolistic retailers in a retailer commission case.

Third, Apple claims that allowing consumers to sue will result in "conflicting claims to a common fund—the amount of the alleged overcharge." *Illinois Brick*, 431 U.S., at 737. Apple is incorrect. This is not a case where multiple parties at different levels of a distribution chain are trying to all recover the same passed-through overcharge initially levied by the manufacturer at the top of the chain. Cf.

id., at 726–727; *Hanover Shoe, Inc.* v. *United Shoe Machinery Corp.*, 392 U. S. 481, 483–484 (1968). If the iPhone owners prevail, they will be entitled to the *full amount* of the unlawful overcharge that they paid to Apple. The overcharge has not been passed on by anyone to anyone. Unlike in *Illinois Brick*, there will be no need to "trace the effect of the overcharge through each step in the distribution chain."

It is true that Apple's alleged anticompetitive conduct may leave Apple subject to multiple suits by different plaintiffs. But *Illinois Brick* did not purport to bar multiple liability that is unrelated to passing an overcharge down a chain of distribution. Basic antitrust law tells us that the "mere fact that an antitrust violation produces two different classes of victims hardly entails that their injuries are duplicative of one another." Multiple suits are not atypical when the intermediary in a distribution chain is a bottleneck monopolist or monopsonist (or both) between the manufacturer on the one end and the consumer on the other end. A retailer who is both a monopolist and a monopsonist may be liable to different classes of plaintiffs—both to downstream consumers and to upstream suppliers—when the retailer's unlawful conduct affects both the downstream and upstream markets.

Here, some downstream iPhone consumers have sued Apple on a monopoly theory. And it could be that some upstream app developers will also sue Apple on a monopsony theory. In this instance, the two suits would rely on fundamentally different theories of harm and would not assert dueling claims to a "common fund," as that term was used in *Illinois Brick*. The consumers seek damages based on the difference between the price they paid and the competitive price. The app developers would seek lost profits that they could have earned in a competitive retail market. *Illinois Brick* does not bar either category of suit. In short, the three *Illinois Brick* rationales do not persuade us to remake *Illinois Brick* and to bar direct-purchaser suits against monopolistic retailers who employ commissions rather than markups. The plaintiffs seek to hold retailers to account if the retailers engage in unlawful anticompetitive conduct that harms consumers who purchase from those retailers. That is why we have antitrust law.

* * *

Ever since Congress overwhelmingly passed and President Benjamin Harrison signed the Sherman Act in 1890, "protecting consumers from monopoly prices" has been "the central concern of antitrust." The consumers here purchased apps directly from Apple, and they allege that Apple used its monopoly power over the retail apps market to charge higher-than-competitive prices. Our decision in *Illinois Brick* does not bar the consumers from suing Apple for Apple's allegedly monopolistic conduct. We affirm the judgment of the U. S. Court of Appeals for the Ninth Circuit.

It is so ordered.

"This is clearly a case of pass-on"

JUSTICE GORSUCH, with whom THE CHIEF JUSTICE, JUSTICE THOMAS, and JUSTICE ALITO join, dissenting.

More than 40 years ago, in *Illinois Brick Co.* v. *Illinois*, 431 U. S. 720 (1977), this Court held that an antitrust plaintiff can't sue a defendant for overcharging *someone else* who might (or might not) have passed on all (or some) of the overcharge to him. *Illinois Brick* held that these convoluted "pass on" theories of damages violate traditional principles of proximate causation and that the right plaintiff to bring suit is the one on whom the overcharge immediately and surely fell. Yet today the Court lets a pass-on case proceed. It does so by recasting *Illinois Brick* as a rule forbidding only suits where the plaintiff does not contract directly with the defendant. This replaces a rule of proximate cause and economic reality with an easily manipulated and formalistic rule of contractual privity. That's not how antitrust law is supposed to work, and it's an uncharitable way of treating a precedent which— whatever its flaws—is far more sensible than the rule the Court installs in its place.

. . .

II

The lawsuit before us depends on just the sort of pass-on theory that *Illinois Brick* forbids. The plaintiffs bought apps from third-party app developers (or manufacturers) in Apple's retail Internet App Store, at prices set by the developers. The lawsuit alleges that Apple is a monopolist retailer and that the 30% commission it charges developers for the right to sell through its platform represents an anticompetitive price. The problem is that the 30% commission falls initially on the developers. So if the commission is in fact a monopolistic overcharge, the *developers* are the parties who are directly injured by it. Plaintiffs can be injured *only* if the developers are able and choose to pass on the overcharge to them in the form of higher app prices that the developers alone control. Plaintiffs admitted as much in the district court, where they described their theory of injury this way: "[I]f Apple tells the developer . . . we're going to take this 30 percent commission . . . what's the developer going to do? The developer is going to increase its price to cover Apple's . . . demanded profit."

Because this is *exactly* the kind of "pass-on theory" *Illinois Brick* rejected, it should come as no surprise that the concerns animating that decision are also implicated. Like other pass-on theories, plaintiffs' theory will necessitate a complex inquiry into how Apple's conduct affected third-party pricing decisions. And it will raise difficult questions about apportionment of damages between app developers and their customers, along with the risk of duplicative damages awards. If anything, plaintiffs' claims present these difficulties even more starkly than did the claims at issue in *Illinois Brick*.

Consider first the question of causation. To determine if Apple's conduct damaged plaintiffs at all (and if so, the magnitude of their damages), a court will first have to explore whether and to what extent each individual app developer was able—and then opted—to pass on the 30% commission to its consumers in the form of higher app prices. Sorting this out, if it can be done at all, will entail wrestling with "'complicated theories'" about "how the relevant market variables would have behaved had there been no overcharge." Will the court hear testimony to determine the market power of each app developer, how each set its prices, and what it might have charged consumers for apps if Apple's commission had been lower? Will the court also consider expert testimony analyzing how market factors might have influenced developers' capacity and willingness to pass on Apple's alleged monopoly overcharge? And will the court then somehow extrapolate its findings to all of the tens of thousands of developers who sold apps through the App Store at different prices and times over the course of years?

if Apple charges 30%.

This causation inquiry will be complicated further by Apple's requirement that all app prices end in $0.99. As plaintiffs acknowledge, this rule has caused prices for the "vast majority" of apps to "cluster" at exactly $0.99. And a developer charging $0.99 for its app can't raise its price by just enough to recover the 30-cent commission. Instead, if the developer wants to pass on the commission to consumers, it has to more than double its price to $1.99 (doubling the commission in the process), which could significantly affect its sales. In short, because Apple's 99-cent rule creates a strong disincentive for developers to raise their prices, it makes plaintiffs' pass-on theory of injury even harder to prove. Yet the court will have to consider all of this when determining what damages, if any, plaintiffs suffered as a result of Apple's allegedly excessive 30% commission.[2]

Plaintiffs' claims will also necessitate "massive efforts to apportion the recovery among all potential plaintiffs that could have absorbed part of the overcharge," including both consumers and app developers. If, as plaintiffs contend, Apple's 30% commission is a monopolistic overcharge, then the app developers have a claim against Apple to recover whatever portion of the commission they did not pass on to consumers. Before today, *Hanover Shoe* would have prevented Apple from reducing its liability to the developers by arguing that they had passed on the overcharge to consumers. But the Court's holding that *Illinois Brick* doesn't govern this situation surely must mean *Hanover Shoe* doesn't either. So courts will have to divvy up the commissions Apple collected between the developers and the consumers. To do that, they'll have to figure out which party bore what portion of the overcharge in every purchase. And if the developers bring suit separately from the consumers, Apple might be at risk of duplicative damages awards totaling more than the full amount it collected in commissions. To avoid that possibility, it may turn out that the developers are necessary parties who will have to be joined in the plaintiffs' lawsuit. See Fed. Rule Civ. Proc. 19(a)(1)(B); *Illinois Brick*, 431 U. S., at 739 (explaining that "[t]hese absent potential claimants

---

[2] Plaintiffs haven't argued (and so have forfeited in this Court any argument) that Apple's imposition of the 99-cent rule was *itself* an antitrust violation that injured consumers by raising the price of apps above competitive levels. They didn't mention the 99-cent rule in their complaint in district court or in their briefs to the court of appeals. And, as I've noted, they concede that they are seeking damages "based solely on" the 30% commission. Brief in Opposition 5.

would seem to fit the classic definition of 'necessary parties,' for purposes of compulsory joinder").[3]

III

The United States and its antitrust regulators agree with all of this, so how does the Court reach such a different conclusion? Seizing on *Illinois Brick*'s use of the shorthand phrase "direct purchasers" to describe the parties immediately injured by the monopoly overcharge in that case, the Court (re)characterizes *Illinois Brick* as a rule that anyone who purchases goods directly from an alleged antitrust violator can sue, while anyone who doesn't, can't. Under this revisionist version of *Illinois Brick*, the dispositive question becomes whether an "intermediary in the distribution chain" stands between the plaintiff and the defendant. And because the plaintiff app purchasers in this case happen to have purchased apps directly from Apple, the Court reasons, they may sue.

This exalts form over substance. Instead of focusing on the traditional proximate cause question where the alleged overcharge is first (and thus surely) felt, the Court's test turns on who happens to be in privity of contract with whom. But we've long recognized that antitrust law should look at "the economic reality of the relevant transactions" rather than "formal conceptions of contract law." And this case illustrates why. To evade the Court's test, all Apple must do is amend its contracts. Instead of collecting payments for apps sold in the App Store and remitting the balance (less its commission) to developers, Apple can simply specify that consumers' payments will flow the other way: directly to the developers, who will then remit commissions to Apple. No antitrust reason exists to treat these contractual arrangements differently, and doing so will only induce firms to abandon their preferred—and presumably more efficient—distribution arrangements in favor of less efficient ones, all so they might avoid an arbitrary legal rule.

Nor does *Illinois Brick* come close to endorsing such a blind formalism. Yes, as the Court notes, the plaintiff in *Illinois Brick* did contract directly with an intermediary rather than with the putative antitrust violator. But *Illinois Brick*'s rejection of pass-on claims, and its explanation of the difficulties those claims present, had nothing to do with privity of contract. Instead and as we have seen, its rule and reasoning grew from the "general tendency of the law . . . not to go beyond" the party that first felt the sting of the alleged overcharge, and from the

---

[3] The Court denies that allowing both consumers and developers to sue over the same allegedly unlawful commission will "result in 'conflicting claims to a common fund'" as *Illinois Brick* feared. *Ante*, at 12. But Apple charged only one commission on each sale. So even assuming for argument's sake that the 30% commission was entirely illegal, Apple can only be required to pay out in damages, at most, the full amount it received in commissions. To their credit, even plaintiffs have conceded as much, acknowledging that because "there is only *one 30% markup*," any claim by the developers against Apple would necessarily be seeking "a piece of the same 30% pie." Brief in Opposition 12. It's a mystery why the Court refuses to accept that sensible concession.

[handwritten margin note: will be messy regardless of who the money go to.]

complications that can arise when courts attempt to discern whether and to what degree damages were passed on to others. The Court today risks replacing a cogent rule about proximate cause with a pointless and easily evaded imposter. We do not usually read our own precedents so uncharitably.

Maybe the Court proceeds as it does today because it just disagrees with *Illinois Brick*. After all, the Court not only displaces a sensible rule in favor of a senseless one; it also proceeds to question each of *Illinois Brick*'s rationales—doubting that those directly injured are always the best plaintiffs to bring suit, that calculating damages for pass-on plaintiffs will often be unduly complicated, and that conflicting claims to a common fund justify limiting who may sue. *Ante*, at 11–13. The Court even tells us that any "ambiguity" about the permissibility of pass-on damages should be resolved "in the direction of the statutory text," *ante*, at 8— ignoring that *Illinois Brick* followed the well-trodden path of construing the statutory text in light of background common law principles of proximate cause. Last but not least, the Court suggests that the traditional understanding of *Illinois Brick* leads to "arbitrary and unprincipled" results. It asks us to consider two hypothetical scenarios that, it says, prove the point. The first is a "markup" scenario in which a monopolistic retailer buys a product from a manufacturer for $6 and then decides to sell the product to a consumer for $10, applying a supracompetitive $4 markup. The second is a "commission" scenario in which a manufacturer directs a monopolistic retailer to sell the manufacturer's product to a consumer for $10 and the retailer keeps a supracompetitive 40% commission, sending $6 back to the manufacturer. The two scenarios are economically the same, the Court asserts, and forbidding recovery in the second for lack of proximate cause makes no sense.

But there is nothing arbitrary or unprincipled about *Illinois Brick*'s rule or results. The notion that the causal chain must stop somewhere is an ancient and venerable one. As with most any rule of proximate cause, reasonable people can debate whether *Illinois Brick* drew exactly the right line in cutting off claims where it did. But the line it drew is intelligible, principled, administrable, and far more reasonable than the Court's artificial rule of contractual privity. Nor do the Court's hypotheticals come close to proving otherwise. In the first scenario, the markup falls initially on the consumer, so there's no doubt that the retailer's anticompetitive conduct proximately caused the consumer's injury. Meanwhile, in the second scenario the commission falls initially on the manufacturer, and the consumer won't feel the pain unless the manufacturer can and does recoup some or all of the elevated commission by raising its own prices. In *that* situation, the manufacturer is the directly injured party, and the difficulty of disaggregating damages between those directly and indirectly harmed means that the consumer can't establish proximate cause under traditional principles.

Some *amici* share the Court's skepticism of *Illinois Brick*. They even urge us to overrule *Illinois Brick*, assuring us that "modern economic techniques" can now mitigate any problems that arise in allocating damages between those who suffer them directly and those who suffer them indirectly. Brief for State of Texas et al. as *Amici Curiae* 25. Maybe there is something to these arguments; maybe not. But there's plenty of reason to decline any invitation to take even a small step away from *Illinois Brick* today. The plaintiffs have not asked us to overrule our precedent—in fact, they've disavowed any such request. So we lack the benefit of the adversarial process in a complex area involving a 40-yearold precedent and many hard questions. For example, if we are really inclined to overrule *Illinois Brick*, doesn't that mean we must do the same to *Hanover Shoe*? If the proximate cause line is no longer to be drawn at the first injured party, how far down the causal chain can a plaintiff be and still recoup damages? Must all potential claimants to the single monopoly rent be gathered in a single lawsuit as necessary parties (and if not, why not)? Without any invitation or reason to revisit our precedent, and with so many grounds for caution, I would have thought the proper course today would have been to afford *Illinois Brick* full effect, not to begin whittling it away to a bare formalism. I respectfully dissent.

Notes

1.   After the Court's focus in *Ohio v. American Express* on the substance of platforms, is *Apple v. Pepper* a switch to formalism? Is the App Store a two-sided transaction market? If it is, who are the parties to the transaction? Note that the Court says that both consumers and app developers can sue Apple. If it is not, does that explain the different approach? Or does the two-sidedness play different roles for substance and procedural/standing rules?

Geoffrey Manne and Kristian Stout argue that it follows from *American Express*'s approach to the relevant-market question that both app developers and app purchasers are part of the same relevant market, so that both should have standing. *See* Geoffrey Manne and Kristian Stout, *The Evolution of Antitrust Doctrine After* Ohio v. Amex *and the* Apple v. Pepper *Decision That Should Have Been*, 98 NEB. L. REV. 425 (2019). Is it clear, given *American Express*, what it means to be part of a two-sided market? Is the idea that both app developers and app purchasers purchase the same product, app distribution, and that merchants and customer purchase the same product, credit-card services? Is that true in the same sense, say, that both food sellers and cigarette manufacturers purchase cellophane? *See* United States v. E. I. du Pont de Nemours & Co., 351 U.S. 377 (1956). If not, then in what sense *is* it true, and what are the implications for antitrust? As Manne and Stout point out, procedure and standing to sue do not determine substantive antitrust rules, and these questions are yet to be answered.

2.   Is it important that the claim alleges injuries in Apple's market, not the app developers' markets? Is the price set by app developers dependent on Apple's commission rate? If so, is Apple's "who sets the price" theory convincing? Would the result have been different if Apple's commission were just a few percent, like those of credit-card companies? Should it matter? What if Apple charged the app developers more than $99 as their annual fee and took no commission?

3.   Does it follow from this case that the only consignment clothing store in an isolated small town, if it profits from commissions, could be sued by consumers on a claim that the commission rate is supracompetitive? The Court notes that just

because consumers can sue Apple does not mean that they will win. Assuming the clothing store can be sued by consumers, would the consumers win? Is Apple in a different position?

4.   Is the key to the decision that the indirect-purchaser doctrine, unlike much of antitrust law, is inherently a formalistic one? Could the decision here be defended on the ground that, like the section 1 *per se* rule, the indirect-purchaser rule sometimes produces the wrong result, but that conducting a more thorough case-by-case inquiry would not be worth the cost and trouble?

6.2. Procedural Issues

Procedural issues can also present obstacles to plaintiffs in novel antitrust cases. Articulating the nature of competitive harm in novel cases can be difficult, particularly given antitrust's reliance on categorization of antitrust offenses. The *1-800 Contacts* case above, for example, seems most logically to be characterized as a market allocation case, but that is not a label used by the F.T.C. in the case itself. Another example is the following case:

EJ MGT LLC v. Zillow Group, Inc.
Civil Action No. 18-584 (JMV) (JBC) (Feb. 28, 2019)

This case primarily concerns antitrust allegations against a market leader in online real estate information. Plaintiff EJ MGT LLC brings this action against Defendants Zillow Group, Inc., and Zillow, Inc. (collectively "Zillow") for conspiracy under the Sherman Act, 15 U.S.C. § 1 and other alleged violations. The gist of Plaintiffs allegations is that Zillow illegally contracts with certain real estate brokers and agents to remove Zillow's estimated price, or "Zestimate," as to certain properties while not offering this option to other brokers, agents, and property owners, such as Plaintiff. Plaintiff does not claim that the Zestimate is completely removed from the listings of the "co-conspirator brokers," but that the Zestimate is instead less prominently displayed.

Currently pending before this Court is Defendants' motion to dismiss Plaintiff's Complaint under Federal Rules of Civil Procedure 12(b)(6) for failure to state a claim upon which relief can be granted as well as Rule 9(b) for failure to plead a fraud claim with particularity. . . . For the reasons that follow, Defendants' motion to dismiss is granted without prejudice.

I. BACKGROUND

Plaintiff EJ MGT is a New Jersey limited liability organization that is the owner of 142 Hoover Drive in Cresskill, New Jersey (the "Property"). The Property is 1.5 acres of land and includes a single-family home measuring 18,000 square feet.

Plaintiff spent significant time and resources restoring the Property since purchasing it in March 2015.

Zillow is a market leader in online real estate information. Among other things, it manages websites[3] that serve as the central database for all real estate listings (including those that are not for sale) in the United States. Its flagship website, www.zillow.com, includes property facts (such as the number of bedrooms, number of bathrooms, and lot size), tax assessment information, prior transaction data, and listing information for over 110 million United States homes.[4]

For all listed properties, Zillow includes a Zestimate — Zillow's own estimate of the current market value of a home based on an algorithm that considers property facts (location, lot size, square footage, number of bedrooms/bathrooms, etc.), tax assessments, prior transactions (both of that property historically, and neighboring properties), and user data. Zillow represents that the Zestimate is the "starting point" for determining a home's value. Plaintiff alleges that "Zillow itself acknowledges" that this starting point is "false, inaccurate, or otherwise misleading." Yet, Plaintiff fails to mention that Zillow also publishes the error rate of its Zestimate publicly on its website (7.9% nationally as of January 5, 2015), and discloses the shortcomings of this estimate, namely, "homes in luxury markets" that have new renovations or "many custom features, which aren't' accounted for in the Zestimate model." Paul Moore, The Zestimate Home Value Explained, Premier Agent (January 5, 2015), https://www.zillow.com/agent-resources/blog/the-zestimate-explained/.

In January 2017, Plaintiff listed the Property for sale. Keller Williams served as the broker and listing agent; Zillow displayed the Property on its website. Plaintiff alleges that Zillow's use and placement of its Zestimate on Zillow's website has prevented the Property from being sold. For example, on January 2, 2018, Plaintiff's Property was listed on Zillow for $7,788,000. Immediately under the sale price, the Zestimate reflected a price of $3,703,597. Plaintiff alleges that potential buyers have advised Plaintiff that the difference between the listed sales price and the Zestimate informed their decision not to purchase the Property.

Plaintiff alleges an anticompetitive conspiracy in Zillow's contracting with specific brokers and agents, or "co-conspirator brokers," to omit Zestimates of particular properties from under the listing price. As noted, the Property's Zestimate was listed directly below its sales price, which is the typical placement of the Zestimate. Plaintiff alleges that Defendant entered into "Zestimate Agreements," which allows certain brokers to relocate the Zestimates of their properties so that they do not appear directly under the listing prices. The co-conspirator brokers include Sotheby's International Realty, Inc.; Coldwell Banker

---

[3] In 2014, Zillow purchased its top competitor, Trulia, and now operates both of the leading online real-estate databases.

[4] An address' Zillow page is also one of the first links to appear when someone uses a search engine, such as Google, for the address.

Real Estate LLC; Century 21 Real Estate LLC; The Corcoran Group ERA; and Weichert Realty. To be clear, Zillow does not completely remove the Zestimate for any listing. Even when it removes the Zestimate from under the listing price, Zillow still makes the Zestimate available under the "Zestimate details" tab on the property's Zillow page.

Plaintiff contacted Zillow to remove the Property's Zestimate from directly underneath the Property's listing price, but Zillow refused. A Zillow representative explained that "this feature is only available on our premiere agent program for real estate agents" and forwarded Plaintiff information on that program. The Zillow representative later clarified that "Zillow has various partnerships with Agents, Brokerages, and Vendors that may display a listing page differently than others." Plaintiff alleges that even premier agents cannot gain this preferential treatment unless they are members of the co-conspirator brokers. Plaintiff asserts that all others -- brokers, agents, and individual homeowners -- who are not associated with the co-conspirator brokers "are left no choice but to have the inaccurate and otherwise misleading Zestimates appear prominently" on their properties' Zillow pages, putting them at a distinct competitive disadvantage and harming overall competition in the local and national real estate markets.

Plaintiff does not claim that the Zestimate provided for the Property did not reflect fair market value. Similarly, Plaintiff does not allege that its listing price represented the fair market value of the Property. Plaintiff also does not argue that it has not been able to sell the Property due to the positioning of the Zestimate below the asking price. Instead, Plaintiff claims certain, unnamed "[p]otential buyers" indicated that the difference between the Zestimate and the list price for the Property has "impacted and/or informed" the potential buyers' decision not to purchase the Property.

. . .

IV. ANALYSIS

. . .

Here, Plaintiff alleges that "vertical Zestimate Agreements are directly aimed at restraining horizontal competition in both the market for the sale of residential real estate and for the listing of residential real estate." The Third Circuit has ruled that certain horizontal agreements can be subject to the per se or quick look analysis, but vertical agreements are subject to the full rule of reason review. Thus, the Court conducts a full rule of reason review.

Defendants argue that (1) not offering Plaintiff a Zestimate Agreement was not a concerted effort, but Defendants' own unilateral decision, (2) that Plaintiff has not sufficiently alleged anticompetitive effects, (3) that Plaintiff has not sufficiently alleged proximate cause, and (4) that Plaintiff has not sufficiently alleged an antitrust injury.

Plaintiff first disagrees that Zillow's decision was wholly unilateral and argues that it adequately alleged agreements to support this position. Regarding this point, the parties appear to be talking past each other. Defendants appear to argue that they have taken unilateral action in determining whether to enter into the agreements with the alleged co-conspirator brokers. In other words, it appears that Defendants are claiming that there are no plausible allegations indicating that Defendants are prohibited – through the Zestimate Agreements – from entering into similar agreements with any other party, including Plaintiff. Plaintiff responds that the alleged Zestimate Agreements are sufficient proof of an agreement to satisfy Section 1. For purposes of the current motion, the Court finds that Plaintiff has sufficiently alleged vertical agreements for Section 1 purposes.

. . .

Plaintiff also asserts that Defendants' argument falls short because they have not demonstrated the procompetitive aspects of the Zestimate Agreements. However, such an argument puts the cart before the horse, because under a rule of reason analysis, Plaintiffs must first demonstrate the harm (or potential harm) to competition before the Court (or Defendants) turn to the pro-competition attributes. In this regard, Plaintiff fails to analyze, much less cite any relevant authority regarding, the fact that the Zestimates are not completely omitted from the alleged co-conspirator brokers' listings. Instead, the Zestimates are still displayed but not immediately under the listing price. In that regard, this case concerns the prominence of certain information as opposed to the information's complete omission.

More fundamentally, Plaintiffs opposition takes a position inconsistent with the allegations in its Complaint. In its Complaint, Plaintiff argues that the Zestimates are unreliable and inaccurate. Plaintiff continues that the Zestimate Agreements create a competitive disadvantage because the misleading Zestimate is displayed directly under its listing price, while the same is not true for the Zillow listings of the co-conspirator brokers. The thrust of Plaintiff's entire case, as alleged in the Complaint, is that it wants the Zestimate removed from directly under its listing price.

Yet, in its opposition, Plaintiff makes a materially different argument. Plaintiff asserts that the Zestimates reflect "critical" price information and that consumers are harmed by Zillow and its alleged co-conspirators "suppress[ing] [this] price-related information from consumers' view." Plaintiff alleges that Defendants facilitate the selective suppression of this "critical" price information and give co-conspirators the ability to conceal it as well. Essentially, in its opposition, Plaintiff claims that Zestimates are critical pieces of information and that the Zestimate Agreements reduce the usefulness of Defendant's product for consumers because the Zestimates are not displayed in a prominent position. This is an entirely new theory of liability that was not pled in the Complaint.

As a result, the Court is unable to conduct the appropriate analysis in light of the motion to dismiss. The Court dismisses Plaintiff's Section 1 and analogous New Jersey Antitrust Act claims (Counts I and II) without prejudice.

. . .

Notes

1.   What exactly is or should be the claim here? One possibility is that the plaintiff alleges a nonprice vertical restraint under which the co-conspirator brokers that are parties to the Zestimate Agreements have more freedom to control the information Zillow provides. But those brokers are not really "dealers" in the information that Zillow "manufactures"; instead, Zillow is the only provider of the information and allows the dealers to, in some sense, filter the information.

2.   In some respects, this case resembles a non-antitrust case, *Levitt v. Yelp! Inc.*, 765 F.3d 1123 (9th Cir. 2014), in which the plaintiffs alleged that Yelp required businesses to purchase advertising from Yelp to avoid Yelp's manipulation of the businesses' ratings. The plaintiffs alleged violations of California's Unfair Competition Law, under which they claimed that Yelp had engaged in "extortionate" conduct. The Ninth Circuit disagreed, taking the view that because there was "no contractual right pursuant to which Yelp must publish positive reviews, nor does any law require Yelp to publish them," Yelp could condition such publication on the purchase of advertising. The court did say, though, that other claims might succeed, though none was adequately pled.

3.   Suppose that Zillow requires payment from brokers as a condition of entering into Zestimate Agreements and thus being permitted to remove Zestimates from its listings. How, if at all, should that be characterized as an competition problem? Is it the requirement of a payment in order to avoid (some degree of) exclusion by possibly misleading information, and thus exclusive dealing? In what market? The market for real estate information, in which Zillow presumably could be alleged to have market or monopoly power?

This would admittedly be an unusual exclusion claim, but information markets are unusual markets. Perhaps a suitable analogy would be to treat Zillow as an information supermarket, akin to a typical supermarket, and to treat the Zestimate Agreements as agreements to give favorable treatment to information from particular suppliers. On that view, the Zestimate Agreements are similar to so-called slotting allowances, which are typically viewed as a species of exclusive-dealing arrangements. But the competitive effects then would be dependent on the functioning of the information ecosystem: How much power does Zillow have? Since the potential harm would be at the broker level, how competitive is that market? And should competition in that market be viewed as involving sales of houses or provision of information?

On the other side of the ledger, what would be the procompetitive effects of the Zestimate Agreements? It is not at all clear that they have any of the sort of product-integration or risk-reduction benefits that are the usual justifications for exclusive arrangements. It therefore seems that if the plaintiff could establish an anticompetitive effect, Zillow would have difficulty overcoming that showing. The failure to make its *prima facie* case in fact appears to be the issue, according to the court in a later opinion:

For example, Plaintiff alleges that "[t]he Zestimate Agreements ... have the purpose and effect of stifling and distorting the flow of price related information, anticompetitively tilting the playing field in favor of the co-conspirator Brokers, and creating and heightening barriers to entry in the market for residential real estate listing services." As a result of these effects, Plaintiff alleges that Zillow users are injured because they, inter alia: (1) "are forced either to make decisions based on selectively distorted information or to expend additional time and effort to scour each listing for potentially concealed information"; (2) are forced to pay "increased [costs] in the form of advertising fees, brokers' commissions, or other costs incurred solely to alter or conceal the display of Zestimates"; and (3) face barriers to entry and expansion in the listing and sale of residential real estate. Notably, Plaintiff fails to provide adequate factual support for such allegations.

Ultimately, however, the court dismissed the case on standing grounds "[e]ven taking these allegations as true." This is a not-uncommon solution for courts faced with difficulty in justifying a motion to dismiss in a novel case. *Cf.* PHILLIP E. AREEDA & HERBERT HOVENKAMP, ANTITRUSt Law ¶ 360f, at 202-03 (rev. ed.1995) ("When a court concludes that no violation has occurred, it has no occasion to consider standing. An increasing number of courts, unfortunately, deny standing when they really mean that no violation has occurred.") If competition law is to overcome the challenge of ensuring competition in the information economy, it will have to confront these issues, not evade them.

Made in the USA
Middletown, DE
08 August 2020